**More praise for *The First Sex***

"Striking . . . An original and often quite enjoyable book."
—*The New York Times Book Review*

"Thought-provoking . . . We're not getting older, we're getting better."
—*USA Today*

"Full of interesting anecdotes, lively commentary, and a wealth of information."
—*The Dallas Morning News*

"This controversial compendium of bold statements, supported by vast amounts of biological and anthropological research, is persuasive—partly, no doubt, because Fisher's writing style makes the material accessible."
—*BookPage*

"Provocative . . . Fisher, an anthropologist at Rutgers University, synthesizes the insights of her own discipline and those of psychology, sociology, ethnology, and biology into good news for women."
—*Publishers Weekly*

# THE FIRST SEX

# HELEN FISHER

# THE
# FIRST
# SEX

## THE NATURAL TALENTS OF
## WOMEN AND HOW THEY
## ARE CHANGING THE WORLD

BALLANTINE BOOKS

NEW YORK

Grateful acknowledgment is made to the following for permission to reprint previously published material:

*Elizabeth Barnett for the Edna St. Vincent Millay Society:* Lines from "I too beneath your moon, almighty Sex" and excerpt from Sonnet XXIX of *Fatal Interview* by Edna St. Vincent Millay. From *Collected Poems*, HarperCollins. Copyright © 1931, 1939, 1958, 1967 by Edna St. Vincent Millay and Norma Millay Ellis. All rights reserved. Reprinted by permission of Elizabeth Barnett, literary executor.

*Farrar, Straus & Giroux, Inc.:* Eight lines from "Valediction" from *Poems 1965–1975* by Seamus Heaney. (Published in the U.K. as *Death of a Naturalist*) Copyright © 1980 by Seamus Heaney. Rights in Canada and the open market are controlled by Faber and Faber Limited. Reprinted by permission of Farrar, Straus & Giroux, Inc. and Faber and Faber Limited.

*Harcourt, Inc.:* Excerpt from "True Love" from *View With a Grain of Sand* by Wislawa Szymborska. Copyright © 1993 by Wislawa Szymborska. English translation by Stanislaw Baranczak and Clare Cavanagh copyright © 1995 by Harcourt, Inc. Reprinted by permission of the publisher.

*HarperCollins Publishers, Inc.* and *Faber and Faber Limited*: Excerpt from "Three Women: A Poem for Three Voices" from *The Collected Poems: Sylvia Plath*, edited by Ted Hughes, pp. 176–187. Rights throughout the world excluding the United States are controlled by Faber and Faber Limited. Reprinted by permission of HarperCollins Publishers, Inc. and Faber and Faber Limited.

*Shambhala Publications, Inc.:* "Song" by Tzu Yeh from *The Erotic Spirit*, edited by Sam Hamill. Copyright © 1996. Reprinted by arrangement with Shambhala Publications, Inc.

Ballantine and colophon are registered trademarks of Random House, Inc.

This edition published by arrangement with Random House, Inc.

www.randomhouse.com/BB/

Library of Congress Catalog Card Number: 99-91716

ISBN 0-449-91260-4

Manufactured in the United States of America

First Trade Paperback Edition: February 2000

10 9 8 7 6 5 4 3 2 1

*For Ray Carroll*

If ever the world sees a time when women
shall come together purely and simply for the benefit
and good of mankind, it will be a power such as
the world has never known.

MATTHEW ARNOLD

# ACKNOWLEDGMENTS

I thank my friend Ray Carroll for his breadth of knowledge and his sophisticated insights. I thank my agent, Amanda Urban, for her astute guidance during the conception of this project and her unflagging enthusiasm for this book. I thank Kate Medina, my editor, for her critical eye and valuable commentary. I am indebted to Edie Weiner and Arnold Brown, trend analysts, for allowing me to sit in on their think-tank sessions about the future. I am grateful to Bob Alford, Arnold Brown, Ray Carroll, Fletcher Hodges, and Barbara Pillsbury for their careful reading of the manuscript, and to Michelle Cristiani, Janel Tortorice, and Jenny Overman for gathering some of the research materials. I also thank my friends and colleagues who took the time to read sections of the book or had valuable conversations with me during the years of writing: Judy Andrews, Art Aron, Sydney Barrows, Laura Berman, Laura Betzig, Lucy Brown, Matt Clark, Ellen Dissanayake, Perry Faithorn, Bob Fisher, Ron Fletcher, John French, Larry Frolik, Lynn Goldberg, Jack Harris, Mariko Hasegawa, Toshikazu Hasegawa, Kim Hill, Gene Katz, Laura Klein, Jane Lancaster, Edwin Laurenson, Marie Lugano, Deb Masek, B. Kay Manuelito, Anne Moir, Peter Moore, Merry Muraskin, George Newlin, Roger Pasquier, Michelle Press, Audrey Redmond, Carolyn Reynolds, John Munder Ross, Pepper Schwartz, Gregg Simpson, Barb Smuts, Susan

Stautberg, Fred Suffet, MacGregor Suzuki, Martin Tandler, Barbara Tober, Edie Weiner, Franny Whitney, Lorna Vanparys, Jeff Zeig, Caroline Zinsser, and my associates at Rutgers University. I also thank Meaghan Rady, as well as Sally Marvin, Sybil Pincus, Carol Schneider, and everyone else at Random House who contributed to the publication of *The First Sex*.

# CONTENTS

# DEEP HISTORY

## An Immodest Proposal

There is only one way of seeing things, and that is
seeing the whole of them.

JOHN RUSKIN

What is a woman?" Simone de Beauvoir asked this question in her celebrated 1949 book, *The Second Sex*. She believed that a woman is solely the product of economic and social forces. As she said, "One is not born, but rather becomes, a woman."

Times have changed since Beauvoir wrote these words. A great deal of scientific evidence now demonstrates that all human beings emerge from the womb with circuits in the brain that enable them to act in human ways. Moreover, in some fundamental respects the sexes are not alike. For millions of years, men and women did different jobs, tasks that required different skills. As days turned into centuries and natural selection weeded out less able workers, time carved subtle differences in the male and female brain. A woman is born a woman.

I am a clone; I am an identical twin. My twin sister and I are alike in many ways and different in many others. We laugh alike and our gestures are uncannily similar, but I am an anthropologist and she is a hot air balloon pilot and a painter. Because of this lifelong personal experience, I am acutely aware that parents, teachers, friends, jobs, and myriad other cultural forces dramatically influence how one thinks and acts. Environment and heredity are eternally intertwined, locked in a pas de deux. No two human beings are alike.

Yet men and women emerge from the womb with some innate tendencies and proclivities bred on the grasslands of Africa millennia ago. The sexes are not the same. Each has some natural talents. Each is a living archive of its distinctive past.

Beauvoir's central tenet was correct, however. She endorsed the nineteenth-century view that social traditions emerging during our farming ancestry had forced women into a secondary place in society.

Since the 1970s scholars have established that before humankind adopted a settled farming lifeway, women were powerful economically and socially. On the savannas of ancient Africa women "commuted" to work to gather fruits and vegetables. They left their children in day care with relatives and they returned to camp with much, often most, of the evening meal. In "deep history," as Edward O. Wilson calls humanity's primordial beginnings, the double-income family was the rule. Anthropologists believe that women were regarded as roughly equal with men.

As the agricultural revolution took hold, however, men assumed the primary economic tasks: clearing land, plowing fields, and harvesting crops. Soon they also became the traders, warriors, heads of household, and heads of state. Women in many farming cultures were and still are treated, in many respects, as what Beauvoir called the "second sex."

With the Industrial Revolution in the West, powerful economic forces began to draw women into the paid workforce. It is no exaggeration to say that this has led to one of the most extraordinary developments in the long journey of *Homo sapiens:* the return of economically powerful women. Women around the world are gradually reacquiring the economic clout they enjoyed hundreds of thousands, even millions of years ago.

They bring to the marketplace many natural talents.

So here is my immodest proposal: As women continue to pour into the paid workforce in cultures around the world, they will apply their natural aptitudes in many sectors of society and dramatically influence twenty-first-century business, sex, and family life. In some important parts of the economy, they will even predominate, becoming the first sex. Why? Because current trends in business, communications, education, law, medicine, government, and the nonprofit sector, known as civil society, all suggest that tomorrow's world will need the female mind.

How do men and women vary? Why did these gender differences evolve? How will women's uniquely feminine attributes change the world?

Winston Churchill once said that in an author's mind a book begins as a toy, turns into a lover, and becomes a tyrant. I don't know about the toy part, but when I began this book, these questions immediately became lovers. I couldn't get them out of my mind. I pored over reams of data on subjects as diverse as brain anatomy, animal behavior, psychology, gender studies, world business, and demography. In no time, I found hundreds of scientific studies documenting biological and psychological differences between women and men.

Women have many exceptional faculties bred in deep history: a talent with words; a capacity to read postures, gestures, facial expressions, and other nonverbal cues; emotional sensitivity; empathy; excellent senses of touch, taste, smell, and hearing; patience; an ability to do and think several things simultaneously; a broad contextual view of any issue; a penchant for long-term planning; a gift for networking and negotiating; an impulse to nurture; and a preference for cooperating, reaching consensus, and leading via egalitarian teams.

Men have many natural talents, too. Among them is a superb understanding of spatial relations, a talent for solving complex mechanical problems, an ability to focus their attention, and a gift for controlling many of their emotions. All, I will contend, were built into the architecture of the gendered brain millennia ago.

This is not to say that women and men are puppets dangling from strings of DNA. With the emergence of humanity came the evolution of the cerebral cortex. We think. We weigh a vast array of possibilities. We make choices. We learn new skills. We regularly rise above our inherited nature to make decisions about our lives.

Nevertheless, we do have luggage from the past. These gender differences appear in cultures around the world. They reemerge decade after decade in the same society, despite changing attitudes about women. Many appear in infancy. Many are associated with male or female sex hormones, the androgens and estrogens. Some have been traced to specific genes. Some emerge long before a baby leaves the womb.

Scientists have even discovered how some of these gendered proclivities become installed in the male and female brain. At conception the embryo is neither male nor female. Around the eighth week of fetal life, however, a genetic switch flips. If the embryo is to be a boy, a gene on the Y chromosome directs the gonadal buds to become testes. These developing sex organs then produce male hormones that further build the male genitals. Later they also mold the male brain.[1]

If the embryo is genetically destined to be female, no male hormones act on it and female gonads appear by the thirteenth week of fetal life—followed later by the female brain.[2] Recently scientists have begun to think that a gene on the X chromosome and fetal estrogens also play active roles in constructing the full composition of "woman."[3] But all agree that if male hormones do not kick in to sculpt the growing embryo, it will become a girl.

As a result of these findings, scientists regularly refer to woman as the default plan.

I read these data differently. "Woman" is the primary sex—the first sex. You have to add chemicals to get a man. Hence the first sex from the biological perspective is emerging as the first sex in many spheres of economic and social life.

The distinction between "man" and "woman" is far from simple, however. Each of us is a complex mix of feminine and masculine traits. As Susan Sontag has written, "What is most beautiful in virile men is something feminine; what is most beautiful in feminine women is something masculine." Nobody is wholly male or wholly female.

Even this intriguing amalgam of male and female in each of us is shaped by biology. The fetal brain grows slowly and unevenly, so different parts of the brain become susceptible to sex hormones at different times. Levels of these fetal hormones also change continuously.[4] So tides of powerful sex hormones can masculinize one part of the brain while they leave another region untouched. As a result, every human being lies somewhere along a continuum that ranges from superfeminine to hypermasculine, depending on the amount and timing of hormones the individual was doused with in the womb.[5]

Then environmental forces take up the job of shaping who you are. "It's a girl!" "It's a boy!" As you emerge from the womb, someone announces your gender. In this instant, you are assigned to a category that pigeonholes you all your years. Blue for boys, pink for girls; trucks for one, dolls for the other: many, many social forces direct youngsters, adults, and seniors to behave as one sex or the other. Environmental forces also alter the secretion of neurotransmitters in the brain, the ebb and flow of the sex hormones, even the activities of genes, subtly changing biology and behavior throughout our lives.[6]

Albert Einstein once said of the intellect, "It has powerful muscles, but no personality." Upon the intricate scaffolding of our unique brains, culture builds our unique personalities. Yet the scaffolding remains. Women as a general group do carry within them a host of specific aptitudes—innate talents they will use to make tremendous changes in our modern world.

Two oddly correlated phenomena, the international baby boom and the biology of menopause, will accelerate women's impact on tomorrow.

The huge baby boom generation is reaching middle age. As anthropologists have documented, middle-aged women around the world tend to become much more assertive. This is partially due to cultural forces.

But middle-aged women also get a dividend from nature. With menopause, levels of the estrogens decline, unmasking natural levels of testosterone and other androgens in the female body. Androgens, male sex hormones, are potent chemicals regularly associated with assertiveness and rank in many mammalian species, including people. As this tidal wave of baby boomer women reaches middle age, they will be equipped—not only economically and mentally but also hormonally—to make substantial changes in the world.

"Such a critical mass of older women with a tradition of rebellion and independence and a way of making a living has not occurred before in history," writes historian Gerda Lerner. We stand at the doorway of what may become an age of women.

Each of the first six chapters in this book examines specific male/female differences—using data on the brain, information from many cultures, and evidence from anthropology, psychology, sociology, ethology, and other behavioral and biological sciences. Each chapter explores why these biological variations evolved and shows how women's specific gifts are beginning to affect some sectors of society. I give examples of women's impact on the media, education, the service professions, law, medicine, corporations, government, and civil organizations.

In chapter 7, I discuss menopause, show how women around the world become more influential in middle age, and propose that as women of the international baby boom generation move into their fifties their force will increase—not only in the workplace but in the voting booth. In chapters 8 through 10, I explore the effect that economically powerful women will have on patterns of sex, romance, and marriage. Chapter 11 expresses my hope that men and women will begin to acknowledge their differences, employ women's natural talents in the workforce, and use these data to build rapport with one another. It concludes that men and women are regaining a relationship of equality that is natural to humanity and was common in deep history.

I am optimistic about the future—not only for women but for men. Women's propensity to think contextually and their intense curiosity about people will add variety and texture to what we watch on television. Their faculty for language and appetite for diversity and complexity will enrich what we read in newspapers, magazines and books—and influence our feelings and beliefs. With their people skills, women will continue to invigorate the service professions, adding comfort and novelty to our work and leisure hours.

Women already bring compassion and patience to hands-on healing. They offer imagination in the classroom. They are broadening our perspective of justice. Their facility for networking and reaching consensus will become more and more important as companies dismantle hierarchical management structures and emphasize egalitarian team playing. With their long-term and contextual view, their need to nurture, and their prominent role in civil society, women will also make major contributions toward solving our worldwide social and environmental ills.

More and more, women are expressing their sexuality, adding zest to life in the bedroom. They are changing the meaning of intimacy and romance. And as society's "kin keepers," they are transforming family life in extraordinary ways.

Women are better educated, more capable, and more interesting than ever before. If there ever was a time in human evolution when both sexes had the opportunity to make satisfying careers and happy marriages, that time is now.

# THE FIRST SEX

# CHAPTER 1

# WEB THINKING

## Women's Contextual View

What man has assurance enough to pretend to know
thoroughly the riddle of a woman's mind?

CERVANTES

G od created woman. And boredom did indeed cease from that moment." Friedrich Nietzsche was no feminist, but he apparently appreciated the female mind. He was not the first. Women have been adding zest, wit, intelligence, and compassion to human life since our ancestors stoked their fires in Africa a million years ago.

Now women are about to change the world. Why? Because during the millions of years that our forebears traveled in small hunting-and-gathering bands, the sexes did different jobs. Those jobs required different skills. As time and nature tirelessly propagated successful workers, natural selection built different aptitudes into the male and female brain. No two people are the same. But, on average, women and men possess a number of different innate skills. And current trends suggest that many sectors of the twenty-first-century economic community are going to need the natural talents of women.

Please do not mistake me. Men have many natural abilities that will be essential in the coming global marketplace. Nor have men been laggards in the past. They have explored and mapped the world; produced most of our literature, arts, and sciences; and invented many of the pleasures of contemporary life, from the printing press to light-bulbs, sneakers, chocolate, and the Internet. Men will continue to make enormous contributions to our high-tech society.

But women have begun to enter the paid workforce in record numbers almost everywhere on earth. As these women penetrate, even saturate, the global marketplace in coming decades, I think they will introduce remarkably innovative ideas and practices.

What are women's natural talents? How will women change the world? I begin with how women think.

I believe there are subtle differences in the ways that men and women, on average, organize their thoughts—variations that appear to stem from differences in brain structure. Moreover, as discussed throughout this book, women's "way of seeing" has already begun to permeate our newspapers, TV shows, classrooms, boardrooms, chambers of government, courtrooms, hospitals, voting booths, and bedrooms. Feminine thinking is even affecting our basic beliefs about justice, health, charity, leisure, intimacy, romance, and family. So I start with that aspect of femininity that I believe will have the most ubiquitous impact on tomorrow.

In this chapter I maintain that women, on average, take a broader perspective than men do—on any issue. Women think contextually, holistically. They also display more mental flexibility, apply more intuitive and imaginative judgments, and have a greater tendency to plan long term—other aspects of their contextual perspective. I discuss the scientific evidence for these female traits and the probable brain networks associated with them. Then I trace women's outstanding march into the world of paid employment and conclude that women's broad, contextual, holistic way of seeing will pervade every aspect of twenty-first-century economic and social life.

### The Female Mind

"When the mind is thinking, it is talking to itself," Plato said. Everyone has tossed around in bed at night churning over a business problem or a troubled love affair. Images appear, then vanish. Scenes unfurl. Snippets of conversation emerge from nowhere, dissolve, then repeat themselves. A rush of anger engulfs you. Then pity. Then despair. Then rationality takes over for a moment and you resolve to do this, then that. On goes the debate as clock hands wind from three to four. A committee meeting is in progress in your head.

"The mind is a strange machine which can combine the materials

offered to it in the most astonishing ways," wrote the British philosopher Bertrand Russell. Both men and women absorb large amounts
of data and weigh a vast array of variables almost simultaneously.

Psychologists report, however, that women more regularly think
contextually; they take a more "holistic" view of the issue at hand.[1]
That is, they integrate more details of the world around them, details
ranging from the nuances of body posture to the position of objects
in a room.[2]

Women's ability to integrate myriad facts is nowhere more evident
than in the office. Female executives, business analysts note, tend to
approach business issues from a broader perspective than do their
male colleagues.[3] Women tend to gather more data that pertain to a
topic and connect these details faster. As women make decisions, they
weigh more variables, consider more options and outcomes, recall
more points of view, and see more ways to proceed. They integrate,
generalize, and synthesize. And women, on average, tolerate ambiguity better than men do[4]—probably because they visualize more of the
factors involved in any issue.

In short, women tend to think in webs of interrelated factors, not
straight lines. I call this female manner of thought "web thinking."

## The Male Mind

As a general rule, men tend to focus on one thing at a time—a male
trait I first noticed in my twenties. At the time I had a boyfriend who
liked to watch the news on television, listen to rock music on the
stereo, and read a book—presumably all at once. In reality, he just
switched channels in his head. When he was imbibing from one mo-
dality, he tuned the others out. Not I. The flashing of the TV screen,
the throbbing music, the printed words: all of these stimuli swamped
my mind.

Men are good at compartmentalizing their attention. Just ask
a man who is reading the newspaper a simple question. Often he
doesn't hear you. When he does, he appears to rouse himself as if
returning from a different planet. Men tend to tune out extraneous
stimuli. Their thinking process is, on average, more channeled.

Faced with a business problem, men tend to focus on the immediate dilemma rather than putting the issue in a larger context. Unless

facts are obviously pertinent, men are inclined to dispense with them. Then they progress in a straightforward, linear, causal path toward a specific goal: the solution.[5] As a result, men are generally less tolerant of ambiguity. They like to weed out what appears to be extraneous, unrelated data to focus on the task at hand.

This capacity for focusing attention is particularly evident in the male attitude toward work. As psychologist Jacquelynne Eccles puts it, many men show a "single-minded devotion" to their occupation.[6]

Charles Hampden-Turner, a business consultant and member of the Global Business Network in Emeryville, California, believes that American business managers epitomize this male perspective.

He and his colleague Alfons Trompenaars conducted research on the values and business practices of American male and female executives. Men, Hampden-Turner reports, tend to analyze business issues in distinct parts, such as facts, items, chores, units, and other concrete segments. They often view a company as a set of tasks, machines, payments, and jobs—a collection of disparate components.[7] Female executives, he believes, see a company as a more integrated, multilayered whole.

I call men's focused, compartmentalizing, incremental reasoning process "step thinking."

## Juggling Many Balls, Wearing Many Hats

Janet Scott Batchler has described this gender difference succinctly. She writes feature films with her husband and partner, Lee Batchler. She says of her spouse, "He does one thing at a time. Does it well. Finishes it and moves on. He's very direct in his thought processes and in his actions. And he deals with people in that same focused way, meaning exactly what he says, with no hidden agenda. I'm the one who can juggle a hundred balls at once, and can realize that other people may be doing the same thing, professionally or emotionally."[8]

The scripts that Hollywood film writers create illustrate these different ways of thinking vividly. The scripts that men write tend to be direct and linear, while women's compositions have many conflicts, many climaxes, and many endings.[9]

American's national pundits express this gender difference, too. Essayist Barbara Ehrenreich declares flatly, "Women historically don't compartmentalize as well as men."[10]

When political scientist Roger Masters of Dartmouth College asked men and women about their political views and then showed them videotapes of politicians with various facial expressions, the sexes' responses were noticeably different, too. Masters concluded that "information about a leader and the nonverbal cues of the leader are integrated more fully by women than by men."[11]

Spokeswomen for the National Foundation for Women Business Owners say that American female business owners stress intuitive thinking, creativity, sensitivity, and personal values. Male business owners stress focused thinking, methodical processing of information, and concrete analysis of data. They report that "women business owners are thus more easily able to switch among multiple tasks."[12]

Demographers for the United Nations Development Programme have documented this gender difference in many cultures. In 1995 they canvassed the working habits of men and women in 130 societies. In places as different as Norway, Botswana, Argentina, and Mongolia, they report, "women in particular have developed a facility for juggling many activities at once."[13]

As women around the world do multiple tasks simultaneously, they are mentally assessing and assimilating an abundance of data— engaging in web thinking.

## Web Thinking in Childhood

This feminine way of mentally processing information begins in childhood. In the classroom, boys are more task-oriented.[14] They concentrate intently on one thing at a time. Girls have a harder time detaching themselves cognitively from their surroundings. When playing on the computer, boys are likely to head straight for their desired goal, while girls tend to browse through a host of alternatives before settling on one.[15] And when asked about themselves, boys stress the particulars, while girls are more inclined to locate themselves in a broader, more contextual environment.[16]

Classic examples are Jake and Amy, participants in the well-known study of rights and responsibilities conducted in the early 1980s by psychologist Carol Gilligan of Harvard University. Jake and Amy were both bright, ambitious American eleven-year-olds in the sixth grade. When Jake was asked how he would describe himself, he discussed his talents, his beliefs, and his height—a set of discrete, particular, concrete facts. Amy, on the other hand, placed herself within the context of the wider social world. She said she liked school, she saw a world full of problems, and she wanted to be a scientist so that she could help others.[17]

When these youngsters were asked about a situation in which responsibility to oneself and responsibility to others conflicted, they also responded differently. Jake replied: "You go about one-fourth to the others and three-fourths to yourself." Jake compartmentalized the task; he divided his responsibility into parts and allocated specific amounts in specific ways. Amy's reply was contextual, characteristic of feminine web thinking. "Well," she said, "it really depends on the situation." Then Amy launched into the multitudinous variables one must consider before acting. As Gilligan points out, "Amy responds contextually rather than categorically."[18]

This gender difference continues into adulthood. When Gilligan queried college students about their concepts of right and wrong, women were more willing to make exceptions to rules, probably because they weighed more variables and saw more possibilities.

When men and women are given Rorschach inkblot tests and asked to examine these blotches of splattered ink, men tend to talk about the details that they see. Women integrate these minutiae into larger patterns and talk about whole creatures they envision instead.[19] When men and women write stories, men are more likely to discuss the contests they have won, or when they received a free vacation or caught the biggest fish—concrete, isolated events. Women write about people, places, or embarrassing situations, tales that encompass a broader social context.[20]

When psychologist Diane Halpern of California State University at San Bernardino did a comprehensive analysis of hundreds of studies examining men's and women's verbal, mathematical (quantitative), and visual-spatial abilities, she concluded that the tasks that each sex excelled at required different cognitive abilities. Women's skills all required "rapid access to and retrieval of information that is stored in memory." Men's skills required the ability to "maintain and manipulate mental representations."[21] These differences reflect web thinking versus focused linear thought.

"All thought is a feat of association; having what's in front of you bring up something in your mind that you almost didn't know you knew." Poet Robert Frost perfectly captured the triumph of mental association so characteristic of the female mind.

## Crossroads of the Mind

Web thinking versus step thinking; an emphasis on the whole versus a focus on the parts; multitasking versus doing one thing at a time: scientists are far from understanding, even properly defining, these subtle differences between women and men. But they do know where in the brain these thinking processes take place: the prefrontal cortex.

The prefrontal cortex is the front (anterior) part of the cerebral cortex—the outer rind of the brain. It lies directly behind your brow, occupying approximately one quarter to one third of the entire cerebral cortex.[22] It is far more developed in humans than in even our closest relatives, chimpanzees; in fact, it does not fully mature in people until the teenage years.[23]

Yet the prefrontal cortex is essential to human thinking. In fact, it is known as the "central executive" or the "crossroads" of the mind.[24] It acquired these names because it has many specific regions. Each region processes different kinds of information, and each connects with many other regions of the brain and body.[25]

Doctors first listened in on the traffic at this crossroads in the 1930s, when they began to treat depressed patients with the procedure known as a prefrontal lobotomy. Surgeons worked a scalpel into the skull and sliced the brain from top to bottom, severing the prefrontal cortex from all other brain parts. This cured most patients of their depression. But the patients acquired new problems. For example, they could no longer perform several simple parallel tasks at once.[26]

More recent studies of patients with injuries to the prefrontal cortex have confirmed that damage to this area makes multitasking impossible.[27]

From these now-discredited operations, as well as many other studies of the prefrontal cortex, scientists have learned that this part of the brain also controls your ability to keep track of many bits of information at once, to order and weigh these data as they accumulate, and to find patterns in the information. Moreover, it enables you to predict outcomes from the patterns, display mental flexibility, reason hypothetically, manipulate contingencies, and plan for the future.[28] All of these tasks are aspects of web thinking.

Other regions of the prefrontal cortex govern the brain functions associated with step thinking. These areas enable you to focus your attention, encode data in serial order, plan sequentially, construct hierarchical plans of action, and process data linearly—all aspects of step-by-step, compartmentalized thought.[29]

## Genes for Web Thinking

Could regions of the brain's prefrontal cortex vary between women and men, predisposing more women than men to assimilate larger chunks of data, think in webs of factors, and view the world more contextually? Could other areas of the prefrontal cortex also vary by sex, predisposing more men to focus their attention on fewer bits of data, compartmentalize this information, and think sequentially?

New data on the brain support these possibilities. In 1997 neuroscientist David Skuse of the Institute of Child Health in London and his colleagues examined girls and women with Turner's syndrome, a genetic disorder in which the girl or woman possesses only one X chromosome instead of the normal two. They also collected data on normal men and women. From this ingenious and complex study, they concluded that a gene or a cluster of genes on the X chromosome influences the formation of the prefrontal cortex.

What is even more remarkable, Skuse established that human patterns of inheritance and bodily interactions cause this gene or cluster of genes to be silenced in all men—but active in about 50 percent of women. In other words, this strand of DNA expresses itself only in women. Moreover, when this gene or cluster of genes is active it builds the feminine prefrontal cortex in specific ways, giving women an advantage at picking up the nuances of social interactions, as well as remaining mentally flexible.[30]

These data suggest that about 50 percent of women are genetically better equipped than all men to coordinate multitudinous bits of information—the basis of web thinking.

There is more evidence that the prefrontal cortex is constructed differently in women and men—architecture that could affect the ways the sexes organize their thoughts.[31] For example, scientists have established that at least one region of the prefrontal cortex is larger in women.[32] This difference, they believe, is due to male hormones that bathe the brain at critical periods before and after birth.[33]

Whether this size difference in part of the prefrontal cortex has any influence on women's holistic approach and on men's more linear view, we do not know. But this sex-linked difference could conceivably relate to variations in how men and women "think."

### Women's Well-Connected Brains

Other parts of the brain also show structural variations that could play a role in women's web thinking. Of particular relevance are the cables of tissue that connect the two hemispheres of the brain.

One such tissue bridge is the corpus callosum. It is composed of some two hundred million fibers that link the two brain halves from the forehead to the back of the head. A least one section of the corpus callosum is somewhat thicker in women than in men.[34] The second main tissue bridge that connects brain hemispheres is the anterior commissure; it is 12 percent larger in women than in men.[35]

Tests of stroke victims, patients with other brain injuries, and normal subjects indicate that these thicker connecting links in women allow for greater communication between the two brain hemispheres. In males, the two brain halves are less in touch; each side operates more independently. Perhaps women's well-connected brains facilitate their ability to gather, integrate, and analyze more diverse kinds of information—an aspect of web thinking.[36]

The human brain is also somewhat "lateralized." This means that some mental functions are carried out predominantly in the left hemisphere, while others take place largely in the right. The male brain, however, is more lateralized than the female brain; each hemisphere is more rigidly dedicated to doing one task or another.

Psychiatrist Mark George of the National Institute of Mental Health proposes that this brain structure may enable men to focus their attention more intensely than women.[37] I would add that women's less lateralized (more integrated) brain probably helps them to embrace the larger view. As psychiatrist Mona Lisa Schultz of the Maine Medical Center puts it, "Because women's brains are less lateralized, they may have access to this area in both the right and left hemispheres. They don't see things as cut and dried, the way men do."[38]

## The Evolution of Web Thinking

It is not difficult to surmise how and why men's step thinking and women's web thinking could have evolved.

A million years ago ancestral men were building fires, chipping stone hand axes, and hunting big animals in East Africa. As they pursued these dangerous beasts, men had to concentrate—peering from behind a bush, crouching near a water hole, slipping past a sleeping leopard in a tree, trailing cantankerous wounded creatures, then attacking when the time was right.

Century after century of this perilous work must have favored those who could focus on the task at hand. Those who didn't pay strict attention were gored, trampled, or eaten. So as our male forebears tracked warthogs and wildebeests, they gradually evolved the brain architecture to screen out peripheral thoughts, focus their attention, and make step-by-step decisions.

Women's facility for web thinking most likely also arose from their primordial occupation. Ancestral women had the hardest job of any creature that ever trod the earth: raising long-dependent babies under highly dangerous conditions.[39] In order to rear helpless infants, ancestral mothers needed to do a lot of things at the same time. Watch for snakes. Listen for thunder. Taste for poison. Rock the sleepy. Distract the cranky. Instruct the curious. Soothe the fearful. Inspire the tardy. Feed the hungry. Mothers had to do countless daily chores while they stoked the fire, cooked the food, and talked to friends.

Psychologists argue that contemporary women *learn* to do and think several things simultaneously.[40] Just watch a working mother in the morning, dressing children, packing lunches, feeding goldfish, pouring cereal, and arranging day care on the phone—all at once.

But I suspect that women's talent for contextual thinking—and the related skill of multitasking—evolved in deep history. Thousands of generations of performing mental and physical acrobatics as they raised helpless infants built these outstanding capacities into the architecture of the female brain.

## Web Thinking in the Office

This feminine faculty of web thinking may give women an advantage in the morning whirl of getting children off to school. And it certainly will help them as they tackle complex business puzzles. But it can also cause problems in the office, as the following story illustrates.

An office manager was trying to decide which worker to promote to an important job, a young man or young woman. He gave both candidates a vexing business puzzle with three potential solutions, A, B, and C. He asked both aspirants to see him the following morning with their appraisals of the situation.

The man came in first and told the boss that he had thought it over, considered all of the aspects of the situation, and selected solution B. When the young woman entered, she said thoughtfully, "Well, solution A would be the best—if issues one or two can be solved first. Solution B would be most appropriate if issue X gets solved instead. Solution C is definitely the best alternative if—" The boss did not want to hear such a web of reasoning. He looked at her in dismay and said, "I think you should try another line of work."[41]

Because women, on average, do not think in a linear, step-by-step fashion as regularly as men do, men often regard them as less logical, less rational, less concrete, less precise, even less intelligent.

This gender difference can cause real troubles when the sexes work together.

"The road is all," Willa Cather wrote. Many women would agree. How you arrive at a conclusion is important to most women.[42] Women are "process-oriented." They are "gathering." They want to explore the multiple interactions, the multidirectional paths, all of the permutations of the puzzle. So women regard men as careless, unimaginative, or "tunnel-visioned" when they ignore what women think are important aspects of a problem.

Men get frustrated when women raise a host of variables that the men regard as superfluous. To most men, the immediate goal is more important than the process of arriving at the decision. They are "hunting"—focusing on the solution. They don't want to linger in the process; they want to complete the task.[43] So men think women are trying to undermine a business meeting when women introduce what men see as piles of unnecessary data.

Because of this gender difference in perspective, people of each sex often regard those of the other as poor team players.

## Web Thinking in the Future

Why can't a man be more like a woman? Why can't a woman be more like a man?

Because each sex is playing with a different deck of evolutionary cards. Both web thinking and step thinking are perfectly good ways of making decisions, depending on the circumstances. Both can be logical. Both, I think, are lodged in the gendered brain. Both emerged in a time long gone when the sexes did different jobs. And both decision-making styles are employed by each of the sexes at one time or another. As Christie Hefner, CEO of Playboy Enterprises, said during a speech in New York City in 1998, "The best managers are those who adopt both male and female strategies for doing business."

Still, for generations American executives have admired and rewarded those who analyzed issues on a component-by-component basis—the atomistic approach. An example is the common American obsession with the bottom line.

This focus is changing. As the information age and globalization develop even greater momentum, business leaders are becoming obliged to weigh and integrate more and more factors as they make decisions. Some business consultants have even begun to recommend ways to avoid linear thinking and acquire the holistic point of view.[44]

Peter Senge, former director of the Center for Organizational Learning at MIT's Sloan School of Management, has advised thousands of American business managers on preparing for the future global market. Among his clients have been Ford, Procter & Gamble, and AT&T. His recommendation: systems thinking. "Systems thinking," Senge explains, "is a discipline for seeing wholes. It is a framework for seeing interrelationships rather than things, for seeing patterns of change rather than static snapshots."[45]

Certainly linear thinking will remain an essential tool in the business community, particularly among the leaders of industry in capitalist societies. To make key decisions, these individuals often need to compartmentalize issues and focus their approach. In a crisis they are obliged to disregard much of the context of the situation in order to move assuredly with a single-minded view. Linear thinking is often dynamic thinking.

But the feminine propensity to look at business problems contextually, to concentrate on the whole of an issue rather than its parts, is becoming more and more valuable.[46] As businesswomen weigh more variables, consider more alternatives, pursue more options, and introduce new issues, they will bring balance and innovation to the office world. In fact, executives note that one of women's outstanding contributions to corporate America is their introduction of more varied, less conventional points of view.[47]

## Women's Mental Flexibility

A related gender difference is how the sexes reason. Psychologists have established that men tend to think and plan according to abstract principles more regularly than women do.[48] During committee meetings, for example, men argue more abstractly and make more categorical statements of right and wrong, while women use more examples and personal experiences—contextual data.[49]

Men also tend to become wedded to these abstract principles.[50] On average, men are more rule-bound, probably because context is less meaningful to them. Women are more inclined to make exceptions, probably because they can visualize a wider range of alternatives.

This feminine mental flexibility has a genetic component. Mental suppleness, David Skuse and his colleagues report, stems from the same gene or genes on the X chromosome that produce other aspects of feminine mental acuity.[51] As you may recall, this string of DNA is silenced in all men and expressed in about 50 percent of women.

Feminine mental flexibility is not always an endearing quality, of course. Women are notorious for changing their minds. But I am convinced that women's mental malleability will become an essential asset in the coming global marketplace. Peter Drucker, the eminent business analyst, and many other business experts believe that companies today must be able to alter plans, products, and services quickly and frequently to keep pace with their competitors.[52]

As competition increases, the demand for flexibility should escalate. Women's innate mental elasticity should become a valuable planning asset.

## Women's Intuition

"A woman's guess is much more accurate than a man's certainty,"
Rudyard Kipling wrote. Kipling was voicing a classic perception about
women's insight. At least since the ancient Greeks appealed to the
oracle at Delphi, folklore has reflected the view that women are the
more prescient seers.

Today this feminine gift can be explained. Women's intuition is a
composite of several female traits. As I point out in chapter 4, women
are far keener than men at noticing the creases in your clothes, the
tension in your voice, your tapping foot, the faint annoyance on your
lower lip. Women pick up more messages from your posture, gestures, emotional expressions, and voice. Then, with their uniquely
constructed and well-connected brains, women are more apt to assimilate all of these disparate little facts faster, achieving what appears to be a clairvoyant view.

In fact, "women's intuition" is probably another aspect of feminine
web thinking—arising from the prefrontal cortex where the brain as-
sembles and integrates information.

## Gut Thinking

But intuition is more than rapid assimilation of myriad data. People
regularly describe intuition as a gut reaction.

Even this can be explained. The prefrontal cortex and all other
brain parts are widely connected to one another and to bodily organs
via specific circuits.[53] Neurologist Antonio Damasio of the University
of Iowa College of Medicine calls these brain-body circuits "body
loops."[54] He believes these brain-body connections produce that "gut
reaction" that people report as they get a "hunch."

He and his colleagues demonstrated this brain-body connection in
an experiment involving gambling. They hooked up subjects to a de-
vice that measures responses of the skin. Then they encouraged them
to gamble with decks of cards.[55] Some of the subjects were normal
healthy adults; others had incurred injuries to the prefrontal cortex.
All were given four decks of cards to work with, as well as several gambling tasks. None was told that two of their decks had been stacked
to ensure heavy gaming loses.

The healthy subjects soon developed a "hunch" that they were playing with two kinds of decks, two "good" decks and two "bad" decks.
As they began to get their first inkling that certain decks were riskier
than others, their skin began to respond. Concurrently with this skin
response, they unconsciously began to avoid playing with the risky
decks. Only later did they become fully aware that two of the decks
were rigged. Nevertheless, their bodily responses had already begun
to help guide their behavior.

What is equally telling, the individuals with a damaged prefrontal
cortex never registered any skin response—and they continued to select cards from the "bad" decks. Their brains had failed to integrate
data from their body loops.

Damasio proposes that the skin, stomach, heart, lungs, bowels, and
other body organs send subliminal signals about the environment to
the prefrontal cortex. He calls these body cues "somatic markers." He
believes they help the rational mind make decisions.[56] In short, gut
reactions add emotional value to the brain's rational list of potential
options—and help steer behavior.

"All learning has an emotional base," Plato said. He perceived the
relationship between the rational mind and the feeling body. With
their facility for collecting and integrating myriad stimuli in the brain,
women may pick up and assimilate more of these body cues—the
handmaidens of intuition.

### "Chunking" Data

Intuition also comes from stored experience, says psychologist Herbert Simon of Carnegie Mellon University.[57] As a person learns how
to analyze the stock market, run a publishing company, diagnose an
illness, or play professional bridge, he or she begins to recognize the
quirks of the system, see regularities, and organize these patterns into
blocks of knowledge—what Simon calls "chunking."[58] With time,
more patterns are chunked. And linked. And these clusters of knowledge are stored in long-term memory.

Then, when a single detail of a specific complex pattern appears,
the experienced person instantly recognizes the larger composition, bypasses the time-consuming step-by-step analysis of each segment, and anticipates and predicts things that others must figure out

with plodding sequential thought. The chess master, for example, sees individual chess moves as tiny details of a larger military plan. The primatologist analyzes a baboon's yawn within the larger context of baboon social life. Simon believes that intuition stems from the ability to call upon organized, stored expertise.

"From long habit the train of thoughts ran so swiftly through my mind that I arrived at the conclusion without being conscious of intermediate steps."[59] So says Sherlock Holmes as he explains one of his deductions to the less quick-witted Watson. Thus did Sir Arthur Conan Doyle accurately describe this thinking process, chunking data.

Men and women most likely chunk data in much the same way. But each sex probably excels at chunking different kinds of facts. I would expect men to chunk knowledge about football because men spend more time watching football. Because women excel at reading people's faces and processing the nuances of social interactions (more on this in chapter 4), they are probably better at chunking—and intuiting—the nuances of social exchanges.

Men do use their intuition. When journalist Roy Rowan interviewed the chief executives of some of America's biggest corporations in the 1980s, many conceded that they used their gut reactions regularly, particularly when making important decisions. Rowan concluded, "The last step to success frequently requires a daring intuitive leap."[60]

Businesswomen are somewhat more intuitive, however. A 1982 survey of more than two thousand corporate managers discovered that female managers score higher than male managers on scales of intuition.[61]

Why have women developed a keen intuitive sense? It is not difficult to surmise. Ancestral women were constantly obliged to decipher the needs of their prelingual, highly dependent young.

I saw a contemporary instance of this at an airport while I was waiting in a coffee shop for a flight. It could have taken place a million years ago. Two women were sitting in the booth behind me with an infant. The child began to wail. "I just changed him," one said. "I know he isn't hungry," the other replied. Together the women reviewed dozens of possible reasons for the tears, trying to intuit the solution to this primordial human puzzle: a baby.

Psychologists and business analysts currently believe that intuition plays a productive, if often unrecognized, role in managerial decision making.[62] As the expanding global business community thrusts more executives into situations where they must size up foreign clients and colleagues, assess unfamiliar markets, and travel in novel environments, intuitive judgment may well become more highly valued—giving women a business edge.

### Women as Long-Range Planners

"Women are the best index of the coming hour," Ralph Waldo Emerson wrote. The American philosopher correctly discerned another feminine faculty that is related to web thinking: women's keen sense of future possibilities.

Both men and women have some ability for planning long term. I have found no concrete evidence that either sex is more skilled at this essential task. However, a few business analysts do believe that women are apt to think long term more regularly, while men are more likely to focus on the here and now.[63]

Men, for example, more frequently pile up business sessions back-to-back, sacrificing valuable respites they might have used for reevaluating their progress and considering future moves. Career women, on the other hand, take more time to catch their breath, reflect, and contemplate between meetings or appointments. Five minutes here, ten minutes there: women squeeze in time to assimilate what is happening around them and envision the future. Women "keep the long term in constant focus," says business journalist Sally Helgesen.[64]

Women's tendency to think long term is particularly visible in their attitude toward their own money.

When Terrance Odean and Brad Barber, economists at the Graduate School of Management at the University of California, Davis, examined the trading records of some thirty-five thousand clients at a large brokerage firm, they found that men traded 45 percent more often than women did. Odean said of women, "They don't churn their accounts the way men do."[65] In fact, three out of four female investors have no short-term investment goals, as a 1997 Gallup poll of six thousand investors done in collaboration with PaineWebber demonstrates.[66] Women also put more money into retirement plans, thinking of the distant future.[67]

This feminine attitude toward money is a winner in all but the worst financial markets. The National Association of Investors Corporations reports that women-only investment clubs earn a 21.3 percent average annual return on their purchases, while men-only clubs make an annual return of 15 percent.[68] NAIC also notes that women pay more attention to the overall operations of the companies they invest in and ride out market fluctuations more regularly. A financial planner in Washington, D.C., summed it up: "Women don't have a racetrack mentality about risk. They say, 'I'm not in it for the big kill, I'm in it for the long haul.' "[69]

## Biology of the Long-Term View

Women's long-term view of money might be explained by contemporary social realities. In order to rear their children, women move in and out of the job market more frequently than men do. So they have smaller pensions and fewer retirement benefits.[70] Women also live longer. So women are considerably less confident than men that they will have enough money to live comfortably in their senior years.

But women's propensity to think long term may also stem from feminine brain architecture. Why? Because long-term planning is unquestionably a mental process lodged in the prefrontal cortex of the brain—as an accident in the summer of 1848 vividly illustrates.

It was late afternoon along the Black River in Vermont, hot and sunny. Phineas P. Gage, a young construction foreman for the Rutland & Burlington Railroad, was preparing to blow up a rock escarpment so that his gang of railroad workers could lay ties. He had drilled the hole in the rock and placed the powder and fuse inside. Then he began to tamp at the hole with a three-foot-seven-inch iron bar.

Alas, Gage had forgotten a crucial step: covering the powder and the fuse with sand. The explosion erupted in his face. Worse yet, the iron rod, a little over an inch in diameter, entered with its pointed end into his left cheek and exited from the top of his skull, then sizzled through the air until it landed a hundred feet away.

Miraculously, Phineas Gage survived this accident. He talked to those around him as he lay waiting for an oxcart to take him to a nearby inn. He even sipped a cool drink on the porch of the hotel as the doctor examined him. With the exception of being blind in his left eye, he seemed to be physically restored in about two months.

But Gage's personality had changed entirely. A tranquil, competent, persistent, energetic, shrewd work leader became irreverent, capricious, obstinate, indecisive, impatient, shiftless—and hopelessly unable to carry out any long-term plans. Moments after he devised a scheme for the future, he would abandon it. He displayed no fore-thought about or interest in tomorrow. He lost job after job, then joined the circus, then drifted to South America to work on a horse farm and drive a stagecoach. Finally his mother and sister in San Francisco took him in.

From studying Phineas Gage and many other patients with injuries to the prefrontal cortex, neuroscientists now know that long-term planning takes place largely in this crossroads of the brain.[71] As you may recall, women and men display differences in the structure of the prefrontal cortex. So it is possible that these brain differences con-tribute to women's tendency to plan long term.

Long-term thinking would have been adaptive for women across the eons of deep history. Hunting required men to think about the habits of the animals and birds, the cycles of the moon, positions of the stars, patterns of the winds and rains, where creatures roamed last year, and where they would be heading next month or a year from now. Unquestionably, men had to think of events that would occur months, even years, ahead. But rearing and educating babies required women to prepare for exigencies that could occur decades down the road. As Dorothy Parker said of this feminine responsibility, "It takes eighteen years for a wise women to make a man of her son."

From millennia of planning for crises that could occur in the distant future, women may have evolved intricacies of brain architecture that predispose them to take the long-term view more regularly than men.

### The New Holism

Some men are certainly skilled at long-term planning. Financial offi-cers and CEOs of almost all major companies are, overwhelmingly, men. These men must be adept at long-range and strategic planning. But women are good at "the vision thing," as former U.S. president George Bush once called it.

Many business analysts and executives believe that the ability to cast issues within an even broader long-term perspective will become more and more relevant in the expanding global marketplace.[72] "Breadth" of vision and "depth" of vision have become buzzwords in many executive offices and boardrooms. As this trend accelerates, women should make major contributions.

All they have to do is be themselves.

## The Power of Imagination

"The problems of the world cannot possibly be solved by skeptics or cynics whose horizons are limited by the obvious realities. We need men who can dream of things that never were," said John F. Kennedy. JFK celebrated the imagination; he believed it was an essential ingredient for progress.

What is imagination but the ability to reach into the depths of one's stored knowledge, assemble reams of information in new ways, and suppose how various combinations of things would play out? These abilities are aspects of web thinking. So it seems likely that the capacity to imagine arises from specific areas of the prefrontal cortex where patterns are assimilated, plans are made, and novel responses are generated.[73]

With their specially constructed prefrontal cortex and well-connected brain, women are likely to excel at envisioning future outcomes in innovative ways.

"The possible's slow fuse is lit by the Imagination," wrote Emily Dickinson. With their natural talent for web thinking; their mental flexibility; their intuition; their broad, contextual long-term perspective; and their imagination, women have the innate talents to transform the business world.

They will have the opportunity, too. Women are entering the workforce in unprecedented numbers.

## The Rise of Working Women

"A woman's place in society marks the level of civilization," said the nineteenth-century feminist Elizabeth Cady Stanton. On the farm, women worked long and hard. American women also sold their surplus jam, soap, candles, quilts, and knitted sweaters in their parlors or at local farmers' markets. Some made commercial leather goods or clothes at home or cleverly ran a family business. But women rarely owned their own money or ran businesses by themselves.

By the 1830s, American women began to leave the farm for domestic service and low-paying factory work. In 1870, however, only 14 percent of American women of working age were employed outside the home and most of these were unmarried. They made up only 16 percent of the labor force.[74] Nevertheless, these female pioneers came home for holidays with stories, money, and store-bought clothes. They launched women's march into the modern world of paid labor.

After the Civil War an era of swift economic development enticed more young women into the swelling urban centers to teach, shuffle paper, or do factory work, at least until they married. More and more clerical and sales jobs became available by 1900. Then, after World War I, droves of young unmarried women took to typing, filing, answering phones, and tidying up the office world. By 1930, some 20 percent of all clerical jobs were taken up by women.[75] Many women even returned to work after their youngest child had completed high school.

The Great Depression of the 1930s saw more American unmarried women working from nine to five, mostly in repetitive, boring, subordinate, dead-end jobs. But the number of working women doubled between 1870 and 1940. During World War II it doubled once again.[76]

Women's participation in the paid workforce took a temporary plunge when men returned home from military service to resume their "rightful" positions in the working world. With the postwar economic boom, however, the demand for secretaries, teachers, nurses, and salespeople soon expanded job opportunities for women. By 1950, even married women were being pulled into the American workforce. By 1970, roughly 43 percent of women over the age of sixteen in the United States held paying jobs. By 1996, almost 60 percent of these women worked.[77]

In 1998, 46 percent of the American workforce was made up of women.[78] Less than 3.5 percent of Americans worked on a farm.[79]

### Fewer Babies

This historic trend toward women in the workplace is certain to persist, for several reasons. First, today women can work outside the home: they are bearing fewer babies.

On the farm, women needed many children to pick the beans, milk the cows, collect the eggs, and help in making candles and mending socks. Children were a cheap, reliable, essential part of the farm labor force. But as ambitious young men and women packed their carpetbags and caught trains for Chicago and New York in the nineteenth century, they left this necessity behind. Urban families did not need children by the dozen. Throughout the 1800s, American birthrates steadily declined.

This trend continues. Today American women bear an average of 2.2 children that live to adulthood. Across most of Europe, women bear even fewer young.[80]

New inventions have accelerated the decline in birthrates. Vastly improved medical technologies now save many more infants from untimely death. So a woman no longer has to conceive several infants in hopes that two or three will live. With modern methods of contraception, and the legalization of abortion in 1973, American women can also plan when they will bear young—and when they won't.

Thus, married women generally have more years to work before getting pregnant. They also remain at work longer during pregnancy, return to work sooner after bearing babies, and have fewer pregnancies that interrupt their careers.[81] In fact, today women, on average, spend less time being pregnant and caring for children than at any time in human evolution.

### Housework Is Getting Easier

Women's home lives are also far less demanding than in the past. Today most women are surrounded by ingenious gadgets. They don't grow the peas or raise the chicken that they serve for dinner; instead they hunt and gather in the grocery store. They go through catalogs or department stores to buy clothes instead of shearing sheep, carding wool, and weaving cloth for skirts and coats and blankets.

Hot running water, lightbulbs, washing machines, dishwashers, electric stoves, microwaves, refrigerators, baby bottles, Crock-Pots, Cuisinarts, canned foods, telephones, even Saturday morning television: an endless stream of inventions has made the tasks of cooking, washing, cleaning, shopping, and rearing babies easier for women. Women are finally liberated for work outside the home.

## More Jobs for Women

And work is available. The decline of smokestack and assembly-line industries and the growth of higher-skilled and service-sector jobs favor women. For example, all of the paper-shuffling and computer-clicking clerical jobs; work in the medical and technical professions; and teaching, nursing, home care, child care, retail sales, and service industry employment continue to expand.[82] These jobs, as a rule, do not require the physical strength of men. Many are part-time or have flexible hours as well—factors that appeal to women.

The contemporary workforce does require some education. But women have used their extra time to educate themselves, as you will see in chapter 3. As women become better educated, they bear even fewer children, continuing the downward trend of childbirth and the steady entry of women into the labor force.[83]

Moreover, many women must work. Due to a constantly rising cost of living, women in most dual-income families say they cannot maintain a decent standard of living unless both spouses keep a job. Other women work because a husband has lost his job, returned to school, or prefers to raise the children as a house dad. Some women work because they have divorced. In fact, as women in industrial societies join the paid workforce, they gain the economic means to depart unhappy marriages more easily. Many do, thereby increasing the number of years they will be obliged to work.

## Women Want to Work

Fewer children, more gadgets in the home, more jobs outside the home for women, more educated women, more divorce: all these factors encourage women to join the workforce. There are still other reasons. Women are marrying later. This means they have more premarital years to support themselves. Women are also living longer, extending the number of years they will work.

Women also work because they want the things that money buys. Television sets, cars, fancy meals, aerobics classes, massages, designer blue jeans, concert outings, vacations to Key West, Kyoto, or Kathmandu: in America and other prosperous nations, many women have become accustomed to comforts and entertainment.

As the necessity of bearing babies has declined, the attractions of working are mounting—drawing women into the world of paid employment.[84]

"Money is the most egalitarian force in society. It confers power on whoever holds it," according to New York social commentator Roger Starr. The Bureau of Labor Statistics reports that in 1993 American full-time working wives brought home, on average, 41 percent of the family's earnings. In the United States in 1998, some 20 percent of working wives earned more than their husbands did.[85] Also, men are retiring earlier, and more of them are working part-time.[86]

As a result, the "pay gap" between the genders is gradually closing—albeit slowly and unevenly.[87] American women are gradually gaining economic equality with men.

## The Worldwide Rise of Women in the Workforce

What happens in the United States often happens elsewhere later on. This is particularly true with regard to women.

Women in most of the world are having fewer children. Far fewer women are dying in childbirth.[88] More are getting an education.[89] And in many largely agrarian countries, insecticides, weed killers, tractors, and other technological innovations are freeing women from some farm labor, enabling them to enter more lucrative positions in the salaried world.[90]

As Ma Shuozhu, the patriarch of a large family in rural China, put it, "Farming is easy, there is time for business now."[91]

Overall, women currently make up 40 percent of the labor force in the countries of the European Union and the rest of the industrial world.[92] In 1990, women made up 39.5 percent of the worldwide labor force as well.[93] In fact, during the past two decades more women have begun to work outside the home almost everywhere in the world, while men's participation in the labor force has declined.[94]

Japan, for example, has lifted several restrictions on overtime and late-night jobs from which women were formerly barred. As a result, Japanese women currently account for 35 percent of all paid working hours. Women in Qatar, one of the strictest Muslim countries in the world, are beginning to work outside the home—without a veil. Even in the mountain jungles of Papua New Guinea, women are defying ancient customs to join the modern labor force.

Miriam Wilngal is among them. In 1997, Miriam appeared in *The New York Times* soon after a prestigious clan leader was killed in a jungle struggle. To compensate for the murder, the offending clan was fined $15,000, twenty-five pigs, and one girl in marriage: Miriam. Miriam Wilngal refused to wed, defying centuries of tribal custom, toppling an elaborately balanced structure of social debts and credits, and infuriating her relatives.

"I want to learn to be a typist," Miriam said to reporters in Port Moresby. "I want to have my own money; I don't want to have to depend on a man."[95]

## The Female Advantage

The world will see more women like Miriam.

In 1995, the United Nations Development Programme devised an ingenious index to compare women's advancement relative to men, using multiple measures of men's and women's health, life expectancy, educational attainment, literacy, access to knowledge, relative income, and standard of living. The UNDP then used these figures to rank each of 130 countries according to its degree of equality between the sexes.

Women fared best in Sweden, Finland, Norway, and Denmark, in that order. The United States ranked fifth. Japan placed eighth. Women fared worst in Niger, Mali, Sierra Leone, and Afghanistan. No society treated its women as well as it did its men. But over the past two decades, women moved toward equality in every single one of these societies. According to this 1995 survey, "Not a single country has slipped back in the march towards greater gender equality."[96]

Afghanistan must have slipped back since these data were published; the fundamentalist Taliban government has stripped women of all vestiges of equality.

Nevertheless, women are advancing in the paid job market in almost all contemporary societies. And many national and international organizations have launched projects that can only accelerate women's progress.[97]

## Web Thinking Will Be Valued

" 'Tis true: there's magic in the web of it," Shakespeare wrote. A remarkable confluence of technological and economic forces is enabling women to join the paid labor force around the world.

Moreover, with the growing complexity and sharpening pace of the global marketplace, more and more companies are likely to need employees who can collect, assimilate, and weigh a wide range of data; construct intricate relationships among constellations of ideas; imagine unexpected business developments; embrace ambiguity; intuit appropriate actions in puzzling business situations; strategize in multiple directions; devise complex long-term plans; envision a broad range of consequences; anticipate rapid, unexpected changes; prepare fallback options; set business objectives within their broader social context; think in systems; remain mentally flexible—and juggle a lot of office demands at once.

All these abilities are aspects of web thinking; all are characteristic of the female mind. Many may come to agree with Amy Pascal, president of Columbia Pictures: she says, "My greatest power as an executive is that I'm a woman."[98]

# CHAPTER 2

# THE ORGANIZATION WOMAN

## Feminine Team Playing

Nature is in earnest when she makes a woman.

OLIVER WENDELL HOLMES

Absolute power is absolutely delightful," it has been said. Both sexes seek and enjoy this ambrosia. But to men and to women, power is often a different thing. Men regularly associate power with rank and status. Women more often see power as a network of vital human connections.

Not every man or woman fits neatly into these psychological patterns. But sociologists, anthropologists, psychologists, even business analysts have extensively described this multifaceted gender difference: women's interest in personal contacts, their drive to achieve interpersonal harmony, and their tendency to work and play in egalitarian teams versus men's sensitivity to social dominance and their need to achieve rank in real or perceived hierarchies.[1]

Many psychologists believe that men's love of rank and women's appetite for connections develop in childhood, created by parents' attitudes, children's games, and the different ways that boys and girls attach to Mother. But men's striving for rank has been widely associated with the male hormone testosterone. Although the data are far less clear, I believe that women's taste for egalitarian harmonious connections is associated with the female hormone estrogen.

So in this chapter I maintain that men's and women's views of power come not just from childhood experiences but also from physiology and deep history. Moreover, I argue that men's biological drive for rank has helped them reach the top in traditional hierarchical corporations, while women's desire for connections (particularly connections to their young) has inhibited their rise into the highest echelons.

Corporate management and mores are changing, however. Organizations are replacing pyramidal office structures with lateral networks and work units composed of coequal team players. The business world is transforming in this and many other ways that will suit—and need—the female mind.

## Men Seek Rank, Women Love Connections

"Man is the rival of other men; he delights in competition." So wrote Charles Darwin. He understood men.[2]

Men tend to place themselves in a hierarchy; then they jockey for position. Men are more willing to endure exhausting workloads to attain rank. They more regularly sacrifice their health, safety, and precious time with family and friends to win status, money, and prestige.[3] Men and women exhibit no difference in what psychologists call "internal competitiveness," the desire to meet personal goals and display excellence. But men score much higher in "external competitiveness," the willingness to elbow others aside to get ahead.[4]

Women are, on average, more interested in cooperation, harmony, and connections—a network of support.[5] Women cast themselves in a web of friendships; they make lateral contacts with others, and they form cliques. Then women work to keep these ties intact. Women can be determined and clever at climbing the social or corporate ladder. But when they do achieve high rank, they more regularly downplay their authority. Fewer women are interested in power for power's sake.

## Feminine Flat Packs

Lateral connections versus ranked hierarchy; cooperation versus competition; interaction and sharing versus status and independence: these related gender differences emerge in childhood.

Little girls rarely engage in outright contests with clear winners and losers when they play informally. Instead, they arrange themselves in "flat packs," nonhierarchical, leaderless groups of about five or six who are sensitive to one another's needs.[6] These games have endless give-and-take. Girls take turns. They offer suggestions. They appeal to reason and try to persuade. Girls almost never resort to force. If a conflict erupts, girls will stop the game, ignore the rules, change the rules, or make exceptions. Somebody's feelings are at stake.

For girls, peace, harmony, social stability, and noncombative, nonhierarchical play are essential to having fun.[7] When girls play informally, winning is not vital; they seek applause and admiration. Paramount to most girls is "being liked."

Boys play war. Little boys sort themselves into large hierarchical packs; then they spend their days on the playground competing to be top dog.[8] If girls want to be liked, boys want to be respected. Boys interrupt, give orders, take orders, tease, and barter status to achieve and retain rank. Their games are more structured and complex than those of girls. Boys focus on the score. And unlike girls—who will quit a game when they get bored—boys stop when they have won or lost. Boys' games have clear winners and losers.[9]

Boys are much more concerned about rules. Their games, like baseball and football, have set and accepted regulations. Boys more often emphasize the principles of justice, fair play, and duty.[10] In a dispute, most boys fight about the rules and search for equitable ways to apply them. But bending the rules is out of the question. To boys, the point is to play by the rules—and win. As football coach Vince Lombardi allegedly summed up this male attitude, "Winning isn't everything, it's the only thing."

When journalist Peggy Orenstein studied a group of eighth-graders in two schools in northern California in the early 1990s, she immediately noticed these gender differences in the classroom. Students in one school were largely middle-class whites; students in the other were mostly low-income minorities from an inner city.[11] But boys were boys and girls were girls. Race, class, family background made no difference.

Girls in both schools, for example, disagreed courteously so as not to demean others who had spoken. Boys dissented directly and noisily. They skipped the protocol of hand raising to holler out answers, right or wrong. And boys manipulated their classmates, undermining or agreeing with one another to get attention and score points. Boys wanted credit for their remarks. As one boy from the middle-class school put it, "I think my opinions are important, so I yell them out. Girls will sit there until the bell rings with their hands up."[12]

## Women's Win-Win Attitude in the Office

These gender differences are particularly apparent in the business world.

Women's style of management is based on sharing power, on inclusion, consultation, consensus, and collaboration.[13] Women work interactively and swap information more freely than men do. Women managers encourage their employees by listening to, supporting, and encouraging them. Women give more praise—and praise is more valuable to women. Women also compliment, thank, and apologize more regularly. Women ask for more advice in order to include others in the decision-making process. And women tend to give suggestions instead of giving orders. In fact, women managers sometimes soften their criticisms so much that men don't realize they have been criticized.[14]

As Esther Dyson, an entrepreneur of the Internet, says, "The men are trying to do all this explicit, hierarchical, formal stuff. Women pay more attention to human factors."[15] Women personalize. They are more likely than men to join a company if they believe the atmosphere is cordial. Many even proceed to form a strong relationship with the company itself. Business analyst Carolyn Duff writes that women often see the organization "as if it were a live, caring person."[16]

As a result, women express greater commitment to the company and support company values more frequently than men.[17] They also spend less on expense accounts and take fewer rewards for themselves.[18] Women characteristically believe everyone can succeed in business: they take a win-win attitude in the office world.

## Men Play to Win or Lose

"Business is a combination of war and sport," said the French writer André Maurois. Men tend to see business in terms of win or lose.

Books written by men on how to succeed in business often advise that the best way to motivate employees is to keep them "off balance" and "in constant competition."[19] As a result, men tend to have difficulty sharing information. They collect it and hoard it.[20] Instead of focusing on office relationships, men are more likely to pay attention to who is dominant over whom.[21]

Men assign greater value to titles, office space, a high salary, and perks—the flags and emblems of rank.[22] Even the way men follow their investments reflects this interest in status. Men are much more likely to compare the investment performance of their portfolio against the performance of the Dow Jones Industrial Average than women are.[23]

## Men, Women, and Office Stress

These gender differences—men's passion for rank and women's love of connections—permeate almost every aspect of office life, including the ways in which the sexes handle office stress.

When scientists queried 2,000 male and 670 female workers in an American manufacturing business about depression, anxiety, and sleeplessness, they established that men agonize when they feel a lack of control over what they are doing at work. Women become stressed when they feel they have little or no social support. Men cope by going to the boss—a hierarchical move. Women manage by talking to friends and kin—a lateral rescue mission.[24]

Men suffer less stress than women from inflexible office rules, boundaries, and procedures. They grew up with inflexible rules on the playing field; the rigid rules of the workplace are nothing new. Besides, as discussed earlier, most men respect abstract rules; they construct them and abide by them.[25] But women have a different orientation. As girls they changed the rules on the playground to suit their more important social needs. With their proclivity for web thinking, women also embrace alternatives more easily. So women become much more stressed than men when confronted with office rules they cannot bend.

Women also become more stressed when they feel others are taking credit for their ideas. Because women tend to share power and swap information more freely than men, they are more careful with attribution. So if a woman comes up with a solution to a problem and a man paraphrases her ideas—and gets the credit—the woman feels slighted, even robbed.[26]

Men, on the other hand, are used to feeding off one another. They have borrowed ideas since boyhood. Men can't imagine why women are so sensitive about a minor theft.

### Jockeying During Office Presentations

These basic gender differences can create trouble when men and women make office presentations.

Men are more restless when they are tense, so they are inclined to take up more space as they speak.[27] Men also tend to spread their papers across the table, put an arm or elbow on the back of a woman's chair, and lean across her to make a point. Because women have sharp peripheral vision and a keen sensitivity to body postures (as discussed in chapter 4), they see these gestures as hostile intrusions on their personal space—as well as a hierarchical move. They feel stressed. But if a woman asks an overbearing, gesticulating male colleague to remove himself from her territory, he thinks she is being petty or trying to show that she outranks him.

Men will more regularly break a thoughtful silence to seize the floor.[28] They also deliver more take-charge speeches.[29] Men are more apt to attack with words, and they take coworkers more seriously when they argue back. As one speaks louder, the other follows, stimulating a spiral of "dominance matching" that can end in a shouting match.[30]

Women shrink from these verbal assaults. They are less likely to confront others during a presentation or to defend themselves when others confront them. To women, verbal jousting is stressful, irrelevant, even counterproductive to the task at hand: reaching consensus.

Even when men and women command, they generally do it differently. A man will simply state, "I need your report by Friday." A woman is more likely to ask obliquely, "Will this be done by Friday?" Women don't wish to dominate.

## Office Banter

Sociolinguist Deborah Tannen of Georgetown University, as well as other social scientists, has examined the ways the sexes use words in the office.[31] Because women regard conversations as ways to cultivate closeness, connection, consensus, and confirmation, says Tannen, they work to make the conversation flow smoothly and equally among office participants. If another person raises an issue or topic, a woman will support this direction of conversation. They respect one another's "turn" to speak and ask questions designed to include others in the conversation. They look for common ground and commiserate to build rapport. So women downplay their certainty with phrases like "I'm not sure."

"No two people can be half an hour together, but one shall acquire an evident superiority over the other," Samuel Johnson wrote. Spoken like a man. For men, conversations are often negotiations for rank. So men typically downplay their doubts. They brag more. They ask fewer questions, feeling these are appeals for help and admission of lower rank. Men are also more likely to give directives.

All is well when members of each sex talk among themselves; everyone knows what is going on. The problem comes, Tannen notes, when men and women talk to one another. Women ask for advice more regularly than men, even when they really don't want counsel. <u>Women are searching for connection.</u> Men don't ask for guidance unless they need it. So when a woman asks a man for advice, she often does not achieve her objective. Instead of feeling included, the man may feel superior.

And men cannot fathom why women apologize so much. I once saw a male photographer's assistant become dumbfounded by this female trait. His boss, Joyce Ravid, was taking my picture. I would cock my head; she would snap the shot. I would change my pose; she would click again. We had a rhythm going. But we would get out of "sync," wasting film and time. So I kept mumbling, "I'm sorry." She would chirp back, "I'm sorry." On we went, peeping like canaries. Finally her assistant demanded to know what we were so sorry about.

In what are known as "ritual apologies," women say "I'm sorry" to smooth out small imbalances in relationships.[32] Men don't "get it." They don't apologize unless they have made a genuine mistake and wish to admit their fault—and their lowered status. So when women make their ritual apologies, men often think this is an expression of weakness, subservience—and lesser rank.

Words, words, words. Even what men and women choose to talk about in the office can lead to friction. Men gravitate to jokey, teasing one-liners and impersonal chat about politics, business, or sports. To women, this teasing banter is a put-down; it establishes rank and disrupts a woman's need for connection and equality. Women generally don't like impersonal chatter about sports or politics, either. They find these topics evasive and distancing.

So women banter with stories and anecdotes. They disclose minor secrets about themselves, and they often mock themselves.[33] These personal references and self-deprecating humor leave most men cold. To them, self-mockery is passive and pathetic. They regard self-disclosure as entirely inappropriate in a business setting. To reveal one's personal life is to be weak and vulnerable.

### Are Boys and Girls Taught to Define Power Differently?

How we talk is shaped by factors other than gender, of course. Class, age, economic and social power, and cultural traditions often define who asks the questions, who speaks politely, who uses direct language, who hedges here or there. So, to see if any of these differences between the sexes also occur in other societies, psychologist Marilee Monnot examined videotaped conversations between Masai men and women, nomadic cattle herders of Kenya. She also recorded conversations among the Hamar herders and gardeners of southwest Ethiopia and the Baka Pygmies of the tropical forests of southeast Cameroon.[34]

Women in all of these societies were more likely than men to use language to emphasize cooperation and connection. Men's speech more regularly reflected competition and the pursuit of rank.

Scientists in many disciplines believe that men and women, boys and girls, *learn* to behave in these gendered ways. They say that children's games, parents' rules, teachers' demands, and society's subliminal messages direct little girls to seek cooperation and connection and train boys to form hierarchies and compete. Some theorize that these gendered behaviors are instilled in infancy. Because girls are not encouraged to separate from their mothers, they develop a world-view in which secure relationships are primary. Because boys more regularly sever this close bond to adopt male friends, male games, and male ways of interacting, they develop a sense of self as separate and autonomous instead.[35]

Infancy, childhood, and society certainly do influence how the sexes perceive and construct the world around them. But the lifeways of virtually every other primate species support the view that men's thirst for rank and women's craving for connections also stem from our human heritage.

## Monkey Politics

In almost all primate communities where more than one male resides, males form what primatologists call a "male/male dominance hierarchy."

These dominance ladders vary according to the particular species, the amount of food and safety in the environment, the number of males and females in the group, who has kin nearby, even the time of year. Some hierarchies are quite rigid; some are remarkably flexible. Some are linear, like beads on a hanging chain. Some are based on complex combinations of alliances.[36] But at any single moment the social lattice is defined. Every male knows who's who and who's the boss. Male primates rarely form egalitarian congregations.[37]

Among chimpanzees, our closest relatives, males are preoccupied with rank. At the Arnhem Zoo, in the Netherlands, male chimps wrangle over power at least five or six times every day.[38] Often one male will try to intimidate another by staging a "bluff over." He rises on his hind limbs, arches his back, rocks from side to side, hoots, and tears past his rival, ignoring him. Then he falls to the ground, pounds the dirt with his fists, and crows triumphantly.

Perhaps you have felt humiliated at a business meeting or party when a colleague or acquaintance looked over your shoulder to scan the room or rushed past you to greet another. This "cold shoulder" is a simian gesture of contempt.[39]

Male chimps even form coalitions to maneuver for position in the community. In one hideous status battle at the Arnhem Zoo, two underlings ganged up on the alpha male in their common night cage. It happened after the last of the scientists and keepers had gone to bed. By morning, the alpha male lay dying on the cage floor, a mass of blood and broken bones. Several of his fingernails, his toes, and both of his testicles had been bitten off.

"Politics is the gizzard of society, full of gut and gravel," Thoreau once said. Female primates also rank themselves. They can be calculating social climbers, too, making clever ad hoc coalitions to get their way.[40] But female hierarchies are generally more stable—and much more subtle.

Female competition is "low key" and "chronic," says primatologist Barb Smuts of the University of Michigan, while male disputes tend to be more "episodic" and much more "intense."[41] Female chimps attack and maim one another far less often than males do.[42] And they fight over different things. Female chimps compete for food or to protect their young; they rarely bicker over rank.[43]

## Power as an Aphrodisiac

So modern men's compelling drive for rank undoubtedly stems from prehistoric times, when male/male dominance hierarchies prevailed. And it is easy to see why men regard rank, status, money, titles, and office space as power: these accessories attract women.

"Nothing agreeth worse than a lady's heart and a beggar's purse," wrote the English satirist John Heywood in the sixteenth century. Women in tribal societies, be they Zulus, Aleut Eskimos, or Mbuti Pygmies, are more interested in marrying "big men," individuals with rank.[44] American women polled in both the 1930s and the 1980s considered a potential mate's financial prospects about twice as important as men did.[45] Even female mice, deer, and bighorn sheep find high-ranking males more attractive.[46]

"Power is the great aphrodisiac." Henry Kissinger's well-known insight is right on target. Women have probably been "turned on" by high-status men since their ancestors were living in the trees. For an important reason: ancestral women reared babies as a living. Those who mated with socially powerful men reaped the payoffs of their mates' intelligence, savvy, charisma—and their ability to protect and provide.[47]

So the teenage boys who join a gang to look important, the New Guinea tribesmen who parade their coveted feathers at a feast, and the American businessmen who work late, take business risks, and check their net worth in the stock market every morning are all stepping to one of nature's oldest tunes—the mating dance. Some men even die of overwork, trying to achieve. In Japan this is known as _karoshi_. Men expire from heart attacks provoked by exhaustion from the office grind.

"The tragedy of life is not so much what men suffer, but rather what they miss," Thomas Carlyle once said. True enough. But those who rise to the top of the male/male dominance hierarchy usually get more opportunities to mate and breed, passing their seed toward eternity— as well as selecting for the male appetite for rank.

## The Origin of Female Friendships

How and why did women evolve their tremendous drive to connect with friends, assemble in flat packs, and nurse these egalitarian social webs? Data indicate that these feminine proclivities also lie in our primordial past.

Most female primates do not cultivate female friends; they build relationships mainly with their female kin. But the human female habit of making close, relatively egalitarian social bonds with female nonrelatives does occur among our nearest relatives, common chimps and pygmy chimps, also known as bonobos.[48]

Female common chimps cultivate female friends when they live in captivity. In the Arnhem Zoo, mothers form stable long-term friendships with mothers of other families.[49] These females maintain their friendships daily, giving gifts of leaves and twigs, sitting beside female companions to clean their fur, or supporting friends by standing near them during disputes.

Each female knows who is dominant over whom, just the way women know the subtle status differences between the members of their female groups. But differences in rank are generally expressed delicately. In fact, these chimp friendship networks look quite similar to girls' flat packs and women's cliques.

Bonobos are much more eccentric at making and keeping female friends. These apes live in the jungles of the Democratic Republic of the Congo, formerly Zaire. Females leave their natal community at puberty. When they arrive at a new locale they begin to cultivate relationships with older females. They start by gazing at a particular female, sitting close to her, and grooming her when permitted. After a few weeks these two individuals generally become close companions. This friendship is the newcomer's passport into a network of females she will cultivate and count on all her life.[50]

That bonobos build female/female networks and maintain these friendships in the wild is remarkable. How they sustain these ties is even more unusual. They engage in "genito-genital rubbing," or *hoka-hoka,* as the local Mongandu people call this form of coitus. One female reclines; the other embraces her face to face, and they rub their pendulous clitorises together. Often both reach orgasm. Female bonobos engage in *hoka-hoka* almost every day to calm a nervous comrade, reconcile after a spat, relax before meals, or relieve social tension at other times. Their sexual exchanges enable them to tighten the sisterly coalitions they will use to control food sources and gain status—as a team.[51]

These female friendships have genetic payoffs.[52] Among bonobos, females with influential connections gain food and social support they will use to rear their young.[53] Female primates with the "right" connections and higher status tend to bear their infants in faster succession, too.[54] In short, they bear more young. Among chimps, the infants of high-status females also mature faster to bear infants of their own. Hence females with the right connections spread more of their DNA into the future.[55]

Ancestral women who made friends and built a team of ever-ready supporters undoubtedly also bore more young and had access to more food and protection as they reared them. Their young survived—and passed along the feminine tendency to regard power as connections.

## The Biology of Women's Appetite for Connections

No one knows what it is in the female brain that drives women to seek and build harmonious lateral connections and assemble in flat packs or egalitarian teams. This issue has never been addressed. But I'll hazard a guess that these feminine proclivities are associated with the female hormones, the estrogens.

At puberty the ovaries begin to secrete great quantities of these powerful chemical compounds. At puberty the feminine urge to connect, cooperate, and sustain a system of support also intensifies.[56] At menopause the levels of estrogen decline. And with menopause, women become far more assertive, outspoken, and independent (this is discussed in chapter 7). Moreover, estrogen is directly related to nurturing behaviors in many mammalian species, including humans.

So I have come to suspect that estrogen contributes to women's deep drive to connect with others, achieve harmony and consensus, and work and play in relatively egalitarian flat packs.

### Testosterone: The Hormone of Attainment

There is a great deal of evidence that testosterone, the predominantly male hormone, is associated with men's drive for rank. As sociologist Steven Goldberg of City College of the City University of New York sees it, testosterone wires the male brain during fetal life for a trait he calls "male attainment," leaving men more motivated than women to fight for status.[57]

Scores of scientific studies support Goldberg's thesis. When testosterone is injected into castrated Mexican swordtail fish, female *Anolis* lizards, low-ranking male and female ring doves, and low-ranking hens, they all advance up the social hierarchy.[58] High rank has been associated with high levels of male hormones in an all-male group of rhesus monkeys, in female monkeys and chimps, and in several other mammalian species.[59]

High levels of testosterone are commonly associated with rank in people as well.[60]

Aggressive criminal lawyers, hockey players, and actors often have higher levels of testosterone than ministers do.[61] Before a contest, such as a competitive video game or a chess match, testosterone levels rise abruptly in most men.[62] After men compete at wrestling, tennis, or chess, levels of testosterone are higher in winners than in losers for at least an hour.[63] Even male spectators at a soccer match often get a jolt of testosterone when their team wins. Perhaps this is why male fans like to cheer and why they sometimes become so aggressive when their team triumphs.

The relationship between testosterone and assertiveness is more complex in women. In one study of 350 women, those who had been subject to high levels of testosterone in the womb were less likely to marry, had fewer children, regarded career as more important than family, pursued more male-dominated occupations, and achieved higher-status jobs.[64] Women in professional, technical, and managerial jobs tend to have higher levels of testosterone than do female clerical workers, housewives, and women in service occupations.[65]

Still, in women, levels of testosterone do not go up and down as they win or lose at sports, as is the case with males.[66] Scientists therefore believe that women's competitive behavior is less governed by levels of testosterone.

Nature isn't tidy. There is no simple correlation among hormones, aggressiveness, and status. For example, professional men tend to have lower levels of male hormones than do blue-collar and unemployed men.[67] Bodily testosterone needs to be at a specific level to correlate with high rank. In addition, your social maturity, who you know, how long you have lived in the community, how you conduct yourself, and a host of other cultural and psychological phenomena contribute to the creation of your rank.

Nevertheless, young men have at least seven times more testosterone than young women do. And like males of many other species, men everywhere in the world are much more likely to compete aggressively for rank.[68]

## The Biology of Risk Taking

Many other chemical compounds have been associated with the drive for titles, status, and prestige.[69] The most interesting to me is monoamine oxidase (MAO), a substance that plays a role in risk taking.

Both men and women like novelty; both like variety; both like intense experiences. But boys and men seek thrills more regularly than women do—on the road, in the sky, under water, at the gambling table, and in the financial markets of the world.[70] Men buy more high-risk stocks and bonds.[71]

Psychologist Marvin Zuckerman calls this drive for intense novel experiences "sensation seeking." He reports that seeking thrills is associated with low levels of the calming agent MAO. And he notes that men tend to have lower levels of MAO than women do.[72]

We all know that women like adventure. For many years my identical twin sister got up every morning to ride the winds above Aspen, Colorado, in her hot air balloon. But, on average, men appear more predisposed to do or die. Women are the cautious sex.

## Women Hold Grudges

Men's need for rank has its drawbacks. Overwork, lack of sleep, less time with friends and family: this form of ambition takes its toll.

But women also suffer from the pursuit of *their* version of power: harmonious connections. Many suppress their personal views, their interests, even their careers to accommodate others and maintain harmony in their social worlds. As Elizabeth Cady Stanton said of this feminine proclivity, "The thing which most retards and militates against women's self-development is self-sacrifice."

Women's appetite for connections can be debilitating in the office. Because women generally seek consensus and harmony with those around them, they have much more difficulty working with people they dislike or disagree with. Women, more than men, tend to distance themselves from their rivals.[73] Men, for example, will join one another for a drink after a divisive meeting in the office; women flee.

Even worse, women remember slights; they are thinner-skinned than men.[74] Women get visibly upset at inappropriate times, as when someone disagrees or argues with them. Men were bullied or insulted on the playground since they began to walk; they learned early to handle verbal attacks, shrug off their losses, and try again. Moreover, men are biologically primed to fight for rank. So they try to bury their resentments to move ahead.

Not women. Women grew up in egalitarian groups, where they took pains to respect one another's feelings. They form cliques at work. And they are built to strive for cooperation and consensus. So when a colleague picks a fight or besmirches a woman's work or reputation, the woman remembers. As Dawn Steel, former president of Columbia Pictures, said of her female employees, "They take things too personally; way, way too personally."[75]

When Deloitte & Touche, in collaboration with the Fortune Marketing Research Group, polled hundreds of businessmen and businesswomen about the skills they thought women needed to acquire to be more effective in business, these executives responded with several suggestions.[76] Among them: Women should separate their emotions from their business decisions and take things less personally.

Girls and women hold grudges, too.[77]

Holding grudges is probably an ancient practice among humans—female chimpanzees also nurse their grievances. Male chimps tend to make peace with one another within hours after a fight. But when a female is betrayed by another female who has handled her infant carelessly or eaten too much of the communal lunch, she may slap or shove this transgressor, then ignore her for days or weeks.[78]

This feminine trait may be yet another adaptive mechanism that arose in deep history. Ancestral women, like other mammalian females, could not afford to misjudge another's character more than once. A careless or hostile peer could seriously harm a woman's child. Women also had to judge their lovers carefully. They risked nine months of pregnancy and years of child rearing. So our feminine forebears had to remember minor slights and treat offenders accordingly, thus possibly selecting for the tendency of women to hold on to their resentments.

"The female of the species is more deadly than the male," wrote Rudyard Kipling. Men can be venomous creatures, to be sure. But for "getting even," women take the cake.

When girls and women feel snubbed, they often stop speaking to you—unlike boys and men, who tend to express themselves with direct physical confrontation.[79] Women exclude a colleague from informal meetings, ignore him or her at conferences and other business gatherings, and use their connections to present a united front against him or her.[80]

Women prefer not to confront—so they skillfully spread false rumors behind one's back.[81] In a study of 350 men and women, psychologist Donald Sharpsteen found that women are far more likely than men to use gossip for revenge.[82] As one female executive in the investment business said, "I see a lot of backstabbing among women."[83]

H. L. Mencken saw women as "enormously dangerous and hence enormously fascinating." Women, like men, unquestionably have a dangerous side. But from millions of years of rearing helpless babies, women also evolved a powerful arsenal of valuable skills. They are good at doing many things simultaneously, thinking contextually, using their intuition, remaining flexible, planning long term, seeking connections, generating consensus among peers, and working in egalitarian teams.

I will discuss how these feminine attributes are becoming highly useful in the emerging global marketplace. But first I must look at the question of why women have not achieved parity with men in the traditional corporate world.

## The Organization Woman

"I would prefer not to," said Bartleby whenever his boss asked him to carry out his clerical duties. This strange fellow in Herman Melville's story "Bartleby the Scrivener" expressed what most men have come to feel about clerical work.

In 1900, men held 75 percent of all clerical jobs in the United States.[84] By 1990, women performed 68 percent of all computer and data processing and 79 percent of all secretarial and administrative services.[85] About 98 percent of secretaries and over 90 percent of all personnel clerks, data-entry keyers, bookkeepers, stenographers, and receptionists were also women.[86] Over 80 percent of all billing clerks, file clerks, payroll clerks, and information clerks were women.

Women are also rising up the corporate ladder. In 1990, 40 percent of those in middle management in America were women.[87]

But few women have become the highest-ranking business executives or board members in major corporations. In 1995, 95 percent of the senior-level managers of the Fortune 1000 industrial and Fortune 500 service companies were men, whether these jobs were defined by title, paycheck, or responsibility.[88] Of the top five earners in each of the Fortune 500 companies, only 2 percent were women.[89]

Relatively few women have been named to boards of directors. A survey by Catalyst, a New York research organization that promotes the advancement of women in the workforce, indicates that 84 percent of Fortune 500 companies had at least one woman on their board of directors in 1997, up from 69 percent in 1993.[90] "The woman's seat," male members sometimes call it. In 1997, women held only 10.6 percent of all board seats in major companies in America.[91]

Interestingly, women are not entering business schools in anywhere near the numbers in which they are entering medical schools or law schools. In the 1970s, only 5 percent of MBA students in American business schools were women.[92] As of 1997, 30 percent of students at the Harvard Business School were women. But that figure had not changed in five years.[93] This static enrollment level of women is also true of the other major business schools in the United States.[94] Moreover, today only 8 percent of the tenured faculty of the country's top twenty business schools are women.[95]

If women's climb to the topmost levels of the American corporate business community has been unimpressive, conditions are similar or worse in other countries. Today women shuffle the papers, take the notes, arrange the meetings, and keep the office in working order in all of the advanced industrial countries.[96] But no more than 5 percent of senior management positions in major corporations are held by women in any industrial society.[97]

## Why Women Don't Reach the Top

Felice Schwartz, founder of Catalyst, once said, "I don't know a CEO in the country who wouldn't like to have at least one or two really talented women in high levels in his company."[98] Why don't more women reach the top in the corporate world?

Male managers point out that women are newcomers to this sector of the marketplace; hence few have been in the pipeline long enough or had enough experience to reach the top. Others say that women who pursue a career in business generally do not have the benefits of the old-boy network. Many analysts report that superiors still do not choose to mentor or sponsor women as regularly as men. And women generally don't get invited to the golf games or sports events where men mix fun with office matters.[99]

In short, managers still discriminate against women by the ways they hire, whom they choose to train on the job, the duties they assign workers, and how they pay and promote.

Even a miniscule bias in how a company promotes its staff can make a difference—as researchers discovered when they constructed a computer model of a fictional company. Their fantasy company had eight job levels, equal numbers of men and women on the bottom rung, and a standard policy for promoting staff up the ladder. But they built into the system a 1 percent bias favoring the promotion of men.[100] Then they simulated a series of promotions.

It did not take long before 65 percent (instead of 50 percent) of those on the highest rungs were men.

## A Delicate Balance: Work and Family

But discrimination is only one of the reasons why women are not achieving parity with men at the highest-ranking jobs of the traditional corporate world. I suspect there is a biological component to this complex situation: as testosterone and other male hormones contribute to men's drive to reach the top of the business ladder, estrogen most likely contributes to women's drive to take time out to rear their children—undermining their ability to achieve these high-status jobs.

As discussed in chapter 5, estrogen is clearly associated with nurturing behavior in many mammalian species, including humans. And there is a great deal of evidence that women are more inclined to try to balance work with family than men are. In a 1989 *New York Times* poll of 1,497 American working parents, for example, 83 percent of working mothers reported that they were torn by the conflicts of work and family life; some 72 percent of working fathers said they felt the same way. But far more of these working women than men thought their career was too big a sacrifice; it wasn't worth it.[101]

A striking example is the much-discussed case of Brenda Barnes, former president and chief executive officer of Pepsi-Cola, North America, and mother of three children, ages ten, eight, and seven. In 1997 she resigned from her high-pay, high-status job to rear her young. As she said, "Every time you would miss a child's birthday, a school concert or a parent-teacher discussion, you'd feel the tug."[102]

Unquestionably, many, many women are ambitious. All sorts of women work ten hours a day to save their families from poverty and malnutrition. Many delay giving birth until their mid-thirties to build careers. Some have fewer children in order to concentrate on office duties. Large numbers leave children in long hours of day care to stay late at work. Often, women in senior positions have no children.

But as a rule, women are not as willing as men to stay late in the office, travel constantly, skip school events, entertain clients in the evening, or relocate, sacrificing their family lives and their personal interests for their careers.[103] Many more women drop out of high-salaried jobs if they feel their work jeopardizes their ability to rear their children.[104] As a female executive in Seattle put it, "I think I'll always work outside the home. But make no mistake about what comes first. He has red hair, and he weighs thirty-six pounds."[105]

Catalyst reports that "commitment to family responsibilities" is among the primary hindrances to women's progress into rarefied business circles.

This delicate balance between work and child rearing is seen everywhere in the world. In a 1995 study of work habits, the United Nations documented women's balancing act in 130 societies. In remote villages of Argentina, for instance, women more regularly choose informal employment, such as street vending, over steadier indoor jobs. They say they want to take their children with them when they work.[106]

From the strictly evolutionary perspective this feminine proclivity to balance work and family makes sense: nothing is more important to a woman's future than the survival of her children. Men have opportunities to breed throughout their lives. But women can bear only a few babies. They are obliged to rear these precious creatures if they are to spread their DNA into perpetuity. This is nature's law.

Despite these biological realities, more and more women will undoubtedly reach the highest echelons of the corporate world in coming decades. Women have more education than in earlier times and greater expectations for careers. Federal and state laws concerning job discrimination and judicial decisions concerning affirmative action have helped somewhat. And companies have begun to take women's needs seriously, providing more flexible work schedules and other mechanisms that enable women to balance work and family.

Still, women's rise to the highest corporate ranks will be slow and uneven. Even in Sweden, where policies on child care and flexible work hours rank among the finest in the world, those men and women who take time off still jeopardize their careers. As Claes Tell, a father, said of his time on parental leave, "Top management, in general, still holds traditional values. You can't get to the top this way."[107]

So I am not convinced that women will ever reach parity with men in the highest echelons of the traditional corporate world. Not because women lack the education or intelligence. Not because women fear failure. Not because men will monopolize these trophy jobs. But because fewer women are willing to work long hours, take job risks, transfer to other cities, and jeopardize their family and personal lives in other ways to gain the summit. They feel they have something more important to do.

But the business climate is changing. Segments of the evolving corporate community are beginning to need women's flexible, co-operative spirit—and offering new avenues to the top.

## The Rise of the "Flat" Corporation

In past economic eras, most large businesses were structured as pyramids.[108] Each hierarchy operated with similar management principles and comparable processes. Each company had similar regulations, similar expectations, similar financial and accounting systems, and comparable worker benefits. From family farm to megacorporation, the social contract was generally the same between worker and workplace—one based on mutual loyalty, lifelong employment, paternalism, and a ranked, linear ladder of authority. The "organization man" started at the bottom and worked his way up, slapping backs, talking sports, taking risks, and working late.

But the late 1980s saw unprecedented organizational upheavals in the American business community. Mounting global competition accelerated the need to cut fixed costs and increase efficiency, driving many companies to slash their workforces. Moreover, the expansion of companies around the world, in tandem with the revolution in telecommunications (such as fax machines, e-mail, and satellite-transmitted telephone conferencing), has undermined the ability of a few people at the top to broker or withhold vital information and connections.

Even male business leaders no longer see the old hierarchical order as sacrosanct. To avoid what some call "corporate Alzheimer's," to ride the information highway, to keep in touch with their expanding business networks, and to attract capable staff, many have begun to believe that they must restructure their organizations. They are doing this by replacing the pyramidal command-and-control model with far more flexible, decentralized, less hierarchical office structures, as well as work units composed of team members who see themselves as coequals.

## Corporations Are Linking Instead of Ranking People

What will these nontraditional structures be like?

A number of business experts and trend analysts have devised versions of tomorrow's corporation.[109] Bruce Pasternack and Albert Viscio, business consultants at Booz Allen & Hamilton, voice a common theme: the "centerless corporation."[110]

These management experts interviewed chief executives and examined the structure, functions, and performance records of hundreds of companies around the world. They have come to believe that one important emerging business model will be a global enterprise engaged in several lines of business but lacking a huge central home office.

A minimal "global core" of senior executives, they say, will provide high-level strategies, develop leaders, place key workers, and oversee the company. But the loosely connected interdependent business units will basically run themselves. Working in teams will be essential. Layers of middle managers will be dismantled to create "flatter" organizations. And the company's primary assets will be its knowledge, its skilled workers, and the links between disparate, largely autonomous company parts.

Business analyst Sally Helgesen has mapped out a variant of this nonpyramidal or "flat" corporation.[111] The emerging corporation, she proposes, will be centered around a hub with spokes radiating out to satellite units. Each manager will be at the center of a circle of employees, with spokes of direct communication radiating out to still more circles of employees—a spiderweb or giant wheel of fortune, as Peter Drucker calls it.

According to Helgesen, each component unit will be relatively autonomous. Individuals will work in cooperative teams, units that may change weekly, seasonally, or annually. Managers of these teams will be more like team leaders who define, organize, allocate assignments, inspire, provide assistance, and build a network of team players. Basic to this kind of structure is flexibility—with all of its advantages. Managers can make connections with a wider range of colleagues and convene teams to focus on a particular issue, then disband the teams when their work is done.

In this schema, the chief executive still leads; he or she just does it more subtly. No longer "alone at the top," these CEOs are at the center of the action—able to collect data from all sectors of the company. In fact, everyone is privy to a wider range of knowledge. Most important to stockholders, this business structure gives the company the ability to change rapidly in an age when fast-changing technology and global competition prevail.[112]

Many companies have already adopted some version of this less hierarchic, "flattened" wheel of fortune. Some have reduced their echelons of middle management; others have created a greater number of semiautonomous teams or built new lateral connections among company units. Among these reorganized companies are the Body Shop, Ford Motor Company, Kodak, Hewlett-Packard, Wal-Mart, and one of America's largest nonprofit organizations, the Girl Scouts of the U.S.A.[113]

Peter Drucker believes there will be many more. In the "Knowledge Economy," as Drucker calls this evolving economy, skilled workers "are not amenable to the command-and-control methods of the past."[114] Instead of being ranked, like workers of the past, Drucker advises, knowledge workers must be "linked."

As political analysts Francis Fukuyama and Abram Shulsky put it in a report of the Rand Institution, "large, vertically integrated corporations will either flatten their managerial hierarchies or else evolve into networks of smaller, more agile firms."[115]

## Virtual Companies

The most extreme form of the flat, decentralized business is the so-called virtual corporation. Such organizations range from "office-less" firms to traditional companies whose units communicate via computer.

In the officeless company, members may meet weekly in a rented space. Most tasks are given to freelancers. Managers lease workers from other companies or hire employees short term as needs arise.

And colleagues conduct business affairs on the Internet. Preposterous? I don't think so. Every day in the United States, more freelance workers are becoming laced to one another in networks that can be perceived only by messages left on an answering machine and a trail of paper spewing from a fax.

Edie Weiner and Arnold Brown, trend analysts of Weiner, Edrich, Brown, a business consulting firm in New York City, call all these new organizations "hyborgs," short for "hybrid organizations."

Each hyborg, they maintain, will be unique—with its own idiosyncratic mix of structures, means of communication, worker-management relations, and job benefits. Permanent versus contract employees; knowledge-based versus tangible assets; management jobs that rotate; work done in the United States, China, or Haiti; subsidiaries; joint ventures; subcontracting; strategic alliances; licenses; leases; offshore or transnational connections; global assets; multiple purposes; multiple products; flextime; job sharing; profit splitting; paid or unpaid leave; variable-pay programs: each company will be a mix-and-match organism unlike any other.

"It's cafeteria-style business," Edie Weiner says. But relationships will be based on results rather than loyalty; on self-reliance, not paternalism; and on change as opposed to permanence.[116] As Weiner recently said to me, "The model of the future organization is that there is no model."

## Women in Hyborgia

Here's the point. These trends toward decentralization, a flatter business structure, team playing, lateral connections, and flexibility favor women's ways of doing business.[117]

This flexible, flat organizational form is similar to the flat packs that little girls naturally construct on the playground. It is similar to the cliques that women form in offices, and to the cliques that female chimpanzees naturally compose. It is similar to the foraging parties that ancestral women naturally formed on the plains of ancient Africa. And it fits the way that women naturally view power. From the evolutionary perspective, women should be particularly effective at working in these nonhierarchical business webs.

Women should be attracted to many of these hyborgs, too. Where team playing is the rule, where lateral, more egalitarian relationships are valued, where the eight-hour day is obsolete, and where rigid, uniform rules governing leaves of absence, vacations, and retirement have been replaced by more flexible working conditions, women will find the versatility they need to rear their children.

Political scientist Harlan Cleveland anticipated this kind of flexible business structure in 1972, when he predicted that "the organizations that get things done will no longer be hierarchical pyramids with most of the real control at the top. They will be systems—interlaced webs of tension in which control is loose, power is diffused, and centers of decision are plural."[118]

What Cleveland did not anticipate is that this emerging office climate would be especially hospitable to women's natural talents: an interactive style of management, a proclivity to share information, a need to strive for group consensus, a desire to empower workers, a comfort with ambiguity, and a tendency to seek win-win solutions to sticky business problems.[119]

As more women assume positions of authority, either in traditional corporations or in some of the newer kinds of companies, they will inevitably bring change to the office world.

Female executives will undoubtedly exchange ideas with a wider range of colleagues, thereby increasing the flow of information. They will conduct meetings that emphasize inclusion and the sharing of power. They will add flexibility to work regulations and schedules. Some women managers will hold informal business discussions in new kinds of settings; instead of doing business on golf courses, they may make deals during evening telephone conversations, at women's clubs, or in meetings on women's issues. Some will rearrange office furniture to minimize displays of rank and title. Others will devise new ways to gain and distribute office perks.

But around the world, women managers and executives will subtly build more flexible, diverse, egalitarian, cooperative work environments more suited to the female mind.

Many will also choose to work for themselves and mix career, family, and leisure in unconventional ways.

## Women Entrepreneurs: Trendsetters

More women than men step off the corporate ladder.[120] When career women leave high-power jobs, however, they rarely retire to bake cookies.

In one study of executive women who had resigned, some 90 percent continued their career somewhere else.[121] As Sheila Wellington, president of Catalyst, reports, "Invariably they tell their employers they are leaving to go home. But very few actually do so. Women do not want to burn their bridges. They start their own businesses. Or they look for jobs where they can have a better balance, or where the opportunities for advancement are better."[122]

Many women are going into business for themselves. Fortune 500 companies employed some 16.3 million people in 1979; today they employ only 12 million.[123] In 1994, 16 million Americans were "lone eagles," free agents working for themselves. Most were women. The number of women going into business for themselves is twice that of men.[124]

Women-owned businesses are flourishing, too. In 1996, the National Foundation for Women Business Owners reported that women-owned businesses numbered nearly eight million, almost one third of all American businesses.[125] It is estimated that by the year 2000 women will own half of all U.S. firms. Their enterprises are more likely to stay in business, too. Women-owned businesses in the United States have a two-year success rate of 80 percent, well over the national average of about 50 percent.[126]

Women are starting small businesses in many other parts of the world as well.[127] Today more than 790,000 women in the United Kingdom run their own firms; 40 percent of new businesses in Germany are started by women; and one of five businesses in Singapore is owned by women.[128] Yang Yurong, age forty-two, began her company in rural China in 1979, when she borrowed 150 yuan to buy a few ducklings, a pig, and books on how to raise ducks. In 1988 she earned more than 10,000 yuan from her farm.[129]

Rapidly changing technology should enable even more women around the world to go into business for themselves—because the "electronic cottage" has come of age.

I am sitting in one. As I type these words on my computer, my e-mail is collecting business messages. My fax machine could pump out a business letter at any time. My dining-room table long ago turned into a second desk on which to stack articles and correspondence. Antique file cabinets serve as bedside tables. Part of the kitchen counter is now the mail room. And my answering machine records my incoming calls. I used to say I worked at home, but it would be closer to the truth to say I sleep in my office.

With the revolution in telecommunications, I am one of millions who have abandoned a stuffy, fluorescent-lit, monitored cubbyhole in the business world to work at home. In this era of stunning change, creative women will find a hole in the diversifying economic landscape, fill this "business space," and get rich, if that is their objective.

Many more will have the opportunity to rear children as they continue their career—largely at home.

## Stewardship

"The reports of my death are greatly exaggerated," cabled Mark Twain to the Associated Press in 1897. The same might be said of traditional companies where leaders command, workers conform, information flows in structured ways, and managers do or die for the bottom line. Many are thriving.

Nevertheless, Peter Drucker and many other business analysts believe that an age of "stewardship" is emerging. Corporations are changing from hierarchical structures where leaders command from on high to laterally connected webs where managers favor team playing, egalitarian connections, consensus, and flexibility.[130] Although both men and women unquestionably possess all of these traits, such ways of thinking and behaving are more characteristic of women.

"The best preparation for business is motherhood," contends trend analyst Arnold Brown. From millennia of rearing impetuous babies, women have evolved many special skills. As women fill the ranks of middle management and some of them reach the top, they are bound to bring flexibility, imagination, intuition, cooperation, consensus, and a broad, contextual, long-term view to every sector of the business world.

Judy Rosener, professor in the Graduate School of Management at the University of California, Irvine, feels that companies that make full use of women's talents will become more innovative, more productive—and more profitable. As she warns, "organizations that ignore the competitive advantage women represent do so at their own peril."[131]

# CHAPTER 3

# WOMEN'S WORDS

## Educators in
## the Information Age

> The difference between the right word and the almost
> right word is the difference between lightning
> and the lightning bug.
>
> MARK TWAIN

S peak the speech, I pray you, as I pronounced it to you, trippingly on the tongue." So spoke Hamlet to his actors, encouraging them to speak smoothly, appropriately, and eloquently. Women can be clever, broad-minded, intuitive, and many other things. But of all of women's gifts, their most outstanding, I think, is the talent that Shakespeare cherished—a flair for language.

In an era where television may soon offer five hundred channels, and more and more people around the world are beginning to need an education to make a living, the ability to communicate with written and spoken words is becoming essential in much of the workplace—including, of course, television and radio, journalism, and the expanding universe of education.

In this chapter I contend that women will come to dominate many sectors of the communications and education fields. With their contextual perspective, their mental flexibility, their imagination, and their superb linguistic faculties, they will also enrich our airwaves, print media, and classrooms with more diversity and range of subject matter, more intricate discussions of issues and ideas, and a more detailed and sensitive depiction of minorities, foreigners, women, and human relationships.

## Born to Talk

At talking, women have the edge. Infant girls in the United States often babble more than infant boys. They begin to speak earlier in childhood.[1] As they grow up, girls use longer utterances, as well as more complex grammatical constructions, such as the passive voice.[2] Their speech is smoother. They make fewer slips of the tongue, omissions, and repetitions, and utter fewer incomplete sentences. Girls are three to four times less likely to stutter, and more than three times less likely to be dyslexic.[3] Far fewer girls require remedial reading.

Girls like words. They enjoy word games, riddles, puzzles, making up stories, and talking to grown-ups. By age twelve, they excel at grammar, punctuation, and spelling and at understanding and remembering what they read.[4] There has been much debate about men, women, and SAT exams—tests that many say have been refashioned to minimize gender differences.[5] But on aptitude tests that record language abilities more precisely than SATs, girls regularly outperform boys.[6]

Boys never catch up. Girls and women excel at what psychologists call verbal fluency—rapidly finding appropriate words, phrases, or sentences.[7] On average, mature women can list almost twice as many synonyms for common words like *sharp* or *wild*. They can repeat tongue twisters more accurately. And they can rattle off more words starting with a specific letter. Although men and women have vocabularies of the same size, men are less able to reach quickly into their memories to find the appropriate words.[8]

When psychologists reviewed six large surveys of gender differences conducted between 1960 and 1992, they found that females excelled at several language skills in all three decades.[9] Some 150,000 Americans ages thirteen to twenty-two were included in this analysis, and the average differences between males and females were small. But many more females than males scored in the top 5 percent to 10 percent range in reading comprehension, writing, perceptual speed and associative memory.

American women share this gift of verbal expression with women in other cultures. Girls in Japan, for example, come up with appropriate words, phrases, and sentences faster than boys do.[10] Women also excel at verbal tests in such vastly different societies as England, the Czech Republic, Japan, and Nepal.[11]

In 1996, the International Gallup Organization polled men and women in twenty-two countries in Asia, Europe, North America, and South America, asking them which sex they thought was more talkative. In Canada, Chile, Estonia, France, India, Honduras, Thailand, the United States, and eleven other countries, representing 3.05 billion people and 53.3 percent of the world's population, the vast majority of men and women thought women were more verbal. Only Mexicans and Icelanders regarded women and men as equally loquacious.[12]

"The pleasure of talking is the inextinguishable passion of a woman," wrote the French dramatist Alain-René Lesage in the early eighteenth century. People around the world agree.

As usual, however, much depends on the circumstances. Men speak more when they are in a formal group, particularly in a mixed group of men and women. You have probably noticed this during the question-and-answer part of a public lecture. Men invariably ask more questions, as well as longer ones. Psychologists believe that men use more words in public settings, such as conferences and business meetings, to establish, display, or bolster their rank.[13] Women, on the other hand, do more talking at home and when they are with other women—undoubtedly to strengthen connections with family or friends.

It is impossible to say which sex has the more interesting conversations or writes the more compelling letters or reports. Gardening or fishing, philosophy or history: both sexes can be fascinating—and boring. Men chat more about business, sports, and politics, while women converse more about people.[14]

But leaving substance aside, in test after test and in culture after culture, women excel on how they construct their sentences, choose their words, and pronounce the little sounds of spoken language. Women are, on average, more articulate at saying what they say.

## The Female Brain for Talking

"The nightingale will run out of songs before a woman runs out of conversation." So says the Spanish proverb. How do women conjure up their verbal magic?

With uniquely female brains. When neuroscientist Sandra Witelson of Canada's McMaster University, with her colleagues, examined the brain tissue of five deceased women and four deceased men, she found that the female brains had 11 percent more neurons (nerve cells) in specific areas that specialize in perceiving and differentiating sounds associated with language.[15]

Distinguishing sounds is indeed essential to sophisticated communication. If you say "good morning" with a growl, your message is distinctly different than if you sing out a high, soft-pitched "hello." We size up a person's verbal message by listening to the cadence, the lilt, the inflection, the pitch, the music of his or her words. In fact, women's use of this mental equipment begins in infancy. Baby girls listen more intently to music. They also pay greater attention to people's voices.[16]

At deciphering a person's tone of voice, women would appear to have a biological edge. But Witelson collected data on only nine subjects. Moreover, counting brain neurons is known to be exceedingly difficult and often inaccurate. We plainly need more evidence before the brain physiology underlying women's linguistic facility is firmly established.

That evidence is mounting. In 1995, neuroscientists Bennett and Sally Shaywitz of Yale University and their colleagues put nineteen men and nineteen women into a magnetic resonance imaging (MRI) machine. After each participant was lodged comfortably inside this brain scanner, the researchers used a system of mirrors and a computer screen to flash nonsense words before them.[17]

*Lete, jete, loke, jote:* the task was to decide whether these and other scrambled noises rhymed. As the male subjects mentally verbalized these sounds, areas on the left side of the brain became active. Among most of the female participants, however, corresponding areas in the right hemisphere became active as well. For these women, the language centers for rhyming were spread across both sides of the brain.

## Larger Brain Areas Are Better for Language Skills

Women use both sides of the cerebral cortex for talking because they can. As discussed in chapter 1, neuroscientists now think that the corpus callosum, the tissue bridge that connects the two brain hemispheres, bulges in one or more sections toward the rear in women while it is more evenly cylindrical in men.[18]

To see if this brain architecture also enables women to be more efficient with their words, Melissa Hines of the University of California and her colleagues put twenty-eight women in an MRI brain-scanning machine and took pictures of the corpus callosum.[19] Hines also gave these women several tests of verbal abilities, including tasks that asked them to list synonyms for words and list words beginning with the letter S. Indeed, bigger was better. Those women with a larger posterior bulge in the corpus callosum excelled on these verbal tests.

Another plus for women: Their language centers are located in a "safer" place. Women's primary language centers lie toward the front of the left hemisphere of the brain, while men's primary language centers are more spread out—some lie farther toward the rear of the left hemisphere.[20] Because more paralyzing brain strokes occur in rear portions of the left hemisphere in both sexes, men undergo more injuries to their language centers than women do.[21]

Of all women's biological equipment for conversation, however, most outstanding is the female hormone estrogen.

## Estrogen: The Mother Lode for Language

Oliver Wendell Holmes called a woman's tongue her "mighty member." Had he known what we know today, he would have extolled the powers of estrogen instead. To understand how a mute bodily hormone, estrogen, can help to trigger a woman's swift rejoinder at the dinner table or a business meeting, however, one must know a bit more about the wiring of the brain.

The human brain is a bundle of some ten billion nerve cells, or neurons. Each nerve cell has at least one long arm, its axon, and lots of bushy projecting tendrils, its dendrites. Each cell sends impulses to other nerve cells through its axon, which divides to contact several neighboring neurons. Each cell receives thousands of impulses through its many branching dendrites.[22] These impulses hop across an infinitesimal gap between nerve cells, the synapse. Some ten trillion of these synaptic connections between nerve cells integrate brain parts.[23]

Not every neuron talks to every other neuron, of course. Instead, each talks to a select few; these talk to others; these talk to still others. In this way, interconnecting nerve cells connect brain regions with one another and with other bodily areas in specific circuits, known as systems or modules.[24]

Here's where estrogen comes in. Estrogen builds more dendritic projections or spines on each nerve cell, thereby increasing the number of connecting links between nerve cells.[25] Hence estrogen facilitates the flow of information among neurons.

Estrogen is effective, too. A woman's capacity to pronounce words increases during her monthly menstrual cycle when estrogen levels peak.[26] As estrogen levels rise, a woman's verbal memory and her ability to find the right word rapidly also heighten.[27] When postmenopausal women take hormone replacement therapy (HRT) to increase their levels of estrogen, they also improve their scores on tests of several verbal skills, including verbal memory and articulation.[28]

This link between estrogen and linguistic facility is particularly noticeable in girls with very little circulating estrogen due to the genetic condition known as Turner's syndrome. These girls have difficulty remembering verbal information and speaking quickly and appropriately.[29]

"Does estrogen make you smart?" This question was raised on the cover of *New York* magazine in 1997. *Smart* means different things to different people. But estrogen does multiply the linguistic highways of the brain, enhancing a number of verbal skills. And speaking well is often equated—not always justifiably—with intelligence.

## Genes for Talking?

Specific genes may also enable some women to speak more effectively than men, as an intriguing study indicates.

As discussed in chapter 1, neuroscientist David Skuse of the Institute of Child Health in London and his colleagues have located a gene or cluster of genes on the X chromosome that influences several female traits, including language skills, reading ability, and speech disorders. Due to patterns of inheritance and complex bodily interactions, however, this gene or cluster of genes is silenced in all men but active in about 50 percent of women. This explains, Skuse writes, why "males are substantially more vulnerable to a variety of developmental disorders of speech, language impairment and reading disability."[30]

Talking is one of the supreme achievements of humanity. Even Darwin, who believed that humankind was simply another animal species, said, "The lower animals differ from man solely in his almost infinitely larger power of associating together the most diversified sounds and ideas." At this hallmark of humanity, verbal communication, women regularly excel.

Why is the female of the species so well made for language? I think this feminine faculty evolved to enable ancestral women to rear and educate their young—womankind's most important job.

## Baby Talk

Infants know no grammar. To them, words have no meaning either. So babies begin to learn language by listening to the prosody of speech, the rhythms and intonations. They begin in the womb, listening to the rhythm, melody, pitch, and intonation of their mother's words.[31]

Because infants are more sensitive to higher-pitched sounds, mothers naturally compensate by speaking in a higher voice.[32] Mothers also speak slowly and smoothly and use a singsongy, wide tonal range. The point: to be conspicuous. This exaggeration helps the baby to distinguish the mother's voice from all the other surrounding sounds. Mothers unconsciously know this. In America, Germany, France, Italy, Latvia, and Japan, as well as among the Comanche, the Sinhalese of Sri Lanka, and the Xhosa speakers of South Africa, mothers use these same vocal tricks.[33]

Mothers in a wide variety of cultures also use short words, a small vocal repertoire, and long pauses between their mellifluous, high-pitched phrases. Mothers are verbally repetitious.[34] And they alert their infants to pay attention with linguistic devices, such as calling the baby's name, exclaiming "Look!" or saying "What's that?"[35]

Fathers use some of the same vocal techniques. So psychologist Anne Fernald of Stanford University argues that this suite of stereotypic vocal patterns is universal to human parenting, and that it evolved from the musical signals of lower primates.[36]

Fathers spend far less time caring for infants, however. In a survey of 186 societies done by the Population Council, fathers had "regular close relationships" with their infants in less than 2 percent of them.[37] Even where men do have close relationships with their infants, fathers spend far less time cuddling and talking to their children. Among the Aka Pygmies of central Africa, for example, fathers hold their infants for about 57 minutes in any twenty-four-hour period, whereas mothers cuddle infants some 490 minutes.[38]

Women everywhere in the world spend much more time in direct infant care, holding their babies in front of their faces hour after hour, cajoling, soothing, reprimanding, and educating their young—with words. As they interact, mothers are more verbal than fathers are.[39] Mothers also discern their infant's moods and anticipate its needs by listening to the cadence and melody of the baby's sounds.

Throughout the centuries of our deep history, mothers who talked to and listened to their babies probably reared more healthy, well-adjusted offspring. These young survived to adulthood to breed themselves. Thus the steadfast processes of natural selection gradually built into the female brain all of the biological equipment that gives women their linguistic edge.

## You Tarzan, Me Jane

We will never know when in the course of human evolution women began to outtalk men. But it must have been long ago.

Women's voices are more variable, more musical, and more expressive than men's[40]—traits shared with other female primates. Female apes and monkeys produce a larger array of whimpers, coos, barks, and other middle-range "social" calls, while male primates have a more restricted repertoire of growls and roars, aggressive strident sounds.[41] So ancestral women probably acquired the brain circuitry for a somewhat more intricate tonal range even before our ancestors descended from the fast-disappearing trees of East Africa some four million years ago.

As our forebears began to venture onto the grassy plains that were spreading across the African landscape, both sexes needed to communicate on a more sophisticated level.

With new sound combinations they could coordinate their march. With more complex grammatical constructions they could describe yesterday and plan tomorrow. With the rudiments of human language, they could frame arguments, make offers, strike deals, support leaders, dupe foes, teach skills, spread news, set rules, stop tears, define kin, seduce lovers, placate gods, and tell stories late into the night. As psychologists Steven Pinker of the Massachusetts Institute of Technology and Paul Bloom of the University of Arizona view our distant forebears, "They could no more live with a me-Tarzan-you-Jane level of grammar than we could."[42]

No one knows exactly when human language began to develop. But by two million years ago, fossil skulls indicate that at least one basic language center, now called Broca's area, had started to emerge in the human brain.[43] Along with this brain reorganization must have come some of the intricate brain circuits necessary for language. With time more of the complex architecture of the brain and vocal tract emerged.

The linguistic arms race had begun. Those individuals who possessed this mighty weapon, language, were able to outmaneuver enemies and build more secure relationships with friends. They lived, and bred, and passed along this magnificent hallmark of humanity, talking. But throughout this human journey, mothers were the designated educators of the very young. Nature would build into the female brain superior verbal skills.

"A single word often betrays a great design," declared the French dramatist Racine. Words are still humankind's essential tool for explaining complex phenomena in simple ways. As we move further into the Information Age, it seems likely that women will have an innate advantage in any career that depends on words—particularly in the communications industries and in all of our educational fields.

## Media Women

"These impossible women! How they do get around us!" Aristophanes wrote in 411 B.C.E. With words, women still have the capacity to command attention and make their points convincingly. So it is no surprise that women have moved rapidly into radio and television.

Today more than half of all reporters on National Public Radio are women; many radio anchors and producers are also women.[44] Despite the popularity of television, radio is still a powerful influence. Some 91 percent of American households have access to NPR and about twelve million people tune in to it every week.[45] In fact, NPR is expanding. Some 395 stations were members in 1990; this increased to 540 in 1996.

Radio listening (on all kinds of stations) fits our modern habits. As

John Robinson, director of the Americans' Use of Time Project at the University of Maryland, writes, "one of the dominant trends in media use over the last 30 years is an increased tendency to watch or listen to a program while doing something else."[46] He terms this kind of listening "secondary activity."

Today Americans tune in to radio for some ninety minutes a day, up from fifty-four minutes in 1965; this is more than ten hours a week. Ninety percent of this radio listening is done while working, driving, cooking, tinkering in the garage, sunning, picnicking, or doing something else. Moreover, after country music, which ranks first, Americans listen mostly to news and talk shows.[47] Many of these programs are now written, produced, or presented by women.

Women's influence on the radio airwaves is rising in other countries, too. According to United Nations statistics, between 1970 and 1991 developing countries doubled their share of all the radios used in the world.[48] Moreover, over 25 percent of the jobs in radio in Africa, Latin America, Europe, and Asia are currently held by women.

## Women in Television

Women have also invaded TV land. Men are the CEOs of all three major American TV networks,[49] and men predominate on their boards. But women are flooding into middle management.[50]

In 1994, 35 percent to 50 percent of middle management in most American film studios and television networks were women.[51] By the late 1980s, some 25 percent of all television writers and announcers in the United States were women, and some 50 percent of prime-time TV series had at least one female producer.[52] Ken Auletta, media commentator for *The New Yorker*, reports: "In the television industry, women hold key positions in the entertainment divisions of six broadcast networks."[53]

Women are also entering the communications industries in many other parts of the world. In some forty countries polled by the United Nations in 1995, more than 50 percent of students in the communications fields were women.[54] Roughly 45 percent of all television announcers in Western Europe and Latin America were women, as were 35 percent to 40 percent of all TV producers in Germany, New Zealand, Australia, Sweden, Malaysia, Africa, and Latin America.[55]

Some 30 percent of TV producers in India were women.[56] Even in Japan, where women hold less than 10 percent of all managerial and professional positions, some 19 percent of TV announcers were women.[57]

Prospects for women in the media look very good. Women have not yet reached the highest echelons of corporate management, undoubtedly for reasons discussed in chapter 2. But women are active players in story conferences, where producers decide what will air. As Sally Steenland, former deputy director of the National Commission on Working Women, concludes, women in broadcasting are "primed for power."[58]

## Producer Power in Media Land

TV producers have a remarkable amount of influence. They determine the focus of each segment and pick the people the crew will interview. They match specific visual images with particular verbal points and decide how each segment will be concluded. And their ideas and images reach into our living rooms and grab us by the throat.

Over 89 percent of American men and women watch television—on average, a little over four hours a day.[59] "Without a TV, how would you know where to put the sofa?" This ironical slogan has an element of truth. People in many other countries also view between two and four hours of TV daily.[60]

All this absorbed gazing inevitably affects how we think. The vivid TV portrayal of the massacre at Tiananmen Square in Beijing in 1989 unquestionably influenced world opinion toward China, for example. But the classic story of the impact of television came into being at a particular moment in 1968.

President Lyndon B. Johnson was watching Walter Cronkite, America's leading news anchor, on *The CBS Evening News*. Cronkite had just returned from a trip to the war zone in Vietnam. On this evening, he rejected the rosy official predictions of eventual victory in Southeast Asia, saying he was "more certain than ever that the bloody experience of Viet Nam is to end in stalemate."[61] With that, Johnson switched off the television and remarked, "If I've lost Cronkite, I've lost middle America."[62]

Television is the global campfire. It is immediate, direct, personal, emotional, and ubiquitous. There is now a TV set for every two people in the industrial world.[63] Eighty-five percent of homes worldwide have a TV set.[64] And as men and women sit around this glowing screen, they inevitably adjust what they think and feel.

As the printed word helped to topple European monarchies and galvanize American citizens to fight in the American Revolution in the eighteenth century, television sways contemporary opinions and stirs contemporary emotions. Washington pundits and politicians now take into account the "CNN effect," the worldwide impact of this cable network on people's views.

Male producers and commentators generally orchestrate international news coverage on TV.[65] But this coverage is only a small fraction of what we watch. National and local news shows also mold our views on politics and affect how we vote. Situation comedies subtly shape our standards of morality and decorum. Talk shows sway our beliefs. Nature, arts, and entertainment programs alter our tastes and ideas, even change the ways we buy and work and spend our leisure time.

Television starts to manipulate us when we are toddlers. All too often, it retains this grip throughout our lives. And it showers opinions, values, judgments, and lifestyles on every human being in the world who has access to its screen.

This became eminently clear to Peter Drucker one evening in the early 1990s, while he was traveling in a remote northern province of China. Drucker was addressing a group of twenty-two managers of the surrounding cotton plantations in the village meeting hall. Promptly at 6:00 P.M., however, they politely excused themselves and vanished. At 6:30 they returned, looking refreshed. They had gone to watch *Dallas* on TV.[66]

Another example of American TV's remarkable reach is a remote village in India. Here many children are named Lucy, Ricky, Ethel, or Fred. The popular American TV show *I Love Lucy* had been popular in this hamlet.[67]

Many have begun to fear that television is becoming more powerful at influencing worldwide tastes, opinions, and moral codes than schools, politicians, religion, books, or newspapers. That is debatable. What is not debatable is that television's power is expanding. The Bureau of Labor Statistics reports that TV producers will be among the twenty-five fastest growing professions in the United States by the year 2005.[68]

Because women are so skilled with words, I think they will increasingly fill these middle-level jobs, as well as some of the upper-tier positions in TV land—and shape how millions, even billions, of human beings think and act.

## What Women Want to Watch on Television

"Television is the first truly democratic culture—the first culture available to everybody and entirely governed by what the people want. The most terrifying thing is what people do want," wrote drama critic Clive Barnes. Sophocles, Shakespeare, Ibsen, Chekhov, and most of the other great scriptwriters of the past were men—and they didn't always produce rip-'em-up action plots. But modern producers and writers for television and film have tended to focus on guns, monsters, nonemotional men, shallow women, and dazzling action plots—all catering to the tastes of a putative male audience.

But now women are 52 percent of all American TV viewers.[69] As David Poltrack, executive vice president of Research and Planning at CBS, notes, "The primary, No. 1 audience segment in television is adult women under 55 years of age." As a result, producers are increasingly tailoring their shows to feminine tastes. During the Olympics in Atlanta in 1996, for example, NBC reduced its coverage of boxing and added human interest stories and profiles of players—for women.[70]

Script consultant Linda Seger, author of *When Women Call the Shots,* believes this shift is just a start. When she polled some two hundred American women, as well as women in China, Australia, Mexico, Spain, India, the Philippines, and several other countries, she found that women want to see more diversity and balance on television and in films—including more believable female characters, more lifelike partnerships between women and men, and more complex dramas.[71] These tastes reflect women's contextual view. Women are also more likely than men to prefer musical and dance events.[72]

At an international conference in Bangkok in 1994, over four hundred women who worked in the media in some eighty countries met to express their own vision of the future of the communications industries. They, too, wanted more storytelling in programs, more visual and performance arts, the integration of more humane values such as compassion and cooperation in programming, and the global dissemination of women's views.[73]

Seger thinks that as women continue to enter television and film producing, we are likely to see less violence, less action-adventure, a more sensitive depiction of people and issues, more complex stories, more sequels to stories, more ethnic and age diversity in actors and commentators, a wider range of topics in the news and in film, more talk shows, and much broader and more intricate and accurate depictions of women.[74]

TV shows have begun to reflect women's tastes. Psychologist Sonya Friedman hosted a superior talk show on CNN in the 1990s that covered a wide range of complex topics. Now many women discuss "serious" issues on TV.

Today women are also playing major television roles as doctors, lawyers, and detectives—and these characters behave as educated, competent women instead of female versions of men. For example, the two women detectives in *N.Y.P.D. Blue,* the nationally popular show about the New York City Police Department, are never shown pulling their guns or engaging in violence. Instead they use calming, diplomatic words and a degree of empathy when dealing with actual or alleged perpetrators.

Women's ways of thinking and acting are becoming more and more visible on U.S. radio and television—and being exported around the world.

## The Writing Trade

For the past three thousand years of recorded history, men have been the world's most celebrated authors, poets, and playwrights. Many women wrote, of course, producing letters, memoirs, or reams of poetry. But few women had the time or education to pursue their primordial love affair with words. In nineteenth-century America, Harriet Beecher Stowe wrote novels of great social consequence and Sarah Orne Jewett created works of outstanding literary merit. But they were not welcome in the male-dominated world of arts and letters. In Europe, George Eliot and George Sand even felt obliged to write under a male name.

Times have changed. In the early twentieth century the strong, insightful works of such American writers as Willa Cather and Edith Wharton won great critical acclaim. The floodgates were opening. Since then, American and European women have produced thousands of novels, poems, plays, and critical works, adding tremendous depth to the literature of our time.

Fifty-four percent of all contemporary American book authors are women.[75] Women have also written thousands upon thousands of scholarly papers, magazine articles, newspaper stories, and commentary. Today roughly 53 percent of all American editors and reporters are women, and 54 percent of all technical writers are women.[76]

Women hold more than 25 percent of all jobs as reporters, correspondents, and editors in at least six other industrial nations as well.[77]

Contrary to many dour predictions, reading is not a dying art. Ever since Gutenberg invented the movable-type printing press in 1455, more and more people have enjoyed reading. Readership is still growing. In 1994, one out of three people in the industrial world read a daily newspaper.[78] Americans alone spent over $20 billion that year on magazines and newspapers.[79] Americans also bought more than one billion books, a 31 percent increase over 1991.[80]

Although sales of books fell slightly between 1996 and 1997, some book dealers actually expect book buying to increase in the years ahead.[81] They reason that television, videos, movies, and the Internet stimulate interest and prompt people to buy books. For example, the novel *Forrest Gump* originally sold ten thousand copies. After the tremendous success of the movie, it sold 1.6 million more.[82] Technological developments also stimulate reading. Len Vlahos, of the American Booksellers Association, says, "Every time there's a new technology or Internet development, dozens of books are published, and they all sell."[83]

The world will see even more readers. Middle-aged individuals tend to read the most, and huge numbers of international baby boomers are reaching middle age. Moreover, women read more than men do[84]—and women are gaining the money and leisure time to indulge their taste for words.

As more people become educated, they, too, will read. American adults currently regard reading as one of the most important gifts they can give their children. In a study done by Yankelovich Partners, researchers found that 75 percent of parents read to their young more often than their parents had read to them as children.[85] The sooner children are introduced to reading, the more they will read throughout their lives.

"For a country to have a great writer is to have another government," wrote Aleksandr Solzhenitsyn. Indeed, words—even those of lesser writers—can sway the mind and rally people into action. In a 1992 survey of managing editors of one hundred American daily newspapers, 84 percent agreed that the tastes and attitudes of women journalists are changing what their papers print. The content of the news they disseminate is broader in scope. They have also added coverage on health, family, homelessness, and many other social issues that concern women.[86]

As women's written words filter into the minds of billions of people around the world, women are exercising a new form of feminine leadership and power—and giving the educated public a more contextual, holistic, diversified view of every issue on their minds.

## Gossip Columnists

"If you can't say something good about someone, sit right here by me," Alice Roosevelt Longworth reportedly quipped. Women love to gossip, perhaps because this intimate word-filled pastime connects them to their confidantes, making and sustaining ties that women see as power.

Men gossip, too, of course. But boys and men speak more about sports stars, politicians, or themselves, while girls and women talk more about friends, enemies, and lovers. Women also note and discuss many more of the nuances involved in social interactions.[87] Women are far more avid at juicy rumormongering, face to face and in print.[88] As editor Richard Johnson of "Page Six," the gossip section in the *New York Post,* says, "Women are generally much better at not only gathering the information but also spreading it."

The Chinese would agree. In past decades every neighborhood in Shanghai, for example, was under the watchful eye of a neighborhood committee. Committee members kept an eye on every resident and reported what they saw and heard to the local government. These much-feared neighborhood committees existed across China, and they were typically staffed by older, retired women.[89]

Whatever you think of female gossip, it has a distinguished history as well as vital social uses. Long before television or radio, before the telephone, before the typewriter or fountain pen, even before written language, women politicked with words. With their whisperings, women glued friendships, exposed philanderers, undermined cheaters, criticized laggards, galvanized followers, swayed leaders, convinced doubters, ridiculed pretenders, honored Good Samaritans, ostracized criminals, set moral standards, and spread the daily news. Women used words to include, persuade, educate, and punish.

Their words traveled, too. "Gossip needs no carriage," the Russian proverb goes. So went their whispering, around campfires, into other communities, off to nearby tribes. Women were undoubtedly our gossip columnists and social commentators a million years ago, subtly broadcasting to all around them what was doing in the neighborhood. Gossip was humanity's social glue.[90] British anthropologist Robin Dunbar believes that gossip was so crucial to our earliest forebears that it spurred the evolution of human language.[91]

Gossip still allows us to air our grievances and express our views, not only about friends, foes, and lovers, but about politicians and other public figures. As we share opinions about the president of the United States or the British royal family, we learn about the values of our friends and neighbors. We also form our beliefs, examine our principles, and keep the rich and powerful in line.

As gossip columnist Joanna Molloy of New York's *Daily News* says, "I feel a little uncomfortable setting myself up as a moral arbiter . . . but we want our gods and goddesses to follow the same rules we do."[92]

Our culture will probably become even more gossipy as uniform standards of morality continue to give way to the more pluralist views generated in this age of diversity. Afternoon talk show hosts, newspaper columnists, pundits, politicians, and laymen speaking off-the-cuff during media appearances: this growing horde of gossip makers will definitely affect moral standards by promoting their heroes and favored causes and maligning those on the other side.

Most of these talk show hosts and gossip columnists will be

women—harnessing their primordial skills to fit our modern world. Author and *New York Times* columnist John Tierney believes these women have an impact, too. As he says, "As women gain status in society and the media, they are using their gossip expertise to enforce the rules that men preferred to ignore."[93]

## Women on the Internet

Women's facility with words will also serve them well on the Internet. Cyberspace is teeming with syllables. Teenagers and adult singles are wooing potential lovers. Professors are holding classes. Doctors are counseling patients. Lawyers are advising clients. Even businessmen who used to count on secretaries to unscramble their thoughts in memos are now winging it on the Internet.

Schmoozing in cyberspace: it's a blizzard of mangled syntax and bizarre phraseology. These Web surfers are devotees of Andrew Jackson when it comes to spelling. "It is a poor mind indeed," said our seventh president, "that can't think of more than one way to spell a word."

The Internet features laissez-faire scribbling at its worst. Recently, however, some computer buffs have begun to worry about their writing styles.[94] Good grammar is clear thinking, Net users have just begun to reason. If this taste for grammar, punctuation, and clear writing takes hold, employers will begin to hire more women to conduct their business on the Internet.

They will also hire women if they need employees who can use the Net effectively. This feminine edge was demonstrated recently by managers at the telecommunications company MCI. Using its own Web site, MCI asked tens of thousands of male and female computer users to answer five "general interest" questions about the Net. Women, they discovered, use the Web faster and more efficiently than men do.[95] If women begin to provide much of the programming in this powerful communications medium, their interests and perspectives will surely saturate the world in coming decades.

## Women in Education

"Brains are an asset, if you hide them," Mae West once said. Women are clever enough to play dumb when necessary. But one place where women usually do not try to hide their intelligence is in the school-room. Women are vitally interested in learning—in part, I think, be-cause contemporary educators impart their information primarily with spoken and written words.

This form of learning is relatively recent in the course of human evolution. Our chimpanzee cousins learn by watching: watching their mothers as they crack nuts, watching siblings as they pluck ripe fruit, watching males threaten one another in status duels. Likewise, after our ancestors descended from the trees, children watched their fa-thers chip stone tools and watched their mothers gather herbs for headaches and sore throats. In the beginning, our hominid ancestors learned very little by verbal instruction and, of course, nothing whatsoever from written words.

The development of alphabets, writing tablets, and eventually pa-per, ink, and the printing press changed the course of human educa-tion. Our forebears began to capture and spread knowledge by using symbols on paper and disseminating these written words to all who had the opportunity and the curiosity to learn to read. Today we learn predominantly by listening to or reading words. This kind of learning favors those with superior verbal and reading skills—most frequently women.

In the knowledge economy, blue-collar laborers are being sup-planted by what Peter Drucker calls "knowledge workers."[96] Many of those who are smart, educated, and computer literate, the "gold-collar" workers, will even write their own career tickets.[97] Given this powerful economic impetus, it is hardly surprising that women are motivated to employ their feminine advantage and go to school.

In the 1980s, American men and women were acquiring an educa-tion at just about the same pace. But in the 1990s, women began to pull ahead. In 1997, 89 percent of American women aged twenty-five to twenty-nine had graduated from high school, whereas 86 percent of men in the same age group had received a high school diploma.[98] More women than men in this age group had also completed college, 29 percent of women and 26 percent of men having received college degrees.[99] At the postgraduate level, 46 percent of all U.S. doctorates awarded in 1996 were earned by women.[100] Interestingly, most of these advanced degrees were in education.[101]

Women in other countries, too, are seizing the opportunity to go to school. In contemporary Germany, Britain, and Italy, the numbers of

men and women with university degrees are almost equal.[102] Even in
countries where rigid cultural traditions keep women in the home,
more are getting educated. The *1995 Human Development Report* of
the United Nations Development Programme states that the worldwide gender gap in education has "narrowed rapidly in the past two
decades."[103]

About 33 percent of women in the world are now literate, a huge
advance over earlier years. In contemporary China, Sri Lanka, and
Zimbabwe, to name but a few developing countries making progress
with literacy, women have come much further. Roughly 70 percent of
adult women in these countries can read and write.[104]

"Education is not the filling of a pail, but the lighting of a fire,"
wrote William Butler Yeats. For women, the fire has ignited. They are
earning the essential currency of the information age: knowledge.
And what women learn, they want to teach.

## The Teachers

"Educate a man and you educate an individual; educate a woman and
you educate a family," it has been said. Women do like to teach. In
1996, 98 percent of all prekindergarten and kindergarten teachers in
the United States were women, as were 94 percent of teachers' aides,
84 percent of special education teachers, 84 percent of elementary
school teachers, 57 percent of secondary school teachers, 68 percent
of vocational and educational counselors, and 45 percent of college
and university teachers.[105]

Not many women have reached the highest administrative echelons of the education system. The vast majority of deans, chancellors,
and college and university presidents are still men.[106] Given men's
greater preoccupation with rank, this is not surprising. Yet in the
United States women dominate the direct day-to-day education of the
growing mind.

It seems probable that even more women will be teaching in coming decades. Teachers will be needed.

In 1910, only 10 percent of eighteen-year-olds in New York City
had finished high school, a figure that probably reflected the national
educational level at the time.[107] By 1993, 88 percent of all American
adults had earned high school diplomas.[108] Today some 51 million

children are enrolled in U.S. primary and secondary schools—more than at any other time in American history. Educators project that by 2005 some 55.9 million children will be enrolled.[109]

Americans have come to believe Ben Franklin's dictum "If a man empties his purse into his head, no one can take it from him." As students pour into classrooms, schools will need more teachers to give them information and help them convert this resource into knowledge. I think women will respond enthusiastically to this need for teachers, since the educational system is changing in ways that will appeal to women.

## The Rise of Creative Teaching

Sociologist Nathan Glazer pointed out that the quality of public education in America began to decline as highly talented women acquired more and more opportunities in other sectors of the economy and stopped becoming teachers. This may be so. But the educational system is changing, offering teachers new opportunities that may encourage talented women to enter and remain in this profession.

One of the new options is the much-debated charter schools. Charter schools are publicly funded schools, free and available to any child living in the school district where the charter resides. These schools are generally launched by nonprofit organizations, parents, and/or teachers who wish to pursue their particular educational vision. Most charter schools are released from many of the educational regulations and hiring standards of their district and their state, and they promise dedicated teachers and an enriched education.

How often charter schools actually deliver on that promise remains to be seen. But Bobby Washington, a postal worker in Jersey City, New Jersey, summed up some attitudes on the subject, saying, "I walk into the public school, I see people doing a job; the charter is a mission."[110]

Charter schools are popular and spreading. As of June 1998, more than thirty states permitted the creation of these schools and 786 had opened; more than 400 more were expected to open that fall.[111]

These schools have many critics. But they are already shaking up the world of public education, offering choices, innovations, and, in some cases, the kind of autonomy and teaching flexibility that attracts women. Beth Mackin of the Gateway Charter School in Jersey City is among them. She left a career in publishing to teach at Gateway, saying she was excited about working with a small staff and drawn by the freedom she would have in a small setting.[112] Beth was expressing views characteristic of women.

Magnet schools have also become an option in many cities. These schools are within the traditional public school system, but each is formed specifically to offer a more varied and enriched curriculum. They are less controversial than charter schools. Yet like charter schools, magnets offer teachers more autonomy and greater latitude to express their own ideas and use imaginative teaching methods.[113]

Another growing trend is enrollment in private schools. Private schools have always been favored by the well-to-do in the United States. But as criticism of public schools has mounted, private schools have become an attractive alternative for a wider range of people. In 1996, 10 percent of American children attended a private educational institution.[114] In some cities, poorer parents are even getting vouchers, a form of public funding, to help pay the tuition for their youngsters in private schools. Generally speaking, these schools offer teachers a less structured work environment and more opportunities to use their imagination in the classroom—options that appeal to women.

"Mother wanted me to get a good education, so she never sent me to school," Margaret Mead reportedly said. More mothers have come to agree. Armed with computers, the Internet, and outlines of appropriate curricula, they are educating their children at the kitchen table.

Currently some 1.2 million American children learn to read, write, multiply, and sing at home, and their numbers are increasing by at least 15 percent a year.[115] Some public school systems even permit home-taught children to use the school library and computer rooms, sign up for a few courses, or join extracurricular activities like the baseball team or school band.[116]

With charter schools, magnet schools, private schools, and home schooling, teachers (and parents) are being offered a wider range of opportunities to express their personal visions of education. Even traditional classrooms are becoming less rigid, more idiosyncratic, and more innovative. Bruce Fuller, professor of public policy at the University of California at Berkeley, thinks these trends in education are here to stay. As he says, "This is a breeze now that's picking up to become a major wind. I think it's a movement that will just keep growing."[117]

This wind of change may propel more women into an occupation their ancestors almost certainly practiced as they sat with children beside the lakes of East Africa a million years ago. As women acquire greater autonomy in the classroom, they will also redefine how and what our children learn. Many will emphasize ethnic diversity and a broader, more contextual approach to any subject they choose to teach.

## Higher Learning's Future

Go down Interstate 10 in Arizona, pass the Phoenix airport, and turn in at a group of unprepossessing brick buildings set among a cluster of corporate offices. Here is a campus of the University of Phoenix. It is one of many; the university has now spread across a number of states. The University of Phoenix has been called "the biggest challenge to higher education" in America. Not because it has grown, almost overnight, to be the largest private university in America. Not because it is a for-profit business. But because it is modeled on what may be—for good or evil—some twenty-first-century realities.

The university pays taxes like any business, rents space, owns no library, and accepts only men and women who are gainfully employed and at least twenty-three years old. Students work at their regular jobs during the day and take classes in the evening. Each class is limited to twenty individuals. Students work regularly in small cooperative groups—team learning. The curriculum claims to tackle the issues of the "real world." The teachers are not full-time faculty. Instead they are often working professionals who teach other working adults. As a result, the teachers act more as facilitators of discussion than pedagogues instructing disciples.

Gone is the rigid intellectual hierarchy separating teacher from student. Enter a form of learning that humankind employed for several million years: practical learning as a group. At the University of Phoenix, education focuses on career training rather than psychic transformation.

Although he by no means endorses the University of Phoenix, Peter

Drucker does believe that this kind of education is the wave of the future. He maintains that traditional colleges and universities will gradually collapse under their high costs and be replaced by cheaper, more flexible, more expedient, more focused, more utilitarian, and more egalitarian systems of higher education. As Drucker says, "Thirty years from now the big university campuses will be relics."[118]

Drucker's forecast is, I believe, unduly pessimistic. For one thing, occupational majors are becoming popular in traditional colleges and universities. These institutions are also gradually adapting to practical contemporary needs, scheduling classes in locations available to adult working students on subjects of relevance to their business lives. Moreover, I doubt that the University of Phoenix represents the future of higher education. Many people in the world of education are convinced that America's largest private university is just another profitable diploma mill.

Yet the University of Phoenix may well be one face of tomorrow's educational landscape. And institutions like this do offer students and teachers more flexibility and autonomy—innovations that will attract women as teachers and pupils.

## The Virtual Classroom

Changes in the corporate environment may also present opportunities for women teachers. Many executives have begun to feel that courses and faculty in most traditional colleges and universities no longer provide graduates with the kind of education they need to work productively in the business world. So business leaders have begun to arm-twist some of them into adding certain courses to their curriculums and creating internships that build networks and rapport with corporate America.

Some corporations have even set up their own schools. There, hired-gun professors teach skills designed to meet their corporation's particular needs.[119] America has some twelve hundred of these "corporate universities." The American Council on Education has accredited some of their courses, although none of these schools is fully accredited as yet.

Corporations are also collaborating with accredited universities and business schools to create "satellite classrooms" on the Internet.

Employees can log on and take career-boosting courses at home—an educational option known as distance learning.[120] In 1998, there were 762 of these cyberschools for distance learners. Because many of these virtual classrooms are extensions of accredited American universities, students can even earn academic degrees.

Virtual classrooms are likely to grow in number. Today American workers can earn over 80 percent more in annual income if they come to the job market with a college education, rather than just a high school diploma. The traditional college experience, however, often costs more than $20,000 a year. Economic realities will undoubtedly drive more and more Americans to become distance learners educating themselves in nontraditional ways.

The University of Phoenix, corporate college courses, and virtual classrooms have a number of things in common.

For one, students come to these classes with a powerful incentive to learn. So if a student isn't learning, the teacher is probably at fault. This kind of educational environment puts a new emphasis on useful, clearly stated, empathetic instruction—women's forte. Moreover, these educational forums provide flexible work schedules for both pupils and teachers. Women are much more likely than men to seek these part-time jobs to accommodate the demands of rearing young.

Part-time employment generally offers lower pay, fewer benefits, and little or no job security. Nevertheless, these new educational forums will offer women more flexibility and autonomy in the classroom and more avenues for employment in the field of education.

There are still others.

## Learning Throughout One's Life

Senior citizens and working adults are pursuing new skills and interests in community colleges. These local institutions have expanded some 250 percent since the 1960s.[121] Some vacationers are beginning to take classes in calligraphy, archaeology, art history, and myriad other topics during their holidays in resort hotels. Others are learning while they cruise around the Galápagos Islands or in the Banda Sea. By the year 2000, even couch potatoes will sink some $1 billion a year into courses they can play on their VCRs or CD-ROM players.[122]

In 1996, 40 percent of American adults engaged in some kind

of adult education, mostly to further their careers. As those of the "baby boomlet," the children of the baby boom generation in America, reach college age, even more men and women will be filling out college application forms or looking for alternative ways to acquire knowledge. Although traditional professorships may dwindle as more people grumble about the tenure system, conventional universities are also expected to expand their activities.

James F. Carlin, chairman of the Massachusetts Board of Higher Education, says of higher education, "Whether you like it or not, it's going to be broken apart and put back together differently. It won't be the same. Why should it be? Why should everything change except for higher education?"[123] The genie, as the saying goes, is out of the bottle. Education is becoming flexible, diversified, entrepreneurial, practical—and exportable.

With the spread of the Internet, people in the developing countries will almost certainly want to avail themselves of Western education, too.

Who will educate all these people in traditional public schools, charter schools, magnet schools, private schools, and traditional colleges and universities; at adults-only universities, summer schools, community centers, and senior citizen associations; on ships, in boardrooms, at resort hotels, on television and radio, on CD-ROM, and in cyberspace? I think most of these educators will be women.

An emerging force will be women's words.

## The Knowledge Economy

For millions of years our forebears lived in small egalitarian groups where clever, charismatic, industrious individuals rose to lead. But just about everybody had access to the knowledge of the tribe and could convert it into power if they had the ability to use this information. We are, in a sense, returning to those prehistoric times. Computers, satellites, interactive television, telephones, and radios are enabling more and more people to gather vast amounts of information, convert data into knowledge, and sell it in the marketplace.

Today women are grabbing the opportunity. They increasingly outnumber men on American college and university campuses of every kind, from public to private to religiously affiliated institutions. Demographers predict that by 2007, 9.2 million American women and only 6.9 million American men will be enrolled in college. The contrast is even greater among part-time, adult, and minority students. Women are also gradually closing the education gap in much of the rest of the world.

"Knowledge is power," Sir Francis Bacon said. Trend analysts of every stripe agree that education and information are the coinage of tomorrow.[124] Women will have the tools to move into some of the most lucrative jobs in the industrial world. Many will make careers in the communications industries and in our expanding educational facilities. And as they educate us on the radio, on television, on the Internet, and in every other medium and educational avenue available in this vast communications age, they will disseminate their tastes for diversity, flexibility, cooperation, and egalitarian team playing, as well as their broad, contextual view of issues and ideas, to every corner of the world.

# CHAPTER 4

# MIND READING

## People Skills at Your Service

> The ability to deal with people is as purchasable a
> commodity as sugar or coffee. And I pay more for that
> ability than for any other under the sun.
>
> JOHN D. ROCKEFELLER

Intelligence is quickness in seeing things as they are," wrote philosopher George Santayana. Women have a remarkable talent for "reading" people. Their social antennae are always on. They pick up the tiny signals that people send, detect their motives and desires—and deftly navigate their way into the human heart.

Women are built for mind reading. Touch, hearing, smell, taste, vision: all of women's senses are, in some respects, more finely tuned than those of men. Women also have a knack for decoding your emotions by looking at your face. They swiftly decipher your mood from your body posture and gestures. They remember more of the things in the room or office around you, putting you in social context. Many even have a genetic advantage for interpreting the nuances of social interaction, what neuroscientists call "executive" social skills.

Women are socially smart. And their abilities to read others, understand their concerns, and help them cope are becoming valuable commodities in our modern world.

As more women work outside the home, millions of men and women are paying others to do the shopping, walk the dog, teach the children how to swim, help them with their exercise routine, even balance their checkbook. Restaurateurs, take-out food shop operators, entertainers, retail salespeople, diet specialists, decorators, financial advisers, travel agents, private detectives, interpreters, lawyers, mediators, therapists: never before have so many been so dependent on the services of so many others to help them deal with their concerns, from the mundane to the complex.

With their contextual view, their imagination, their networking abilities, and their linguistic and social skills, women have already established a strong presence in the service occupations and professions. They will dominate many of these fields in the years ahead, bringing people around the world inventive solutions to their daily concerns, as well as ingenious new ways to play.

I will start at the beginning: how women read your mind.

## Woman's Special Touch

Women are, on average, more sensitive to touch.[1] This female responsiveness begins a few hours after birth and continues throughout life.[2] Women feel another's touch more acutely and they perceive sensations more accurately when they touch.[3] Women often stroke their lovers too delicately; they assume that men are just as sensitive to touch.

Women like to touch. Cashmere, mahogany, rawhide, garden dirt, or furry peaches: as dramatist Jean Giraudoux says, "in a woman's mind, beauty is something she needs to touch." Infant girls reach out to touch their mothers more often than baby boys do.[4] Boys do more rough-and-tumble play; men shake hands more regularly; and men are more likely to touch strangers.[5] But studies of people in several societies indicate that girls and women touch those they know more frequently than men do.[6]

This feminine proclivity probably derives from millions of years of rearing babies. In parts of Nigeria today, mothers massage their infant's whole body daily.[7] "Massage the legs of your daughter, so she will walk with grace" is a saying among the Maoris of New Zealand.[8] !Kung San mothers of the Kalahari Desert of southern Africa keep their infants in bodily contact 90 percent of the day. A woman holds her infant on her hip as she tends the morning fire and puts her baby in a shawl slung across her back as she gathers fruit, roots, and greens. She sleeps next to her baby every night.[9] No cribs, strollers, high chairs, or car seats for the !Kung. In some societies infants never go through the "crawling stage." They are held until they learn to walk.

Babies need this motherly touch. "The great source of terror in infancy is solitude," wrote William James. Orphans left to hospital cribs and institutional care often suffer mental and physical disabilities from lack of loving touch.[10] Fondled infants, on the other hand, are much more alert and active; they also achieve much higher scores on tests of growth and development.[11] In fact, cuddled infants gain weight almost twice as fast as those who are rarely handled.[12]

Scientists now know why this touching is so therapeutic. Massage has been shown to trigger the release of oxytocin in the brain. This hormone produces feelings of sedation and relaxation, lowers blood pressure, creates a metabolic environment that encourages the storage of nutrients, and stimulates growth.[13] Data on rats suggest that motherly touch also stimulates the release of growth hormone (GH) and reduces levels of cortisol, a hormone that can depress the immune system and render one more susceptible to disease.[14]

"Did you hug your child today?" This suggestion is medicinal. A mother and her infant are a symbiotic pair. To thrive, a baby must be cuddled, patted, and groomed. To detect its needs, the mother must touch her infant regularly. Cool? Rough? Supple? Rigid? Shaky? Soggy? For millennia, women needed sensitive fingertips to collect clues about their infant's health, thus selecting for women's exquisite tactile sensitivity.

But this keen sense of touch is not restricted to the nursery. Your sweaty cheek, your clammy hand, the firmness of your grip: women pick up these subtle cues in the office, at conferences, at parties, even on the street. Then they use these tiny signals as they piece together who you are.

### Women Are Good Listeners

Women, on average, also have superior hearing.

For one thing, women are better than men at hearing high sounds, an advantage that begins in girlhood and increases with age. Women are also more sensitive to loud noises. Men tend to prefer music and spoken words much louder at every frequency from bass to treble.[15] This may be why spouses argue over the volume on the TV set or car radio. And who hears the water faucet dripping as husband and wife drift off to sleep? The woman.

A vivid example of this auditory gender difference occurred in a health club in Massachusetts in 1998. Erlinda McGinty of North Quincy began to think that the disco music in her aerobics class might make her deaf. So she asked the manager, a man, to turn it down. He ignored her. An argument ensued. The situation escalated. So outraged was McGinty that she finally launched a legal campaign to require Massachusetts health clubs to post warnings to customers about loud music.[16] The health club manager—along with many other men—probably wonders why McGinty got so riled.

The answer lies in deep history. An ancestral woman needed superb hearing to rear her precious packet of DNA, her child. Her baby's slightest whimper, its sigh, its troubled breathing: a woman had to distinguish among these inchoate sounds to know when her infant needed sleep or food or hugs.

Her excellent auditory sense probably also roused her to protect her child—by igniting her feelings. Sounds can rally the emotional core of the brain, tripping feelings of nostalgia, yearning, ecstasy, despair, or fury. Music can inspire a person to march toward the enemy, charge the goalposts at a football game, even recall an incident that took place thirty years ago.

On the plains of ancient Africa, women listened to their infants, listened to the wind and rain, listened for snakes and cats and rapacious birds, then "listened" to their own hearts to save their young. Those with keener hearing attended to their babies; their babies lived to pass along this trait, and gradually natural selection favored women with a keen ear for sound.

Ancestral women probably used this superb sense to listen to their mates and lovers as well. They needed to distinguish if these men were honest, kind, and fatherly before they bore them babies and devoted their lives to rearing these men's genes.

Today this natural talent can also tell a woman something about her colleagues in the workplace. A slightly raised voice, a dropped syllable, a quiver, a note of urgency: women pick up all these subtle auditory cues as they listen to you on the phone, in the boardroom, or over lunch. Then they replay this vocal information mentally—and use the cues to size you up.

## "Odor Prints"

Human beings can detect over ten thousand different scents; we wade through smells with every breath. We also produce and absorb fragrances, acquiring an individual "odor print" as distinctive as our face and hands. But women can detect fainter scents than men can.[17] During the monthly menstrual cycle when estrogen levels peak, a woman's ability to detect odors gets even better.[18] And a woman's sensitivity to aromas declines less markedly with age than a man's.

Women live in a richer olfactory world. They also recognize odors more accurately than men.[19]

Women's outstanding sense of smell probably evolved for the same evolutionary reason that women acquired their excellent sense of touch and hearing: to protect their young. With their impressionable noses, ancestral mothers detected dangerous smoke, rotting meat, even the scent of a stranger in the dark.

Their sense of smell probably helped them to react immediately, too. Smells have a direct line to the brain's primitive memory and emotion centers. Here they detonate, triggering elemental feelings. As Rudyard Kipling wrote of this, "Smells are surer than sights and sounds to make your heart-strings crack." So when an ancestral mother smelled danger, she became engulfed with fear and sympathy—and leaped to protect her child.

Women still use their sharp sense of smell to rear and protect their infants. When mothers are blindfolded, they can pick out their own baby from a group of infants just by smell, something fathers cannot do with as much success.[20]

But women also use this fine sensory equipment at the office and in social situations. "The nose knows," as Jimmy Durante used to say. Women note the perfumes and body lotions that you slap on, last night's alcohol on your breath, the smells on your coat and hair, and the aromas you cart into the office from the gym, the beauty parlor, the library, or the park. Women log these aromatic messages in their memory banks as they build their impression of you.

## Taste Buds

"He was a bold man that first ate an oyster," wrote Jonathan Swift. There are many things in the human diet. We are omnivores, after all; we devour an incredible range of plants and animals. But women and men have a somewhat different sense of taste.

Raisins, grapefruit juice, chili peppers, root beer, salty potato chips: women consume these and other strongly flavored foods with far less relish than men do,[21] largely because women, on average, can taste sweet, sour, salty, and bitter flavors in lower concentrations.[22] In one taste study of sweets, for example, scientists added sucrose to soft white cheese and to heavy cream. As it turned out, women liked their cheese and cream when the sucrose level was about 10 percent. Men liked these foods twice as sweet.[23] Small boys relished cream with 40 percent sucrose!

I have noticed this gender difference in restaurants. I like super-sweets such as pecan pie and cherry tarts. But I have watched in awe as male friends have washed down chocolate mousse with a Coca-Cola, then topped off dessert with macaroons.

This feminine acuity probably also evolved from women's primordial need to protect and nurture babies. With their ability to detect bitterness, ancestral mothers could guard against poisons—since most poisons in the plant kingdom are bitter.[24] With their ability to discern degrees of sweet and sour, mothers could reject unripe, less nutritious fruit. With their sensitivity to salt, our female forebears could recognize brackish water before they gave their child a drink.

The mouth has been called the body's gatekeeper. The taste buds inspect incoming substances so nothing harmful will pass into the stomach. Prehistoric women almost certainly sampled food before they fed their young.

Today, however, women pick up subtleties of your personality as they sit beside you in the office cafeteria and share food.

## Night Is Woman-Time

Our most vital human sense is vision. For at least sixty million years our forebears lived in the trees, where one misstep could cost your life. Monkeys do fall to the ground and die. As a result of this long heritage in the foliage, nature has given women and men superb vision, at least when they are young.

But the sexes see somewhat differently. Men excel at seeing in the light. Curiously, they also suffer more in very bright light. In the dark woman have superior eyesight. Women adjust their vision faster to the dark and see more accurately in the dead of night.[25]

This is probably another legacy from deep history, when mothers needed good night vision to perform essential chores—feeding, doctoring, and comforting teary infants in the moonless grass. But today this special acuity favors women in dimly lit restaurants, during slide presentations in the office, and in all pursuits that require seeing when the lights are low.

Women also have keener peripheral vision. Because of the way the eyeball is constructed, men are slightly better at depth perception while women have a somewhat wider field of vision.[26] Women literally see the "bigger picture." In the deep past, women may have used this sharp peripheral vision to keep an eye on children while they worked nearby, perhaps beside some marshy lake, catching crabs or pounding nuts.

Today they use this aptitude to evaluate your shuffle, your slouch, your entwined feet or tapping fingers during an office meeting. Superior peripheral vision also enables women to make a quick visual survey of guests at a crowded business or social gathering.

## Women and Color

"The purest and most thoughtful minds are those which love color the most," opined John Ruskin. No one knows which sex loves color more. But women usually distinguish colors, particularly the various shades of red and green, more accurately.[27]

One out of eight American Caucasian men is born with some deficiency in red/green color vision. Either they have trouble distinguishing most reds from most greens or they confuse more subtle hues, such as light pink and pastel blue-green, or brown and olive green.[28] Only 1 in 230 women is born with any sort of difficulty sorting red from green or seeing any of the more subtle shades of each.[29]

This feminine talent for perceiving shades of red and green is genetically determined. The genes for red/green color vision and all combinations of these colors lie on the X chromosome. Because women have two X chromosomes, the normal genes on one chromosome mask any defective genes on the other. Men have only one X chromosome, however. So if a man inherits the defective genes for red/green color vision, he has no normal gene to hide its effects. As a result, he can make some bad mistakes as he shops for a sweater, tries to connect color-coded electric wires, or approaches a traffic light.

Women can also remember shades, tones, and color values more accurately than men. This color memory, as well as their superior ability to distinguish red and green, undoubtedly derives from women's long ancestry of foraging for fruit and vegetables—the forerunner of shopping. Are the berries red—and ripe? Or green—and sour? With their sensitivity to color, ancestral women could tell what was edible and what was unnutritious, even dangerous. Those with good color vision lived. They fed their children more wholesome fare. And as seasons turned into centuries, time selected for women with a superior color sense.

Women's ability to see shades of the color red may have helped them heal their infants, too. We judge people's health by the color of their lips and cheeks. That's why women wear rouge and lipstick: to advertise their vigor to friends and suitors. But shades of red are also the color of fever, rash, and inflammation, of crying eyes and infected wounds. Those ancestral females who could interpret the subtle hues of red in an infant's face and eyes detected early signs of sickness, as well as fear or shock. Keen-eyed females disproportionately cured their young.

In today's workplace, however, women are more likely to discern a slight blush of embarrassment, the pallor of despair, or the glow of health—and use these signals to appraise you.

## Reading Faces

Touch, hearing, smell, taste, night vision, peripheral vision, color vision: women's sensory acuities give them a remarkable advantage in any occupation where understanding and getting along with people is required. Yet women have even more arrows in their social quiver. They have an outstanding ability to read facial expressions.

In a revealing demonstration of this aptitude, neuroscientists Ruben and Raquel Gur of the University of Pennsylvania and their colleagues showed twenty-four male and fifteen female volunteers slides of human faces and asked them which ones were sad. The participants rated each photograph on a seven-point scale.[30]

Women were somewhat more sensitive to sadness in a man's face than in a woman's. Men, however, were extremely insensitive to unhappy expressions in a woman's face. As the Gurs noted, "A woman's face had to be really sad for men to see it. The subtle expressions went right by them."[31]

Many studies confirm the Gurs' results. Women are, on average, better than men at deciphering emotions by looking at a face. Preschool girls, grade school girls, and high school girls are better at reading emotions in a face than are boys of the same ages.[32] Women are particularly skilled at reading babies' faces. Experience as a babysitter or a mother does not contribute to this gender difference, either. Single women with no experience in child care are just as keen observers of infants' facial expressions as are mothers with years of practice.[33]

American women share this aptitude for reading faces with women in at least ten other countries.[34] Even in the jungle villages of New Guinea, women are better than men at judging emotions by looking at faces.[35]

Socially subordinate people often excel at interpreting the facial expressions of their bosses and others of higher rank.[36] Thus women's superior ability to perceive sadness and other facial emotions might derive partially from centuries of being treated as inferior to men.

But the ability to recognize emotions in a face is also linked to the female hormone estrogen. Girls born with only one sex chromosome (Turner's syndrome) have less circulating estrogen as adults—and they are relatively poor at recognizing emotions in others' faces.[37] Evolution, it appears, has chemically designed women to excel at this essential social talent: reading your inner world by looking at your face.

It is not difficult to speculate on why women surpassed men at reading facial expressions. In ancestral times, a man who misread an enemy's face probably received a spear in the belly. Males needed to discern the facial nuances of hunting companions, too. But if a man misread a woman's face, he incurred no more than a few angry words, perhaps the primitive equivalent of a night on the living-room couch. Even the man who misread a child's face lost little from the misinterpretation. For men, misreading faces was serious only under dangerous—and infrequent—circumstances.

If an ancestral woman misread a baby's face, however, or the faces of her growing sons and daughters, she missed vital information about their daily health. Women also had to read the faces of men, especially those they chose as mates or lovers. Would he be deceptive, cruel, indolent, or cowardly? A woman needed to know as much as she could about a man before she made love to him and bore his child.

In yesteryear the ability to read faces enabled women to care for helpless preverbal babies and judge potential mates. Today it is becoming a vital skill in the global marketplace as well. More and more businesspeople must deal with a wide range of colleagues and clients, including individuals from many foreign cultures. To operate effectively in this unknown social world, they need every social detail they can collect.

## Body Language

Women are also more skilled at reading all of the nonfacial bodily clues that we unthinkingly transmit.

People's emotional messages are 90 percent nonverbal.[38] We may say we are having a lovely time at the party, but our body-clasping arms send a different message. In fact, in conversation, words often make up only a fraction of the communication. Tone of voice delivers as much as one third of the message.[39] Gestures, posture, and facial expressions provide an additional one half or more of the communication.

We emit these cues naturally: just watch men or women talking on mobile phones as they stride down the street, waving their arms, smiling, and frowning, sending a host of signals to someone who isn't there.

Tests on thousands of men and women in nineteen countries demonstrate that women excel at reading a person's emotions from his or her tone of voice, posture, gestures, and other nonverbal cues.[40]

Girls and women pay more attention to body language, while men are more likely to concentrate on words. As a result, women pick up more of these nonverbal signals and notice them faster.[41]

"All I want is a fair advantage," W. C. Fields once said. When it comes to appraising people, women have a decided edge—with a host of biological tools they have evolved to read your body and your face.

They also notice just about everything around you.

## Remembering Physical Context

"You can send a man and a woman to church, but it is the woman who will be able to tell you what everyone had on," paleontologist Louis Leakey once remarked.[42] Women are generally superior at noticing and remembering physical contexts.[43] For example, when women and men are shown a group of objects and then some of these objects are moved or removed, women are generally better at noting the changes.[44]

This aptitude for discerning context could relate to women's ability to notice and remember landmarks.[45] In one memory test, men and women were ushered into an office where they were told to wait a few minutes for someone to arrive. After being escorted out of the office, they were asked to recall the location of the objects in the office. Remarkably, women remembered 70 percent more of the articles than the men did.[46] Women also recollect more details of a city, a college campus, or a home they have visited, and they recall these details faster.[47]

Women even navigate by means of stationary objects spread across a landscape. "Take a left after the grocery store, then turn right when you see the high stone wall." When women give directions, they specify twice as many concrete landmarks as men do.

Known as "location memory," this feminine ability to recall stationary items emerges with puberty, when estrogen levels rise.[48] So psychologists Irwin Silverman and Marion Eals hypothesize that this feminine form of spatial orientation comes from bygone times, when ancestral women were obliged to remember the location of water holes and the berry patches, termite mounds, and fig trees where they did their gathering. Women must have used these immobile features of the landscape as guideposts to find their way back home.

Men usually navigate by distances and cardinal directions instead. "Go a quarter of a mile north on highway 9, then east on route 21 for about five hundred yards." When men give directions, they give twice as many of these quantitative and cardinal references as women do.[49]

In a number of studies, this male method of orientation has been associated with male hormones, particularly testosterone.[50] So this male trait most likely stems from men's primordial occupation, hunting. It would have been difficult for ancestral hunters to notice specific berry bushes as they stared at darting antelope or watched vultures overhead. Noting the position of the sun and sensing how far they had come in one direction was a more practical way to orient themselves as they followed moving quarry.

In the past, both means of navigation must have been vitally useful. But women's location memory is taking on new significance in the workplace. When a woman walks into another's office, she notices the miniature sailboat on the bookshelf, the photographs of Nepal, the Russian novel on the windowsill, the squash racquet behind the door. Then she uses these personal details as she deals with this colleague.

For people who need help finding things, women's superior locational memory can often save the day. Eyeglasses, opera tickets, car keys, running shoes, business cards, engagements scratched on notepads: sometimes we are swamped by our belongings. At remembering where things are, women take the prize.[51]

## The Nature of Tact

So women have an arsenal of people skills. With their delicate sense of touch, they gauge your grip. With their sensitive hearing, they note a hesitancy in your voice, a faltering or lilt. With their superior peripheral vision and ability to detect nonverbal cues, they register your impatient foot—even in the dim light of an office slide presentation. They detect from your face that you are confused or bored. They smell the odors in your clothes and in the room. They observe the fabric of your suit, the cut and hue. And they notice your surroundings, the crystal on your desk, the swizzle stick on the floor. Then they employ this battalion of data to fathom what it is you want to hear—and proceed to manipulate you with words.

"Tact is, after all, a kind of mind reading," wrote Sarah Orne Jewett.

Across the countless ages of rearing preverbal infants, women evolved a host of aptitudes for understanding the needs and desires of those around them.

Women still use these abilities in child rearing. But their feminine talents also enable them to excel at all sorts of jobs where one must work cleverly, intuitively, and tactfully with people. Translators, interpreters, police officers, detectives, therapists, social workers, advertisers, financial advisers, lawyers, arbitrators, mediators: many more of these "people professionals" will be women in the years ahead.

Many will bring to their jobs one more outstanding feminine social talent, too. Dozens of psychological tests show that women are, on average, more skilled at what psychologists call interpersonal sensitivity.

## Women's Genes for "Executive" Social Skills

Neuroscientists currently believe that interpersonal sensitivity, a conglomerate of aptitudes they call "executive social skills" or "social cognition," resides in the prefrontal cortex, the area behind the brow considered to be the crossroads of the mind.

When your prefrontal cortex is well built, you are, for example, aware of the feelings of others. You easily pick up emotional expressions in faces. You notice and integrate the cues of body language. You are flexible, responsive, and appropriate during social interactions. You are tactful and clever at making and keeping friends. You maintain good relationships with siblings, parents, and teachers. And you can override the impulses that distract you from completing your social goals.[52]

Neuroscientist David Skuse posits that women are more likely than men to acquire the genetic endowment for this suite of related social aptitudes. Why? Because he and his colleagues have traced these social skills to a specific gene or cluster of genes on the X chromosome that influences the formation of the prefrontal cortex; his study was discussed in chapter 1. As previously noted, due to patterns of inheritance and bodily interactions, this gene or gene cluster is silenced in all men but active in about 50 percent of women. Hence about half of all women have the brain architecture to excel at perceiving the nuances of social give-and-take.[53]

Another aspect of brain architecture could contribute to women's superior executive social skills: the tissue bridges that connect the two brain hemispheres.

The two hemispheres of the cerebral cortex have some specialized functions. For example, the right hemisphere plays a larger role in identifying facial expressions and in detecting emotions in one's tone of voice.[54] But people interpret these nonverbal data in verbal centers lying in the left cerebral cortex.

Here's the point: Because men's brains have somewhat smaller connective highways between the brain hemispheres, they may be less agile at interpreting the nonverbal data they have collected, hence less gifted at executive social skills.[55]

## Women Are Born People Watchers

"Who are *you*?" asks the Caterpillar of Alice in *Alice's Adventures in Wonderland*. Like the Caterpillar, women want to know.

They begin in infancy. Newborn girls spend more time than newborn boys maintaining eye contact with adults.[56] At four months of age, an infant girl can pick out facial features more accurately than a boy and better distinguish one person from another.[57] An infant girl smiles more intently at a human face while a boy smiles just as readily at a blinking light.[58] By age one, girls also approach their mothers and adult female strangers more often than boys do and remain closer to them.[59]

This feminine curiosity about people continues throughout life. Girls and women pay more attention to faces. They recognize faces more readily than boys and men do and they employ a "friendly gaze" more often when they interact. They are also comfortable speaking and listening to others at closer distances.[60] Girls are drawn to people. And as they grow up, they begin to work the crowd.

Friendship, Samuel Johnson remarked, should be kept in "a constant repair." Women believe it. Women send the majority of greeting cards. Women give the parties, keep the telephone companies in business on weekends, and expend more time and energy maintaining family ties.[61] As discussed in chapter 2, women cast themselves as actors in webs of affiliations, obligations, and responsibilities. Then they nurture these connections by talking, listening, sympathizing, and employing all of their other people skills—including, of course, a winning smile.

Women smile more in social situations than men do[62]—most likely to connect with others. Women even smile more when they are alone, such as in restaurants or while listening to a tape-recorded story.[63]

Because socially subordinate people smile more often than dominant ones,[64] some psychologists regard this feminine trait as an expression of deference and appeasement, the result of centuries of social subordination. But feminine "social smiling" begins in infancy and increases with age.[65] So psychologists have come to believe that feminine smiling and laughing serve as a kind of social glue. It relieves tensions, synchronizes moods, punctuates thoughts, and solidifies social bonds.[66]

Women's innate people skills will be a valuable commodity in almost every sector of the twenty-first-century economy. Peter Drucker and many other respected business analysts have come to regard people as a company's most crucial resource.[67] "The organization of the future," Drucker says, "must be nonbureaucratic and based on the concept of human capital."[68]

With their people skills, their language abilities, their drive to network, and their faculty for contextual thinking, women will be extremely valuable human capital in almost any business setting. No segment of the marketplace, however, requires people skills more constantly than the service occupations.

### At Your Service

Brenda Scharlow of Clarksville, Indiana, installed a three-foot-deep swimming pool in her revamped 1954 fire truck. When she gets your call, she hops into the cab and wheels into your front yard to teach your children how to float and swim.[69]

Today some 239,000 people, mostly women, are licensed "nail technicians"; they paint your toenails while you read or chat.[70] Entrepreneurs will sell you hot meals in train stations, return your library books and video rentals, fill your prescriptions, redecorate your living room, plan your vacation, edit your manuscripts, even clean out your closets.

Personal fitness trainers will test your wind capacity and muscle power, then prescribe and oversee your exercise regimen. Personal chefs will educate your palate, put you on a special diet, and design, cook, and present your meals. Personal shoppers will buy you dresses to match your shoes and scarves. Personal financial advisers will listen to your plans for school, marriage, or retirement, then buy your stocks and bonds for you.

Forget about cooking. In 1994 Americans spent some 44 percent of their spare cash on food cooked outside the home.[71] Neighborhood restaurants and take-out food shops are burgeoning. In fact, demographers predict that at least 20 percent of supermarkets will go out of business in the years ahead as we continue to buy our food at convenience stores and go out to eat.[72]

If you work as a restaurant cook, baker, manicurist, or bellhop, in the dry-cleaning or laundry business, or in a nursery selling special houseplants, the Bureau of Labor Statistics predicts that your services will become even more in demand in the years ahead.[73]

In fact, the fastest-growing sector of the U.S. economy is made up of self-employed people who run small service businesses.[74] As more and more working women—and men—need help to do their chores, even more little businesses will open. Welcome to a new stratum of society, what trend analysts Edie Weiner and Arnold Brown call the "professional servant class."

Who are all these people?

According to the 1996 *Statistical Abstract of the United States*, 60 percent of those working in the service industries are currently women. Some four million businesses in the service industries are owned by women; they add up to 52 percent of all women-owned businesses in America.[75]

Women in America are not the only ones taking over the service trades. In 1990, women in Europe and other developed nations held over 60 percent of all service jobs.[76] In almost all of the 174 developed and developing nations surveyed by the United Nations in 1995, women held roughly 50 percent of all clerical, sales, and service jobs as well.[77]

Women around the world are converting their ancient people skills into cash.

## Women as Detectives, Police Officers, and Advisers

A remarkable professional service provider—and probably a harbin-
ger of things to come in the twenty-first century—is Marie Schembri.
Schembri calls the third floor of her brownstone in New York City
"bat cave." Here she keeps her wigs, her tiny cameras, her binoculars
and dark glasses, her Red Cross uniform, her combat boots. For a fee,
Schembri dresses appropriately and then combs the caverns of Forty-
second Street or the East Village to find a drug-addicted daughter, ex-
poses a husband with his lover, finds out why an ex-wife is spending
so much money, locates stolen merchandise, or provides almost any
other service you need from a private eye.

Schembri's wits are for hire—and she is convinced that women
make good private detectives, a traditionally male pursuit. "Women
haven't had force," she says, "they've had to rely on cunning."[78]

Chances are good that Schembri and her fellow gumshoes will
have plenty of work to do in the years ahead. The Bureau of Labor
Statistics reports that the job of private investigator is among the
twenty-five fastest-growing occupations in the United States.[79]

Women are also slowly making their way onto America's police
forces, in part because of their people skills. Only 13 percent of all
police officers and detectives in the United States are women.[80] But
police departments have begun to recognize that female cops have
some vitally important qualities. Female officers are, for example,
outstanding at coaxing perpetrators into squad cars. Women keep
their voices calm and their batons at their sides. They are more soothing and less confrontational than men. They tend to sweet-talk
suspects into custody without provoking violent reactions.[81]

Policewomen are also clever at eliciting confessions. Captain Margaret York and her partner have the highest rate of confessions in the
homicide division of the Los Angeles Police Department. As York says
of her success rate, "These people either look at us as a mother figure, or they think we are too stupid to know what to do with the information."[82] Policewomen are also becoming recognized for their
special effectiveness at working with juveniles and with cases of domestic violence and rape.[83]

Women lawyers put their feminine wiles to work as well. Because
female lawyers tend to be quieter and more sympathetic than their

male peers, witnesses sometimes forget they are talking to an adversary. As a result, female interrogators get more information out of witnesses during depositions.[84]

Advertising agencies, public accounting firms, and companies in the securities industry are recognizing women's special talents with clients.[85] Fifty-eight percent of public relations specialists are women, as are 35 percent of advertising executives and 52 percent of accountants and auditors.[86]

More and more women are also becoming financial advisers. As Hardwick Simmons, president and CEO of Prudential Securities, explains this trend, "Investors are looking more and more for a relationship with their financial advisers. They want someone they can trust, someone who listens. I don't know if it's nature or nurture, but in my experience, in general, women may be better at these kinds of relationship-building skills than men are."[87]

It's nature, Mr. Simmons. At least in large measure. As personal and professional services continue to flourish, women will flourish, too.

## Retail Sales

"A woman is always buying something," Ovid observed in ancient Rome. In this regard, much has remained the same. But today's women are not only buying, they are selling—certain kinds of selling. Men sell televisions, automobiles, and appliances, and 85 percent of those who sell to business firms are men. But 77 percent of those who sell retail clothing are women.

Today's retail industry is booming—particularly for women. While sales jobs have increased at least fivefold for men since 1900, they have increased more than thirteenfold for women.[88] American women currently hold 65 percent of all jobs in retail sales and personal services and 75 percent of all jobs in sales-related occupations.[89] The job of salesperson currently ranks among the top three fastest-growing occupations in the United States.[90]

Women currently hold most of the service and retail sales jobs in European countries, too, as well as in some countries in Africa, Asia, and Latin America.[91]

One of Trollope's characters called women "the most successful swindlers of the age." Perhaps he was thinking of women's uncanny ability to read your mind, then tell you what you want to hear. As more people buy more clothes, jewelry, and God knows what else in America and abroad, they will surely fatten the collective female purse.

## Creative Leisure

"The future ain't what it used to be," Yogi Berra reportedly said. In the past, Americans hoped to fill their leisure hours with scenery and a nap on the beach. No more. Today many of them plan to spend their precious spare time at much more inventive play. "Creative leisure" is on the rise.[92]

Bisbee, Arizona, an old mining town, has replaced its deserted saloons with twenty-seven art galleries, three museums, and a summer arts festival. American opera companies have increased in number from sixty to over one hundred since 1975. Thirty-six new museums for children have come into being since 1990. All sorts of creative camps are popping up. Camp Start Up offers girls aged thirteen to eighteen two weeks of summer leisure while they learn about careers in the corporate world. The girls make business presentations, attend "power lunches," design business cards, and learn to play the corporate world's most important sport, golf. In a resort on Disney's Orlando, Florida, property, you can take any of eighty courses while your children play with Mickey Mouse.

Jerry Mallett, president of the Adventure Travel Society, reports that "the women's market is driving the travel industry."[93] Not coincidentally, I think, learning and exploring are "in." Some 5 million Americans boarded cruise ships in 1996, up from 1.4 million in 1980. People are also joining religious pilgrimages; some twenty thousand of these trips are listed on the World Wide Web.[94] They are also flocking to theme parks, megachurches combined with amusement parks, working farms, and dude ranches.

Vacationers in the United States spent more than $416 billion in 1995, reports the Travel Industry Association of America. They are not alone. People in other affluent countries are also spending heavily on entertainment, travel, and dining out.[95] In fact, tourism is now regarded as the world's largest industry.[96] In 1997 the total economic value of all goods and services tied to tourism was $3.6 trillion, some 10 percent of the global gross product.

Wide-bodied aircraft, lower fares, the opening up of formerly Communist countries, travel shows on television, business trips that include family members: many current forces stimulate the human urge to wander.

As people in industrial societies retire earlier, as they live longer, and as the baby boomers move into their fifties and sixties, even more people will use their leisure time for travel, entertainment, and education. Globe-trotting has become the thing to do. As a result, the job of travel agent will be one of the twenty-five fastest-growing occupations in America by 2005. Flight attendants will not be far behind.[97]

"It is a happy talent to know how to play," Emerson wrote. The world is practicing. As Deborah Luhrman of the World Tourism Organization says, "travel is one of the basic human rights now."[98] Women, of course, will be prominent among those who hit the road. But many other women will take jobs in the travel or entertainment industry and prosper from these wanderlusts.

### Gracious Homes

Women will prosper from those who stay at home, too. Martha Stewart may be the bellwether of this market, inspiring millions to repot plants, flip omelettes, and decorate for holidays in innovative ways. But many other women have entered the "gracious home" trades.

Linens, glassware, bath gels, 300-thread-count cotton sheets: people are decorating their living quarters again. The sale of home-improvement goods in America has increased some 30 percent since 1990.[99] Gardening is in, along with $15,000 statues and ornamental ponds stocked with $10,000 goldfish. One gentleman gardener I know swelled with pride as he told me that his prize carp was ten inches long!

In an age when vegetables come in plastic bags, cakes appear in boxes, and dresses materialize from catalogs, people want some connection to the natural world. Feminine entrepreneurs will oblige them.

American women are not the only ones who have begun to profit from our growing reliance on services. Women in Russia, Poland,

and other Eastern European countries, for example, are going into business for themselves. Besides engaging in such traditional small businesses as selling baked goods and home furnishings, they are also producing magazines, making textiles, and forming media companies, language schools, and training centers for accountants and secretaries.

International investment groups are even beginning to finance this growing development, women starting small businesses in the service, retail, and entertainment industries.[100]

## Culture Brokers

No single trend is more widely discussed in contemporary business circles than globalization, the expansion of business operations and capital flow into foreign lands. Most agree that this deeply rooted crosscultural phenomenon will continue unabated for many decades, if not centuries.

Who will build all the necessary bridges among foreign people in foreign worlds? Enter the culture brokers, professionals who know the language and customs in the countries on your business schedule or vacation itinerary.

One of them is a friend of mine, Barbara Pillsbury, an anthropologist who reads or speaks thirteen languages. Barbara, a founding member of the Pacific Institute for Women's Health, has taken on special assignments in dozens of countries for the U.S. Agency for International Development and other organizations. But she also works on her home turf, the United States, often as a culture broker.

For example, Pillsbury was hired to help a group of physicians from China who were sent for training in a dozen medical schools across North America. These Chinese doctors wanted to know how to engage American colleagues in casual conversation, how to say no without sounding hostile, how to conduct themselves at professional conferences or when invited to an American home for dinner, and how to understand certain American phrases, gestures, and vocal tones.

Pillsbury carefully explained American habits, attitudes, and expectations. She also held practice sessions, simulating actual situations that these Chinese doctors might confront and coaching them on how to act.

Do you bring your wife along when a traditional Muslim man invites you to supper in Beirut? How do you respond when someone bows from the waist in Tokyo? What do you give as a gift in Namibia? As more of us interact with foreigners in the office and buy business or vacation tickets to Turkey, Thailand, or Patagonia, we will need to be savvy enough to avoid the potential land mines of daily communication in foreign climes.

Some 60 percent of business ventures between American and foreign companies fail. Arlene B. Isaacs, a New York–based corporate consultant, believes this is, in large part, because Americans do not spend enough time learning local traditions before they depart for foreign places. To deal in the global marketplace, she advises, you should spend at least 10 percent of your preparation time learning key phrases like "hello" and "good-bye" and familiarizing yourself with some of the country's landmarks, artists, writers, and personalities.

Will executives spend this time? The smart ones will. I think many will employ others to help them, though. Most of these savvy culture brokers will be women.

With their language abilities, their aptitude for reading body postures and facial expressions, and their other social skills, women should also excel as interpreters in societies around the globe.

### Women Lawyers

"The first thing we do, let's kill all the lawyers," exclaims a character in one of Shakespeare's plays.

It hasn't happened. Americans currently support some 864,000 lawyers—a lot of them women. In 1960, 2.5 percent of lawyers in the United States were women; today about 26 percent are women. Around 80 percent of legal assistants are women, as are almost 50 percent of law students.[101] The U.S. Supreme Court has two female justices. A woman is also U.S. attorney general, head of the Justice Department.

Not many women have made it into the upper echelons of the legal profession. Some 90 percent of state and federal judges are still men. In 1996, only 13 percent of the partners in the 1,160 largest law firms in America were women.[102]

There are many reasons why women have not achieved the most prestigious, highest-paying positions in the law. For one, they only recently began to enter the profession in sizable numbers. Sociologists report that (male) senior law partners are more inclined to choose men than women to become partners.[103] As Cynthia Epstein of the CUNY Graduate Center in New York sees it, these men have in their mind's eye a template for the model lawyer—and the ideal is not a woman.[104] Hence women must demonstrate extraordinary dedication and ability to achieve partnership rank.

Another factor, however, is that fewer women are willing to sacrifice precious time with family to meet the grueling schedule and demands these jobs regularly require.[105] Young female lawyers proudly sign up with influential law firms just as men do. But after a few years of trial by fire, more women than men resign.[106] To accommodate women, some of America's large law firms now offer women maternity leave, part-time positions, even part-time partnerships.[107] Yet women still abandon these choice jobs more often than men.

This reality—women's need to balance work and family—is central to understanding women's progress in every sector of the economy. It will continue to be crucial as the twenty-first century proceeds.

Nevertheless, women will make exceptional contributions to the law, particularly in those areas in which the lawyer must deal directly with a variety of people. In these situations, one must size up the client and the adversary, combine brainpower with empathy, weigh the data within a broad social context, work with all parties diplomatically, and strive to achieve a frequently ambiguous commodity: justice. All lawyers need these skills, but women's natural social aptitudes should give them an advantage.

Unquestionably, women are infiltrating the American legal system in growing numbers. But they often take different career paths than men. More women become temporary lawyers, individuals employed for a particular job. More take jobs as in-house counsel in corporations, at nonprofit institutions, and in banks and government agencies. Some teach. Many gravitate to smaller "boutique firms." Others start small law firms of their own.[108] In short, women are drawn to lawyering positions where rank, competition, and specialization are less important, and where working with people and thinking within a broad social context are central to the job.[109]

The specific kinds of law that women and men pursue also differ.

Male lawyers are often more interested in raising capital, buying and selling real estate, transacting mergers and acquisitions, and the other functions of corporate law. These forms of lawyering "grease the wheels of capitalism," as Dean Robert C. Clark of Harvard Law puts it.[110] Men are also more attracted to litigation. In the courtroom, it's win or lose—a situation that appeals to more men than women.[111]

In general, women are more interested in improving social conditions.[112] So they tend to be attracted by public interest law, health law, civil rights law, and environmental law, which directly affect the well-being of large numbers of people. As you might expect, women are also more interested in family law, trust and estate law, and other kinds of law in which they work directly with individuals and mediate personal disagreements.

Our contentious times promise to provide these women lawyers with plenty of cases that suit their interests.

## Litigation

"Litigation is becoming the new frontier," writes Patrick Garry of the Columbia University School of Law.[113] America's high divorce rate and the advent of prenuptial agreements have contributed to the flood of lawsuits between former lovers. Children are suing parents over personal rights. Students are suing teachers over grades. Employees are suing coworkers for sexual harassment. Patients are suing doctors for malpractice. Tenants are suing landlords over heat and water. Prisoners are suing states over cafeteria food. Individual workers are suing corporations for personal injury, industrial diseases, negligence, abusive sexual climates, and discriminatory practices.

"Mad plaintiff disease," it's called.[114] For good reason: some thirty million lawsuits are filed every year in American local, state, and federal courts.[115] A new term has even come into use: the "serial suer"—the individual who brings legal action again and again. Mad plaintiff disease is even spreading to other cultures, as men and women around the world depend less on traditional customs to solve their problems and more on modern legal practices.[116]

The current frenzy in litigation in the United States has led to a new interest in procedures other than court actions: arbitration and mediation. Both of these offer women opportunities to use their superb people skills.

## Win-Win Solutions

"We are witnessing the birth of a new arm of civil justice," reports Lewis Maltby of the American Civil Liberties Union.[117] More and more companies, trade organizations, and state and local governments wish to avoid the time and costs of court proceedings, so they offer in-house arbitration services for a variety of disputes.

Arbitration procedures can differ. But usually the two parties must agree in advance on the selection of the arbiter or arbitration panel and state whether they will accept the judgment rendered. Arbiters are not necessarily lawyers, but many are; all have expert knowledge in the subject of the dispute. If the parties have agreed to accept the decision, then the arbiter's judgment is final and enforceable by law.

Several industries, some states, and many nonprofit organizations administer arbitration programs. The two largest organizations are the American Arbitration Association and the Council of Better Business Bureaus. Representatives at the the American Arbitration Association report that businesses of all kinds are using their services. In fact, the demand for arbiters is at an all-time high.[118] The association also reports that an increasing number of the hearing officers in these arbitration disputes are women.

Mediation, unlike arbitration, is a legally nonbinding negotiation process in which both parties try to work out a solution to their dispute with the help of an impartial, diplomatic, trained mediator. The mediator has no authority to impose a decision. Instead his or her job is to enable the disputants to negotiate and arrive at a compromise. Very often the mediator is a woman.

I am not surprised. Women have a remarkable evolutionary heritage for this kind of work.

## Women's Heritage as Mediators

Female chimpanzees are experts at settling disputes. At the Arnhem Zoo, older females are particularly skilled at mediation. When juveniles squabble, an elderly female chimp saunters into the fray and stands there, barking and waving her arms. Her very presence disheartens callow troublemakers.[119]

When an argument erupts between adult males, females also try to intervene; males are more likely to take sides or even join the fight. If the argument gets vicious, the alpha male of the community generally breaks up the quarrel. But after the warriors have retired to preen or sulk, females begin to mediate between these enemies.[120]

Each has her own mediating style. One female begins by sitting close to one of the defeated males, grooming his hair and encouraging him to groom hers. Then she presents her buttocks. He inspects her genitals, then follows her as she inches toward his adversary. Moments later, she goes to his enemy and does the same. Back and forth she shuttles. Gradually the two combatants find themselves side by side. Then with a little encouragement from this mediator, they turn to one another, kiss, and groom each other's fur.

Some female chimpanzee peacemakers drag one adversary by the hand until he is sitting near the other. Some jab the victor in the ribs with fingers until he moves toward the defeated male to make amends. One older female even strode up to a male who was about to throw a rock and peeled his fingers from around the missile. When he picked up another rock, she took it, too. Six times he found a new projectile. Six times she interceded. Finally he gave up and sat down to mope.

These older female chimps are excellent mediators. They seek win-win solutions to a spat. Often they achieve a settlement and community harmony as well.

Ancestral women, particularly older women, undoubtedly also acted as mediators. Using their verbal tools, their natural talent at handling people, their ability to embrace ambiguity, and their facility for seeing issues in a broad context, contemporary women will carry on this long, long feminine tradition—and achieve win-win solutions to many modern legal problems.

## Feminizing Justice

Will the influx of women into many areas of the law have any significant long-term consequences for the American justice system?

It is too early to tell. But there are some portents of what the future might hold. A number of major law schools have introduced new programs on public interest and environmental law, fields that particularly interest women.[121] Some schools have also established ways to give students credits for working in legal aid clinics for low-income clients.[122]

But will our concepts of justice change?

According to some legal experts, male and female lawyers view justice somewhat differently.[123] Women lawyers, these experts say, are more likely to look at alleged or convicted criminals within the wider context of their poverty and lack of education; male lawyers are more likely to view them within a narrower context of the crime itself and the legal rules of society.[124] Moreover, male lawyers tend to focus on the rights and duties of autonomous individuals, the atomistic details, while female lawyers more often consider relationships between people, the larger social milieu.[125]

Male and female lawyers also often differ in how they define rape, sexual harassment, and domestic violence, as well as how they view pornography, child support, abortion, and the rights and obligations of parents.[126] And female judges are more inclined than male judges to favor plaintiffs in cases alleging gender or race discrimination in employment.[127]

"Every new time will give its law," said the Russian writer Maxim Gorky. The growing presence of women will not create a sea change in the American legal system. The justice system changes slowly and carefully.

Nevertheless, women lawyers and judges will probably examine cases within a broader social context. Judges may subtly base some of their decisions on the mitigating circumstances of individuals rather than on the strict dictates of the law. And as legislators, female lawyers may write and support different kinds of laws, particularly laws regarding health, education, the environment, and other broad social issues. All will incrementally change some of the ways we define and administer justice.

"Yesterday is not ours to recover, but tomorrow is ours to win or to lose," said Lyndon B. Johnson. Women will win. With their ability to read minds and with their executive social skills, many will make shrewd business deals. Their people skills may become priceless commodities. And as women around the world come to dominate many sectors of the service industries and professions, they will bring comfort and novelty to millions of people's daily lives.

CHAPTER 5

# HEIRS TO HIPPOCRATES

## Women as Healers

Seeing's believing, but feeling's the truth.

THOMAS FULLER

The first wealth is health," wrote Ralph Waldo Emerson. Many women have bestowed this blessed gift. Women have brewed teas, confected potions, applied poultices, set bones, massaged muscles, cleaned gashes, administered tranquilizers and stimulants, and prescribed diets throughout recorded history—curing friends and relatives with their knowledge of the natural world.

This feminine talent for healing has long been overlooked or minimized by Western society. But today women are becoming a major force in almost every sector of the healing professions. They bring tremendous innate assets to these jobs: a natural emotional expressivity, empathy, a tendency to nurture, patience, and the special feminine physical ability to manipulate small objects, such as a surgeon's scalpel.

Several trends in medicine will strengthen their presence and their impact. More and more patients are eager to avoid high-tech treatments; they seek old-fashioned hands-on curing by experts who listen compassionately—primordial female fortes. A growing number of people also want to supplement conventional Western treatments with preventive medicine and alternative cures, areas of medicine that have long been the domain of women. And the aging population is stimulating the expansion of medical facilities, from establishments for "assisted living" to health centers for the middle-aged. These facilities will need women's people skills and hands-on care.

Men have made and will continue to make enormous contributions to all of the healing professions. They have built and currently operate most of the essential equipment used to treat the very ill. They have erected and run many of the hospitals. And they have saved millions from undue pain and misery.

But women bring new attitudes to the job of healing. They spend more time with patients. They tend to work in teams with other professionals more regularly than men. They are more likely to treat the whole patient, rather than just the symptoms of the disease. And women are more inclined to mix traditional Western medical practices with alternative or "complementary" cures.

I will maintain that as women continue to enter the medical professions they will substantially enrich our Western concepts of and procedures for healing.

## Women as Healers in Traditional Societies

In a sense, Western women are reclaiming a role that was never lost in more traditional societies.

In these cultures, more men become the shamans, practitioners who heal with magic and their contacts in spirit realms. But women are the hands-on healers of everyday ills of the flesh. Saraguro Indian mothers of the southern highlands of Ecuador, for example, treat some 86 percent of all family complaints.[1] By age twelve, girls begin to be proficient at diagnosing symptoms, helping their mothers mix remedies, even applying cures. Saraguro boys know almost nothing about healing.

Life in modern Taiwan, westernized in many ways, is much the same; 93 percent of all illnesses are first treated at home—by women.[2] In fact, anthropologists have come to realize that in traditional societies mothers and grandmothers are often the diagnosticians and healers, the primary providers of bodily well-being. The sick turn to professionals only when they cannot cure their illnesses themselves or find relief at home.[3]

Many traditional peoples even believe that women are naturally imbued with the power to heal. The Sinhalese of Sri Lanka say that women are the curers because women are more regularly graced with *athquniya*, "the touch."[4] In Jamaica, male shamans sometimes don feminine dress to acquire women's empathic, curative aura.[5] In bygone eras, women in European societies were often thought to have natural healing powers, too, although some were unfortunately regarded as dangerous witches instead.

Women's talent for healing was widely acclaimed in the West for a short period during the nineteenth century. The Englishwoman Florence Nightingale became a legend during the savage midcentury Crimean War between Russia on one hand and the Ottoman Empire, France, and England on the other. As Lytton Strachey wrote of Nightingale in *Eminent Victorians,* "Her sympathy would assuage the pangs of dying and bring back to those still living something of the forgotten charm of life. . . . A passionate idolatry spread among the men: they kissed her shadow as it passed."[6]

Clara Barton received similar acclamation during the American Civil War, when she organized nurses for the Union army and earned the nickname "Angel of the Battlefield."

For a time, the United States became a leader in training female physicians.[7] As men and women poured into America's swelling cities in the 1870s, a great demand for professional medical services emerged, and more and more medical schools began to accept and train women.

Women's role in medicine declined during the first half of the twentieth century, however, when many of the medical institutions that admitted women were forced to close for lack of financial support.[8] Several women's colleges also shut, and new anti-nepotism rules barred women from following their spouses into the expanding co-educational colleges and universities.

Then, after World War II, staying home and having babies became the fashion, even among educated women. Hardly any American women pursued careers in medicine. As a result, a lower percentage of doctors were female in 1950 than in 1900. But in the decades that followed, the feminist movement, affirmative action programs, and the determination of millions of women made a profound impact on academic institutions.[9] Doors began to open. Women poured into colleges and universities—and into the various healing professions.

## Women's Irreversible Gains in Medicine

They are there to stay. In 1995, 95 percent of registered nurses and licensed practical nurses in the United States were women.[10] In the mid-1990s, over 90 percent of speech therapists, occupational therapists, and dieticians were women.[11] Ninety-nine percent of dental hygienists were women. Seventy-five percent of physical therapists were women. Some 36 percent of pharmacists were women, up from 23 percent in 1980. Thirty-two percent of health diagnosticians were women, up from 12 percent in 1980.[12] Women were also providing 79 percent of home health care.[13]

Women are flourishing in the more lucrative and prestigious medical fields as well. Less than 1 percent of dentists were women in 1960, but this number rose to 15.4 percent in 1990. By 1995, 37 percent of all dental students were women.[14] In 1990, about 14 percent of optometrists were women, up from 8 percent in 1980. What is most remarkable, only 5.5 percent of American physicians were women in 1960, but between 1970 and 1990 the number of female physicians in the United States increased some 310 percent. By 1990, 25.5 percent of all American doctors were female. By the mid-1990s, almost 45 percent of all medical students were women.[15]

Women are making significant and irreversible gains in many areas of the healing professions—and returning to a profession they probably practiced a million years ago. They bring with them many natural endowments, among them a tremendous ability to express compassion.

I begin with this compelling aspect of the female mind.

## Women's Emotional Expressivity

The emotions are the furnace of the brain.

Fueled by chemical compounds, people are impelled to save a drowning child, declare their love, or savor the satisfaction of a job well done. Anger, pride, piety, envy, patriotism, chagrin, jubilation: feelings are powerful, sometimes overwhelming tides that surge through the brain, coloring everything one thinks. Ceaselessly they ebb and flow. And just as the finite keys on a piano can play infinite melodies, the basic chemical compounds that produce the emotions can mix in numberless combinations, creating subtle variations of sorrow, loathing, disgust, fear, anxiety, or joy.

Both men and women feel an incredible variety of emotions; both feel them with piercing intensity and dogged regularity. Yet the ability to express these emotions is the special trait of women.

Feminine emotionality is a worldwide phenomenon. After Gallup pollsters asked people in twenty-two societies which sex was more emotional, they concluded that "More than any other trait, this one elicits the greatest consensus around the world as more applicable to women than men."[16] Eighty-eight percent of Americans think women are more emotional, as do 79 percent of the French, 74 percent of the Japanese, and 72 percent of the Chinese.

Men express poignant feelings all the time. But they often express their feelings less directly, less openly than women do. When they are depressed, men are much more likely to joke, drink, or just fall silent. Women prefer to talk about their anxieties, fears, or sorrows.[17] Psychological studies report that men "internalize" their feelings; they keep them to themselves.[18] In fact, men have a remarkable ability to restrain their feelings, an aptitude I call emotional containment.

## Men's Emotional Restraint

Men's emotional containment may be due, in part, to child-rearing practices. American mothers, for example, use fewer emotional words when they tell stories to their little boys. They express a narrower range of feelings when they play with their sons. And they avoid discussing complex emotions, choosing to explore these feelings with daughters instead.[19]

Several factors suggest, however, that men's emotional containment also stems from biology. Despite the dissimilar ways that mothers treat sons and daughters, young boys are no better than girls at restraining their feelings. At age ten, both sexes express the same amount of anger, for example. But as boys mature and their levels of testosterone rise, they become skilled at masking feelings of vulnerability, weakness, and depression. Boys begin to avoid expressing sadness, grief, fear, loneliness, anxiety, guilt, and hurt.[20] They camouflage these emotions with silence.

When asked, teenage boys often refuse to discuss their feelings.

They become fluent at "joke-speak," all of the quips and gags and seemingly offhand remarks that boys and men employ to mask their emotions.[21] Some even drive these feelings into their unconscious; they have no idea how they feel.[22]

Then, as young men age, they continue to avoid emotional conversations. During marital spats, for example, men are more likely to retreat from verbal confrontation, fleeing into stormy silence and stonewalling a wife's attempts to talk about feelings.[23] When psychologist John Gottman of the University of Washington recorded hundreds of marital quarrels, he found that 85 percent of stonewalling was done by men.

This male emotional containment is apparent in many cultures. Women canvassed in the United States, Finland, Norway, and Sweden all complain that men are "emotionally stingy."[24] Even in India, China, and Japan—societies where little boys have traditionally received much more pampering and privilege than little girls—men do not express emotions as regularly as women.[25]

## Biology of Male Emotional Containment

Gottman and his fellow psychologist Robert Levenson have an intriguing explanation for men's emotional containment, particularly the containment of negative feelings.[26]

They point out that negative emotions like fear, jealousy, and anger activate or act in conjunction with the autonomic nervous system (ANS), the bodily system that gets the heart pumping and revs up the body to fight or flee. But in men, lower levels of negative feelings trigger this bodily arousal system. Moreover, once aroused, men recover from the bodily symptoms more slowly than women do.[27]

Chronic ANS arousal is harmful to both sexes. So these psychologists hypothesize that men unconsciously withdraw from conflict, particularly marital discord, to avoid the harmful effects of this bodily stimulation. In short, men avoid emotional interactions to preserve their health.[28]

I suspect, however, that gender differences in the brain also play a role in men's emotional containment. To follow my reasoning, you must know something about how the brain coordinates thinking with feeling.

The prefrontal cortex, discussed in earlier chapters, is where humans think about and modify their feelings. Here we process our emotions, tempering sensations, integrating feelings with ideas, and regulating the degree of our emotional arousal. For example, using our prefrontal cortex, we contain feelings of petty envy of friends or transform these feelings into those of joy at their good fortune.

Below the prefrontal cortex is a group of structures in the middle of the head that actually register, generate, and activate basic emotional responses, such as fear, anger, disgust, joy, sadness, and passionate love. These brain regions are known collectively as the limbic system, although this term is going out of style as scientists begin to isolate more precisely those areas involved in generating the emotions.[29] All agree, however, that at least one primary factory for producing feelings is the amygdala, an almond-shaped region deep in the side of each brain hemisphere.[30]

Connections between the prefrontal cortex and the amygdala probably play a role in men's emotional containment. Here's how.

## Body Loops

Specific neuronal circuits connect the amygdala with the prefrontal cortex, as well as with other brain regions.[31] The heart, stomach, muscles, and virtually all other bodily organs are also linked to the amygdala and the prefrontal cortex, as well as to other brain regions.[32] Several of these body loops are devoted specifically to the integration of reasoning-plus-feeling. This is why your heart may pound or you may feel "butterflies" in your stomach as you think about your sweetheart and feel romantic passion.[33]

In people with brain damage to a particular region of the prefrontal cortex, however, these circuits are disrupted. The patients are perfectly rational—but almost totally emotionally contained.[34]

Such a person is Eliot, a patient of Antonio Damasio, a neurologist at the University of Iowa College of Medicine. Eliot had had a tumor removed from the region of the prefrontal cortex. During the operation, surgeons also excised some surrounding brain tissue that had been damaged. Eliot recovered successfully, but he was no longer Eliot. He was lucid and pleasant, even charming. He could remember names and dates. But he could not make simple decisions or follow any plan. And he showed no sorrow, no joy, no frustration, no resentment, no worry, and only rare, brief outbursts of anger. Because a primary reasoning-plus-feeling circuit of the brain had been disrupted, Eliot thought but did not feel.[35]

Here's the theory: Perhaps these emotion circuits connecting feeling and thinking areas of the brain are different for the sexes— enabling most men to contain their feelings more easily than most women.

Related aspects of brain architecture could also contribute to men's ability to contain, even repress their emotions. As you know, the brain's two hemispheres are somewhat specialized. The ability to shut off or contain negative emotion, for example, is a skill that goes on predominantly in the left prefrontal cortex.[36] This brain region may differ between the sexes in some way that enables men to contain their sadness or despair.

As discussed in chapter 1, the two brain hemispheres are also less integrated, less well connected, in men. In one study, for example, men and women were put into a brain scanner and asked to think sad thoughts. In women, the prefrontal cortex in both hemispheres showed activity, whereas in men only the left hemisphere was predominantly active.[37] This compartmentalization of the male brain may also help men to divorce themselves from their feelings.

## Emotional Flooding

When men do tap into their feelings, especially into powerful ones such as fear, anger, sadness, or anxiety, they are more likely than women to be swamped by these emotions, a condition that Gottman calls "emotional flooding."[38]

The heart pounds; muscles tense; sweat appears; blood pressure rises; breathing deepens; adrenaline and the stress hormones flow. Some flooded individuals revert to primitive responses, such as hurling fists or shedding tears. Emotional flooding is particularly evident when men get mad. As you will see in chapters 6 and 9, men are much more likely than women to become overwhelmed by rage.

Men's proclivity toward emotional flooding may be related to their tendency toward emotional containment. Men have fewer neuronal avenues connecting some brain regions. Perhaps they are unable to integrate—or exit—their emotions as rapidly or effectively as women.

Scientists will eventually pinpoint the neurological basis of men's emotional containment, as well as their susceptibility to emotional flooding. In the meantime, it is not difficult to imagine why men could have evolved these traits.

"The happiness of a man is in the mastery of his passions," Tennyson wrote. This must have been particularly true in deep history. It was not adaptive for an ancestral hunter to be consumed by fear as he stared into the yellow eyes of a leopard, nor by pity as he cut the throat of a baby gazelle, nor by compassion as he raided an enemy camp. Primitive hunters who could contain, even stifle, their emotions must have survived disproportionately.

Psychologist Howard Gardner of Harvard University proposed that humans possess several different kinds of intelligence, including "interpersonal intelligence," the ability to understand the moods of others, and "intrapersonal intelligence," knowledge of one's own feelings.[39] Men may be somewhat less equipped to get in touch with their own emotions.

Emotional containment could be an asset in some medical situations, as when a doctor must give a patient extremely bad news. But in most doctors' consultation rooms, in the emergency rooms of hospitals, in rehabilitation centers and physical therapists' offices, patients often seek practitioners who can empathize as well as prescribe in their hour of need.

### Feminine Empathy

Poets, playwrights, and philosophers have long remarked on women's emotionality—often with a tinge of scorn. This contempt still thrives. For example, in a 1995 poll of 14,070 Americans using the Prodigy computer network, 65 percent of the men questioned were of the opinion that women are too emotional.[40]

I often think we are. Like many women, I am easily moved by plays, operas, movies, parades, church rituals, and touching human moments. Something happens in my brain; although I feel ridiculous, I weep. Women's emotions can spill out at inappropriate, inconvenient times. Nevertheless, I think women's emotional expressivity is a byproduct of natural selection for one of humankind's most admirable traits, empathy—the capacity to experience vicariously the feelings of others.

On hundreds of tests of empathy, emotional responsiveness, nur-

turance, and affection, girls and women—from infants to octogenar-
ians—get higher scores than boys and men.[41] Little girls cuddle and
pamper dolls, expressing sympathy for these human replicas. When
girls play, they are more nurturing with one another than boys are.
Psychologists Eleanor Maccoby and Carol Nagy Jacklin report that
"women throughout the world and throughout human history are
perceived as the more nurturant sex, and are far more likely than men
to perform the tasks that involve intimate care-taking of the young,
the sick, and the infirm."[42]

Freud saw women as so self-sacrificing that he called them "moral
masochists." Even Darwin, who doggedly held that men were more
courageous and intelligent than women, agreed that women were
more empathetic. As he wrote in 1871, woman differed from man
"chiefly in her greater tenderness and less selfishness."[43]

Today scientists are beginning to understand the biology behind
women's emotional expressivity and their empathy.

In 1996, psychiatrist Mark George of the National Institute of
Mental Health and his colleagues put ten men and ten women into a
brain-scanning machine and asked these subjects to recall sad events,
such as the death of loved ones, separations from loved ones, illnesses, or career disappointments. As these individuals recalled the
bitter experiences of their past and present, George recorded the activity in emotional and thinking centers of their brains.

Here are the astonishing results: While thinking sad thoughts,
the women's brains were eight times more active than the men's.[44]
George concluded, "Women seem to experience a more profound sadness than do men."[45]

Women's brains most likely show greater activity because they are
better integrated, as neuroscientists Arne Ohman, John Morris, and
Ray Dolan discovered.[46] These researchers put subjects into a brain
scanner and showed them slides of angry faces. When the subjects
saw and recognized these furious expressions, their left amygdala became active. But when the angry face was flashed too quickly to be
consciously seen, the right amygdala reacted instead. The researchers
concluded that the right amygdala registers and generates the emotions of the unconscious mind, while the left amydgala is more active
when the brain actually perceives these emotional responses and con-
verts them into conscious feelings.[47]

Here's the point: The amygdala in the right brain hemisphere is not in direct communication with the one in the left hemisphere. They do interact, but the network is circuitous. With their better-integrated brains, women probably have more communication between the right and left amygdalas. This may provide them with better access to their unconscious feelings.

## Winter Doldrums, Spring Fever

Mark George is one of many psychologists who report that women experience their emotions more profoundly than men do.[48] I have not decided whether I agree. The female brain becomes more active when women think sad thoughts. But does a larger web of brain activity signify more depth or complexity of emotion? Hard to say. I have no doubt, however, that women are affected by their emotions more regularly. Numerous studies confirm, for example, that women experience almost twice as much depression as men.[49]

Mental health experts do not agree on the meaning of these statistics. Some argue that women are more willing to admit their turmoil and seek help. Some maintain that more women are stuck in dead-end jobs and social predicaments that generate depression. Some say that our very definitions of depression single out women more often than men.[50] They contend that if health professionals were to define alcoholics, drug addicts, murderers, and vagrants as depressed, these professionals would find more depressed men than women.[51]

Despite this dispute, surveys done in more than a dozen countries, including Canada, France, Germany, Italy, South Korea, Lebanon, New Zealand, and the United States, have reported that women actually do express more symptoms of classically defined clinical depression than men.[52] Particularly in the spring.

"April is the cruellest month," wrote T. S. Eliot. The highest rates for admissions to mental hospitals are in February, March, and April. More of these patients are women. Women also express more of the symptons of spring fever. Helios, Ra, Mithra, Sol—call it what you will, the god of sunlight cheers up women more regularly than men. Women are more sensitive to seasonal changes in light and dark.[53]

In short, women express the entire range of positive and negative emotions (except rage) with greater intensity and regularity than men do.[54]

This emotional expressiveness begins in infancy. In a classic experiment, psychologist Martin Hoffman exposed day-old infants to a battery of sounds, including wild animal calls, a monotonous computer-made language, and the unhappy wails of other infants. All the babies cried the most when they heard the cries of other infants. But girls cried more.[55]

"It is as healthy to enjoy sentiment as to enjoy jam," wrote G. K. Chesterton. I suspect many women would agree. Women not only express their emotions more regularly, they express their feelings more accurately.[56] Be it joy, disgust, horror, or surprise, women are more skilled at expressing exactly how they feel with nonverbal cues, particularly with facial expressions. In fact, women's faces are, on average, simply more expressive.[57]

Nature has designed women to feel and display empathy—regularly and clearly.

## Evolution of Feminine Empathy

It is not difficult to surmise why and how feminine emotional expressivity and women's capacity for empathy evolved.

According to one study, when American mothers interact with their babies, they respond to their infant's cries and squeals at least once a minute. If the infant gurgles happily, the mother squeals back—not to imitate but to acknowledge the infant's feelings. This way she affirms what her baby is feeling and coordinates her own state of mind with her baby's mood, a practice known as "emotional attunement."[58]

Surely ancestral women also needed to coordinate emotionally with their young. Those who suffered when they saw a sick or unhappy infant devoted more time and energy to keeping this child alive. Emotionally attuned mothers raised children who were well adjusted. These children disproportionately lived—gradually selecting for women's superior ability to express sadness, pity, empathy, compassion, and other nurturing emotions.

As a result, almost all healthy human mothers seem compelled to hold, look at, talk to, check on, and talk about their infants. Many women never put their infant completely out of mind. As poet Sylvia Plath expressed it, "I see her in my sleep, my red, terrible girl. / She is crying through the glass that separates us."

Some mothers even seem to merge emotionally with their young. Siriono Indian mothers of Bolivia are extreme examples of this fixation. These mothers adopt their newborn's name for their own and add a suffix to indicate "mother of."[59] "Every beetle is a gazelle in the eyes of its mother." This Moorish proverb describes the feeling of women around the world: almost all dote on their young.

I am not suggesting that all women are highly empathetic. Nor do I believe that men make poorer parents. But everywhere in the world, no matter what kind of culture one examines, women expend far more time at hands-on infant care than men do.[60] They always have. And among almost all of our primate relatives, females do all the nurturing of infants.

To ensure that their young are cared for, women have evolved a powerful capacity to feel and express empathy.

## The Chemistry of Empathy

"God could not be everywhere, and therefore he made mothers." So goes the Jewish proverb. Nature has made mothers; feminine nurturing is driven by a host of chemical compounds ubiquitous among mammals.

During the birthing process, for example, levels of estrogen increase, triggering motherly behaviors in all female mammals: they begin to nuzzle, carry, and protect infants.[61]

The basic brain chemical oxytocin is also linked to nurturing. Although both sexes produce this pituitary hormone, mammalian females produce much more of it—particularly as they give birth. The surge of oxytocin produces the contractions of labor and triggers the "letting down" of mother's milk. But oxytocin also primes females to become acutely responsive to the sight of, sounds of, and odors of their infants—predisposing them to accept, lick, warm, and nurse their tiny offspring.[62]

Even specific genes are associated with maternal nurturing. Female mice that lack the fosB gene fail to gather up their newborns or crouch over them to nurse and warm them. Hungry and cold, these infants die.[63] The Mest gene, too, seems to promote maternal behaviors in mice.[64]

"Oh, what a power is motherhood," Euripides exclaimed. The great dramatist knew what he was talking about. Nature has built a mag-

nificent machine for the incredibly important job of nurturing infants. But this feminine empathy has nonmaternal uses as well—in
the modern workforce.

## Emotions in the Workplace

Darwin reasoned that the female of the species naturally extends her
empathy, selflessness, and nurturing "toward her fellow-creatures,"
not just her young.[65] Yet many contemporary women seem determined to deny that women are emotionally expressive and nurturing,
that women's compassion stems from nature, or that women are predisposed to extend their empathy toward their fellow creatures in
general. These doubters seem to believe that if they acknowledge
these feminine attributes, they will be marking women as emotionally
fragile—not tough enough for demanding jobs.

    In the past, they had solid reasons for their fears. Most business-
men were wary of what they saw as excessive feminine emotionality.
But attitudes are changing. Employers and managers are beginning
to see women work effectively at high-pressure jobs. Equally important is that many managers are beginning to value cooperative team
spirit and an empathetic attitude toward colleagues and clients[66]—
qualities that women offer.

    Women's emotional expressivity and compassion are becoming
particularly important in the medical professions. More patients are
demanding hands-on care—by individuals who have a sympathetic
bedside manner. Medical schools have even begun to instruct students on how to relate to patients, advising them on how to listen and
interact—in short, how to express concern and compassion. These
talents come naturally to most women.[67]

    But women's emotional expressivity and empathetic nature would
be of little practical value in the nursery or the office without another
feminine quality: patience.

## Women's Patience

"Genius is nothing but a great aptitude for patience," French naturalist Comte Georges-Louis Leclerc de Buffon reportedly said.
Women of all ages have more of this precious gift than men. American girls, on average, have longer attention spans than boys. Girls de-

vote more time to fewer projects, and they are more likely to finish the projects they start.[68] Women are more patient in the office.[69] They are even more patient when they invest money in the stock market.[70]

The feminine gift of patience is recognized around the world. In the 1996 International Gallup Poll on Gender and Society, men and women in twenty-two societies were asked whether patience was more characteristic of men or women. The overwhelming response: women are the patient sex.[71]

This feminine gift has a corollary among our closest relatives, chimpanzees. Female common chimps spend almost three times longer than males at tedious, time-consuming jobs like cracking nuts and collecting insects.[72]

Females of just about every mammalian species do much more parenting than males do. Rearing infants takes perseverance, tolerance, and patience—whether you are a chimpanzee, a hedgehog, or a fox. So I suspect that women share this trait with just about all other female mammals.

The method of natural selection for patience may have been quite simple. Impulsiveness, the opposite of patience, is associated with low levels of serotonin, a basic neurotransmitter in the mammalian brain. Men have fewer receptor sites for this neurotransmitter in at least one brain area associated with the emotions.[73] Women probably evolved more of the physiological machinery required for patience.

"Our patience will achieve more than our force," wrote the eighteenth-century British stateman Edmund Burke. He might have added that patience is itself a force. Women's outstanding aptitude for this gritty perseverance will serve them well in many sectors of the workforce—particularly medicine.

### How Women Will Grip the Scalpel

Compassion. Patience. Besides these qualities, women have a particular physical aptitude that should serve to their advantage in the healing professions: their skill at manipulating small objects.

This may be due in part to their more slender, agile hands. But this dexterity is also associated with the female hormone estrogen. A woman's skill at manipulating little objects increases during the monthly menstrual cycle when estrogen levels peak.[74] When estrogen levels are high, for example, women are much better at experiments like putting pegs into holes. Postmenopausal women who take estrogen also increase their manual dexterity.[75]

This fine motor control also resides in the architecture of the female brain. In women, the areas for organizing the complex control of the arm and hand reside in the front part of the left hemisphere, near the motor cortex, the central station that tells the body's muscles how to act. In men, the same areas lie farther to the rear of the left hemisphere. This proximity in women, psychologists believe, gives them their ability to make more precise hand movements.[76]

Women's "fine motor control" undoubtedly evolved in our deep evolutionary past. Chimpanzees use fine manual dexterity when they "fish" for termites. First they insert a long thin twig into a termite tunnel. Then they twiddle it, provoking the insects to attack and stream out along the twig. Female chimps do three times more of this patient, dextrous work than males do.[77] Female chimps and orangutans also manipulate leaves and twigs and other objects more often than males.[78] And female primates do much more grooming of their young, picking off specks of leaves, bugs, and dirt from their infants' coats.[79]

We humans also groom one another. You must have seen a bit of lint on the jacket of the person in front of you in a supermarket line. Didn't you have an urge to pluck it off? No one, to my knowledge, has yet done a study to see whether men or women groom others more regularly. But since women do so much more hands-on tending of very young children, it seems likely that they also do more social grooming.

Did eons of chimplike twiddling, picking, and grooming others predispose our tree-dwelling female ancestors to manipulate small objects easily? Did ancestral women perfect this fine motor coordination when they descended to the ground and began to spend hours, decades, lifetimes collecting tiny seeds and berries, cleaning babies, and sprucing up their friends?

The existence of special feminine brain architecture for this task, along with the link between estrogen and fine motor control, suggests that women have been busily manipulating small objects for several million years. In the past they used this talent to feed and care for young. Today they have begun to use it in intricate surgery as well.

## Man the Engineer

Most men are at a severe disadvantage at performing fine motor chores.[80] Try asking almost any man to unfasten your necklace; then wait five minutes while he struggles with the clasp. "Men build bridges and throw railroads across deserts," journalist Heywood Broun once noted, "and yet they contend successfully that the job of sewing on a button is beyond them." There is more than a kernel of truth in this stereotype. Men are generally built for strenuous action and power instead of fine, precise work.

This is easy to notice in the spring, when men begin to "hum the pea," as my father used to call throwing a baseball. Men are, on average, more proficient at throwing, catching, kicking, running, and jumping—"gross" body movements.[81] These skills are associated with specific aspects of male brain architecture as well as with the male hormone testosterone.[82] So they almost certainly come from millennia of stalking, chasing, surrounding, and felling prey.

It is difficult to see how men's gross motor abilities will be useful in the many desk jobs that are coming to dominate the workplace. They are certainly of little use to doctors, dentists, or most others in the healing professions. Only exceptionally dexterous men succeed as surgeons, for example. But men do have a related talent that will be crucial to the practice of twenty-first-century medicine, as well as in many other pursuits: an outstanding spatial sense. On average, men are far more spatially and mechanically talented than women.

Boys begin to express this spatial acuity early. An infant boy is better than a girl at tracking a blinking light across a TV monitor. Little boys excel at predicting the path of a moving object.[83] Boys like toy cars, blocks, trains, and other things they can move around or use in construction. They pack the video arcades to play spatial games, zapping electronic prey. When it comes to computers, girls use them deftly—but boys love them. By age ten, boys are better, on average, at anticipating where specific patterns will appear in paper-folding tests and in matching a three-dimensional object with a second one drawn from a slightly different angle.[84] When testosterone floods the male brain at puberty, boys generally begin to outstrip girls in geometry, mechanical drawing, and other spatial tasks.

In studies of over 150,000 Americans aged thirteen to twenty-two, tested over thirty-two years, those individuals whose scores fell in the top 5 percent to 10 percent in science, math, mechanical reasoning, and engineering overwhelmingly were male.[85]

Male spatial aptitudes are evident outside the United States as well. Studies in Japan and several other countries have yielded similar results.[86] Spatial acuity is a hallmark of men.

## Testosterone Creates Spatial Acuity

Scientists now believe that the brain architecture for this spatial prowess is created in the womb—by fetal testosterone. Just as fetal testosterone produces the asymmetry of the male brain, it also builds spatial skill. Then bodily levels of testosterone continue to fuel men's spatial dexterity throughout their lives.[87]

There are many examples of the relationship between testosterone and spatial skills. When healthy male senior citizens receive injections of testosterone, their spatial acuity increases.[88] Women become better at finding their cars in parking lots, as well as at other spatial chores, around menstruation—when estrogen levels are at their lowest and bodily testosterone becomes unmasked.[89] And middle-aged women who take estrogen as therapy do much better on spatial tasks when they are off their medication, when bodily testosterone can express itself more fully.[90]

The correlation between testosterone and men's spatial aptitudes is not simple. Too much or too little can dampen one's spatial talent.[91] Moreover, estrogen can play a substantial role in a person's spatial sense.[92] Nevertheless, testosterone is associated with many spatial abilities—and men have much more of this hormone than women have.[93]

A million years ago, men used their spatial genius to track zebras and wildebeests. Ten thousand years ago they shot tiny birds on the wing. In the past hundred years, men have used their spatial and mechanical wizardry to string the world with telephone cables, enliven our homes with radios and TV sets, and walk on the moon. Tomorrow men will continue to design and operate our complex computers—as well as high-tech medical equipment.

Because men are so technically proficient and so concerned with rank, male doctors tend to seek the top-level jobs in the most presti-

gious medical specialties. Men run America's hospitals, HMOs, and
health-oriented insurance companies. As of 1995, over 95 percent of
medical school deans and department chairs were also men.[94] I think
men will continue to maintain their presence in these financially lucrative positions throughout the many fields of medicine.

But a major shift in thinking is occurring in the medical
professions—toward a more contextual, holistic view of illness and
recovery. With their compassion, their patience, their manual dexterity, their people skills, their verbal gifts, and their contextual view,
women will establish a strong presence in many of the healing professions—and make changes in the curing arts.

This trend has started.

## How Women Heal

Female physicians schedule fewer patients per hour, when not con-
strained by the pressures of "managed care." In 1992, female doctors
averaged 97 patients per week, while male doctors saw 117.[95] These
women say they spend more time with patients to build rapport. They
believe this extra talking and listening is an essential part of a holistic healing process.[96]

Videotaped office visits confirm this gender difference. Female doctors do talk more to their patients. They ask more questions, listen
more to the answers, and spend more time with patients, be they male
or female.[97] As Yvonne Mart Fox, a consultant who advises doctors on
patient relations, puts it, "I tell the men to try to bond as much as possible. But women definitely have the edge."[98]

Not everyone is looking for a nurturing connection with his or her
physician. Some people, particularly men, come into a doctor's office
only to solve a problem. They are not seeking an emotional relationship with this professional. Nevertheless, many men and women do
say they are more satisfied after seeing a female doctor.[99] They prefer
the hands-on, empathetic care that women give.

Patients of both sexes are definitely interested in this nurturing
touch when they must face a serious operation. Dr. Susan Love, a surgeon and former clinical professor at the University of California, Los
Angeles, says that she always takes her patient's hand as he or she begins to feel the anesthesia in the operating room. "And I'll tell you,"

Love remarks, "every man I ever operated on has grabbed my hand just as quickly as every woman—and held on just as tightly."[100]

In a 1994 poll, medical students reported that female physicians are "more sensitive, more altruistic, and less egoistic" than male doctors.[101] Anthony I. Komaroff, professor of medicine at Harvard Medical School, agrees. "Male doctors," he says, "tend to be puzzle solvers, whereas women tend to be healers."[102]

Part of women's healing gift are their abilities to listen, talk, touch, empathize, and nurture—talents that come from feminine deep history.

## Women Doctors Choose Different Paths

Not surprisingly, women choose different career paths in medicine, choices that reflect their evolutionary heritage and their approach to healing.

Women gravitate to internal medicine, pediatrics, obstetrics and gynecology, family practice, and other primary-care subspecialties that emphasize hands-on, nurturing treatment. Men tend to choose high-tech specialities, such as vascular surgery, cardiology, radiology, anesthesiology, and pathology—fields that use their spatial and mechanical aptitudes and require less long-term, person-to-person interaction.[103]

Women are also more interested than men in healing as members of a team. Current changes in health care are pressuring more and more doctors who are in solo practice to join a group. Nevertheless, female doctors are almost twice as likely to work for a hospital, for an HMO, or in group practice, while more men work for and by themselves.[104] This may stem, in part, from women's natural proclivity to form egalitarian cliques.

Team doctoring may also appeal to women because female physicians are generally more interested in treating the whole patient, rather than focusing narrowly on the symptoms of a disease. As you know, women tend to take a broader, more contextual view of almost any issue or problem, while men are more likely to compartmentalize and focus intently on one element at a time. So it is not surprising that women have a more holistic approach to curing.

These feminine proclivities toward providing empathetic hands-on care, working as part of a team, and treating the whole patient may well be the wave of the future. The late physician Marcia L. Storch, former chair of the American Menopause Foundation's medical/ scientific advisory board, was one of many who believe that team healing will be the new exemplar in medicine. As she said to me, "A group of doctors will collect data on several aspects of a patient's life, then treat all parts of a person's multifaceted disease."[105]

As women continue to move into the practice of medicine, we will probably see more and more compassionate, hands-on, holistically oriented team practice.

## Nurse-Practitioners

One bellwether women's team is a group of four highly trained nurse-practitioners who opened a primary health care practice in New York City in 1997.

Sore throats, abdominal pain, cuts and bruises from the play-ground, kitchen accidents, asthma: these women treat all of these minor illnesses and chronic diseases just as doctors would, referring those with more complex medical conditions to specialists or sending them to hospitals. But these licensed nurse-practitioners devote more time to the whole patient than most doctors. Like most nurses with advanced training, they also tend to recommend diet and exercise regimens, rather than the more costly treatments more often pre-scribed by technology-minded male physicians.[106]

Current economic forces will almost certainly enable more of these teams of nurse-practitioners to thrive. Health care providers, particularly HMOs and hospitals, regard these independent nurse-practitioners as a way to cut costs and increase efficiency.[107] So Medi-care, Medicaid, and private insurers are helping these nurses to expand their practices into more areas normally dominated by doc-tors. Today more than twenty-five states permit highly trained nurses to practice in some areas of medicine without the supervision of a doctor. In every one of these states, except Illinois, they can also pre-scribe a wide variety of medications.[108]

Nursing, a specialty of women in traditional societies around the world, is expanding its scope—a trend that almost certainly will strengthen the power of women within the American medical community.[109] In fact, some demographers predict that the United States will soon experience a glut of doctors and a shortage of highly skilled and highly regarded nurses.[110]

## Healing the Whole Patient

Health professionals are finally beginning to pay attention to some of the social and psychological factors that contribute to illness.[111]

It has long been recognized that social isolation can be hazardous to health. Hundreds of studies link it with heart disease, cancer, depression, and other illnesses.[112] Aging men and women who have no one with whom to share their experiences and feelings are twice as likely to get sick or die.[113] Studies indicate that social isolation can kill you just as fast as smoking, obesity, or lack of exercise.[114] In a ten-year study of men and women in California, for example, those with little social contact died at three times the rate of those with full social lives.[115]

To deal with these problems, gerontologists and other doctors have begun to recommend a full round of social engagements for patients as a way to retard decrepitude and disease.

There will be many jobs in these medically related fields. Much of the world is graying. Fewer children are being born almost everywhere in the developed world, and more men and women are living into old age. It is estimated that by the year 2015, roughly 20 percent of the world population will be over age sixty-five. Even now, these elderly want to live at home. And politicians listen to this powerful group of voters. The Netherlands, Scandinavia, and the United States are among the leaders in this regard, providing the frail and elderly with housing and social services—including exercises, dancing, and theater outings, as well as round-the-clock medical care.[116]

"Assisted living" is the wave of the future. Ten years ago private home care companies that provided assistance to the sick and elderly in their homes grossed some $1.3 billion annually. Today they take in $8.5 billion.[117] By the year 2020, these home care companies are projected to make $20 billion.[118] Their services focus on the social and personal needs of their clients, as well as health care.

"Wellness centers" have also begun to proliferate. These facilities provide state-of-the-art exercise, nutritional advice, and medical professionals who give physical therapy to people of all ages.[119] The objective is not to treat illness but to keep people fit and well. Many such centers, demographers report, will be operated by hospitals and other health care providers. Creative entrepreneurs have also begun to set up lifestyle centers, combining training in diet and exercise with meditation and spirituality.

Me! { Who will be the providers of all these medically related social needs? I think it will be largely women—bringing compassion, hands-on treatments, and a holistic view of illness and health to the frail, the sick, and all those who wish to prevent disease.

## Complementary Medicine

Of all the current trends that favor women's interests and women's healing skills, the most widespread is the shift in attitudes toward alternative medicine.

"The best doctors in the world are Doctor Diet, Doctor Quiet, and Doctor Merryman," wrote Jonathan Swift. A growing number of Americans have come to agree. They finally understand what shamans around the world have known for at least thirty thousand years: there is a connection between the mind and the body. Since too many impersonal, hurried, expensive, high-tech Western doctors treat them like engines with faulty parts, rather than as whole human beings, more and more patients have begun to turn to alternative remedies.

Black cohosh root to fight hot flashes. Passionflower and kava to contain mood swings. Gotu kola for mental alertness. Many Americans are in the mood to treat their illnesses and other physical problems with unconventional methods. Homeopathy, naturopathy, acupuncture, biofeedback, meditation, self-hypnosis, visualization, aromatherapy, reflexology, chiropractic, osteopathy, organic diets: Americans spent some $14 billion in 1996 on unconventional therapies, an increase of 69 percent since 1989.[120]

One out of three Americans uses some kind of alternative medical treatment.[121] Some 40 percent believe that herbal remedies can be effective in treating major illnesses, including cancer.[122]

Given these public attitudes, purveyors and supporters of conventional Western medicine are beginning to dismount from their high

horse. About half of all American medical schools now offer courses
that include discussions of previously disdained techniques, such as
homeopathy, acupuncture, and massage. Microsoft, Donna Karan,
and other major businesses now offer employees insurance coverage
for several forms of nonmainstream medicine. Oxford Health Plans is
one of several insurance companies that cover some forms of alternative healing, including acupuncture and chiropractic.[123]

Interestingly, some 60 percent of American doctors have actually
referred their patients to practitioners of alternative medicine. Even
the term is changing: "alternative medicine" is evolving into "complementary medicine."

These nonconventional treatments promote self-reliance; they empower. After all, you can buy vitamins, herbal teas, organic foods, and
bottled water at the corner store. You can do yoga while you watch
TV. You can employ a masseuse to unfold her table in your living
room. You can purchase health care books, attend conferences, or
consort with like-minded people in health food stores or on the Internet. More than one hundred Web sites are now devoted to alternative
treatments.

True enough, conventional Western medicine can transplant a
human heart, scan the brain, and offer drugs of undoubted potency.
But can it alter all of the horrible daily habits that made the patient
sick in the first place? Or quell the postoperative depression that
slows the healing process? The many devotees of complementary
medicine think not. Americans are joining traditional peoples around
the world who mix conventional and alternative therapies in dealing
with their ills.

The aging of the baby boomers should only accentuate the
trend toward complementary treatments. Skeptical middle-aged
boomers may even be arm-twisted into adopting some of its precepts.
Managed care organizations are currently thinking of requiring participants to pay more of their medical bills if they cannot show that
they are paying sufficient attention to maintaining their health.

High-tech science, the god of modern Western medicine, is being
coupled with an ancient mistress, home cures from the natural world.
These are women's specialties. As complementary medicine continues to flourish, women should assume powerful, profitable positions
in the healing arts.

## The Return of Midwifery

The ancient practice of midwifery is also regaining some of its former respectability. It was widely practiced in the United States in colonial times. By 1900, midwives attended about half of all births.[124] With the rise of standardized medicine, however, midwifery declined. In some states it was even made illegal.

Today a growing number of states again permit midwifery. Some hospitals and medical schools now give courses and practical training in this profession. Some offer alternative birth centers staffed with certified nurse-midwives, registered nurses with special training in obstetrics who are certified by the American College of Nurse Midwives.[125]

Women also still practice a more traditional kind of midwifery, particularly in the rural South, in Appalachia, and in the American Southwest, often without a license or formal education. A growing number of educated yet uncertified midwives are in practice too. So just about everywhere in America, women pursue this primordial female occupation—legally or illegally.[126] In much of Asia, Africa, and Latin America, village midwives still deliver just about all of the infants.

Anthropologist Wenda Trevathan of New Mexico State University maintains that midwifery is womankind's oldest profession. She hypothesizes that our female ancestors began to pursue this special trade sometime after the human brain began to take form, some two million years ago. A series of evolutionary events, she believes, led to the development of this feminine profession.

It all began as our ancestors began to walk erect. With this revolutionary shift to bipedalism, Trevathan reasons, the human pelvis began to take on its modern shape, becoming broader from side to side and compressed from front to back. The end of the spine began to curve in, too, reducing the size of the female birth canal even more. Then, with the further development of the human brain by 1.5 million years ago, infants began to become too big-headed to slip easily through the constricted birth canal. Babies had to be born in a premature state to be born at all; they emerged in an increasingly helpless and immature (altricial) state.

With more enlargement of the human brain and additional remodeling of the pelvis for efficient walking, mothers began to need help in bearing their young.[127] Midwives, Trevathan proposes, could have been practicing their crucial art a million years ago.

These women had a tricky job. Human infants must twist themselves inside the birth canal as they exit. Even worse, most emerge from the womb facing downward, away from mother's face. So our female forebears, particularly first-time mothers, needed someone to help guide the infant, unwind the umbilical cord, and catch the baby before it plunged to the ground face first.

Females of other species rarely help a mother as she delivers her infant. Dolphins are an exception. In one instance, scientists saw a mother dolphin having difficulty delivering her newborn; its fin was caught in her pelvis. In moments, a second female dolphin pulled the infant from its mother's womb and helped her hold it at the water's surface to breathe—even though it had already died. Meanwhile, a third female gently pulled the protruding placenta from the mother's birth canal.

What is equally remarkable, on one occasion a male orangutan carefully ushered an infant from its mother's womb, first with his mouth, then with his hands. As soon as he gained control of the infant, he handed it to the mother.[128]

But only among humans is midwifery commonplace—undoubtedly because human births are almost always difficult and dangerous. In fact, Trevathan believes that women's deep anxiety about childbirth— found in many cultures—is an adaptive emotional mechanism that evolved to encourage ancestral mothers to seek help during this arduous process.[129]

Modern birth attendants make a difference. One recent study reports that women with midwife attendants had 50 percent fewer cesarean sections than did those with doctors. Their periods of labor were 25 percent shorter. They needed 40 percent less oxygen and 30 percent fewer painkillers during childbirth. They also suffered less postpartum depression.[130] Results like these, plus rising medical costs in the United States and the growing interest in natural childbirth, have led to greater public and professional acceptance of midwifery.

As the Western world continues to embrace complementary medicine of many kinds, more women will use midwives. And more women will return to this ancient female calling.

## Twenty-first–Century Shamans

The flood of women into the practice of all forms of primary health care is a welcome change—for patients and for our collective pocketbook. As Patricia Braus wrote of female physicians in *American Demographics* magazine, "If current trends continue, their increasing numbers could help reduce the cost of health care, increase the availability of much-needed primary-care physicians, and change the way medicine is practiced."[131]

Indeed, women bring to the curing arts a compassion, a patience, a precision touch, people skills, an interest in healing as a team, a tendency to seek holistic cures, and a view of the patient as a whole human being with social and psychological needs. These feminine aptitudes for curing come across the eons, from ancestors who roamed the plains of Africa millions of years ago. Women have long employed their healing powers in traditional societies. Soon they will dominate many sectors of contemporary Western medicine as well.

Many will be heirs to Hippocrates.

CHAPTER 6

# HOW WOMEN LEAD

## Women in Civil Society
## and Government

I suppose leadership at one time meant muscles; but
today it means getting along with people.

INDIRA GANDHI

T he more we realize our minuteness and our impotence in the
face of cosmic forces, the more astonishing becomes what
human beings have achieved," wrote Bertrand Russell. Many
of these achievements were born of the ambitious human brain.

Which sex is more ambitious?

In 1996 the International Gallup Organization polled men and
women in twenty-two societies in the Americas, Europe, and Asia
about ambition. People in Japan, China, Taiwan, and France thought
men were a great deal more ambitious than women. Spaniards regarded women as slightly more ambitious than men. Thirty-seven
percent of Americans considered men more ambitious; 26 percent regarded women as more ambitious; and 37 percent thought the two
sexes were equally eager to get ahead. At least 40 percent of the people sampled in fourteen of these countries believed that both genders
were equally ambitious.[1]

Worldwide business and social trends demonstrate women's ambitious spirit. In much of the industrial world women are now as educated as men; in the United States women have begun to outnumber
men at colleges and universities. Women make up 40 percent of middle management in corporate America and the rest of the industrial

world. Women start more new businesses than men do, and their enterprises are more likely to stay in business. They predominate in the service occupations. They may soon make up 50 percent of all lawyers in the United States. They have taken over many sectors of the healing professions. Women write over 50 percent of the books published in America, and produce more and more of what we watch on television, hear on the radio, and read in the newspaper.

Yet often women and men are ambitious in different ways. One outstanding difference is how the sexes seek to lead.

Despite the opportunities that women have to enter politics and win elective office in all industrial societies, far fewer women than men seek positions at the highest levels of government anywhere in the world.

In many parts of the democratic world, however, politics and government are no longer the only routes to local, national, or international leadership. Governments are being supplemented, even somewhat undermined, by new social forces. Extragovernmental entities such as multinational corporations, the global financial marketplace, the Internet, international judicial tribunals, and nongovernmental organizations (NGOs) are increasingly able to control huge sums of money, sway public opinion, and influence the policies of national governments.[2] At the same time, ethnic and religious groups are stirring in many parts of the world, gradually shifting power from the nation to the tribe or sect. As political scientist Harlan Cleveland writes of these directions, "The nation-state is leaking upward to globalism and downward to tribalism, but it is leaking—it isn't finished."[3]

Of all these forces that challenge the state, the one that will give women the most access to power and leadership is the growth of nongovernmental, nonprofit organizations: civil society. This chapter discusses women's growing role in civil society and their lesser participation in formal government and the military. Then it looks at the career paths that men and women pursue in societies around the world. It concludes that as women gain power in nonprofit organizations of all kinds, they are applying their people skills, their compassion, and their broad holistic approach to solving some of our most vexing social and environmental ills.

## Civil Society

Ernest Gellner defines civil organizations as all those intermediate nonprofit institutions, such as trade unions, political parties, church groups, pressure groups, interest groups, foundations, and other kinds of clubs and associations, that are not related to the family or the state.[4]

One well-known example is the organization formed by women to keep drunk drivers off the road: Mothers Against Drunk Driving, or MADD. Planned Parenthood, the Girl Scouts of the U.S.A., the Salvation Army, the League of Women Voters, and the Nature Conservancy are just a few of the thousands of American groups dedicated to one cause or another. All these organizations, ranging from local to international, make up what sociologists, political scientists, and others consider civil society.

Civil society has no central plan, no formal code of ethics, no single party line. Instead, each civil association is composed of individuals who have joined together to strive toward a common goal. Most are egalitarian, adjustable, and autonomous. Most can be disbanded or expanded as members see fit. Civil associations are not supported in perpetuity by the family or sustained by governmental force. Hence, individuals are not obliged to join a civil organization as a consequence of birth or mandated to congregate in these associations by law. Members volunteer—and they can depart of their own free will.

As Benjamin Barber of Rutgers University says of civil society, "It is literally constituted of, by, and for the people. It is the power of us."[5]

## The Rise of Civil Associations

Civil society has a long history—and historically women have played major roles in these associations.

In traditional cultures, men and women regularly form informal economic alliances and interest groups. In the European Middle Ages, independent guilds of merchants and artisans sometimes exercised considerable economic and even political power. These were forerunners of modern civil organizations. With the coming of the Industrial Revolution, Europeans began to congregate in sizable numbers in associations that were distinct from family enterprises and independent of the state. Mercantile associations, charities, lodges, funeral aid societies, religious groups, embryonic trade unions, maternal organizations: in the nineteenth century, hundreds of these volunteer associations emerged in America.[6]

Many of them were dominated by women. In the 1830s, Alexis de Tocqueville wrote admiringly of these civil associations in his classic book *Democracy in America*. He was particularly impressed by the women who volunteered in these groups. "If I were asked . . . to what the singular prosperity and growing strength of that people [the Americans] ought mainly to be attributed, I should reply: to the superiority of their women."[7]

In the late nineteenth and early twentieth centuries, women increased their participation in political clubs, worker associations, and professional organizations.[8] In America and Europe, they started settlement houses, joined religious and moral reform societies, and marched for the right to vote.[9] In Asia, women fought for the right to education. Women in India, China, West Africa, and many other parts of the non-Western world were leaders of and participants in social movements as well.[10]

In recent decades, civil associations have multiplied rapidly in the United States and other industrial nations.[11] And women continue to play extremely important roles in many of these organizations. As the United Nations Non-Governmental Liaison Service writes of women, "they frequently form the majority of community and grassroots organizations and play leading roles in movements for social change."[12]

## The Domestication of America

In Fort Greene, Brooklyn, for example, Maxine Croft and Roslyn Williams, two middle-aged, longtime residents of a rundown housing project, recently got fed up with living in what some called a no-man's-land. Gunfire was so prevalent that their neighbors were afraid to venture outdoors after 5:00 P.M. These women sought and won a grant of $10,000 to form the Fort Greene Coalition. They recruited and trained teenagers, who now carry two-way radios and patrol hallways and pathways. The youngsters also escort older residents to grocery stores on violence-prone Myrtle Avenue.[13] A small, sweet victory for civil society—and for women.

"Think global, act local." Americans have taken this aphorism to heart. In Austin, St. Louis, Santa Barbara, and many other American towns and cities, women (and men) have set up community groups to train unskilled people, start youth programs, watch the neighborhood for burglars, or prune trees. Others lobby for boardwalks or raise money for schools, ball fields, or libraries. In some areas, groups of local merchants are hiring street cleaners and private guards to improve their neighborhoods. In 1970, there were some 10,000 of these neighborhood associations; in 1997, there were more than 150,000 of them.[14] Neighborhood crime-watch groups alone have increased tenfold during the 1990s.

Today there are some one million nonprofit organizations in the United States, three times more than in 1967.[15]

One expanding national grassroots organization is Emily's List. EMILY is an acronym for Early Money Is Like Yeast. As the name suggests, Emily's List is a women's political organization that raises seed money for women to run for state or federal office. According to some, Emily's List is currently the third-largest political action association in the United States.[16] Many other women's political organizations have emerged as well, all serving to promote women's representation in the electoral process, heighten awareness of women's issues, and lobby for women's agendas.[17]

This form of advocacy and leadership is thriving—and changing American society. New York City witnessed fewer murders in 1996 than it had in four decades. Murder rates are down in Boston, Los Angeles, and San Francisco as well. This unexpected trend has elicited a wide variety of explanations. The police must be doing something right. Fewer men and women are smoking crack cocaine, a powder keg for violence. The current AIDS epidemic in prisons may be taking some of our criminals out of circulation. But some social critics point to yet another possible source for America's declining crime rate: women.

"We can thank women for getting it started," writes Nicholas Von Hoffman in *The New York Observer*. He refers to the shelters for battered women, clinics to educate men about wife abuse, programs for parents of unruly children, lobby groups on gun control, and thousands of other civil associations that women have started, have led, or in which they have played the dominant role. "It may be," Von

Hoffman concludes, "that as women assume higher place and greater influence, they have used their new power to accelerate the domestication of the United States."[18]

The domestication continues. Today some 93 million Americans volunteer over 20 billion hours of their time annually, overseeing projects that further their special goals.[19] Peter Drucker predicts that by 2010 more than 120 million Americans will volunteer at least five hours a week to some organization in the civil sector that addresses their needs.[20] He regards all these civil organizations as a major growth area, calling them collectively the third sector of society, after government and the corporate world.[21]

Drucker thinks this third sector "may well be American's most important contribution today."[22] Political theorist Francis Fukuyama of George Mason University would agree. He believes this dense network of associations operates as a kind of social glue, creating an environment that enables the market economy and government to work efficiently.[23] When this sector of society is vital and healthy, a nation will prosper.

### Women in Civil Society

Women are emerging as a powerful force in this nonprofit sector of American society. Women managers and professionals hold many more influential positions in the nonprofit sector of American society than in the for-profit business world.[24] The third sector of society apparently appeals to the female mind.

I would expect this—for several reasons.

For one, civil associations are generally composed of like-minded people who come together for a common cause. These organizations often start small. Members are volunteers, and participants work in relatively egalitarian teams or flat packs. As the association grows, members hire staff, take on a governing board, and adopt a set of supervisory principles. But with the exception of the large nonprofit organizations that have CEOs, large boards, and pyramidal staffs, civil associations tend to have less hierarchical structures and more collaborative decision-making processes.

Women enjoy making these lateral connections to others and working in these less formal, less hierarchical settings.

Moreover, women board members in nonprofit organizations do much more than just occupy the "woman's seat." Peter Drucker reports that "many nonprofits now have what is still the exception in business—a functioning board."[25] They even have something more astonishing, in Drucker's estimation: a CEO who is accountable to the board. So women on the board actually have opportunities to lead.

Civil associations also appeal to women, I believe, because women are inclined to think contextually. Women generally look at individual social problems, such as drug abuse or teen pregnancy, and link them to broader, deeper social ills. Women also have a tendency to think long term. Most civil organizations "think" this way, too. They have the same broad focus and long-term social goals.

Women have the necessary people skills to do this kind of work. Many nonprofit organizations regularly depend on volunteers. These people have no binding contractual relationship with the organization. So leaders (who may also be volunteers) must be adept at motivating, organizing, and directing others. In nonprofit organizations women can, even must, employ their exquisite social skills.

These feminine social skills are particularly useful for sizing up major donors and getting large financial contributions. As Roger Pasquier of the Environmental Defense Fund says of this feminine ability, "Women have been particularly skilled at fund-raising—especially with donors of large contributions—because of their style of strategic thinking. Successful fund-raising depends on getting inside the potential donor's mind. It requires attention to detail, sensitive listening, and empathetic responses, all skills possessed by many women."[26]

Western society has no historically based belief about which sex makes better fund-raisers. So women who seek employment in nonprofit organizations don't battle prejudice; they can move relatively easily into important fund-raising positions. With their talent for networking, they excel at finding supporters, too. And in these organizations they can work in an environment where they are less likely to have to travel constantly or relocate to another city.[27]

Perhaps most important, the primary goal of many nonprofit institutions is not to make money but to cure or alleviate some distress of society or the environment. Healing, nurturing: these are among women's callings.

Consequently, large numbers of ambitious, educated women are creating, joining, and leading civil associations of all kinds. As civil society becomes an even more prominent force in the United States and around the world, women's values and interests are increasingly influencing public opinion, public mores, and public policy.

### Women in Foundations

Women's participation in the third sector is nowhere more striking than in foundations. I discovered this when I counted the number of women in senior positions in America's major foundations.

The 1998 *Foundation Directory*, published by the Foundation Center in New York City, includes 8,649 foundations—all of those with at least $2 million in assets or $200,000 in annual giving.[28] Although these foundations represent fewer than 20 percent of all active grant-making foundations, they hold more than $247 billion in assets, 89 percent of all foundation assets. They award annual grants totaling more than $12.4 billion, some 90 percent of all foundation giving. For each entry the directory lists only the primary one or two donors, the trustees, and the top administrator.

When I sorted the individuals named in this directory by gender, I discovered that the number of women listed as donors, trustees, and/or top administrators was 12,541, or 29.12 percent of the total.[29]

A 1998 report by the Council on Foundations describes an even higher participation by women. This organization canvassed 667 major American foundations and corporate giving programs. Of 4,580 full-time staff, 75 percent were women; 92 percent of support staff were women, 68 percent of program officers were women, and 50 percent of all CEOs were women.[30]

By comparison, less than 5 percent of CEOs and board members of the Fortune 500 companies are women. Clearly women are far more likely to play leadership roles in major foundations than in the traditional corporate world.

Women in leadership positions in foundations are likely to increase in number and wield even more power in society at large. Between 1981 and 1996, foundations almost doubled in number, from 22,000 to 39,000.[31] About 1,000 new foundations spring up every year.[32] All told, they distribute almost $14 billion annually. Despite their low profile in the media, foundations clearly have become major players in many parts of American society.[33]

"A president's hardest task is not to *do* what is right, but to *know* what is right," said President Lyndon B. Johnson. Knowing what is right is often difficult for the rest of us as well. The sexes tend to dif- fer in how they believe foundation funds should be allocated. And as more women reach the top of the foundation world, the focus of funding is shifting. A staff member at the Foundation Center tells me that he has become conscious of an increasing number of grants being made to women's causes, although he says he has no statistical information to back up his statement.

Corroborating his hunch are data showing that foundations are giv- ing less to basic research and more to advocacy groups and social service programs—areas of interest to women.[34]

## Charitable Giving

"Give all thou canst; high Heaven rejects the lore / Of nicely cal- culated less or more," wrote William Wordsworth. Nothing says more about your values, fears, and hopes than how, when, where, and to whom you give your money. People have all sorts of reasons for do- nating to charities. Compassion, penance for their sins, a payback for their good fortune, to help improve some aspect of society, to express social responsibility, to get a tax break, or to show off to friends: all are motivations for giving.

Today approximately 65 percent of all American households give to at least one charity. In 1997, they gave $143 billion to charitable or- ganizations.[35] This will increase. Demographers estimate that as the baby boomers inherit property from their more frugal parents, they will set aside some $1 trillion of it for charity. As couples bear fewer children, they will have more money to give away as well. As a result, annual philanthropic giving is expected to triple by 2030.[36]

It seems likely that women will run many of the charitable institutions.

## Domesticating the World

Civil society, with its many organizations, is so pervasive in America and Europe that most of us hardly notice it. Yet different nations have very different attitudes about civil organizations, a fact that became clear to me as I read an article in *The New York Times* about gay culture in contemporary China.

The article reported on homosexual lifestyles in one of China's major cities. The Chinese government apparently permits homosexuals to congregate in sidewalk cafés and nightclubs. But the law does not allow these men and women to organize into formal groups with the purpose of lobbying the political establishment. In Communist China, the state still dictates who can formally associate with whom. In other developing nations, governments require civil associations to register themselves formally and list their members. In that way, the government can make them pay fees and also keep a close watch on their activities.

In much of the world, civil society is a groggy giant just staggering to its feet. But like blue jeans, hamburgers, and democracy itself, civil society is spreading—with the help of international nonprofit organizations often led by women.

For example, the Global Fund for Women, established in Palo Alto, California, in 1987, has given small grants to more than eight hundred women's organizations in some one hundred different countries. The women's groups are free to use the money as they see fit, so long as they work collectively and their goals focus on women's rights.

In 1998, anthropologists Barbara Pillsbury and Michele Andina of the Pacific Institute for Women's Health visited some of these women's grassroots organizations in Brazil, Uganda, Turkey, Pakistan, India, Nepal, Nicaragua, and the Philippines to evaluate their progress. A shelter for women victims of domestic violence in Kathmandu, an education center for Afghan refugee women living in Islamabad, a Ugandan women's club that provides counseling on AIDS: these and many more are thriving, Pillsbury reports. Her conclusion: "Let women's organizations just do it."[37]

Another one of these international organizations is the Women's World Bank. This global organization develops women's microbanks, or loan societies, chiefly in developing countries. In turn, these lending agencies help poor women borrow start-up funds for their own businesses. Some fifty countries now have female-focused micro-banks.[38] The World Bank, the United Nations–affiliated agency that finances large international projects, has hailed these microbanks as a magnificent innovative achievement in the war against poverty.[39]

Women's international civil associations are also creating liter-acy programs, peace initiatives, movements against the arms trade, organizations for the awareness of feminine health and reproduc-tive issues, and programs to aid those who suffer from AIDS, drug abuse, or a life of prostitution, as well as victims of violence against women.[40]

Some call this trend "inchworm economics." But Pillsbury and other leaders in the field of international development believe these women's grassroots organizations will be among the most significant economic catalysts and forces for social justice in the coming century.

### Women's International Leadership

"The strongest pressure in the world can be friendly pressure," wrote Lester Pearson, former prime minister of Canada. Women know it. As they use their innate talents to unite behind common causes, they are becoming a political force.

In 1997, women of Serbian, Bosnian, and Croatian background lay down together in a square in Belgrade every Wednesday for several months to call for peace; they called themselves Women in Black. In the Middle East, Palestinian and Israeli women have joined to rebuild safe areas for children. The Green Belt movement in Kenya has led more than fifty thousand women to plant trees in their yards to com-bat desertification; some of the country's most threatened areas are actually becoming wooded.[41] In Ukraine, women are meeting to fight nuclear pollution.[42] Muslim women of several countries have produced a manual, "Claiming Our Rights: A Manual for Women's Human Rights Education in Muslim Societies."[43]

As Kofi Annan, secretary-general of the United Nations, puts it, "people move governments."[44] An outstanding example is Jody Williams. This American from Vermont jointly won the Nobel Peace Prize in 1997 for leading what became a worldwide campaign to ban the production and use of land mines. In 1997, partially as a result of these efforts, more than 120 governments signed a treaty that severely curtails the use of these indiscriminate killers. "Together," Williams said, "we are a superpower."[45]

Women appeared to have unnerved the Chinese authorities in September 1995, when they descended on Beijing to attend the United Nations–sponsored Fourth World Conference on Women. Chinese authorities decided to house many of the conferees in a community a considerable distance from the central conference, and they rigidly controlled traffic between conference centers and the other forums where participants congregated.

In spite of this, more than thirty thousand women assembled. They came from Canada, Ecuador, India, Kenya, Mongolia, Papua New Guinea, and almost everywhere in between. Village weavers stood by Nobel laureates. Saris mingled with dreadlocks and high heels. Babies perched next to laptop computers. On the agenda: relief from poverty and violence, economic development for women, equal education and training for women, comprehensive health care for women, equality in the workplace, and a fair share of authority for women in the family, the state, and the international community. As the conferees summed it up, "Women's rights are human rights."

Women had also met to discuss a wide range of women's issues in Mexico City in 1975, in Copenhagen in 1980, and in Nairobi in 1985. Women played major roles in several other U.N. meetings as well, including conferences on the environment in Rio in 1992, on human rights in Vienna in 1993, and on population and development in Cairo in 1994. In every one of these assemblies, women were the driving force; in fact, they shaped the policy discussions.[46]

These conferences have made an impact. When an international group of women met in 1998 to take stock of the progress on women's rights since the Beijing conference, even the skeptics had to agree that many gains had been made. Over 50 percent of 187 nations had taken significant steps, mapping out plans to improve women's rights, creating national offices for women's affairs, and creating avenues that enabled women to propose national legislation.[47]

The participants attributed this progress to the "increasingly strong local and international women's organizations."[48]

## Women as Grave Diggers of Dynasties

Arabs call women the "grave diggers of dynasties," presumably because women can undermine established political orders with their facility for meeting, talking, and planning outside officially approved channels.[49] This feminine "grave digging" is certain to increase—because nongovernmental organizations are springing up around the world.

Today Civicus, a world alliance of civil associations, boasts of having 380 members from over sixty countries. The alliance has tripled its membership since 1994.[50] In fact, Civicus is among a new class of civil associations, the so-called supranational civil organizations. Today the United Nations has accredited over fifteen hundred of these international associations.

Some are exceedingly powerful. Friends of the Earth, for example, pressured, cajoled, and shamed many nations into attending the Rio Earth Summit in 1992.[51] Human rights groups have successfully pushed governments into supporting the creation of the International Criminal Court. And a few relief and development organizations are beginning to distribute billions of dollars annually.[52]

"The steady concentration of power in the hands of states, which began in 1648 with the Peace of Westphalia, is over, at least for a while." So thinks Jessica T. Mathews of the Carnegie Endowment for International Peace.[53] Many agree. The rise of nongovernmental organizations has been called "a jaw-dropping transformation in the world's political structure."[54] As states lose some of their sovereignty and NGOs continue to flourish, women will assume influential roles in these prominent international forums.

Women's leadership in civil society will continue to expand, for two reasons. First, women are becoming better and better educated. As trend analysts Pamela McCorduck and Nancy Ramsey write, "Educated women now exist all over the world, in such growing numbers that they amount to a new critical mass, capable of making radical change."[55] Second, women are long-lived. By 2015, 20 percent of the world's population will be over sixty-five—and women in this politically and socially potent age group will outnumber men two to one.[56]

"When spiderwebs unite, they can tie up a lion." Women believe this Ethiopian proverb. With their natural people skills and their primordial drive to network, they will subdue more than lions as the twenty-first century proceeds.

The future of women as leaders in government looks somewhat different. Women are not drawn to this form of power, perhaps in part because they are less comfortable than men in rigid, hierarchical formal settings.

## Women in Formal Government

"The job of a citizen is to keep his mouth open," wrote Günter Grass. When it comes to politics and working one's way up the formal hierarchy of local, state, and national governments around the world, men have been far more vociferous and energetic than women.

Men's predominance in formal governance is seen in every industrialized society. In 1997, women held only 9 percent of the seats in the United States Senate and 12.6 percent of the seats in the House of Representatives.[57] Women have never occupied even 10 percent of the fifty state governors' mansions.[58] As of 1994, among the member states of the European Union, only 13.6 percent of the members of national parliaments were women. In France, Italy, and Ireland in 1998, women held 12 percent or fewer seats in the lower houses of national government.[59]

Women's political representation is highest in the Scandinavian countries, Germany, and the Netherlands, in all of which women hold more than 25 percent of seats in the lower houses.[60] But even in Norway and Sweden, men dominate the policy-making ministerial positions in foreign affairs, finance, and justice. Women hold less powerful and less prestigious ministerial posts in health, education, and labor.[61]

In Russia and Eastern European countries, women actually lost seats in parliament with the introduction of democratic government. Under Communist rule, women in these countries held between 20 percent and 35 percent of seats in lower houses. "Socialist systems gave priorities to workers and to women," reports Pierre Cornillon of the Inter-Parliamentary Union, based in Geneva.[62] After the collapse of Communist rule, over half of the seats women held were won by men.[63]

Asian national governments are also male-dominated. In Japan in 1995, only 2.3 percent of all members of the Diet, the lower house of parliament and key legislative body, were women.[64] In fact, women held less than 15 percent of seats in lower houses or single-house legislatures in almost all countries in Latin America, Africa, the Middle East, and Asia. Among the few exceptions were the Seychelles, Cuba, South Africa, and China, in each of which more than 20 percent of seats were held by women.[65]

Even fewer women hold cabinet-level positions. As of 1995, women held an average of 6 percent of these posts in societies around the world—5 percent in developing countries, 8 percent in industrial societies.[66] Only in the Scandinavian countries, the Netherlands, and the Seychelles did women hold more than 30 percent of cabinet positions.[67]

It is even rarer for women to become heads of state or heads of government. In a 1995 survey of members of the United Nations by the United Nations Development Programme, women held the position of president only in Iceland, Ireland, Nicaragua, and Sri Lanka.[68] At the same time, women held the position of prime minister in Bangladesh, Norway, Pakistan, Sri Lanka, Turkey, and the tiny island republic of Dominica.[69] All told, only twenty-two women have become head of state or head of government in the twentieth century. Even in the few cases where women have become heads of state or government, men held the vast majority of high positions surrounding them.

Women's lack of participation in national government cannot be explained by a country's stage of development, its level of income, or the educational level of its women. The average representation of women in parliament is 10 percent in the developing world and 12 percent in advanced industrial countries.[70]

Women's lack of participation in national government cannot be explained by voting behavior, either. American political pundits often speculate that voters cannot envision women in high executive offices. This is not true. Richard Seltzer, political scientist at Howard University, led a study on 61,603 candidates who ran for state legislatures, the U.S. House of Representatives, the Senate, or the office of state governor between 1972 and 1994. He and his colleagues established that women win just as often as men do—when they run.[71] In a similar study, they established that women are only slightly more likely to vote for women candidates than men are.

In many cultures, more women begin to move into local and state politics in middle age.[72] Some societies, such as India, have begun to establish gender quotas in their representative bodies.[73] But far fewer women than men start in their twenties or thirties to work their way into positions in the highest ranks of government—anywhere in the world.

When the United Nations Development Programme used an ingenious mixture of factors to measure women's status compared to that of men in more than one hundred countries, it found that women worldwide are gradually closing the gender gap in health, education, and economic power. "But," it concluded, "politics remains an obstacle course for women."[74]

## Matriarchy Is a Myth

Female leaders have been even less evident in traditional tribal cultures, past or present. When sociologist Martin King Whyte surveyed ninety-three hunting-gathering, gardening, herding, and agrarian societies, he found that men held the vast majority of positions of formal authority in all of these cultures.[75] In eighty-two of these societies, all local, intermediate, and top political leaders were men. Even in cultures where women were economically and socially powerful, such as the Navajo of the American Southwest or traditional farming societies of West Africa, men were much more likely to attain formal positions of political rank.

Some academics point to female figures on ancient pots and other feminine motifs in archaeological records as evidence that women once ruled in some places.[76] But there is no solid evidence of such matriarchies—and a great deal of evidence to the contrary. In currently existing cultures where female gods prevail, where female figures decorate the water jugs, and where female warriors are present in art, myths, and songs, men still predominate at the top rungs of tribal rule.

There is no evidence that women have held the bulk of governmental offices or ruling positions in any society anywhere on earth.[77] Matriarchy—defined by anthropologists as women as a class holding rule over men as a class—is a myth.

## If Women Ran the World

Despite women's meager participation in the highest echelons of government in any culture on earth, most men and women believe that women's participation would improve their governance.

The 1996 Gallup poll of twenty-two societies confirmed this. The pollsters asked the question, "Would your country be better run if more women held political office or would things just get worse?" In twenty-one of these societies, including China, Germany, India, Japan, and the United States, more women—and more men—thought things would improve than believed things would degenerate.[78] Only in El Salvador were people evenly divided on this question. In the 1991 General Social Survey conducted by the National Opinion Research Center (NORC) at the University of Chicago, 90 percent of Americans reported that they would vote for a woman for president if she were qualified.[79]

As more women acquire an education, it seems almost certain that at least some more women will enter the ranks of local, state, and national governments.

These women will probably make a difference in how governments conduct their business. Former congresswoman Patricia Schroeder of Colorado is an example. As an influential member of the U.S. House of Representatives, she was a prime mover behind legislation to increase women's opportunities in the military. This was not just talk about women's rights. Her work helped many women—and improved the military services.

Women in governmental roles are drawn to public policies that foster community health, public education, children, day care, families, and the elderly.[80] For example, women currently hold 40 percent of the seats in the state of Washington's legislature. They are raising debate on issues such as maternity leave, domestic violence, and divorce law, topics that had received little attention in the past.[81] Women in the Virginia state legislature have ushered in a bill on domestic violence. In Connecticut, thanks to female lawmakers, a new mother can remain in the hospital for forty-eight hours after delivering a child.

Whether women in power would also have a different slant on foreign policy remains to be seen. After being chosen as the first woman secretary of state, Madeleine Albright gained a reputation as a tough-talking defender of U.S. national interests. But her influence as a policy maker has been regarded as minimal.

Some say that governments will need a critical mass of women at the top—they estimate about 35 percent—before women's values begin to make an impact on national policies and priorities.[82] The exact nature of such an impact is hard to predict. Certainly such leaders as Indira Gandhi and Margaret Thatcher illustrate that women can be as decisive and tough-minded as men. However, most women in power will probably be less likely than men to resort to military action to settle disputes. They may be more inclined to agree with Winston Churchill. In a conciliatory mood he once said, "To jaw-jaw is always better than to war-war."

Indeed, more women are entering politics. In America the number of women mayors tripled between 1975 and 1982.[83] In 1996, women held about 21 percent of all seats in America's state legislative bodies.[84] In thirteen of the seventy-eight countries for which the United Nations Development Programme collected data, somewhat more than 25 percent of municipal representatives were women.

But women enter politics for different reasons than men. Surveys of the past twenty-five years indicate that women run for office because they want to improve society. Men are more likely to start a political career to make business connections or to climb the political ladder to the top.[85] As Harriet Woods, former president of the National Women's Political Caucus, says, "Most women begin with community concerns, not ambition."[86]

Given these widely different approaches to political power, women will probably not reach parity with men in the highest ranks of national government in the United States or anywhere else in the world. These formal, ranked, pyramidal avenues to leadership generally appeal more to men. But through their influence in civil organizations, women will sway governments to see the world their way.

## Women, Men, and War

Another sector of national and international leadership where women are unlikely to become preeminent is the military.

In recent years, the American military services have insisted that their ranks are now hospitable to women. Millions of women have indeed joined up and improved their standard of living. Some have graduated from West Point. A handful have even become generals. But the military is a rigidly hierarchically structured arm of the state—not an environment that normally attracts many women, especially educated women.

Moreover, the military's ultimate raison d'être is fighting. Although some women will be drawn to battle, and some will be outstanding warriors, men are built to fight—physically and emotionally. In the 1996 Gallup survey of twenty-two societies, people in twenty-one of them thought men were more physically aggressive.[87] Only in Iceland did both men and women slightly favor the notion that women are more combative.

Aggression is not always emotional, of course; sometimes it is coldly calculating. Even when aggression is emotion-driven, the feelings behind it may vary. Patriotism can impel an individual to annihilate the enemy. Envy can drive a person to launch a tirade at a colleague. Joy can prompt some to riot at a ball game. Ideology, religious beliefs, or ethnic hatred can induce some to join in sectarian violence, "ethnic cleansing," or pogroms. Some fight just for honor. As Napoléon said, "a man will die for a piece of ribbon." Nevertheless, emotion-driven, physical aggressiveness is the bastion of men.

Boys start early. Little boys everywhere do much more rough-and-tumble play than girls.[88] Teenage boys play far more contact sports. Men form aggressive gangs—everywhere in the world.[89] And men commit 87 percent of the violent crimes in America—a percentage that is probably matched in many other countries.[90]

Men's inclination toward physical aggression is not due just to overcrowding, poverty, and the other stresses of modern urban life. Men were more savage than women in the Dark Ages of France, in medieval Spain and Italy, in Chaucer's England, and in Abe Lincoln's America.[91] Evolutionary psychologists Martin Daly and Margo Wilson of McMaster University in Canada report that until recent years even the !Kung bushmen of the Kalahari Desert "had a homicide rate approximately equivalent to that of the most violent urban American ghettos."[92]

Today men continue to be more violent than women in places as culturally different as Botswana, Brazil, Canada, India, Kenya,

Mexico, Scotland, and the Democratic Republic of the Congo (formerly Zaire).[93]

Nowhere in the world are women as physically aggressive as men. Women can be catty, demeaning, and vituperative to your face and slanderous behind your back. But few women attack physically—except in the home. Women in the United States, Canada, Great Britain, and New Zealand commit the same number of physical acts of aggression against sexual partners as men do.[94] In fact, women are slighly more likely to slap, kick, bite, choke, or throw something at a partner.

But women move from verbal attack to physical assault much more slowly than men do, and they do not visibly maim or seriously injure as often.[95] And very few women attack or kill people they do not know. About 12 percent to 14 percent of Americans on trial for murder at a given time are women. Most are accused of killing husbands, lovers, rivals, or their own children.[96] The incidence of male violence exceeds that of females by a rate of nine to one.[97]

Some scientists have argued that women and females of other primate species are just as aggressive as males, that they just express their aggressiveness differently.

It is true that female primates squabble chronically about food and space. They can become nasty during a power shift in the community, too, threatening, chasing, hitting, and biting. Females gang up on others. They attack without warning more often than males. Their attacks often last longer, so their bites and kicks add up. And females can be exceedingly belligerent and unpredictable when they protect their young.[98]

Still, the males of most primate species are more physically vicious than females are. Their battles are more intense and they injure others more often.[99]

## Man the Protector

"It is unfair to blame man too fiercely for being pugnacious; he learned the habit from nature," wrote the American essayist Christopher Morley. The comment is apt: it is easy to see how male militancy arose during human evolution. Ancestral men were obliged to fight among themselves to win women, then fight others to protect the mates they had won. Our male forebears also had to protect the community at large, as males of most primate species still do.[100]

One could even say that women are partially responsible for men's pugnacious nature. Across the eons of our deep history, females chose aggressive males and bore their young, selecting for warlike men.

A stunning example today are the Yanomamo Indians of the Amazonian rain forest. *Waiteri,* the men call themselves, "fierce." Yanomamo men fight among themselves with clubs and axes, usually over women. Their fierceness pays. Yanomamo men who win glory in battle attract more wives and clandestine lovers. As a result, the victors sire three times as many children.[101]

"The last thing a woman will consent to discover in a man whom she loves, or on whom she simply depends, is want of courage," wrote Joseph Conrad. For millions of years, women chose men who could protect and provide for them. Thus, by the tireless processes of natural selection, men evolved their chivalrous yet pugnacious spirit.

### Chemistry of Combat

Nature built a remarkable fighting machine.

In 1995, neuroscientist Ruben Gur and his colleagues placed thirty-seven men and twenty-four women in a brain scanner and asked them to lie quietly, relax, and try to exert no mental effort. Admittedly, it is hard to think of nothing. Nevertheless, brain scans of these "idling" minds revealed a distinct difference between the sexes. The men registered more metabolic activity in primitive, action-oriented emotion centers in the brain. Women registered more metabolic activity in an evolutionarily newer brain region for processing the emotions, the cingulate gyrus, a region that plays a role in symbolic actions. The Gurs propose that this might explain why women tend to express their frustration symbolically, with words, while men are more likely to become physically aggressive.[102]

Men have another natural weapon for combat: testosterone. For centuries farmers have castrated roosters, bulls, and stallions to curtail their aggressiveness. When male bodybuilders and other athletes inject testosterone, they experience " 'roid rage."[103] And approximately half of America's violent crimes are committed by men under age twenty-four—the age when levels of testosterone peak.[104]

The relationship between testosterone and aggressiveness is complex. Having too little testosterone can also cause some people to become violent. Several other chemicals in the brain are involved in male pugnacity.[105] In addition, childhood experiences, level of education, career, religious life, and a host of other environmental factors serve to stimulate, deter, or deflect bellicosity.[106] But the basic ingredient in the chemical and social chowder of aggression is testosterone. Men have at least seven times more of this male hormone than women do.[107]

Today women make up 15 percent of the armed services in the United States. These military women are not, by any means, historically unique. During World War II, the Soviet Union enlisted women to become machine gunners, infantry soldiers, and communications experts; some 8 percent of Soviet soldiers were women. Many Israeli women fought in the 1948 War of Independence. Women have joined independence and liberation movements in countries around the world for centuries.[108]

But a survey of sixty-seven societies—ranging from traditional cultures to industrial democracies—found that fifty-eight excluded women from war entirely. In the remaining nine, women played much smaller, supporting roles.[109] And most of them went home or back to business when peace was achieved.

Males have been society's warriors since long before our ancestors descended from the trees. I think most of the world's soldiers and just about every one of its top military leaders will continue to be men—even as the military changes.

## The New Army

New technology is changing many aspects of warfare. Combat that relies heavily on digital communications, satellite-guided missiles, radar-evading stealth aircraft, computer processing of reams of data, and maneuvers in outer space could require fewer foot soldiers, fewer vehicles, and far less hand-to-hand combat. Even driving tanks and shooting guns could become passé as sophisticated military machines are deployed against the enemy's central computer systems, financial centers, and air-traffic control devices. Computers might even give the orders: "Select enemy; insert weapon; delete."[110]

These innovations could render men's physical strength and propensity for physical aggressiveness less important in many types of military operations—and open the way to female participation in some forms of battle.

I find it difficult to believe that hand-to-hand combat will become totally obsolete anytime soon, however. Conflicts in the forseeable future are likely to be small-scale civil wars, ethnic strife in troubled countries, and the occasional larger-scale, United Nations–sanctioned, punitive operation against an aggressor, such as the war against Iraq in 1991. When outside forces get involved as peacekeepers or even truce supervisors, many will have to be combat-trained ground troops ready to kill or be killed. This is the primordial work of men.

Nevertheless, the American armed forces are currently examining the pros and cons of replacing some of their inflexible, centralized structures with flatter organizational components, eliminating some of their middle echelons, and creating more units of less hierarchic teams.[111] These changes in organizational structure, if made, could draw more women into the military.

Can the military restructure itself? Political theorists Francis Fukuyama and Abram Shulsky argue that flatter, less hierarchic military structures were common in history.[112] Because military organizations suffered from inadequate information in past centuries, leaders were obliged to give each warring unit a degree of independence. These analysts say that the vast managerial hierarchic military organizations of today emerged in Western societies during the nineteenth century, in the same era that the hierarchic factory system came of age.

Fukuyama and Shulsky believe that modern military institutions will gradually adopt some degree of decentralization, a flatter organizational structure, and more units of less hierarchical teams. These changes would attract women.

But a centralized chain of military command is still vital to many contemporary military operations, especially when dealing with large industrial nations. And aggressive ground fighting is far from outmoded. Careers for women in the military may expand to some extent. But I think the military sector in all societies will remain a stronghold of men.

## Will Women Ever Reach Job Parity with Men?

"Job parity" can mean many things; the phrase is a tricky one. If one is talking about income parity, it is almost certain that in many cultures women will eventually achieve equal pay for equal work in many sectors of the economy, even equal pay for "comparable" work. But I do not think that women and men will choose to do the same kinds of work.

In every single traditional society, men do more of the hard manual labor and the physically dangerous work, and much of the protecting and governing of the community.[113] Women spend more time nurturing and educating the young, as well as caring for the sick and elderly. The division of labor by sex has been a hallmark of humanity.[114] And it is still with us.[115]

Today over 95 percent of child care workers and kindergarten teachers in America are women. The vast majority of nurses, secretaries, dieticians, dressmakers, bookkeepers, bank tellers, housekeepers, physical therapists, and information clerks are also women.[116]

Surveys done by the United Nations confirm that women gravitate to child care, nursing, teaching, sales, clerical work, and personal services in many other industrial societies as well.[117]

Men still do the manual labor. Over 95 percent of American garbage collectors, loading-machine operators, oil well drillers, roofers, plasterers, and bricklayers are men.[118] Men gravitate to fields requiring superior spatial and technical skills as well. Ninety-six percent of mechanics are men, as are 97 percent of carpenters, construction workers, and truck drivers. Men are also America's electricians, draftsmen, surveyors, airplane pilots, and navigators. Eighty percent of architects are men. Over 90 percent of almost all types of engineers are men. Men are still the protectors, too. Ninety-seven percent of firefighters and almost 90 percent of police officers are men.[119]

Men gravitate to the heavy manual and technical jobs in European countries and other industrial nations as well.[120]

In America, this sexual division of labor is breaking down to some extent. Some men have entered nursing and library work. Some women are becoming engineers, architects, priests, CEOs of major corporations, and athletic superstars. At present, sales workers, animal caretakers, door-to-door vendors, bartenders, public relations specialists, editors, reporters, economists, real estate agents, accountants, and biological technicians are about equally male and female.

Yet within many of these occupations, the sexes still follow different paths. More women sell cosmetics, for example, while more men sell technical equipment. The majority of fashion journalists are women, while most business journalists are men. In the nonprofit sector, men gravitate to jobs in organizations that deal with international trade, development, and economics, while women join organizations that focus on social services and education. Today very few occupations are completely sex neutral.[121]

Various factors contribute to this sexual channeling in the workforce. How managers and employers recruit; whom they hire; to whom they assign tasks; where they situate employees in the office; whom they choose to train for what positions; whom they promote: all of these decisions can bolster traditional gender roles. But most job-seeking men and women readily accept, even seek, the traditional career paths.[122]

In part, their choices are due to their gendered brains.

### Brain Organization and Job Preference

To investigate the correlation between brain structure and occupation, psychologist Ernest Govier and his colleagues constructed an ingenious test, the "dichotic listening test."[123] The subject is seated wearing a pair of stereophonic headphones while different nonsense syllables, such as *dak* and *gak,* are pumped into each ear simultaneously. The subject is asked to listen to both signals and report on what he or she hears.

Here's the key to the experiment: People generally hear more accurately with the right ear because it is directly connected to the left hemisphere of the brain—where most language processing occurs. Sounds picked up by the left ear travel first to the right hemisphere, then circuitously reroute themselves to language regions in the left hemisphere, causing hearing errors. Hence humans tend to have a "right ear advantage," or REA.

But this right ear advantage is reduced in women because their language processing centers are spread more evenly across both brain hemispheres. Therefore the test can distinguish those whose brain is organized more like a man's from those whose brain is built more like a woman's.

The researchers discovered that most of the men and women in male-typical jobs, such as carpentry, bricklaying, and taxi driving, had a "male-organized" brain. But men and women in female-typical jobs, such as nursing, tended to have a "female-organized" brain.[124] These and several other tests have buttressed the theory that one's choice of occupation is often coordinated with the degree of feminization or masculinization of one's brain.[125]

Hormone levels also seem to be correlated with choice of occupation. Men with very high levels of testosterone are more likely to end up with blue-collar jobs, while men with testosterone levels in the middle range obtain more years of formal education and enter the white-collar and computer-literate gold-collar professions.[126] Women who have received high levels of prenatal testosterone are less likely to marry, and they have fewer children, regard career as more important, enter more male-dominated occupations, and achieve higher-status jobs.[127]

Nowhere is the correlation between gender and occupation more evident than in the fields of science and engineering. In a study of men and women in forty-five countries, men regularly excelled at performing spatial tasks and scored higher on tests of science and engineering.[128] It is no coincidence that men also dominate jobs in the physical and computer sciences, mathematics, and engineering in cultures around the world.[129]

### The Two-Tiered Economy

Because most women are more interested than men in nurturing children and building personal connections rather than in attaining rank, they often end up in professions and positions that pay less. They also do more part-time work. This situation creates what economists call a two-tiered economy. Vivid examples are medicine and the law.

America has already begun to see more male doctors at the top of the medical profession, pursuing the high-tech, high-paying sub-specialties or occupying lucrative hospital administration jobs. The lower financial tier is becoming populated by many more female physicians who do the hands-on care, and who work fewer hours in order to rear their children.[130] Something like this has already occurred in Russia and Western Europe.

The same two-tiered structure is forming in the legal profession. Most lawyers start their careers with equal pay. But as the years go by, men make much more money.[131] In part, this happens because women lawyers tend to leave the lucrative law firms after a few years to seek more cooperative work environments and more flexible schedules—again, to rear children.[132] Male lawyers, on the other hand, often work seven days a week, sacrificing or slighting their home lives to get ahead.

This tendency toward a two-tiered economy is apparent in Denmark, Sweden, England, Russia, and the former East Germany as well.[133] In these societies the sexes regularly enjoy equal educational and economic opportunities, but women gravitate to the "helping professions" while men dominate the more lucrative technical fields and high-ranking executive positions.[134] Not coincidentally, women are paid less just about everywhere in the world.[135]

Although this two-tiered economy is likely to remain, it is not accurate to say that it is always stacked in favor of men. Women end up in the lower-paying jobs. But men land the risky jobs, as well as those with the worst work environments and most physical demands, such as deep-sea fishing, construction work, and policing.[136] Some 90 percent of those who die on the job are men.[137]

## Whisperings Within

"Nature is usually wrong," said James McNeill Whistler. The great American painter saw an imperfect world.

Right or wrong, nature is reality—and human nature still influences occupation. Despite governmental and corporate policy changes designed to give both sexes a fair shot at just about any career they want, the vast majority of men and women everywhere in the world end up—even choose to end up—in the same kinds of careers that their male and female forebears pursued. Ancestral appetites still whisper from within.

But the world is changing in ways that favor women's kinds of work. The U.S. Bureau of Labor Statistics forecasts that the fastest job growth is currently in business services, child care, health services, computer and data processing, residential care, and retail sales.[138] Women dominate these fields.[139] Women are also making great strides in medicine, in law, in educational institutions, in the communications industries, and in the service occupations. Some are even reaching the highest echelons of traditional corporations, government, and the military.

Peter Drucker and many other business theorists regard information and knowledge as the major currencies of tomorrow. Women, it seems to me, are well equipped to acquire this kind of coinage and convert it into power.

In fact, many have begun to lead. This is particularly evident in civil society. In this swiftly expanding world of nonprofit institutions, women have found local, national, and international forums for expressing their views on important issues. And women's influence will only grow. As Hungary's president, Árpád Göncz, puts it, "civic initiative is slowly becoming a world power."[140]

"A leader is a dealer in hope," Napoléon Bonaparte once said. With their people skills, their compassion, their penchant for web thinking, and their networking abilities, female leaders in civil society will bring hope to children, minorities, the disadvantaged, the sick, the elderly, and other women. And they will focus their attention on far-reaching societal and environmental ills—concerns of the female mind.

# CHAPTER 7

# TOMORROW BELONGS TO WOMEN

## How Women Are Changing the Business World

Heart, have no pity on this house of bone:
Shake it with dancing, break it down with joy.
No man holds mortgage on it; it is your own.
To give, to sell at auction, to destroy.

EDNA ST. VINCENT MILLAY

One touch of nature makes the whole world kin": Shakespeare appreciated the deep similarities we share as human beings. Yet nature has roughly modeled two kinds of people, women and men, each with somewhat different faculties, proclivities, and skills.

Women tend to have a way with words: an ability to "read" people from their posture, gestures, facial expressions, and tone of voice; a finely tuned intuitive sense; a keen imagination; patience; an ability to express emotions, particularly empathy; a drive to nurture children, kin, and community; a talent for making egalitarian connections with others; an appetite for networking; a win-win attitude during negotiations; mental flexibility; and a broad, contextual, long-term approach to problems and decisions—all sculpted into feminine physiology as women did their work and chose their lovers millennia ago.

Men have many natural talents, too. But the world is changing in ways that will favor women's innate faculties.

Today television and radio programs are broadcast to millions around the world; the airwaves need people with linguistic skills—an acknowledged forte of women. As more and more people learn to read and write, they are buying more newspapers, books, and magazines; women are filling the expanding ranks of editors, authors, journalists, and technical writers. As vacationers see the world and companies open offices on foreign shores, women are in demand as translators, interpreters, travel agents, and "culture brokers."

Traditional corporations are decentralizing, dismantling some of their rigid hierarchic office structures, and building staff networks based on teams of equals. Women will be especially skilled at constructing and maintaining these office networks. Hyborgs, or hybrid organizations, are emerging, offering flexible work arrangements. Women will gravitate to these companies to balance work and family. The marketplace is also employing more freelance workers. Women launch more of these small businesses, and their ventures are more likely to succeed. In the age of the entrepreneur, many of these savvy, independent women will prosper.

Health care is changing. Many people now want to supplement high-tech Western treatments with more personal hands-on care, as well as preventive medicine and alternative cures—areas of healing often dominated by women. As the world population ages, people everywhere will need more health services of all kinds. Women are adept at caring for the elderly.

Women's verbal and social skills, as well as their empathy and broad social views, are winning them a powerful presence in the burgeoning legal profession. In our highly litigious world, arbitration and mediation are becoming popular alternatives to expensive legal actions. With their win-win attitudes and "people-reading" talents, women are increasingly filling this evolving career niche as well.

Primary and secondary school education has been and will continue to be a stronghold of women. But as women close the education gap, more are also moving into jobs in colleges and universities. And as more and more people need an education to get or keep good jobs, and more take courses simply for pleasure, educational facilities for adults are proliferating. Many will seek those who can impart information clearly and imaginatively—mostly women.

The state, the time-honored realm of men, is gradually being supplemented with a new form of leadership: all of the nonprofit, nongovernmental organizations that constitute civil society. Most of these organizations "think" like women. They take a long-term, contextual view toward solving complex societal ills and often conduct business with fewer trappings of rank or hierarchy. These nonprofit associations need women's people skills, their ability to network, their holistic perspective on life, and their nurturing attitude toward people, society, and the environment.

As more and more women enter the workforce and advance to positions of power, they create business opportunities for even more women. Women already outnumber men in the service occupations, jobs that regularly accommodate working women. And as women's participation in almost every sector of the labor market is rising, men's share in the overall labor force is declining—almost everywhere in the world.[1]

This is not a cause for celebration. It simply shows that at this point in human history the world workforce needs the talents and temperament of women—as well as those of men.

### Demographic and Biological Forces Converge

Two curiously related phenomena are certain to escalate women's progress toward economic equality with men.

After World War II the industrial world became a cradle. Hail the international baby boom. These boomers are reaching middle age. What is equally important, many anthropologists have established that women in widely different cultures around the world become more and more assertive in middle age.

As this tidal wave of educated, experienced, middle-aged baby boomer women rises to powerful positions in corporations, in the communications industries, in education, in the service professions, in law, medicine, and civil society, as a few even make their way into the highest ranks of government and the military, they will accelerate the historical trend toward economic and social equality between the sexes.

Simone de Beauvoir's prediction is coming true. She believed that ancestral women and men shared a rough equality, that this economic and social parity dissolved as the agricultural revolution took hold some ten thousand years ago, and that the day might come when economic forces would enable women to cast off their status as the "second sex." This is happening: women in today's industrial societies

are reclaiming the economic power and social influence that ancestral women enjoyed a million years ago. In some important sectors of
the economy, women are becoming the first sex.

In this chapter, I describe women's journey over the past million
years, from their lifeways on the plains of ancient Africa to their economic decline with the emergence of farm-based living to their recla-
mation of equality with men in our contemporary world. I discuss
attitudes toward menopause in other cultures and explain why the
wave of postmenopausal baby boomers will hasten the reemergence
of powerful women. I show how women vote and suggest that as the
global population ages, women's voting habits will begin to have a significant impact on issues, elections, and governmental policies. Last,
I speculate about the changes women will make in the coming business world.

## Women's Ancestral Equality with Men

"O wad some Pow'r the giftie gie us / To see oursels as ithers see us!"
Poet Robert Burns had watched a louse creeping along the bonnet of
a proud, finely dressed woman sitting in the church pew in front of
him. As the bug made its way to the top of the unsuspecting woman's
hat, Burns pondered the gift of self-knowledge.

How hard it is to shed our cherished perceptions of ourselves and
of others. This seems particularly difficult when scientists and laymen ponder the issue of women, men, and power. "It's a man's world."
Many Americans have believed this since the Pilgrims landed at
Plymouth Rock. Yet it is not true. Women were economically and socially powerful in many societies before the Europeans began to
spread across the world—disseminating their belief that women were
naturally inferior to men.

I discovered this firsthand when I was twenty-two. While I was fin-
ishing college, anthropologist Stan Freed, a curator at the American
Museum of Natural History in New York City, offered me a job doing
research among the Navajo Indians of the American Southwest. After
completing school, I flew to Denver, bought a beat-up Chevy for three
hundred dollars, and drove south to Pine Springs Trading Post near
Window Rock, Arizona. I had never seen a Native American or been
west of Philadelphia.

Within a week of living with a Navajo family, however, I began to see who provided dinner: my Navajo "mother." Mabel Meyers owned the sheep and cattle, the one-room log cabin with its potbellied stove, Formica table, and two big brass beds, and a tiny prefab summer home nestled farther away in the vast desert of sage and pine. Mabel collected wildflowers to make dyes, carded wool from her own sheep, and wove miniature Navajo blankets that she sold in Gallup, New Mexico. Mabel was also a single mother of five. But in the many months I lived with her and her family, I recall no moment when anyone in the community looked down on her as a single parent or the sole family wage earner.

The Navajo are among the roughly 15 percent of human societies that are matrilineal; they trace their descent through the female line. Navajo women customarily inherit the bulk of the family property and give their clan name to their children. These women also diagnose diseases that require communion with the gods, as well as prescribe the appropriate spiritual rituals for recovery.[2] The most powerful deity is a female, Changing Woman. Navajo men run the local council meetings and represent the Navajo nation to the American government. But Navajo women have substantial possessions and spiritual knowledge that they can give away or sell. For centuries they have enjoyed enormous economic and social power.

"Giving is the highest expression of potency," wrote Erich Fromm. So it is around the world. Where women own the land, the livestock, or the fishing rights, where women provide a special service like making beer, curing fevers, or intervening with the supernatural world, they use these resources and talents to build friendships, trade information, make alliances, and seal ties that give them power and prestige.[3] Women in many traditional cultures enjoyed economic and social influence—before the coming of the Europeans.

## Guns, God, and the Subordination of Women

"The penetration of Western Colonialism, and with it Western practices and attitudes regarding women, has so widely influenced women's roles in aboriginal societies as to depress women's status almost everywhere in the world." Anthropologist Naomi Quinn thus summed up a view accepted by many anthropologists.[4]

Before Columbus landed in the Caribbean, before French missionaries paddled into the Great Lakes of North America, before Captain Cook landed in Tahiti, before Europeans thrust into Africa, Australia, Amazonia, and the Arctic—bringing their god, their guns, and their beliefs about the sexes—women in many aboriginal societies possessed valuable goods and information they could trade, barter, or give away.

Hopi, Blackfoot, Iroquois, and Algonqian Indian women of North America were economically powerful. Pygmy women of the Congo were influential, as were Balinese women, Semang women of the Malay Peninsula, women in Polynesia, women in the Trobriand Islands, and women in parts of the Andes, Africa, and the Caribbean. Women in many traditional hunting-and-gathering and "gardening" societies had substantial economic and social status.[5]

A good example are the Tlingit Indians of southeastern Alaska. Anthropologist Laura Klein of Pacific Lutheran University, an expert on women and power in aboriginal societies, has lived among these peoples off and on for several years. She quotes a trader operating among them in the 1880s who wrote, "No bargain is made, no expedition set on foot, without first consulting the women."[6]

"A gift, though small, is precious." Women must have known this a million years before Homer sang these words. From studying the lifeways of contemporary foraging peoples, anthropologists have come to believe that ancestral women regularly left their older children in "day care" with relatives, "commuted" to work to gather fruits and vegetables, and regularly provided as much as 80 percent of dinner.[7] Nuts, melons, wild onions, sour plums, a hare or tortoise, birds' eggs, crabs, or a lump of priceless honeycomb: women returned to camp with staples, luxuries, and information about the whereabouts of fresh water, gazelles, or wildebeests.

Across deep history, the "two-income family" was the rule. And women had goods and information they could barter for power and prestige. So scientists of many disciplines now agree that our hunting-and-gathering forebears almost certainly lived in relatively egalitarian bands.[8] Different but equal was the primordial human way.

This would change.

## The Plow: Death Knell for Women

Women's status as approximate equals with men probably survived humanity's migration out of Africa, the dwindling of the vast tundras and large herd animals across Europe and Asia, the growth of modern forests filled with oak and maple trees, and the proliferation of smaller, more solitary beasts, such as deer, boars, and bears. But social equality between the sexes could not withstand the devastating impact of a totally new lifeway—farming.

By 9000 B.C.E., men and women had begun to settle the hillsides and mountain valleys above the Tigris and Euphrates river plains in what is today's Middle East. By 8000 B.C.E., they started to domesticate wheat—then barley, chickpeas, lentils, grapes, olives, sheep, pigs, goats, cattle, and other animals and plants.[9] Most anthropologists believe that women were the first farmers: they tended fields of edible seeds with a primitive digging stick or hoe. Women do this work in many horticultural or gardening societies today—and women in these societies often enjoy considerable social status.

But in the fourth millennium B.C.E. a primitive plow was depicted on a Sumerian seal.[10]

The plow. This implement would be as important to the growth of civilization as the harnessing of fire, the development of the printing press, the invention of the steam engine, and the creation of the computer chip. But it would destroy the balance of power between women and men.

With the emergence of the plow and the domestication of animals for work and transport, men began to turn away from hunting to fell the trees, plow the fields, irrigate the plants, tend and harvest crops, and cart their extra produce off to local markets. Men also became obliged to defend their precious land.[11] "Sons are guns." Men and women of India still use these words. They know that sons will defend the family and the property.[12]

As the agrarian tradition took hold across much of the world, men became the primary producers. Soon they also came to own the land, the livestock, and the crops, valuable commodities they could convert into wealth and influence. With time, the farming men of Europe, North Africa, and Asia also became the warriors, craftsmen, scribes, priests, traders, heads of household, and heads of state.

## The Decline of Women: The Second Sex

"The major advances in civilization are processes which all but wreck the societies in which they occur," said Alfred North Whitehead. To be sure, the development of plow agriculture had a devastating impact on women: they lost their ancestral economic roles.[13] As barnyards and cultivated fields spread along the riverbanks of the ancient world, farming women were drawn into new kinds of domestic work: spinning, weaving, feeding cows and pigs, making candles, soap, and bread—and rearing a lot more children to help do the chores and work the sod.[14]

Gone were the days when women ranged far and wide collecting staples and luxury items, trading their goods and their information with neighbors, building valuable connections in the wider community, and bringing home much of the family food. Gone were their once-crucial roles in production—the bargaining chips of power and prestige. "Man is an animal that makes bargains," wrote Adam Smith. As women lost the essential leverage to bargain, their status plummeted.

Farming societies are not the only cultures in which men have tended to dominate women in one way or another. But where plow agriculture prevails, a codified sexual and social double standard is particularly prevalent; women are regularly deemed inferior to men.[15]

Many scientists and laymen have offered explanations for this extraordinary cultural transformation—the agricultural revolution—and its negative impact on women's status.[16] Suffice it to say that with the advent of intensive plow agriculture, the origins of substantial private property, and the emergence of a host of related technological and economic changes, women lost their once-vital role in production—as well as the social status they had enjoyed in prehistoric days.

As Simone de Beauvoir put it in her influential work, women became the second sex.

## Myths About Women as Subordinates

"Wives, submit yourselves unto your own husbands, as unto the Lord." So spake the Apostle Paul. Farm living spawned many Western beliefs about women, including the dogmas that women are frail, vain, dependent, less sexual, less intelligent, less ambitious, less savvy in business and financial matters, and eternally dependent on men.

Women were first described as chattels, as possessions of men, in the law codes of ancient Babylon in about 1750 B.C.E.[17] But their status had withered almost universally among the peoples of Europe by the time of the ancient Greeks. Men of classical Greece thought that most women had poor heads for business, poor resistance to stress, and almost no intellectual creativity. Clever courtesans entertained men of the ruling class with poetry, song, and sex. But few women, Greek patricians held, could excel in history or philosophy. Women, they maintained, were by and large weak, emotional, and dumb.

This stereotype of women was to persist as long as farm living dominated Western civilization. Extraordinary women occasionally attained enormous power, of course. Catherine de Médicis, Queen Elizabeth I, and Catherine the Great were the most conspicuous among the many smart, cunning, ambitious women of the agrarian tradition. With the diffusion of Christianity, some women rose to prominence in the Church as nuns. Village women often worked side by side with spouses and occasionally acquired local economic clout. By the 1300s, some female Londoners were grocers, bakers, beer makers, hatmakers, and barber-surgeons. During the Renaissance, upper-class women often acquired an education and became poets, dramatists, musicians, or painters. Highly educated seventeenth-century European women sometimes dominated salons devoted to the arts and letters. And many wives cleverly ruled their husbands and their households.

But during the many centuries of our agrarian past, most women in Europe and other farming societies had little education, few business opportunities, and few legal rights over their property or their children.[18] Their life duty was to raise babies and honor husbands till death did them part.

Charles Darwin even supplied "scientific" explanations for women's subordination. In *The Descent of Man,* published in 1871, he wrote that throughout our human ancestry, men had been obliged to fight other men to win women, then to feed and protect these precious reproductive vessels. Men's jobs, Darwin wrote, required courage, perseverance, determination, invention, imagination, and reason. Thus, by natural selection and survival of the fittest, "man has ultimately become superior to woman."[19]

The Industrial Revolution began to redress the balance of power between the sexes. As factories appeared behind the barns of agricultural Europe in the late 1700s, then later in America, women started to leave the farm for factory work. What did they come home with? Money: movable, divisible wealth—a passport to greater independence and equality. As discussed in chapter 1, women's participation in the paid workforce has increased ever since, not only in the United States but in many other countries.

Women around the world are slowly, fitfully, but inevitably reacquiring the economic leverage they enjoyed ten thousand, one hundred thousand, even a million years ago.

## A Pink Ghetto?

"For every trend, there is a countertrend," reports trend analyst Edie Weiner. A number of countertrends could affect women's economic status adversely.

For example, the world's population is predicted to peak around 2030, then to decline.[20] This population swell will be coupled with advances in the computer industries, plastics, fiber optics, and other technically advanced industries that employ fewer people. We may see more people but fewer jobs. Historically, when jobs were scarce, women were hired last and fired first.[21]

The World Bank predicts that by 2020, the world's biggest economies will be, in rank order: China, the United States, Japan, India, Indonesia, Germany, and Korea, followed by France, Taiwan, Brazil, Italy, Russia, Britain, and Mexico.[22] In a number of these societies, women are largely regarded as throwaway factory workers, field laborers, or office ladies.[23] In many cultures women have a long way to go before they will see any substantial change in these attitudes.

Even in America and Europe, job disparities still hobble women's progress. As discussed in earlier chapters, women often take more low-paying jobs and receive less pay for comparable work—everywhere in the world.[24] Women also hold the majority of part-time jobs, in order to rear their young. As the number of part-time jobs increases, women will probably take even more of these low-paying positions.[25]

"Don't think there are no crocodiles because the water is calm," holds a Malayan proverb. Even when women hold full-time positions, the waters of the workplace are not altogether serene. Flextime, job sharing, contract work: American and European businesses have made a host of innovations in the workplace to accommodate women. But some of these improvements leave women with no retirement, insurance, or medical benefits; no tenure; no paid vacations; and no connections to the wider business community.

The emerging international economy may even sharpen the inequalities between the sexes in some places. In developing societies, women often take the majority of low-paying manual jobs in textile, garment, and electronics factories, while men become the more skilled workers.[26]

In addition, religious fundamentalism still tethers many women to the home. A flagrant example is Afghanistan, where extreme Muslim rulers do not permit women to go to school, hold jobs, even venture into the streets without the chador, the long black robe and veil. Even in Western countries some Muslim girls are still forced into arranged marriages. If they resist, a brother or father has—or claims to have—a duty to slaughter them, a tradition known as "honor killing." Neglect, abandonment, and infanticide of baby girls are still practiced in India and China.

### A Winding Stair

Still, deep political and economic currents are providing women with opportunities to close the economic gender gap in many parts of the world.[27]

Much of the international economy is shifting from one based on natural resources and physical labor to one based on goods and services.[28] This opens the international cash economy to women. Moreover, with the rapid growth of international trade and freer markets, with the expansion of investments across national borders, and with all of the devices of the computer age, money and knowledge are beginning to flow around the world—into women's grasp.

In fact, every year millions of women are finding paid work and raising themselves out of poverty.[29] More will do so. The United Nations estimates that women will make up half of the global labor force by the year 2000.[30] Economist Barbara Bergmann sums up what most economists believe, saying, "For the next several decades we can anticipate that the economic forces bringing women out of domesticity will strengthen."[31]

"All rising to great places is by a winding stair," wrote Sir Francis Bacon. While women will not triumph easily, they have begun to ply their natural talents in the wider world, shedding thousands of years of economic subordination. The second sex is even becoming the first sex in some sectors of the economy in the industrial world.

A quirk of twentieth-century demography, the baby boom, in conjunction with a reality of feminine physiology, menopause, should accelerate this trend: the reemergence of economically powerful women.

### Age Wave: The Boomers

World War II was over. As the troops returned from the battle zones, Rosie the Riveter and her assembly-line sisters in industrial societies put down their tools and went home. This was the only era in the twentieth century when the number of American women in the workforce actually declined.[32]

Middle-class women met at coffee klatches, cleaned house, prepared dinner, and settled on their couches at cocktail hour with their breadwinner husbands to discuss an important matter: babies. They took these conversations to heart. Some seventy-six million Americans were born between 1946 and 1964. Today these boomers make up 30 percent of the American population.[33] In the years following World War II, Canada, Australia, Europe, and parts of South America and Asia also saw a bumper crop of infants.[34]

This was the famous international baby boom. Although the extent and duration of the population surge varied from one country to the next, much of the industrial world teemed with infants.

I am one of these boomers. I started first grade in a local church in my little town, New Canaan, Conecticut, while we waited for school officials to find more classrooms. When I entered college, I slept on a cot in the basement of a dormitory for the first five days while administrators looked for additional beds. When I went to graduate school, record numbers joined me. While the boomers scrambled during their growing years, they also sparked many twentieth-century social trends—burning bras, protesting wars, and ushering uninhibited sex, drugs, and rock 'n' roll into the middle class. They also led the charge for women's rights.

The boomers have finally grown up. This huge cohort of men and women is entering middle age. The oldest American boomers are in their early fifties. These vast numbers are about to shake things up again. Why? Because more and more boomer women are going through menopause.

This sounds far-fetched. But this biological change will, I believe, help boomer women achieve unprecedented social and economic power. Numerous studies show that middle-aged women around the world acquire independence, wealth, property, and connections that give them economic power and prestige. But they get a biological dividend as well. Menopause causes levels of estrogen to decline, *unmasking* women's natural levels of testosterone—a hormone regularly associated with assertiveness and a drive for rank.

## Mighty Menopause

Many Westerners view menopause with foreboding; they believe "the change" augurs a decline of health, sexuality, vitality, and all the joys of life. The prevalence of this fearful attitude was made clear to me by Marie Lugano, president of the American Menopause Foundation. She receives many requests from women for advice and counsel. But, she says, some of the women who seek information from the foundation make it plain that they do not want envelopes to arrive in their mailbox with the word *menopause* on the letterhead.

The fear of menopause that American women express is not common in other parts of the world—particularly in societies where men and women regard menstruation as dangerous and polluting. In these cultures, postmenopausal women actually become free of stringent taboos that cloister younger women. They can finally assert themselves and assume authoritative positions in public life.

Such were the Abkhazians when anthropologist Sula Benet lived among them in the 1960s.[35]

Among rugged foothills of oak, chestnut, and boxwood, in alpine pastures adorned with wildflowers, the traditional Abkhazians lived in a homeland half the size of New Jersey. The natives proudly called their native land "God's afterthought." To the west, the Black Sea. To the east and south, Georgia. To the north, the Caucasus Mountains separated them from Russia and, until recently, protected them from industrial society. Often called the "yogurt people," these are among the longest-living people on earth.

Traditionally, every Abkhazian family had its vineyard. Adults sipped wine and vodka and everyone drank gallons of fermented milk. Before the invasion of modern Western mores, the Abkhazians ate fresh cherries, oranges, and pears; wild persimmons; walnuts; honey; and cornmeal. Little meat, no butter, no refined sugar, no coffee, no tea for the Abkhazians. They refused to have angry or sad conversations as they dined. They had a passion for horse racing. They loved to dance. Sex was considered as important as a good appetite and a good night's sleep. They set no rigid deadlines for themselves. And retirement was unknown. "Without work," the Abkhazians said, "the rest does not give you any benefit."[36] When Benet lived among them, the oldest Abkhazian was reportedly one hundred and forty-five. Many survived to the age of one hundred.

Women of Abkhazia became increasingly important after menopause.[37] As in many traditional cultures, young menstruating women were considered ritually unclean. They could not slaughter animals or join men's conversations while they were bleeding. "The curse," as menstruation has been called in Western cultures since medieval times, kept women in their place. But after menopause, Abkhazian women could begin to butcher meat and attend ceremonies closed to younger women. They also began to assume authority over their homes, their sons, and all of their younger in-laws.

In "God's afterthought," postmenopausal women enjoyed an influential—and long—middle age.

### "The Curse"

Traditional Kaguru gardening people of Tanzania share this view of menopause. They liken menstruating women to fire—dangerous, wild, and polluting. Young women must vigilantly separate themselves from others during menses so as not to contaminate the brewing beer, disturb the ghosts, or upset hunting preparations. At menopause, however, women become free of this monthly stigma. As if from a chrysalis, they emerge to become powerful in community affairs. Anthropologist Tom Beidelman of New York University reports of the

Kaguru, "the shy and pliable young bride sometimes becomes a tough and clever older woman quite the match for any man."[38]

"Time ripens all things," Cervantes said. Many people in the world would apply this aphorism to women. Among the Tiwi of the Australian outback, aging women wield much power in marriage negotiations and crucial property settlements.[39] In Himalayan villages, postmenopausal women brew the beer, distill the liquor, and sell these libations and other luxuries, bringing in substantial amounts of money.[40] On the atolls of Ulithi in Micronesia, the oldest woman in the village becomes equal to the village headman, in charge of supervising gardening, weaving, and other group endeavors.[41] Blackfoot Indians of the American West called older women "manly hearted"; many such women become highly favored wives.[42] Even some Bengali women, traditionally secluded in their homes for some thirty years, cast off purdah, bid their relatives farewell, and march off on expensive religious pilgrimages—after menopause.[43]

Anthropologist Judith Brown writes that around the globe "older women are viewed as being 'like men.' "[44] In fact, postmenopausal women in every traditional society studied become powerful in one way or another—economically, socially, politically, and/or spiritually.[45]

Factors other than freedom from menstrual taboos also play a role. Most postmenopausal women are no longer tied to small children; they finally have time for community affairs, midwifery, or shamanic practices. They also begin to inherit property, acquire wealth, and become centrally situated in the family. In almost all societies, postmenopausal women begin to rule the home and dominate their younger in-laws and their children, particularly sons. They can exact labor from these kinsmen. Middle-aged women often control the household food, too, a powerful function in cultures where food cements interpersonal relations. Because these women can no longer bear babies, even their sexual mischief is sometimes overlooked.[46]

The liberating aspects of menopause have been widely observed. But I believe a biological factor also contributes to women's vigor and assertiveness in middle age.

### "Peaceful Potency"

"No spring, nor summer beauty hath such grace, / As I have seen in one autumnal face." So wrote John Donne about an older woman. Women seem to acquire a new presence in middle age—due, I think, to the physiological changes of menopause.

In a woman's middle forties, some four to eight years before the last menstruation, biological changes cause the ovaries to pump out less estrogen.[47] As levels of female hormones decrease in the bloodstream and other tissues, some women begin to feel the effects. Hot flashes, sweating, a dry vagina, and mood swings head the list. But the climacteric has a virtue. With menopause, levels of estrogen decline, unmasking levels of testosterone and the other male hormones present in the female body.[48] As a result, postmenopausal women have proportionately higher concentrations of male hormones coursing through their bloodstreams.

Some of the effects are unpleasant. Some middle-aged women begin to put on weight around the waist, a male trait. Some grow a little facial hair. Some become slightly bald. Most acquire deeper voices. Some suffer related ailments, such as diabetes, high blood pressure, or heart disease.

But with menopause, women around the world also become action-oriented, confident, forthright, and uninhibited, traits associated with high levels of testosterone in women.[49] Germaine Greer caught the essence of this womanly state when she called menopause "peaceful potency."

People have asked me how hormone replacement therapy, which replaces lost estrogen, will affect their postmenopausal personality. That is hard to answer. But a few things about HRT are clear: Only 8 percent to 12 percent of American women take estrogen in middle age for more than two years; even fewer women in other countries take female hormones for any length of time.[50]

More important, women who do take HRT do not regain the modest, self-deprecating demeanor of young girls—nor the girlish waistline and high voice. These women continue to exude the air of mature confidence that frequently characterizes postmenopausal women. HRT appears to add some healthful estrogen without dramatically affecting the peaceful potency of postmenopausal middle age.

Why has nature bestowed menopause—a condition that frees them to play a larger role in the community—on middle-aged women?

## Why Menopause?

Scientists have argued about the purpose of menopause for decades.[51] To understand this feminine phenomenon, they first had to establish whether menopause was unique to women.

Toothed whales and some types of laboratory mice seem to experience menopause.[52] Some aged female apes and monkeys have irregular menstrual cycles; their fertility declines and they begin to bear infants at wider intervals. A few cease to ovulate completely.[53] In a study of thirteen species of apes and monkeys in captivity, some 60 percent of aged female chimps stopped reproducing; 40 percent of aged female gorillas stopped bearing young; and less than 50 percent of females in the other species became infertile with advanced age.[54]

But menopause did not occur in all these females. And those that did stop ovulating did so only in extreme old age.[55] In contrast, all women experience a complete shutdown of the reproductive system; there are no exceptions.[56] Almost all women go through menopause in midlife, around age fifty—not in old age. And almost all women who survive for the average life span have a long postreproductive life phase.[57]

What a curious phenomenon. All human females are incapable of reproducing for about one third of their healthy adult lives, while most females of every other sexually reproducing species on this planet attempt to reproduce until they are almost dead. Even men are able to breed into extreme old age. And this bizarre female midlife transformation is not just an artifact of our increased human life span in recent centuries.

From studying the life tables of individuals in twenty-four traditional societies, anthropologists Jane Lancaster of the University of New Mexico and Barbara King of the College of William and Mary have calculated that if ancestral women survived to age fifteen, they had a 53 percent chance of living to age forty-five—long enough to experience menopause.[58] In fact, it is estimated that the *Homo habilis* peoples who hunted gazelles beside the shallow lakes of East Africa two million years ago lived to about age sixty-one—if they survived infancy and childhood.[59] More than a million years ago, ancestral women lived long enough for nature to select for menopause.[60]

Menopause must have had a vitally important purpose in ancestral times.

It did: grandmothering.

### The Grandmother Hypothesis

"God gave women menopause so they have the energy to run after their grandchildren," said Jan, a forty-six-year-old African-American baby boomer woman from Los Angeles who was recently interviewed by *American Demographics* magazine.[61]

Jan had it right.

Anthropologist Kristen Hawkes of the University of Utah and several other anthropologists champion the idea that menopause evolved so that women could be effective at grandmothering.[62] Quality over quantity. "Stopping early" enabled women to conserve their strength, avoid reproductive competition with their own daughters, and focus their energy on helping their living offspring, thereby improving the chances that their genes would be passed into tomorrow.

Ancestral grandmothers had a lot to do, too. Unlike infant chimps, who begin to feed themselves as soon as they are weaned, human children are hopelessly inept at collecting food, preparing it, and nourishing themselves. Someone has to help. Across the many millennia, Hawkes reasons, older women got the job, helping to feed their pregnant and nursing daughters and helping to provision grandchildren after these babies had been weaned.[63]

Such are grandmothers among the Hadza, about 750 nomadic individuals who intensely dislike gardening. These men and women still roam the hilly scrub near Lake Eyasi in northern Tanzania, collecting fruits, honey, tubers, and small game—much as our ancestors did a million years ago. But Hadza women in their fifties, sixties, seventies, even eighties provide more dinner than most of the other members of the band.[64] Moreover, these aging women distribute their edibles first to daughters, then to nieces and cousins—younger women who share their genetic makeup. They also baby-sit for free.

Hawkes regards the evolution of menopause and grandmothering as one of the benchmarks of human evolution. She says, "The Grandmother Hypothesis gives us a whole new way of understanding why modern humans suddenly were able to go everywhere and do everything. It may explain why we took over the planet."[65]

## Postmenopausal Wisdom

I would speculate that ancestral postmenopausal women served the community as well as the immediate family.

They were probably also living libraries, wise elders who could remember curious weather patterns, dangerous neighbors, and all sorts of rare plants that could poison, cure, or nourish. They must have stopped squabbles among children, calmed impatient teens, listened to marital complaints, mediated disputes, and spread the news. Some were visionaries or seers. Most helped to keep the peace within the band.[66] Most also had a specialty such as curing, delivering babies, telling stories to educate the young, or communing with the spirit world.

"There is no greater power in the world than the zest of a postmenopausal women," Margaret Mead reportedly said. Long ago, countless wise, clever, patient, knowledgeable, peaceful, middle-aged shepherds expended their energies to serve their kin and their community. Their young survived—selecting for menopause and the peaceful potency of feminine middle age.

As the tidal wave of baby boomer women goes through menopause in coming decades, many will become shepherds of the local, national, and world communities as well.

## Genetic Motives of Social Consciousness

There will be plenty of them.

The twentieth century has been marked by a dramatic change in the human life course: far more people are living into old age. Today fewer and fewer people die in infancy, of infectious diseases, of accidents, or in childbirth. Instead they die of heart disease, strokes, or cancer—in later life. The average life expectancy of people in the United States is currently seventy-six years; by 2050 it is likely to be eighty-three.[67]

Many of these aging men and women will be in good health, too.

Federal studies report that fewer older people are suffering from chronic diseases or disabilities, a trend that first appeared in the early 1980s.[68] Eighty-nine percent of those aged sixty-five to seventy-four report having no disabilities; 40 percent of those aged eighty-five are fully functional.[69]

This cohort of middle-aged and older healthy people can only expand. The earliest of the baby boomers have just turned fifty. The Census Bureau predicts that by 2030 some 20 percent of all Americans will be over age sixty-five.[70] By the year 2050, 15 percent to 19 percent of the world population will be over sixty-five as well.[71] In most Asian countries, less than 10 percent of the population is currently over sixty-five. But demographers report that that number could double or triple in the next thirty years as people have fewer children and the current generation lives into old age.[72]

Most of these people will be women. Currently, in many countries, of people over age sixty-five, there are twice as many women as men.[73] Women simply live longer than men do. And they will play a significant role as shepherds in the years ahead—for an evolutionary reason.

Most older men and women have spread their DNA into the population. These grandparents give advice, baby-sit, provide festive family events on holidays and weekends, and give their children and grandchildren money and property. But today fewer senior citizens live with or near their adult offspring; their adult children have drifted to other towns and cities. In short, these citizens can no longer give direct hands-on care to their descendants. So if they wish to help their children, they are obliged to transfer their attentions to the larger community. As they improve the social and physical environments, they will enable their children and grandchildren—and their DNA—to flourish, too.

Genesis states that God gave man dominion over the earth and everything on it. In the 1960s, Harvey Cox, professor of religion at Harvard University, proposed a different idea: stewardship, the concept that people are the caretakers of the earth. As the world population ages, stewardship is likely to become a buzzword, because aging men and women must build society to nurture their families, their dispersing DNA.

These stewards will change the world in many ways.

## Gray Panthers on the March

The Florida Silver-Haired Legislature, a group of three hundred former judges, doctors, professors, corporate managers, and others whose average age is eighty, has met annually for a week in Tallahassee, Florida, for the past twenty years. They take over the two chambers of the state legislature to discuss issues central to Florida's elderly and to the larger community.[74] No long-winded speakers here. No posturing, either. By the week's end they have chosen five issues of paramount importance that members will then discuss with their own local church groups, civic clubs, condominium boards, or mobile home associations. If they win the support of these organizations, they will lobby state lawmakers and try to get the desired legislation. More than a hundred of their requests have become state law.

Just about half of American states have these bodies of senior citizens. And as families become smaller, even more aging citizens will donate their time, energy, and money to causes not directly related to their own kin group. In fact, this trend has already begun. For example, PlanWise, a financial consulting firm in Bayside, New York, reports that many elderly clients have increased their charitable donations and bequests to people or groups outside the family.[75]

Aging men and women join all sorts of associations to improve life for themselves, for their kin, and for the community at large—not only in America but in many other countries. But this is not the only way they will affect tomorrow. Another will be in the voting booth.

By 2020, people over age fifty-five will make up 45 percent of all American voters, and a large majority of these older voters will be women.[76] Journalist Cheryl Russell of *American Demographics* magazine writes, "These women will become a formidable force in the voting booth."[77] Political theorist Francis Fukuyama agrees, writing that older women will be "one of the most important voting blocs courted by mid-21st century politicians."[78] Here again, women will have the edge.

What kind of world will these older women, and their younger counterparts, engineer?

## How Women Vote

Women have been the majority of voters in U.S. national elections at least since 1964 simply because there are more women of voting age in the population; however, since the mid-1980s they have also turned out to vote at the same or higher rates than men.[79]

Women often vote differently than men.[80] Evidence suggests that women started to do so as soon as they won the right to vote in the United States in 1920.[81] But sociologists report that the gender gap in voting behavior reached modern levels in the 1950s. Moreover, the emergence of women's distinctive voting habits was directly related to women's increasing rates of participation in the paid labor force.[82]

Neither sex is a distinct voting bloc; individuals always vary. Nevertheless, men are twice as likely as women to think the nation's most essential issues are balancing the budget and cutting spending.[83] They are also more likely to want to spend on parks and recreation, mass transportation, and highways and bridges, the infrastructure of the nation. Men more regularly support space exploration.[84] When it comes to foreign policy, men are more interested than women in maintaining superior military power, fortifying the security of allies, protecting weak nations against aggressors, and reducing the trade deficit.

Women, on the other hand, are more inclined to favor all kinds of social programs and social services[85] and to regard issues of education, health care, child care, poverty, and joblessness as essential elements of the national agenda.[86] Women favor more economic and social programs for African Americans and other minorities.[87] They are more likely to support gun control. They uphold capital punishment less frequently. And women are less likely than men to favor conscription, military spending, nuclear weapons, and interventionist foreign policies.[88] When it comes to foreign policy, women are more interested in fighting world hunger, curbing the influx of illegal drugs into the the United States, supporting United Nations programs, and improving the global environment.[89]

These feminine voting habits exist regardless of income, race, age, social class, or residence.[90] Variations definitely occur in some elections; moreover, level of income and occupation can widen or shrink this gender difference. But by and large, old or young, rich or poor, black or white, urban or rural, American women are more inclined to favor social programs for children, health, education, and the disadvantaged than men are.[91]

The gender gap in voting behavior becomes more pronounced as women age. Young men and women often share the same politics. But as women get older, their political orientation increasingly diverges from that of men.[92] By middle age, women are far less financially secure. They hold more part-time jobs, have fewer pension benefits, and have less access to health insurance. So they become increasingly interested in supporting social programs and services concerning education, health care, pension benefits, Social Security and other forms of economic safety, and support for the needy.[93]

As a result, women are less likely to be antigovernment. They tend to see government as a social safety net. They are more likely to believe the government should help the country solve its problems than to choose to leave these issues to individuals and private businesses. Women are more inclined to believe in a stronger role for government.[94]

The United Nations Non-Governmental Liaison Service reports that women in many other cultures share American women's social concerns. Internationally, women are more interested than men in the needs and rights of women, children, the elderly, the disabled, minorities, and the disadvantaged.[95] They are more concerned about health and reproduction, education, welfare, and the environment. They are also less militaristic and more supportive of nonviolence and finding peaceful solutions to international conflicts.[96]

These feminine values have already begun to have a noticeable impact on American elections.[97] Generally speaking, women of all ages are more likely than men to regard themselves as moderates or liberals. So more women vote for Democratic candidates.[98]

## The Growing Impact of Women in the Voting Booth

White suburban women are widely seen as having been the vital component in Bill Clinton's reelection as president of the United States in 1996.[99] These women trusted Clinton, not personally as a man, but as a politician who would fight to help them pay college tuitions for their young, care for their elderly parents, and discourage teen smoking, and who would support their right to choose when they would (or would not) bear a child.

The voices of these "soccer moms" are making a difference in other ways as well. Historian Arthur M. Schlesinger, Jr., recently noted that America has acquired what he calls a new "vital center," a renewed interest in family, work, and community. Questions concerning nuclear proliferation, world trade, and governmental power have taken a distinct back seat to issues of child rearing, Medicare, education, and the environment.

The most avid supporters of governmental action in these areas are white suburban women. These women are in the vanguard of those demanding governmental commitment to the family, the poor, the sick, and the elderly.[100]

As women around the world increasingly vote for presidents, governors, legislators, and others on more local levels who support their views, they will usher into action myriad specific programs that add humanity to humanity.

## How Women Will Change
### the Business and Professional World

"I believe I've found the missing link between animal and civilized man," wrote Konrad Lorenz. "It is us."

In the century unfolding before us, women will have the opportunity to contribute to the further civilization of humanity in ways other than in the voting booth. Throughout this book, and in the beginning of this chapter, I have maintained that the business world is changing in ways that increase the need for women's skills. I have also maintained that as women assume influential roles, they will apply their feminine talents.

Women in powerful positions in the communications industries will change what we watch on television, hear on the radio, and read in newspapers, books, and magazines. We are likely to see less violence and action-adventure, more complicated stories, more sequels to stories, the integration of more humane values into plots, more sensitive depictions of women, more lifelike portrayals of human relationships, more ethnic and age diversity in actors and commentators, a wider range of topics in the news and film, more TV and radio talk shows, more magazine and newspaper columns written by personalities, more visual and performance arts, more programming for children, and a broader, more contextual perspective on just about every issue.

In America today, women have just as much formal education as men; in the future they may have more. As teachers, they will likely bring to the classroom a greater flexibility, imagination, patience, and empathy and a broader range of subjects and views—affecting the thinking of millions of people. They will undoubtedly show greater respect for ethnic, racial, and cultural diversity and endorse more flexible gender roles. Women have already played a major role in introducing courses on women's studies and supporting the inclusion of African-American studies in many schools. They will most likely spend more time delving into the personalities of the people who have made history, thereby unsettling many who wish to see sacred cows left unsullied. They will explore more of the arts and literature of foreign cultures, discuss more of the intricate relationships among species, and examine complex social problems in thoughtful, subtle ways.

As they move into influential positions in corporate America and the rest of the business world, women will unquestionably alter our opinions about millions of consumer products and services. For example, major items like automobiles, once sold only to men, are already being pitched to the female market. Advertisements may become more elaborate to suit the female mind. And home office equipment, like computers and faxes, is likely to be manufactured in a range of colors. Women will introduce more varied, less conventional points of view on business issues, encourage a more egalitarian climate in the office, and create more durable personal ties to clients.

They will undoubtedly support flexibility in the workplace and strengthen programs designed to balance work and home life. They will try to reduce the macho posturing at business meetings, rearrange offices to eliminate the more ostentatious emblems of rank, and establish a wider range of ways to give benefits and perks. Already some businesses use a system whereby one can collect points for overtime work or particular achievements and then apply these points toward acquiring any of several different benefits instead of receiving a standard monetary bonus.

More women will also work for themselves and mix career, family, and leisure in unconventional ways. The traditional dinner hour, already withering, may disappear entirely, but all sorts of creative family outings will be commingled with business trips. The conventional five-day workweek may gradually be replaced by far more flexible schedules.

Women already predominate in the service professions, adding innovative ideas on how we organize our lives and spend our leisure time. For appropriate remuneration, they will buy your clothes, purchase and serve your meals, plan your vacations, balance your checkbook, set up your exercise routine, plan your retirement, or do just about any other thing that harried working men and women need. Hail the emergence of a new "professional servant" class—a sophisticated group not to be confused with the submissive underlings of the past. Female chefs, wine tasters, travel guides, and culture brokers will introduce us to new worlds at home and abroad.

More and more women will enter the management ranks of the police. Even now they rely less on muscle than on verbal skills, ingenuity, and the ability to read people. With their web thinking, policewomen and female private detectives may solve more of our multifaceted crimes. Female lawyers and judges may bring about a broader, more contextual view of crime and justice in the courtroom. They are helping to redefine sexual harassment in the office and to provide reasonable, even win-win solutions in mediation and arbitration. As legislators, women will undoubtedly continue to fight for laws improving education, health, and the environment. They will be more alert to the rights of women, minorities, and homosexuals, and they will take a keen interest in laws on pornography, domestic violence, divorce, child support, and the obligations of parents.

Women in the healing professions are already expanding our views of health and healing. They see fewer patients per hour and devote more time to each, asking questions, listening patiently, and building rapport. Home visits may become fashionable again. Group practices should flourish. More doctors, nurses, and other medical professionals are likely to consider the social and psychological factors that can contribute to an illness. Doctors have already begun to invite traditional healers into some operating rooms to massage patients during major procedures.

Wellness and exercise centers may flower into community centers with health food restaurants, travel agencies, and bookstores. Drugstores are already jammed with racks of natural medications and vials of essences for aromatherapy. Shamanism may become popular again. More TV programs and Internet sites devoted to holistic medicine should emerge. Newspaper and magazine columns discussing natural medicines should expand. Support groups for the very ill and their families will proliferate. Women may even introduce more humane ways to spend one's last days; some have suggested new rituals for dying, such as a serene boat trip with close friends prior to euthanasia.

As nongovernmental, not-for-profit organizations of all kinds continue to flourish, female leaders of civil society will control large sums of money, sway political leaders, and secure governmental programs and policies designed to improve the welfare of women, children, minorities, the elderly, the disabled, and the disadvantaged. They will also play leading roles in national debates on issues of health, safety, education, welfare, and the environment—things of deep concern to women of all ages, classes, and ethnic groups.

Albert Einstein once said, "The significant problems we face today cannot be solved by the same level of thinking that created them." On television, on the radio, on the Internet, in offices, in classrooms, in courtrooms, on vacation tours, in hospitals and doctors' offices, in books and movies, in legislative bodies, at block association meetings, national rallies, and world conferences, women bring a different way of thinking: a cooperative spirit; a gift for understanding people; patience; compassion; a tremendous drive to connect, nurture, and heal; and the ability to examine issues within a broad context.

As women continue to shed the remnants of the agrarian tradition and their second-class status, they will apply their many natural talents in the marketplace. Subtly—at times dramatically—they will change the world.

# CHAPTER 8

# Sexual Civility

## The Feminization of Lust

The sexual embrace can only be compared with
music and with prayer.

HAVELOCK ELLIS

I too beneath your moon, almighty Sex, / Go forth at nightfall, crying like a cat." Edna St. Vincent Millay described the most profound and primitive emotion on earth, the sex drive. Some have regarded this craving as demonic, others as divine; some have seen sex as just a nuisance. But every healthy human being who ever walked the earth has known this urge. You see a picture in a magazine, you replay a fantasy in your head, you feel a lover's fingertip on your neck, and, like a whiff of perfume, sexual hunger saturates your mind.

In this chapter I propose that both men and women have evolved a strong sex drive, but it differs between the sexes in many specific ways. I will contend that women are just as interested in "making love" as men are, but their libido is triggered by different kinds of fantasies and different circumstances. Men are more turned on by visual sexual stimuli and signs of youth, health, and fertility in women. Women are more attracted than men by signals of commitment, status, and material resources. The female sex drive is more flexible; hence women have a greater tendency toward bisexuality. The feminine libido is also more intense (but less constant), embedded in a broader emotional and social context, and just as durable across the life course.

Today sexual double standards are breaking down. Girls are starting to experiment with sex earlier in life. Women are taking more lovers before marriage and engaging in more sexual experiments with their spouses. Some are "swinging"; some are hiring gigolos. Some are bisexuals or lesbians. Women are beginning to express their sexuality from early adolescence to old age—a return to ancient female lifeways.

Many current trends promise to accelerate women's worldwide march toward sexual liberty, including increasing urbanism, more education and literacy, women's economic independence, more divorce, smaller families, and widely available contraception, not to mention factors like satellite television and the Internet.

Helping to set the pace, women are assembling at international conferences, and marching, lobbying, writing, or speaking out in other ways for women's sexual and reproductive rights. Women are also filing most of the current lawsuits on sexual harassment—and winning many of these cases. In these ways they are obliging lawyers, judges, journalists, politicians, and businesspeople of all kinds to redefine sexual codes of decorum according to female standards. Women are gradually feminizing lust.

I conclude that as women's standards of sexual comportment seep across our college campuses, and into offices and bedrooms, women are launching an era of sexual civility.

## The Eternal Thirst

W. H. Auden called the sex drive "an intolerable neural itch." He was anatomically correct. The visceral human appetite for sex begins in a primitive part of the mammalian brain, the hypothalamus. Then, through a complex of networks and reactions, chemicals in the brain pour into the bloodstream and stimulate the gonads to produce the androgens, primarily testosterone, and the estrogens, principally estradiol. As these tides of hormones ebb and swell, you feel that primal ache.

The adrenal cortex also plays a role in human lust. This tissue is the outer crust of the adrenal gland, which sits atop each kidney. At puberty it begins to secrete male sex hormones, as well as small amounts of female hormones. These chemicals contribute to the rush of sexual desire that overwhelms you when you smell a special pungent odor, see a shapely body, or play out a fantasy in your head.[1]

The balance among testosterone, estrogen, and all the other ingredients in the chemical cocktail that drives us to the bedroom is exceedingly complex.[2] Dosage, timing, genes, and social circumstances all play a role in how the sex hormones affect a human being.[3] Nevertheless, testosterone is a central player in what poet Pablo Neruda called this "eternal thirst." When women who have lost their ovaries are treated with testosterone, their sexual desire, their degree of sexual arousal, their sexual fantasizing, even the number of their orgasms increases.[4]

I have two friends, a man and a woman, who get injections of testosterone from a doctor regularly. Both are attractive, hardworking, middle-aged, successful scientists. Both take the injections to boost a flagging sex drive. And both say they begin to feel a tremendous urge to make love about thirty-six hours after receiving an injection.[5] They tell me their libido remains high for several weeks. Women with naturally high levels of testosterone have more sexual thoughts and more desire for sex than do women with lower levels. They also masturbate and make love more often.[6]

Some women feel more sexual desire around ovulation, when levels of estrogen and testosterone peak.[7] Others feel it just before menstruation, perhaps as an aftereffect of higher midcycle levels of testosterone.[8] Environmental rhythms also seem to play a part. No one knows if men's libidos peak in late autumn, but men's levels of testosterone are highest in November and December. And men's and women's daily levels of testosterone are at their highest around dawn.[9]

Are we merely hormones on feet, functionaries that do the bidding of a mindless substance, testosterone? Not at all. As the human cerebral cortex began to expand some two million years ago, our ancestors became increasingly able to control their more fundamental drives. Today we regularly decide when, where, with whom, how, even whether we will express our sexual impulses. Still, the actual bodily sensation of lust comes from nature—and I am convinced that the "feeling" is the same for women and men.

The sexes often experience this emotional sensation under far different circumstances, however.

## Men's Sexual Worlds

"License my roving hands, and let them go, / Before, behind, between, above, below." Poet John Donne liked to touch. Some people are turned on by sex in the woods or in the bathtub. Some like high-heeled boots, candlelight, or Kama Sutra–like coital positions. And every human being has a slightly different opinion about how he or she wishes to be caressed and talked to during coitus.

Much of this variation comes from childhood, from adolescence, and from all of the chance mental associations we make between certain experiences and sexual feelings. But men and women also have some sexual habits that almost certainly originate in the gendered brain.

Men, for example, are more likely to remember specific aspects of a past sexual episode, such as a particular smell, piece of clothing, or time when sex occurred. The feminine psyche is less subject to "conditioning," to associating specific odd things or events with sexual encounters.[10] This may explain why men are more interested in fetishes and exhibit more "deviant" sexual behaviors than women do.[11] For some men, a particular incident or object in childhood becomes linked with sex and they must replay this scenario to trigger lust.

Men's impressionable sexual nature may have evolved for an important reason. Women can find a sex partner almost anytime they want one; after all, women own the precious egg. Men must fertilize this egg if they are to send their genes into perpetuity. So men are obliged to remember the circumstances of successful sexual encounters.

Men also fantasize about sex with different partners and anonymous partners more regularly than women do, most likely because it is biologically adaptive for men to inseminate as many females as they can.[12]

And men like to look.

"Peeking in through / the open window, / your face was / virginal. / But you were / all woman / below." The poet Praxilla wrote these lines in Greece in the fifth century B.C.E. Times haven't changed. In a 1920s study of several hundred American men and women, 65 percent of the men said they had done some peering through a bedroom window. Only 20 percent of the women had done any stealthy ogling.

Men are more turned on by visual stimuli.[13] They use visual porno-graphic materials of every kind more frequently than women do.[14] When they fantasize, they conjure up more images of coitus and body parts, the explicit details of sex itself.[15] Many men are even aroused by looking at their own genitals and by showing their genitals to wives or lovers. This can lead some men to outright public exhibitionism.

Sexual peeping probably gives men a physical jolt. We know that when male monkeys see a sexually available female or watch a companion copulate with a female, their levels of testosterone spike. So primatologist Kim Wallen, of the Yerkes Regional Primate Research Center at Emory University, speculates that men may go to strip bars and look at girlie magazines to boost their levels of testosterone.[16] Not surprisingly, the $500 million porn business in America today is supported almost exclusively by men.

This male urge to look has a Darwinian payoff. By peering at a woman, a man can judge her health and vigor. As levels of testosterone rise, he is also stimulated to woo those who look young, healthy—and fertile.

## What Turns Women On?

Women, too, are excited by visual erotica, although women are not as turned on by it as men are.[17]

Women are much more aroused than men by romantic words, images, and themes in films and stories.[18] Women's sexual fantasies include more affection and commitment.[19] Women often dwell on their own emotional reactions. And they are more than twice as likely to think about a sex partner's emotional characteristics.[20] Women fantasize about familiar partners more regularly than men do. Women also envision more caressing, particularly of nongenital areas of the body.[21]

These feminine tastes are to be expected. Women are interested in words; they verbalize their emotions more readily than men. Women have a more probing curiosity about people, including others' moods and emotional makeup. And women are more sensitive to being touched all over their bodies.

This feminine appetite for talking, touching, and romantic affectionate sex with familiar partners most likely has an evolutionary purpose. A woman risks pregnancy and motherhood when she makes love. As she talks with and touches her suitor prior to coitus, she can evaluate his temperament and his intentions. If he expresses affection, then perhaps he may be willing to become a committed provider, too.

"Too much of a good thing is wonderful," Mae West once said. Publishers know these feminine preferences—and play on them. Romance novels sell in over fifty countries, to women. Even American purveyors of porn videos have begun to cater to these feminine tastes. Visual pornography has traditionally featured casual, anonymous encounters that appeal to men. To attract female customers, some producers now add some conversation and a veneer of romantic plot.

## Feminine Surrender

"One of the magnanimities of woman is to yield," wrote Victor Hugo. In fact, women often like to yield—especially in bed with a lover.

Seventy-one percent of men and 72 percent of women in America fantasize while with a sex partner.[22] But the sexes conjure up different images. Conquest and domination are central to most men's mental scenarios. Submission and surrender are prevalent features in women's sexual thoughts.[23]

American women are twice as likely as men to fantasize about passive sex—being "done to" as opposed to "doing."[24] They see themselves as the objects of a partner's sexual desire, unlike men, who tend to see others as the recipients of their sexual attentions.[25] This gender difference also exists in Japan and Great Britain.[26]

Please don't mistake me: Less than 0.5 percent of men find it appealing to force a women into sex, and less than 0.5 percent of women want to be forced.[27] Rape is entirely different from sex games between consenting partners. But data indicate that women more regularly fantasize about surrendering to a partner.

On one occasion a friend of mine, a good-looking, wealthy, independent woman in her forties, told me a fantasy of hers. She was driving along a country road when a policeman waved her down. As he stood outside her car window writing a speeding ticket, her mind kept flashing to a fantasy in which he demanded that she have sex with him in the bushes. "It wasn't about rape," she told me, "it was about authority—and surrender."

The anonymous stranger, the faceless prince who overpowers: psychologists tell us that women embrace these fantasies of submission and helplessness to avoid feeling guilty about their sex drive or to shed the responsibility of initiating coitus. But women's daydreams of surrender may arise from primitive parts of the female brain—because feminine sexual surrender is exceptionally common in the animal kingdom.

Take the iguana. A male marine iguana courts by puffing up to look dominant and important and then aggressively charging the female. If the female is sexually receptive, she responds by crouching flat on her belly, totally immobile, in a position of utter surrender. Her passivity invites copulation. For iguanas and many other reptiles, signs of submission by the female in conjunction with cues of dominance by the male are essential to coitus.[28] Scientists call this mating dance "agonistic sexuality."

Birds and mammals have added a host of affectionate extras to the reptilian pattern of dominance and submission. Most lick or kiss or tap or stroke or sniff in friendliness prior to copulation, exhibiting "affiliative sexuality."[29] Nevertheless, female lions, female rats, and females of many other mammalian species also hold themselves immobile and available prior to coitus. So ethologist Irenäus Eibl-Eibesfeldt proposes that these leitmotivs of human sexuality—male dominance and female surrender—arise from the primitive reptilian core of the human brain.

Some men also like the passive role. But in the bedrooms of the world, many more women secretly play out this primal fantasy of surrender to spark their lust.

## The Distracted Woman

Women are more likely than men to become distracted during coitus. If a woman hears a baby cry, recalls something that happened at the office, or wonders if she has turned off the stove, her concentration can be interrupted. She has to reset her focus and rebuild her sexual excitement.[30] Men are better able to keep their attention riveted on sex.[31]

This gender difference is also seen in females of other species. If you crumble cheese within the peripheral vision of a pair of copulating rats, for example, the female keeps looking over at the cheese. The male keeps thrusting. I suspect that this feminine distractibility stems from the composition of the female brain. As discussed in chapter 1, the female brain is well connected. Women tend to assimilate many disparate thoughts at once—web thinking. Web thinking may disrupt their concentration as they make love.

Perhaps nature even meant women to be distractible. Sex is dangerous; it disrupts one's vigilance. Males of all species must forgo watchfulness and focus their attention to achieve orgasm and spread their seed. A female's egg drops naturally into the womb; women do not have to focus on orgasm to conceive. On moonlit evenings in ancient Africa, the distractible woman was probably the sentinel for the copulating pair.

## Who Has a Stronger Sex Drive?

The trouble with sex, James Thurber reportedly wrote, is "the other person."

In a 1990s survey of 14,070 Americans, 87 percent thought that women are less interested in sex than men are.[32] Dozens of other studies support this thesis, that men think about sex and engage in sex more frequently than women do.[33]

Women are narrowing the gap. In the 1940s and 1950s, 94 percent of men and 40 percent of women said they masturbated.[34] More recently, 90 percent of men and some 70 percent of women said they pleasured themselves.[35] Nevertheless, even America's most recent sex survey suggests that the male sex drive exceeds that of the female.

This sex survey, published in 1994, is known as the National Health and Social Life Survey (NHSLS), or the "NORC study," because it was carried out by scientists at the National Opinion Research Center in Chicago. It is the first American survey based on a random sample; 3,432 American men and women, ranging in age from eighteen to fifty-nine, participated.[36] Although several scientists have questioned its accuracy on some points,[37] the NORC study is generally regarded as a serious scientific survey.

This national poll shows that the sexes have much in common. For example, approximately 30 percent of men and 26 percent of women have coitus two to three times a week.[38]

But when asked how often they *thought* about sex, 54 percent of men responded that they thought about sex every day, while only 19 percent of the women acknowledged that sex crossed their minds daily. Moreover, 27 percent of men masturbate at least once a week, while only 8 percent of women do so weekly.[39] The gender difference in frequency of masturbation is seen everywhere in the world where data have been collected.[40] American, British, French, and Finnish men also report more sex partners across their lives than women do, a pattern found in other countries, too.[41]

So men lead more active sex lives than women do.

Or do they?

"Man's most valuable trait is a judicious sense of what not to believe." On the issue of sex drive, I side with Euripides. In spite of data to the contrary, I believe that women's sex drive is simply different from men's, more subtle, more complex, and much more misunderstood.

### Women's Different Sexuality

"Winter skies are cold and low, / with harsh winds and freezing sleet. / But when we make love beneath our quilt, / we make three months of heat." Tzu Yeh wrote about the intensity of lovemaking in fourth-century China. Both sexes become ardent during coitus. But, as many sex researchers have pointed out, women are superior performers in bed.

Although the overall duration of orgasm is the same for women and men, the first few major muscular contractions vary in number and duration. Initially, men have three or four strong contractions, followed by a series of irregular minor ones. Women have five or six of these initial gripping muscular sensations, and the contractions proceed in a longer rhythm, drawing out the experience. In fact, this intensely pleasurable first stage of orgasm lasts only three to four seconds in men but some five to six seconds in women—twice as long.[42]

Women's orgasms also engage a larger proportion of the pelvic tissues. And often they become more intense during pregnancy and after childbirth, when vascular networks and blood circulation increase in the pelvic area.[43]

What is equally impressive, women can have several orgasms rapidly in succession, something only a very few young men can do.

Some women can even arouse themselves to orgasm without touching themselves. Only one man in a thousand can achieve an orgasm just by thinking.[44] Although the male libido is definitely more constant, the feminine sexual response is more intense.

If scientists were to measure sex drive by extent and intensity of orgasm, as opposed to the number of daily thoughts about coitus, the number of masturbatory events, or the number of partners across the life span, they would conclude that females' sex drive is at least as strong as that of males.

## Women's Sensuality

The mismeasure of the female libido becomes even more apparent if the definition of sexual activity is expanded to include sensuality. In a poll of 14,070 men and women done by the Prodigy computer network, 75 percent reported that they believed women were more sensual than men.[45]

Flowers, oils, candlelight, satin sheets, fluffy towels: when women fantasize about sex, they conjure up the textures, sounds, and smells, all of the ambience surrounding sex, more regularly than men.[46] Women also like more kissing, hugging, stroking, and cuddling during sex.[47] In short, women place the act of intercourse within a wider physical context.

Women also weave sex into a richer emotional fabric. When husbands and wives are asked to describe the sexual realm of their marriages, women more regularly comment on comfort, communication, love, and intimacy—the emotional context surrounding coitus. Men discuss vigor, arousal, frequency, and other aspects of the physical act of intercourse.[48]

"Men think having an orgasm is having sex. That's the difference," remarked one woman in the Prodigy survey.[49] There is a kernel of truth in what she says. Female sexuality is nested in a broader lattice of emotions, a wider range of physical sensations, and a more extensive social and environmental context—all reflections of feminine web thinking. Men's sex drive is far more focused on the act of copulation itself—yet another example of men's propensity to compartmentalize the world around them and focus their attention on specific elements.

Clearly scientists and laymen who base their measures of the sex drive on such things as frequency of masturbation and number of partners are defining lust from the male perspective. They are compartmentalizing sex and viewing it narrowly. No wonder they mismeasure female sexuality.

## Women, Sex, and Age

"The tragedy of old age is not that one is old, but that one is young," wrote Oscar Wilde. As they age, both sexes still feel young. Nevertheless it is well known that one's sexuality changes with age.

Both sexes have fewer sexual fantasies, masturbate less regularly, and engage in less intercourse as they get older. A man's sex drive peaks in his late teens and early twenties and then gradually declines, along with his levels of testosterone. A woman's sex drive, on the other hand, peaks in her late twenties or early thirties and declines somewhat later, remaining on a plateau for much of her life.[50]

Moreover, contrary to what many believe, most women do not experience a decline in sex drive with menopause. In the late 1980s, Swedish scientists queried 497 middle-aged Swedish women in stable marriages about the caliber of their partnerships and their sex drive. Six years later they asked the same women the same questions again. They discovered that desire was remarkably stable for almost two thirds of them. In fact, 10 percent of these women said their sexual craving had increased.[51]

Some 27 percent did report a decreased libido. But age was not the primary reason for the decline of lust. Instead, most of those whose sex drive had plummeted had alcoholic partners, lacked intimate relationships, were suffering from insufficient financial or emotional support, or had gone through a major depression.[52]

Studies at Duke University of healthy, educated, upper-middle-class women tell a similar story: boredom, stress, drugs, poor health, an uninterested or alcoholic partner, or the death of a spouse can cast a pall over a woman's libido.

But for most women, the sex drive remains stable across middle age—if they are in good financial and mental health.[53] In fact, a *Redbook* study of aging women indicated that almost 40 percent of wives complained that they were not having sex often enough.[54] Perhaps this is because, with menopause, declining levels of estrogen unmask levels of testosterone—the chief hormone of desire.[55]

"Is it not strange that desire should so many years outlive performance?" Shakespeare wrote. Sexual function and sexual desire are separate phenomena, of course. Both sexes struggle with changes in genital function as they age. But scientists report that the aging process takes less of a physical toll on women.[56]

All of these data suggest that women have a robust libido. It is just different from that of men—less constant but more intense, and nested in a broader web of emotions, sensations, and environmental context. But it is just as durable across the life course.

## Do Women Like Sexual Variety?

Of all the differences between the male and female sex drive, the one that seems to intrigue scientists, especially male scientists, the most is the one involving variety. Many staunchly maintain that women are simply less interested than men in copulating with an assortment of partners.[57]

This is their reasoning: Across deep history those men who sought sex with a lot of women spread their seed disproportionately, selecting for men's taste for sexual variety. Because women could have only a few children in a lifetime—and risked pregnancy and motherhood with each copulation—they were predisposed to be choosier than men.

I would agree that most women are somewhat more sexually discriminating than most men. Yet there is compelling evidence that women are designed to seek a good deal of sexual variety.

One line of evidence stems from basic biology. Scientists have proposed that men possess three different kinds of sperm, each with a different job. "Egg getters" swim up the vaginal canal to meet the egg. "Blockers" clump to block an invasion of foreign sperm. And "seek-and destroy" sperm attack and kill alien sperm.[58] If this proves to be the case, the male system of attack and defense against foreign sperm in the birth canal is a remarkable indication that ancestral woman had a roving eye.

What is equally important, our feminine forebears could have gained considerable assets from multiple dalliances: resources, including more food and protection, valuable social connections, even extra sperm, different sperm, or superior sperm.[59]

And their peccadilloes may not have had the dire consequences that some of my colleagues assume. Our feminine forebears spent most of their reproductive years either pregnant or nursing. Scientists have established that women in contemporary hunting-and-gathering societies rarely ovulate while nursing, due to low body weight and the tremendous amount of regular exercise mothers get. So it is plausible that ancestral females who copulated with a variety of partners often could not get pregnant.

Historically, men have gone to extraordinary lengths to suppress female lust. Clitoridectomy in parts of Africa, the veil in many Moslem societies, the seclusion of women in traditional India, foot binding in traditional China, chaperones and chastity belts in medieval Europe: all suggest that men in many cultures have regarded the feminine libido as powerful—and fickle.

Their fears are probably well founded. Everywhere today that women are permitted sexual freedom, such as in Scandinavia, the United States, and some tribal cultures, many women engage in sex with a variety of partners.[60]

Most curious in this debate is the singular lack of attention that scientists have paid to basic mathematics: With whom are all these randy men copulating?

If men have more sexual partners than women do, as all surveys report, then either a few hypersexual women are having sex with an awful lot of men or men are exaggerating their conquests while women are exaggerating their virtue. In a convincing scientific study, psychologist Dorothy Einon of University College, London, concludes that both sexes could be lying about their escapades: women probably have more sexual partners than they report; men have far fewer.[61]

Despite the current scientific orthodoxy that men are more interested in sex with a variety of partners, much evidence indicates that women have a long history—indeed, a prehistory—of concupiscence. Perhaps the most interesting data confirming this come from the research on female prostitutes. From the alleyways of Asia to the jungles of Amazonia, some women seek sexual variety as a way of life.

### Money Is Sexy

No one knows how many American women adopt prostitution. Police book only a few "sex workers." Even in countries where prostitution is legally regulated, many more women engage in secretive, part-time, or amateur whoring than are officially listed.[62]

In the nineteenth century, an estimated 5 percent to 15 percent of young women in Paris and New York City engaged in short-term or long-term prostitution.[63] Historians note that many chose this profession because they thought prostitution was a better job than factory work or domestic servitude.[64]

Prostitution has declined during the twentieth century, probably because women have found other ways to make a living. But women still choose "the life." Some psychologists have estimated that one out of every one thousand to two thousand women in America engages in this line of work, at least part-time.[65]

Given the taboo against prostitution, the danger to one's health, the possibility of violence, and the lack of social benefits, it seems surprising that any woman would freely pursue this vocation. Yet women do. Malay women in Singapore say they become hookers to avoid the drudgery of being a wife. Bemba women of Africa say they want to make enough money to hire others to do their housework. American prostitutes say they like the money, freedom, and adventure. But sexual pleasure may be part of the incentive.

I discovered this after a speech I made to call girls at a meeting of PONY, Prostitutes of New York. These sex workers are not streetwalkers but middle-class women who choose to work for escort services, in massage parlors, or in their own homes. If they work at home, they acquire clients from ads in newspapers and magazines or from others who pass customers along for a fee.

After I made my speech (on the evolution of human sexuality), I asked my audience the classic question: "Do you have orgasms on the job?" One attractive woman, probably in her thirties, told me that some of her clients do not want to leave her apartment until they have given her an orgasm. So she concentrates on bringing herself to climax, then works on the customer. Another told me that her work did stimulate her genitals but she tried not to have an orgasm with clients she didn't like. "I don't like to give them this gift," she said. Another said she tried to avoid having an orgasm because when she did, she felt like quitting work and going out to dinner.

Most agreed, however, that certain clients turned them on. One woman summed up what seemed to be the group consensus: "On a good day I have about five clients, and I often have an orgasm with one of them."

For decades, academics and assorted pundits have speculated on why women would go freely into prostitution. Latent lesbianism, low intelligence, a home life of abuse, greedy relatives, desperate poverty, and various psychopathologies head the list of possible reasons. Evolutionary psychologists believe this feminine predilection is just a way to benefit from men's allegedly stronger interest in sexual variety.[66]

But no one has been able to isolate a specific set of social factors that lead to prostitution. And current books by prostitutes and new scientific studies have prompted sexologists Vern and Bonnie Bullough to conclude that prostitution is, by and large, "simply another occupation."[67]

Various forms of sexual slavery certainly exist. Some streetwalkers are destitute drug addicts. In parts of Asia, young girls, even children, are sold into sexual slavery by parents too poor to feed another mouth. But many American "working girls" say they chose this line of work. These happy hookers have joined exotic dancers, actresses in X-rated films, telephone sex workers, erotic masseuses, and others in the sex industry to build an organization that advocates decriminalization of prostitution. They call their association COYOTE, an acronym for Call Off Your Old Tired Ethics.

"Every woman has her price," madams tell me. From informal discussions with many women, I have come to think that many would indeed engage in part-time prostitution if they were positive they could pull it off unharmed, undiscovered, unscathed by disease or pregnancy—and generously remunerated.

Money is sexy, call girls say. I suspect women are built to seek sexual variety just about as often as men are—provided it meets their primal reproductive need for resources.

### Feminine Sexual Flexibility

Women display another sexual property that undoubtedly comes from their distant past. Female sexuality is more flexible than that of males. As a result, women have a greater tendency toward bisexuality.

Nature is messy. Despite the Western tendency to split the world into two kinds of people, heterosexuals and homosexuals, these are not distinct categories. Individuals vary by degrees, ranging from those who engage in homosexual behavior only under extreme social pressure (like being in jail) to those who knew from childhood that they were attracted to the same sex.

So the 1994 NORC study of American sexuality divides homosexuality into three dimensions: desire, behavior, and self-identity. This survey of Americans reports that some 4.5 percent of men and 5.6 percent of women are physically attracted to those of the same gender. Some 4.9 percent of men and 4.1 percent of women have had at least one same-sex partner since age eighteen. And 2.8 percent of men and 1.4 percent of women identify themselves as primarily homosexual.[68]

These numbers are similar in other recent American surveys, as well as in studies done in Britain, France, and elsewhere.[69] In Japan, for example, 3.7 percent of men and 3.1 percent of women have had homosexual body contact.[70]

But schoolgirls experiment more than boys with bisexuality. Some two thirds of heterosexual women have some attraction to other women.[71] Many self-identified lesbians have some attraction to men.[72] And in an American study of homosexuality done in the 1970s, 20 percent of the usually gay males interviewed had fathered a child, while 40 percent of current lesbians had lived in a heterosexual relationship and given birth.[73] As psychologist Michael Bailey of Northwestern University put it, "Women are more likely than men to have feelings toward both sexes. Men are more channeled one way or the other—there's less choice."[74]

As in so many other aspects of human behavior discussed throughout this book, women's sexual orientation is broader and more generalized, while men's sexual orientation is more focused.

This feminine sexual flexibility could have been adaptive in the distant past. To spread their seed, males had to adhere to a rigid course: wooing females. Ancestral females, on the other hand, needed someone to help them rear their young. Winning the most influential hunter was ideal. But if men were in short supply, a female was obliged to tag along as a second wife or adopt a female companion to help her rear her baby. Women needed a long-term partner— be that partner male or female.

So men and women are not alike in their sexual patterns. Although men think more about the specific act of sexual intercourse and have more partners across their lives, some women probably have many more partners than almost all men. Women experience more orgasms and stronger orgasms. Women's sexuality is nested within a wider context of physical and emotional sensations. Female sexuality is just as durable across the life course. And feminine lust is directed toward a wider array of partners, male and female.

How will women express their sexual drives as they gain economic power and social status almost everywhere in the world?

## The Decline and Reemergence of Lust

Around the spitting bonfire dancers leaped to pounding drums, then faded into the dark to hug and whisper. On hillsides strewn with coconut palms and breadfruit trees, the matted ferns bespoke an afternoon's clandestine meeting. Some girls even skipped church on Sunday, unwilling to give up their sex lives for an hour. Such was life on the island of Tau, Samoa, when Margaret Mead arrived in 1925.

For centuries, Polynesians had held that sex was an art one should learn, practice, and enjoy—as long as it was done with persons of the appropriate class and of the proper kin connection.[75]

Are we headed toward sexual lifesyles akin to those of the traditional Polynesians?

In some ways, yes.

Each era, each culture, and each human being has unique beliefs about sex. Some societies celebrate it; some fear and deplore it. Moreover, attitudes change as people age, as cultures develop or disintegrate, and as eras fluctuate between repression and permissiveness. One of the transforming developments in the history of Western sexual mores, for example, was the rise of Christianity. As Nietzsche wrote, "Christianity gave Eros poison to drink."

The Stoic philosophers of ancient Greece had long proclaimed the evils of coitus. Few listened. Such sects were an island of prudery in a sea of sexual license. The Greeks celebrated lust—as long as sex was between men and courtesans, men and concubines, or men and adolescent boys. Only Greek women of the citizen classes were expected to be chaste before marriage and faithful to their husbands all their lives.[76]

The ascetics of classical Rome also preached chastity throughout the glory days of this empire. But as with the Greeks, few Romans heard their words.

Early Christian fathers embraced the ancient precept of chastity, however. With time, coitus came to be regarded by the Church as filthy, shameful, and ungodly—for both men and women. Only with the intent of procreation, they decreed, should married couples engage in coitus. Even lust for one's spouse was regarded as adultery. In the fourth century, when Christianity became the official religion of the Roman Empire, these credos about sex received the approval of the state.

In some ways these Church doctrines improved the status of women. Since they were thought to be made in God's image, women were entitled to respect. Moreover, these sexual codes aimed to provide women with dutiful spouses, protectors, and providers who could neither divorce nor abandon them. Christianity also curbed male adultery. It even offered women a new avenue for political and social power: the nunnery.

But these early Christian sexual codes certainly dampened lust. As Christianity flowed into the soils of the West, from Ireland to Spain to the steppes of Russia, Europeans came to associate almost every kind of sexual desire with sin.

The Renaissance and the Reformation began to thaw this icy moral code. As urban centers spread and literacy grew in the late 1600s, Western sexual doctrines became more and more liberal.[77] Eighteenth-century European physicians still regarded masturbation as unhealthy. They believed it sapped one's strength and invited ailments, from pimples and constipation to blindness and insanity.[78] But as the Industrial Revolution took hold in the 1700s, adultery and other sexual acts were decriminalized. Enclaves of homosexuals cropped up in London. More and more of those in the professional and bourgeois classes in England, continental Europe, and America came to believe that sex within marriage should be enjoyed.[79] Sex was becoming unlinked from God.

British writer Malcolm Muggeridge grumbled of this trend, "The orgasm has replaced the Cross as the focus of longing and the image of fulfillment."

## Twentieth-Century Libertines

"To spur a willing horse," goes the Latin saying. Economic, social, and technological changes in the twentieth century have increasingly encouraged the expression of our primordial erotic desires.

Margaret Sanger was arrested in 1917 for advocating contraception and running a birth control clinic in Brooklyn, New York. Latex condoms came on the market in the 1930s. Also in the 1930s, the automobile and roadside motel gave men and women more privacy. Penicillin became available in the 1940s—to counteract disease. In the 1960s, the contraceptive pill gave women new control of their reproductive life. Recreational sex came of age.

Today most Americans appear to feel much as the Polynesians do about sex. They believe that any heterosexual activity is acceptable for unmarried adults as long as their partner consents.[80]

Men have also begun to consider women's sexual tastes. In the 1940s, American couples spent about ten minutes at foreplay; today this has increased by some five to seven minutes.[81] In the 1950s, only 12 percent of American married couples engaged in cunnilingus; today about 75 percent of wedded people practice this art.[82] Middle-aged women are also exploring a wider range of sexual techniques.[83]

Some people still spout church dictums, practice macho male ethics, or show Victorian priggishness. But today many American men and women regard sex as fun, a way of relaxing and expressing their love or friendship. Sex has become far more than an act for procreation.

This relaxed Western attitude is spreading around the world. Beijing newspapers have begun to speak of "high tide," their term for orgasm. In Kuwait and Ireland, hosts on radio call-in shows are beginning to discuss sex and romance. In India, people pack the movie houses to watch torrid Italian love stories. A late-night talk show about sex, *About It,* is popular in Moscow; guests air their views on group orgies, sadomasochism, and masturbation. In Warsaw, Poles gather in front of the TV to watch *Clan,* a soap opera about family issues, including sticky sexual situations such as adultery and divorce. And museums of sex have opened in Germany and China. Liu Dalin, the curator of the Shanghai Sex Museum, say the Chinese attitude toward sex lies in the saying "Pale on the outside, glowing within."[84]

Even sex education is increasing in much of the educated world.[85] Signs of sexual liberation are everywhere, particarly among the young.

## Rising Female Sexuality

One Halloween eve a friend and I stopped in a market in New York City to buy some black plastic plates and black napkins. At the checkout counter, we jokingly told the teenage cashier that we were planning on holding a witches' Sabbath. "Do you happen to know a virgin we could sacrifice?" we playfully asked. Taking us seriously, he pondered for a long moment. "No," he said ruefully. "Not one."

American surveys done since the 1960s confirm that teenage boys are more likely than girls to engage in intercourse and have more sex partners. Boys also express less guilt and remorse after their sexual escapades. But girls are changing. A 1995 report from the Carnegie Corporation states that 27 percent of American girls and 33 percent of boys have had sexual intercourse by age fifteen.[86] Several studies corroborate these findings; more young women are having sex at an earlier age, and they are engaging more partners.[87] The sexual escapades of young American women are becoming more like those of men.

American parents have become increasingly tolerant of their daughters' premarital sexual experiments, too. In a 1991 survey, 43 percent of approximately a thousand adult Americans thought there was nothing wrong with sex before marriage; 18 percent thought it was inappropriate under only a few circumstances.[88]

World attitudes about premarital sex vary widely. In India and Iran, for example, men and women still think virginity at marriage is essential.[89] But in a 1990 poll of twenty thousand Chinese men and women, 86 percent approved of sex before marriage.[90] In Finland, France, Norway, the Netherlands, Sweden, and West Germany, men and women tend to regard chastity in a mate as inconsequential. In parts of South Africa and Polynesia, men even prefer a woman who has already borne a child; this way they can be sure that she is fertile.

On the whole, world attitudes about a women's premarital sexuality are becoming more permissive.

## Child Sex

This trend toward premarital sex is not new.

Among the traditional Muria of India, for example, girls and boys as young as six come to the *gotul,* or children's house, at dusk to tell stories, dance, and play. Then all settle down to sleep with a partner until just before dawn, when they return home to work. Older girls often pair up with pubescent boys to teach them to make love. Little girls experiment with caressing, kissing, and intercourse; at puberty they begin to copulate with *gotul* members too.[91] Pelaga Indian girls of Argentina begin to play at coitus around age five.[92] In Arnhem Land, Australia, five-year-old girls and boys curl into one another's arms in explicit copulatory positions. Adults approve; they think children should know how to perform sexually.[93]

Sexologist John Money estimates that children naturally begin to rehearse their sex roles between ages five and eight—playing house, playing doctor, playing other games that include genital stimulation. After age eight these sexual antics become more focused on intercourse—done no longer as a game but for sex itself.[94]

So contemporary girls who experiment with sex long before puberty are returning to habits that were common across our long human prehistoric past.

## Babies Having Babies

There is, however, a dangerous difference between the sexuality of modern girls and that of their hunting-and-gathering forebears. For the past 175 years, age at puberty has been declining about one to three months per decade. Currently in the United States, menarche occurs, on average, at age twelve.[95] Some of these young girls can get pregnant, too. This is new.

Girls in most tribal societies do not reach puberty until around age sixteen. Because these teens eat lean foods and get a great deal of exercise, they go through a period of adolescent subfertility: they generally cannot get pregnant until at least age eighteen. Most do not bear a child until around age twenty.[96] Girls in industrial societies, however, eat a lot of high-protein and fatty foods and get little exercise. These habits raise the critical body weight and trick the body into early puberty.[97]

Here's the point: Nature has programmed girls to experiment with sex at a young age. Modern life enables them to conceive as well. As a result, we will see no end to our current trend of teen pregnancy— except through sex education. Indeed, sex education is now common in much of Europe and becoming more prevalent in the United States.

### Neolibertinism

Many social scientists agree that both developed and developing societies are marching steadily toward more liberal sexual attitudes, including sexual liberty for women.[98] I believe the pace will accelerate, for several demographic reasons.

In America, better-educated people tend to have less restrictive attitudes[99]—and more people are educated. Higher-income earners tend to be more sexually liberal—and the upper-income groups are growing. Those living in metropolitan areas are more sexually permissive—and our urban centers are expanding.[100] People who never marry, as well as those who are divorced, separated, or widowed, are more sexually open-minded—and the number of people in these groups is enlarging.[101] Those who live in small families also tend to be more sexually liberal—and small families are now the most common family type.[102]

Generally speaking, as standards of health rise, and as contraception and abortion become widely available, people become more interested in sex. Satellite television and the Internet now offer a range of programs with sexual information and experiences—and these programs are reaching the farthest corners of the globe. Most pertinent is the fact that as women gain economic independence, they become less likely to exchange their sexual freedom for protection and provisioning from men.[103]

As sexologist and futurist Robert Francoeur of Fairleigh Dickinson University puts it, "one unique feature of this new sexual revolution is that women, not males, are leading it."[104]

Indeed, American women—and women in many other cultures— are starting to experiment with sex earlier in life, taking more sex partners before marriage, living with partners outside of marriage, demanding cunnilingus and other forms of sexual satisfaction from their lovers, using contraception, planning their families, marrying later, and divorcing when spouses do not suit their sexual and social needs. Women are also meeting at national and international conferences to disavow the practices of clitoridectomy and virginity testing, and marching, writing, and speaking out to claim their right to control their sexual and reproductive lives.

Women are actively contributing to, and often leading, the current worldwide shift toward greater sexual expression. I would add that they are also returning to sexual lifeways that are fundamental to the female mind.

Women have begun to express their sexuality in thoroughly contemporary ways as well.

## Cybersex

No longer do girls, boys, women, or men have to pick up sex-laden magazines or sexy romance novels at a shop. In their schools, offices, living rooms, and bedrooms lies sex galore—on the Internet. Some ten thousand porn sites are available on the World Wide Web if you have the right credit card or the ingenuity to break through simple codes. It is all in living color for comfortable browsing after school, after work, or late at night.

It has been said that 90 percent of activity on the Internet is teenage boys downloading images of nudes. I doubt it. Nielsen Media Research showed that employees at IBM, Apple Computer, AT&T, NASA, and Hewlett-Packard tuned in to the on-line edition of *Penthouse* thousands of times a month.[105] A recent poll of ten thousand American households established that some 30 percent of individuals in them tune in to "adult sites." Only 8 percent of all these visits are made by teens.[106] Some 92 percent seem to be men and women sitting at their computer terminals, entering chat rooms, and talking about—or having—cybersex with friends or strangers.

I learned something about this firsthand when I sat beside a stranger, a man in his forties, at a dinner. Conversation was slow until he discovered that I was an anthropologist who often wrote about lust and love. At this, he launched into a soliloquy about his nightly exchanges with various women on the Internet. Usually he and the woman would write "dirty" things to each other until one or the other reached orgasm. If he "came" first, he turned off his computer to go about other business; if the dialogue ended abruptly, he knew his partner had "come" instead.

Sexual discussions on the Internet range from how to please a partner to how to purchase a cage for a human. Pictures range from beauty queens to the obese. But is this entirely new?

I remember sitting on a Mayan ruin during a long day of sightseeing in the Yucatán. After I overcame my weariness, I realized I had perched on a twenty-foot stone penis lying along the ground. Pornography reached artistic heights in ancient China, India, Cambodia, and Japan as well. And cyberporn doesn't begin to compare to the books, magazines, and other adult forms of sexual entertainment that Americans spend billions of dollars on annually.

I am not convinced that cyberporn will be particularly harmful to the populace. Richard Posner, federal court judge and author of the book *Sex and Reason,* concludes that it has never been established that pornography actually leads to sexual deviance.[107] In coming decades, however, anyone curious enough to sit at a computer and push the proper buttons will see more sex at a younger age than was ever possible before in human history. The Internet may well spur both men and women to expand their sexual play.

### Swinging

"All the things I really like to do are either immoral, illegal, or fattening." Today a good many women are beginning to agree with this remark by Alexander Woollcott.

The North American Swing Club Association reports that some three million Americans are swingers. Almost three hundred swinger clubs accommodate them, as well as countless private sex parties. So to understand this world, I interviewed a man of this persuasion, a handsome, witty man in his mid-fifties, an internationally known scientist by day, a swinger by night.

Twice weekly he frequents Le Trapeze, a sex-on-premises swing club in New York City, with one of many girlfriends. He pays seventy-five dollars at the door. Then he and his partner check all their clothes in a locker room, give the key to the attendant, receive two towels, and wander the juice bar, the living room, the dining area, the Jacuzzi, and the mattressed sex rooms as a team. They lie down in one of the sex chambers and relax together, perhaps make love. But if they fancy another couple, they may strike up a short conversation; if all agree, they may switch partners for a while.

Dr. Robert McGinley, president of the Lifestyles Organization, one of the largest organizations of swingers in the world, tells me that more and more women have been expressing an interest in swinging over the past two decades. Access to birth control is part of the reason. But women's rise in economic and social independence is another primary factor. McGinley has interviewed more than ten thousand couples in the past twenty years. He says that single women regularly initiate these escapades, finding the appropriate club or gathering and inviting a partner to accompany them.[108]

## Gigolos

Women are also buying sex.

I have met only one gigolo in my travels: a middle-aged man, tall, thin, white-haired, soft-spoken, intelligent, handsome in a boyish way, originally from California. I was introduced to him through a middle-class call girl and interviewed him over dinner. He services women in their forties, fifties, sixties, and seventies—single women who have boyfriends, women married to much older men, and widowed women.

At the time we spoke, he was employed in New York City by a woman executive in the financial world. Between 10:00 A.M. and 5:00 P.M. he lounged in her huge back office somewhere in midtown. Here he read and watched television. At some point during the day, she would come in to be serviced. She also sent her secretary in to enjoy his skills. On occasion he also serviced two of her clients. At night he lived with another woman and was paid to have sex with her.

Women also paid him to accompany them to art openings and cocktail parties, to go out for dinner, even to accompany them on safari trips in Africa, boat trips to Indonesia, and road trips through the American Southwest. Sex is always part of the transaction, he says. When I asked him how he performed so regularly, he replied, "I find something attractive about every woman I make love to."

A more common route to sexual expression is homosexuality. Studies show that Americans are no more tolerant of homosexuality today than they were twenty-five years ago.[109] Almost 75 percent of Americans still think that sex between two adults of the same gender is "always wrong."[110] But women are far more accepting of homosexuality than men are.[111]

In recent years, a number of American municipalities passed anti-discrimination laws to protect gay and lesbian rights. Homosexuals in some states can get medical benefits from their partner's place of work. Even Harvard University now allows gay and lesbian couples to hold commitment or blessing ceremonies in the university's Memorial Church. In northern Europe, the rights of homosexuals have progressed much further. Even South Africa's postapartheid constitution of 1996 banned discrimination on the basis of sexual orientation.

If not generally approved by the citizenry in most industrial societies, homosexuality is gradually becoming visible—and those who practice it are becoming protected by law against discrimination. In these times when almost anything goes, it is far from surprising that some independent women are choosing the lesbian option.

## Vanishing Double Standards

As women become more and more economically independent and express their sexuality more freely, they are also rewriting our codes of sexual conduct and manners—and curtailing the peccadilloes of men. In short, the old sexual double standard is breaking down.

This is particularly apparent on American college campuses. Since the late 1970s, fliers on date rape and sexual harassment have crammed campus bulletin boards. Student crisis centers have burgeoned. Women have been going to discussion sessions, watching educational films, and forming organizations to combat harassment. Some girls take classes in self-protection. Schools have outlined policies and punishments. Counselors, mediators, and ombudsmen (now called ombudspeople) have become important figures.[112] And students and faculty members have been hauled into campus courts for sexual misconduct.

Almost all of the offenders have been men.[113]

Women's sexual standards are setting the agenda in the office as well. Increasingly, women are speaking out. Researchers report that from 40 percent to 50 percent of American women say they have encountered some form of sexual harassment in the office or on the college campus.[114] In 1995, 59 percent of women who held top-level executive positions in the business world said they had been harassed.[115] Sexual harassment has been legally defined, rules of sexual decorum have been written, and educational forums are being held. Even taboos have emerged.

Men are getting scared. In past decades, the woman's career was generally in jeopardy if sexual misconduct occurred; often she got fired. Today men are much more likely to suffer the consequences of sexual harassment. Currently, women who win these judgments gain an average of $250,000.[116]

Sexual harassment is still prevalent in many countries, however. Nearly 50 percent of working women in Estonia, Finland, Sweden, and the former Soviet Union report being sexually harassed; some 70 percent of Japanese women say they have experienced some form of sexual harassment in the workplace.[117] And although rules will undoubtedly be made in many of these places and offenders will be punished, sexual harassment will persist.

The causes have deep roots in the human psyche.

## Perfect Strangers

For millions of years the sexes did different jobs.[118] Never since our ancestors started to stride across the earth have men and women of reproductive age worked side by side, day in, day out.

Today men and women rise each morning, go through lengthy preparations to look their best and brightest, then join one another in tiny offices. They cram into communal conference rooms and share the communal coffeepot. They meet over breakfast, lunch, and dinner, on weekends, even in hotel rooms in foreign cities—working face-to-face.

Like a pack of hunting dogs, office workers share the same code of ethics, the same goals, the same daily schedule, office jokes, and office gossip. They sometimes spend more hours every week with one another than they do with spouses or lovers. And friends and family are excluded from this office petri dish. A few employees have pictures of spouses or children on their desks. But many work together for years before they meet an office pal's family.

Nothing in our ancestry has prepared us for this amount of intimate contact with strangers.

## The Flirting Gap

What's more, we are born to flirt. We carry within us an arsenal of postures and gestures that we unconsciously employ to woo.[119] We toss our hair, strut, sway, and arch our backs. We raise an eyebrow, gently touch, speak in soft high tones, and beam broad grins that can spark sexual desire even when we don't intend to ignite that madness. Many of these courting cues are universal, too. This is why an American and a Japanese can flirt effectively without either one of them knowing a single word of the other's native tongue.

To make the office even more dangerous, the sexes interpret courting gestures somewhat differently. As psychologist David Buss of the University of Texas at Austin puts it, "When in doubt, men seem to infer sexual interest."[120]

A Washington, D.C., lawyer gave me a remarkable example of this gender difference. It was a steamy summer morning on Capitol Hill. The lawyer was sitting next to a congressman in a meeting. A young woman entered the chamber and chose a chair in front of them. As she settled, she stretched, arched her back, pulled her long hair to the top of her head, piled it there for a moment to cool her neck, then tossed her head and let her hair fall. The congressman leaned toward my friend and remarked, "She's trying to pick me up."

Very few women would regard such a common gesture as a come-on.

When men and women watch films of friendly office exchanges, men are much more likely to interpret a woman's smile and friendliness as sexual interest and seduction than women are.[121] And men are exceptionally sensitive to visual stimuli. High-heeled shoes, tight short skirts, plunging necklines, swishy hair, an arched back, a tilted head, a swaying gait: all are sexual come-ons to men.

Women know their clothing signals sexual interest to men; this is why women dress seductively for an evening date. Many forget, however, that men are just as sensitive to these signals in the office. Men, on the other hand, are remarkably unaware of women's sensitivity to words. Men use sexually explicit words more regularly than women do; they regard them as more acceptable.[122] So when men make lewd

jokes and salacious comments, they generally have no idea how
deeply women react.

This simple gender difference may have played a role in the sexual harassment charges against Clarence Thomas, now a Supreme
Court justice. Thomas allegedly made off-color comments to a subordinate colleague, Anita Hill, about pubic hairs on a can of Coca-
Cola and about a well-endowed male character in a pornographic
film. These kinds of crude allusions don't ruffle men. But women
often find them insulting, even threatening. In fact, women's most
common complaints of sexual harassment concern men's words.[123]
Women also find sexual touching more upsetting than men do.[124]

The office: it is a cocktail for sexual disasters, a neutral zone far
from family and friends, with close quarters, shared hours, shared
stresses, office projects to talk about, flirtatious gestures spilling out,
and time, time, time to let passions brew. Moreover, men and women
see proper sexual comportment differently. So I suspect we will see
more office mates sending confusing signals and taking unwanted
sexual liberties.

In the future, a good number of these offenders may well be
women. Feminine harassment may be slightly different, though.
Frieda Klein, a Cambridge Massachusetts consultant on sexual harassment who works with blue-chip companies, reports, "Women are
less likely to be counting up notches in the belt." Men, she says, have
more "emotionless or acontextual sexual relationships."[125] I suspect
women will pursue fewer targets—but harass them more subtly and
more doggedly.

Trying to outlaw sex and romance in the office is like trying to outlaw the weather. It can't be done. About 25 percent of all American
companies have policies that discuss these issues.[126] Many have even
come to believe that sex and romance are permissible—as long as
the connection is between coworkers with equal power. Nevertheless,
some have hired managers to act as "cupid cops," employees who
make sure that all parties regard the relationship as consensual.[127]

But where sexual advances are not welcome and a harassment case
is filed, women will have their say in court. Men's undesired sexual
advances are being curbed—as women's freedom of sexual expression
comes of age.

## Sexual Civility

Cybersex, swinging, gigolos, and other sexual experiments may become even more popular with some women in coming decades. But most are simply returning to age-old forms of feminine sexuality—with forays into sex earlier in adolescence, freer sex lives before wedding, and more sexual experimentation within marriage. This march toward feminine sexual liberty is occurring in societies around the world; the double standard regarding sexual conduct is breaking down. And several current forces will accelerate the rise of female sexual expression, including the worldwide increase in urbanism, literacy, contraception, divorce, small families, women's economic power, satellite television, the Internet—and the determination of women.

As more and more women demand their sexual and reproductive rights, as they meet at national and international conventions to set feminist agendas, as they lobby governments on women's issues, as they question sexual misconduct in the office and the home, and as they win harassment cases in courts, sexual mores are changing. Men are adopting a more feminine perspective of sexual courtesy—in offices, at schools, in colleges and universities, on dates, at dinner tables, and in bedrooms around the world. Women are feminizing lust.

"Lust is the oldest lion of them all." So goes an Italian proverb. As women fight for female standards of sexual comportment, they are gradually curbing this ancient human drive and creating an international air of sexual civility.

# CHAPTER 9

# INFATUATION

## Romantic Love in
## the Twenty-first Century

Lovers alone wear sunlight.

E. E. CUMMINGS

Thunder, opens chasms of light, in your dark eyes, in the night, on the water, and in me the storm was born." A Catholic priest living in the state of Guerrero, Mexico, wrote down this poem in 1629. It had been recited to him in the native language of Nahuatl by an Aztec Indian.

Romantic love. Obsessive love. Passionate love. Infatuation. Limerence.[1] Call it what you will, almost all men and women have felt the ecstasy and anguish of this madness. In 1992, anthropologists surveyed accounts of 166 varied societies and found evidence of romantic love in 147 of them.[2] In the 19 others, anthropologists had simply failed to examine this aspect of daily living. Everywhere they looked, the anthropologists surveying the literature saw evidence of this passion. People sang love songs or composed romantic verse. They performed love magic, carried love charms, or brewed love potions. Some eloped. Some committed suicide or homicide because of unrequited love. And in many societies, myths and fables portrayed romantic entanglements.

Egyptian legends recount the love between Isis and Osiris three thousand years ago.[3] *The Jade Goddess,* written in China between 960 and 1279 C.E., tells of a young couple who abandoned parents, friends, and honor to elope. Paris and Helen, Orpheus and Eurydice,

Abélard and Héloïse, Troilus and Cressida, Romeo and Juliet, Majnun and Layla in the Middle East, Krishna and Radha in India: thousands of ancient poems, stories, songs, and legends throb with the exhilaration and despair of romantic passion. All spring from the same deep well, the human drive to love.

In this chapter I argue that this primal human emotion, romantic attraction, is associated with specific brain chemicals; that humans share the basic brain circuitry for attraction with other mammals; and that romantic love evolved among our ancestors to encourage men and women to prefer certain partners, thereby conserving their mating energy. I will also explore some distinct gender differences in romantic tastes.

I conclude that romantic love is emerging as a powerful social force in societies around the world. The long human tradition of arranged marriages is waning. Today more and more women and men choose their own partners—and marry for love. As this mighty emotion is unleashed in hamlets, towns, and cities everywhere, the twenty-first century is certain to see more books, movies, talk shows, newspaper columns, and Internet sites discussing love. More people will experience the joy—and the rejection—of love. More will marry—and divorce—to find love. And more will experiment with alternative kinds of romance, such as love on the Internet and "polyamory."

With their empathetic nature, their gift for understanding people, their linguistic skills, and their keen interest in romance, women will be our dedicated pilots on this uncharted sea. They may even set the agenda for how many of us express our romantic passion.

## The Characteristics of Romantic Love

"What 'tis to love?" Shakespeare asked.

Thousands of men and women throughout recorded history have attempted to define romantic attraction. Most conclude that it is a mystery. Westerners do not regard depression, anxiety, or fear as a mystery. Yet they regularly relegate the feeling of obsessive romantic passion to the supernatural. As a result, we know very little about the biology of this madness.

This is unfortunate. Although passionate romantic love can be deeply fulfilling, it can also be wildly destructive. More than 25 percent of American homicide victims are spouses, sexual partners, or sexual rivals. Annually some one million American women are stalked by a rejected lover. And an untold amount of clinical depression and suicide is caused by this emotion.

So I have organized a team of colleagues to study the brain correlates of romantic attraction. In one part of the study, Michelle Cristiani, currently a graduate student in anthropology at the University of New Mexico, and I canvassed the past twenty-five years of psychological literature on romantic love and designed a questionnaire on this topic. To date, 437 American, 402 Japanese, and 13 Navajo informants have answered our survey. With the help of New York statistician MacGregor Suzuki, some of this material has been analyzed.

In the second part of the study, Lucy Brown and Gregg Simpson, both neuroscientists at the Albert Einstein College of Medicine; Art Aron, a psychologist at the State University of New York at Stony Brook; Deb Masek, a graduate student in psychology at SUNY Stony Brook; and I have begun to put infatuated men and women in an fMRI (functional magnetic resonance imaging) brain-scanning machine to measure brain activity. We hope to establish some of the regions in the brain that become active when the love-possessed think about a beloved.

This two-part project is in its early stages; most of the results are too preliminary to discuss. But already three things are becoming clear. Romantic love has some universal properties, including heightened energy and focused attention on the adored individual. Men and women seem to feel this obsession in roughly equal proportions. And at least two of the brain's natural stimulants, dopamine and norepinephrine, appear to be involved in the feeling of romantic passion.

## Special Meaning

"The lane of love is narrow. There is room only for one." So wrote Kabir, a fifteenth-century poet of India. Pierre Teilhard de Chardin, the French naturalist, agreed, calling romantic love "a two-person universe." Gustave Flaubert may have described love best, saying, "She was the focal point of light at which the totality of things converged."

Neither the accumulated wisdom of the ages nor the wonders of technology have changed this salient property of romantic attraction:

It is focused on a single individual. In the beginning, you may waver between several candidates, feeling some passion for one, then obsession for another. But time passes, events occur, a moment of emotional truth comes, and you settle your attention on just one person. As psychologist Dorothy Tennov, a pioneer in the study of this emotion, puts it, a person takes on "special meaning."[4]

In our survey, 93 percent of women and 89 percent of men said they were unwilling to go out on a date with someone other than their beloved. Their hearts were full; there was no vacancy.

### Intrusive Thinking

Then you begin to think about your loved one—relentlessly. You replay tiny moments that you have shared. You wonder if this beguiling creature likes your kinds of books and movies. You fantasize about invigorating conversations and lovely times in bed. Known as "intrusive thinking," thoughts of the beloved invade your consciousness. As a woman living on the tiny South Pacific island of Mangaia summed it up, "Your mind goes wandering."[5]

Seventy-nine percent of men and 78 percent of women in our survey reported that when they were in class or at work their mind would wander to their beloved.

### Focused Attention

Typically, an infatuated person also begins to focus on, magnify, and aggrandize tiny aspects of the adored human being.

If pressed, almost all infatuated people can list what they do not like about their beloved. But they sweep these things aside or convince themselves that these defects are unique and charming. Then they dote on the positive parts of their sweetheart's physical features and personality. Some even adore the beloved for his or her faults.[6]

Stendhal, the French novelist, called this process "crystallization." He likened it to seeing the salt crystals that stick to the barren branches of winter trees: the eye transforms these common chemicals into tiny castles of sparkling beauty.[7] It's life through rose-colored glasses, the "pink-lens effect."[8]

Sixty-five percent of men and 55 percent of women in our survey agreed with the statement "____ has some faults but they don't really bother me."

Infatuated men and women not only dwell on tiny aspects of their beloved's personality and form, they also focus on little moments they have spent together. How he swam playfully beside her in the surf; how she sang to him as they walked arm in arm on a city street: to the love-possessed, these moments breathe. A touching literary example of this comes from ancient China. In the ninth century, Yüan Chen wrote the poem "The Bamboo Mat." "I cannot bear to put away / the bamboo sleeping mat: / that night I brought you home, / I watched you roll it out."

Seventy-two percent of men and 84 percent of women in our survey remembered trivial things that their beloved said and did. Eighty-two percent of men and 90 percent of women said they replayed these precious moments as they mused.

## Mood Swings

"The loving are the daring," wrote the nineteenth-century American writer Bayard Taylor. Infatuated men and women succumb to a barrage of powerful emotions. Elation is paramount. Infatuated people report feeling euphoria, buoyance, and increased energy; some even describe feeling "spiritual" sensations or feelings of "fusion" with the beloved. As a young man on the island of Mangaia described it, he "felt like jumping in the sky!"[9] Many become insomniacs. Many lose their appetite as well.

When infatuated men or women are suddenly with their beloved, they sometimes become exceedingly shy or awkward. Some tremble. Some flush. Some turn pale. Some stammer. Some get sweaty palms, weak knees, or dizzy spells, or feel butterflies in the stomach. Others report a pounding heart and accelerated breathing. And frequently underlying the infatuated person's angst and exhilaration is fear. In twelfth-century France, Andreas Capellanus wrote of this turmoil, "The heart of the lover begins to palpitate." Elvis Presley sang of it, "I'm in love; I'm all shook up."

Typically the smitten man or woman suffers intense mood swings, too. The telephone, the mailbox, a coffee bar or athletic club: you are at the mercy of any place or thing that might connect you to him or her. If the adored one gives some positive response, the lover becomes ecstatic. If rebuffed, the lover becomes what Stendhal called "dead blank." Thus, lovers fall into bleak depression; they are listless and irritable—brooding until they can explain away the setback, soothe their aching heart, and renew pursuit.

Eighty-five percent of women and 87 percent of men in our survey disagreed with the statement "____'s behavior has no effect on my emotional well-being."

In fact, both sexes are willing to sacrifice their time and money, occasionally even their lives, for their sweetheart. Keats wrote of his beloved Fanny Brawne, "I could die for you."

### Craving Emotional Union

The love-possessed also pray their love will be returned.[10]

This yearning for emotional union comes in many forms. Most lovers fantasize about what they hope to do together someday. Some become proprietary, even jealous, of the beloved's affections for family and friends. Many suffer separation anxiety when they are out of touch with their beloved. As a young Moroccan man said to his lover, "If I do not see you for just half a day I go crazy."[11] And most become hypersensitive to the cues that their adored one sends—as Robert Graves put it, "listening for a knock, waiting for a sign."

In our survey, 80 percent of men and 83 percent of women reported that when they were strongly attracted to someone, they dissected their beloved's actions, looking for clues about his or her feelings toward them.

### Out of Control

At the core of this obsession is its fickle power. Infatuation is unplanned, involuntary, irrational, and often uncontrollable. "It was irresistible," wrote Somerset Maugham. "The mind could not battle with it; friendship, gratitude, interest has no power beside it."

Sixty percent of the men and 70 percent of the women in our survey agreed with the statement "Falling in love is not really a choice, it just struck me."

We are not well-built creatures. We are "of two minds." The passion of love erupts from primitive emotion centers in the middle of the head, swamping the rational, thinking cerebral cortex, leaving us helpless in its wake. Romantic love has started wars. It has produced some of the finest literature, the most touching verse, the most compelling art, and the most haunting melodies. It has killed some and saved others. This obsession even stifles our most primal drives, including our need to eat and sleep.

Adversity even fans the flame. In what is known to psychologists as the Romeo-and-Juliet effect, barriers kindle infatuation. Even arguments or temporary breakups can be stimulating. As Terence, the Roman poet, wrote, "the less my hope, the hotter my love."

Sixty-five percent of the men and 71 percent of the women in our survey agreed with the statement "I never give up loving ____, even when things are going poorly."

## The Desire for Sexual Exclusivity

Of all the properties of romantic love, the most interesting to me is the lover's intense longing for sexual union with his or her beloved—coupled with a yearning for sexual exclusivity.

Eighty-three percent of the men and 90 percent of the women in our survey agreed with the statement "Being sexually faithful is more important when you are in love."

This craving for sexual exclusivity suggests to me that romantic love evolved for particular reasons: to enable individuals to focus their attention on specific partners, thereby conserving their mating energy; and to protect ancestral men and women from cuckoldry and abandonment, at least until their primal work of coupling and conceiving had been completed.

But even the desire for sexual intercourse does not supersede the drive for emotional union. In our survey, 75 percent of men and 83 percent of women agreed with the statement "Knowing that ____ is 'in love' with me is more important than having sex with him/her."

## Lust and Romantic Love: Two Different Emotions

Most people easily distinguish between romantic exhilaration and mere sexual release.[12] In fact, people in many cultures have different words for the sex drive and romantic love.[13] The Taita of Kenya, for example, distinguish between *ashiki* (lust) and *pendo* (love).[14]

So I have come to believe that these emotions arise from different, but often related, circuits in the brain. Lust and romantic attraction are distinct emotion systems.

After all, you can copulate with someone you are not "in love" with. You can be "in love" with someone you have never kissed. But the most compelling evidence that lust and romantic attraction are two distinct emotions comes from middle-aged Americans who get injections of testosterone to boost the sex drive. As the testosterone takes effect, their craving for sexual gratification increases—but they do not fall in love.

What happens in the brain when you fall in love?

## The Chemistry of Love

In 1983 psychiatrist Michael Liebowitz of the New York State Psychiatric Institute suggested that the exhilaration of romantic attraction is due to a brain bath of one or more natural stimulants, among them dopamine, norepinephrine, and/or serotonin.[15] As I have cataloged the above traits associated with romantic love, I have come to believe he is correct.

In the right doses, dopamine and norepinephrine give one feelings of euphoria and exhilaration[16]—primary ingredients of romantic love. These chemicals also cause sleeplessness, loss of appetite, excessive energy, and hyperactivity[17]—more primary characteristics of this passion. Very high levels of dopamine can make one feel anxious, fearful, even panicky[18]—further symptoms of intense romantic attaction.

Dopamine is also associated with focused attention, motivation, and goal-directed behaviors[19]—possibly explaining why the beloved takes on "special meaning." Dopamine probably also stimulates the intense motivation to see, talk with, and be with the beloved. Dopamine levels rise when people are in novel situations. Perhaps this is why so many lovers describe their beloved as unique.

Norepinephrine has been associated with imprinting, the curious animal habit of doggedly concentrating one's attention on another and following this individual everywhere that he or she wanders.[20] Infatuation may be a human form of imprinting. Norepinephrine is also associated with increased memory for new stimuli,[21] so it probably contributes to "crystallization," which includes the tendency of the bewitched lover to vividly remember novel moments spent with the beloved.

What causes the love-possessed to suffer from obsessive "intrusive thinking"?

These persistent intrusive thoughts have much in common with the racing thoughts of people suffering from obsessive-compulsive disorder. Obsessive-compulsive individuals continually rerun their ideas and feelings in their heads. Physicians currently treat most forms of obsessive-compulsive disorder with serotonin boosters.[22] So, at the moment, I speculate that intrusive thinking occurs as levels of dopamine and norepinephrine soar—and levels of serotonin plummet.

Passionate romantic attraction takes a variety of graded forms, of course, ranging from pure joy when one's love is reciprocated to emptiness, anxiety, and despair when it is not returned. Undoubtedly a host of chemicals—in varying concentrations and combinations—are involved in this complex range of feelings. But I am convinced that romantic love is a distinct emotion category, associated with a specific set of chemicals, regions, and circuits in the brain. Moreover, this universal human emotion evolved.

### Animal Magnetism

Many birds and mammals display heightened energy and focused attention when they court. In 1871 Darwin wrote of this fever among mallard ducks. Mallards form pair-bonds to rear their young, as most birds do. But one particular female mallard became attracted to a pintail—a duck of a different species! "It was evidently a case of love at first sight," Darwin wrote, "for she swam about the new-comer caressingly. . . . From that hour she forgot her old partner."[23]

The animal literature is filled with such descriptions. Dogs, horses, gorillas, canaries: males and females of many species assiduously avoid mating with some comrades and doggedly focus their attention on others. Scientists call this animal attraction "favoritism," "sexual preference," or "mate choice."[24] Are these creatures "attracted" to one another? I think so. Animal attraction is a simple chemical mechanism, nature's way of ensuring that males and females of any sexually reproducing species notice some within the crowd and draw close to these specific individuals to start the mating process.

Many creatures have even developed distinctive physical traits to trigger attraction in others of their breed. Violet-colored feathers, orange beaks, symmetrical faces, pink rumps: those with gaudy accoutrements made potential partners turn and notice, capturing the fancy of those around them. Along with the evolution of all these display ornaments must have come corresponding brain mechanisms to enable observers to actually feel attraction.

When, where, or how long a creature actively feels this attraction undoubtedly varies from one species to the next. In mice, it may last only seconds. Among our primate forebears living in the trees, this bliss, this fever may have lasted hours, days, or weeks.

But after our human ancestors began to walk the plains of ancient Africa, after the cerebral cortex began to expand, after humankind developed language, fire, song, and art, ancestral men and women must have begun to compose myths and legends, stir love potions, draw love symbols, carve love amulets, sing love songs, and recount joyous tales about this thing we would come to call romantic love.

### Men's Eternal Weakness: Beauty

Judging by our preliminary investigation of this madness, as well as the limited data in the psychological literature, both sexes feel passionate romantic love with roughly the same intensity.[25] Nature has granted neither men nor women immunity from this fire. But unquestionably the sexes have developed different tastes in whom they find attractive.

Men are beguiled by beauty.

Psychologist David Buss of the University of Texas at Austin and his colleagues asked over ten thousand people in thirty-seven societies to examine a list of eighteen traits and rank them in their order of importance in selecting a spouse.[26] Interestingly, men and women put many qualities in exactly the same order. Love, or mutual attraction, came first for both sexes. Next came a dependable character, emotional stability and maturity, and a pleasing disposition. Both men and women also wanted a spouse who was kind, healthy, smart, educated, sociable, and interested in home and family.

But from Zululand to Poland, from Colombia to Taiwan, men were

more interested than women in a partner's physical appearance—
particularly youth and beauty. When Americans place ads in the
personals, men are three times more likely than women to seek a
good-looking partner.[27] And Buss maintains that this male preference
for youth and beauty is inherited. Young skin, gleaming teeth, vibrant
eyes, shiny hair, firm muscles, a lithe figure, a buoyant personality:
these are all visual cues of health, youth, and vitality.[28]

In fact, a pleasing ratio of waist to hips, clear skin, babylike and
symmetrical facial features, and small feet are all associated with high
levels of estrogen and low levels of testosterone—indicators of good
reproductive health.[29] Unknowingly, the Yanomamo Indians of the
Amazonian rain forest put this Darwinian perspective succinctly.
They call their most desirable women *moko dude,* "perfectly ripe."[30]

Women may deplore these masculine tastes for youth, beauty, and
a supple, curvy figure, but many of them exploit these male vul-
nerabilities unmercifully. In parts of Amazonia, women wear a string
belt around the waist. This supports a cord that runs between their
vulvar lips and up through their buttocks to loop around the belt and
form a tassel that swings along the rump as they walk.

American women are only slightly less shameless. We wear makeup
to widen our eyes, redden our cheeks, whiten our brow, fill out our
lips, and smooth our skin—all to look young. We squeeze into tight
shoes to make our feet look smaller. We dye our hair blond, the sweet
yellow of children's hair. Some pay surgeons huge sums to crush
and remold their noses into babylike shapes, strip the skin from
their facial muscles to pull it taut, or suck the fat from their buttocks to achieve the "right" proportions.[31] And women of all ages wear
push-up bras, short skirts, tight belts, and mesh stockings to look
youthful and voluptuous.

Women seem to know that these traits advertise good health to
men. And with the flourishing industries in cosmetics and plastic surgery, many are finding it easier and easier to display youth and beauty.

Because men are so susceptible to visual signals—which are
seen easily and immediately—they generally fall in love faster than
women do.[32]

## Women Love Resources

"The great question that has never been answered and which I have not been able to answer, despite my thirty years of research into the feminine soul, is 'what does a woman want?'" So wrote Sigmund Freud to Marie Bonaparte.

Today scientists have begun to know what women want. Women vary, just as men do. But women often fall in love with men who have resources, men with money, education, or position—assets similar to those that prehistoric women needed to rear their young.[33] Women are attracted to men who sit in a relaxed pose, lean back, nod less frequently, and gesture more—signs of dominance.[34] Women gravitate to men who are three to five years older than themselves, and to men who are industrious, ambitious, and respected. They like smart men. Although both sexes like intelligent partners, women are slightly more interested in a long-term partner who is intelligent.[35]

Women like "good-looking" men, too, preferably those with a strong jaw (a sign of high levels of testosterone) and those with a moderately developed torso.[36] Women generally prefer tall men, perhaps because tall men tend to hold more prestigious positions in the business world, as well as offer greater physical protection.[37] Women also want men who are strong, physically well coordinated, and in good health.[38]

American sports groupies all but line up to copulate with basketball and football players. These stargazers are not extraordinary. In the jungles of Amazonia, Mehinaku girls whisper "*awitsiri*," "beautiful," as they admire the best wrestlers in their village.[39]

Most important, women are looking for a long-term partner who will share his status and financial assets.[40]

And to calculate a man's wealth, status, and generosity, a woman must study him. This takes time. Not that women take months or years to size up a kind heart or plump wallet; sometimes two dates, even two hours, will suffice. But because of the complex nature of what women want, women are less likely to fall in love moments after meeting.[41]

## Love at First Sight

Both sexes do fall in love at first sight, however.

In thirteenth-century England, Chaucer wrote of the moment Troilus saw Cressida, "Looking through the crowd / His eye did penetrate, and went so deep, / That on Cressida it struck, and there did keep."[42] Troilus fell in love in a single glance.

The same occurred to a woman on the tiny island of Mangaia while shopping in a grocery store. "When I saw this man, I wished that he would be my husband, and this feeling was a surprise because I had never seen him before," she told anthropologist Helen Harris.[43] Eventually she married the man. Years later she reflected on the experience, saying the meeting had been "nature's work."

Love at first sight is nature's work. Most animals cannot delay; they have only a few hours, days, or weeks to breed. At the beginning of the breeding season or cycle, they are obliged to select an adequate partner and begin mating. Instant attraction probably evolved to enable them to begin this process swiftly.

Moreover, there is evidence that brain chemistry is involved in their instant attraction. When a female prairie vole, a tiny rodent, receives a drop of male urine on her upper lip, levels of norepinephrine in her brain increase. This surge, in conjunction with other chemical reactions, stimulates the beginning of estrus and mating behavior.[44] Likewise, when female sheep are shown slides of the faces of male sheep, levels of norepinephrine spike in the brain, but only when they are "in heat."

In prairie voles and sheep, attraction may last only seconds; in people it can last months or years.

## Why Him? Why Her?

So men are often attracted to women who show signs of youth and beauty, while women tend to gravitate to men with status and resources. But why do we feel that chemical torrent for one particular person rather than another?

"To every thing there is a season," the Bible says. The timing must be right. If you have just left home for college, are displaced in a foreign city, have recovered from a former relationship, feel comfortable at work or school, have extra time, or are lonely and need a friend, you are in the right condition to fall in love.[45]

Both sexes are also attracted to those who are slightly mysterious. As Baudelaire wrote of this phenomenon, "We love women in proportion to their degree of strangeness to us." The sense that one has a slippery grip on an elusive, impenetrable, boundless treasure is a potent ingredient of romantic love.[46] In fact, scientists now think that sometime between ages three and six, boys and girls lose forever any potential romantic interest in those whom they see regularly. This repulsion from the familiar, they say, is seen in many mammals: it evolved to discourage breeding between close kin.[47]

Attraction to dissimilar others and a distaste for highly familiar people seems to operate on the chemical level. When women are asked to smell men's sweaty T-shirts and report on which they think are the most "sexy smelling," they tend to choose T-shirts of men who have dissimilar immune systems.[48]

Interestingly, women taking contraceptive pills, which partly mimic pregnancy, tend to pick men with similar immune systems. So Claus Wedekind of the Zoological Institute at Bern University in Switzerland reasons that women make these choices because pregnant women are naturally predisposed to surround themselves with kin, whereas those who are ovulating unconsciously seek partners with a different immune system.

The Hutterites of South Dakota are good at picking partners with a different immune system. The members of this tight-knit religious sect are all descendants of sixty-four individuals who migrated to America in the 1870s; they are very closely related. But DNA testing shows that Hutterite men and women regularly choose to wed individuals with different immune systems.[49]

Timing, mystery, differences in the immune system: undoubtedly many other biological factors coalesce to trigger brain circuits when a particular person smiles at you from across a crowded room. But of all the things that can ignite that blaze, the most important is your childhood.

## Love Maps

We grow up in a kaleidoscopic world of experiences and ideas that form our romantic tastes.

Your father's sense of humor and interest in politics or films; your mother's way with words and her aesthetic sense; how parents punctuate their sentences with silence or laughter; what siblings regard as irritating or challenging; how teachers view justice, honor, and kindness; what friends admire or find disgusting or intimate: thousands upon thousands of subtle forces build our individual beliefs, interests, and values. So by our teens, we each carry deep within us a list of characteristics we are looking for in a mate.

Sexologist John Money of Johns Hopkins University calls this unconscious mental template a "love map." He thinks that children begin to develop these maps between ages five and eight and that the maps solidify at puberty.[50] Then these love maps guide us as we row our boats through the sea of mating opportunities—and land us on foreign shores as we fall head over heels in love.

How the love maps of men and women vary is impossible to say. These idiosyncratic psychological charts are too complex to be precisely identified or compared. But I'll hazard a guess at one outstanding difference between the sexes.

From reading the psychological literature and watching my male friends, I have come to believe that one of men's most significant traits is a deep desire to feel needed by a woman. Men want to help, to solve the problem, to be useful by "doing" something. Men often enter a love relationship to "rescue" a woman; many also stay in unhappy marriages because they feel their presence is essential—they are needed. Millions of years of protecting and providing for women seem to have bred into men a deep need to be useful to a mate.

Women, on the other hand, seem to want to feel cherished by a partner. Perhaps women seek to be adored because they instinctively feel a devoted man will also be kind and generous to their young.

So *when* you fall in love, *whom* you fall in love with, *where* you fall in love, *what* you find attractive in a lover, *how* you court your sweetheart, even *whether* you regard this passion as divine or subversive, varies from one society and one individual to the next. But once you find that special person—be it a spouse or a lover—the actual physical feeling you have *as* you experience this passion is chemical. It is built into the human brain. Human beings inherited the capacity to love.

How will this ancient brain circuitry for romantic attraction fare as women become more economically and socially powerful?

Extremely well. One of the outstanding social trends of the coming century, I believe, will be the revival and celebration of romantic love. And it will be women who shepherd us along this tortuous road of passionate romance.

## The Rise of Romantic Love

Americans love love. Most of us regard romance as an elixir—and a sufficient reason to take marriage vows.

But in almost all traditional societies, men and women have felt that romantic passion was an inappropriate reason to wed, at least the first time around. Marriage was regarded an an important business contract. One had to pick a spouse with the right kin and political connections. So parents arranged their children's first betrothal.[51]

Many arranged marriages become romantic, of course. In India, people still say, "First we marry, then we fall in love." Nevertheless, many men and women around the world have entered arranged marriages with tremendous disappointment; secretly they loved another. So in many parts of the world, this passion has been feared. It could make a person do foolish things—as well as topple the delicate balance of social obligation.

The ancient Greeks were of this persuasion: one did not wed for love. They celebrated romantic love—as long as it was between men and boys, patrons and courtesans, or householders and their concubines. But among the upper classes, marriage was a formal alliance between families and clans; it was designed to maintain political ties, secure inheritances, and ensure the correct distribution of property.[52]

Roman nobles also delighted in their slaves, their prostitutes, and their concubines. But they, too, held their lineages and their inheritances together with carefully arranged betrothals.[53]

The early Christian Church fathers sounded a death knell for romantic love of any sort. These ascetics saw obsessive love for another mortal as a carnal pleasure of the flesh, unfit for godly men and women. Only a pure spiritual love of the Lord brought happiness and salvation. Even passionate longing for one's own wife was shameful to God-fearing Christians. So, by the Middle Ages, passionate romantic yearning had come to be regarded as a demonic possession, a form of temporary insanity.[54]

Undoubtedly many village men and women, even lords and ladies, secretly loved one another passionately as they slipped into bed at night. But as Vincent of Beauvais wrote in his *Speculum Doctrinale,* a manual widely followed in the Middle Ages, "The upright man should love his wife with his judgment, not his affections."[55]

## The Pursuit of Happiness

Romantic love gained some respectability among the troubadours of twelfth-century France. These roving bards, entertainers, and knights sang of the anguish and despair of hopeless, unrequited, unconsummated love. They warbled in the vernacular of Provence, not in Latin chants. Everyone could understand their words, so their melodies of torment and desire percolated from court to court across what is today France, Italy, and Germany. To the troubadours, marriage was still bound by duty, property, and alliance. But outside of wedlock, unconsummated, unrequited romantic passion came to be regarded as honorable, even chivalrous.

In the thirteenth century, Dante would immortalize his passion for Beatrice in prose and poetry. Undoubtedly, less erudite men and women also loved passionately throughout the Middle Ages and early Renaissance.

The spread of literacy in the sixteenth and seventeenth centuries intensified the acceptance of romance. The printing press was spinning off Shakespeare's plays and sonnets, as well as other love poems and stories.[56] And by the eighteenth century, intellectuals began to speak out. Jean-Jacques Rousseau thumbed his nose at arranged marriages, for example, proclaiming the virtues of romantic love.[57] The poor agreed with him. About one third of all European men and women had no lands or other substantial property, and eighteenth-century British court recordings suggest that these people often wed for love.[58]

But advice books, medical texts, and religious sermons of the times still discounted romantic love as an appropriate reason to wed.[59]

The Industrial Revolution spurred Western enthusiasm for romantic love. In the late eighteenth and early nineteenth centuries, textile mills began to rise in Europe and America. Trade flourished. Cities spread, pulling our forebears off the farm—away from families that forced them into arranged weddings. In this urban bustle, parents no longer needed the political and economic connections that arranged betrothals bought.

So along with the many economic and social forces that fueled the Industrial Revolution came the belief that matrimony was best achieved when individuals chose their partners for themselves— provided that their parents agreed to the match.[60]

The Romantic poets of England and the Continent enshrined this trend, extolling the joys and sorrows of passionate love in highly charged verse. For the less sophisticated, pulp novels became the rage. "Cupid's fiery shaft," as Shakespeare called this bolt of passion, had struck the Western heart.

## Marrying for Love

The custom of marrying a person whom you are deeply "in love" with has became more and more popular with every decade of the twentieth century.

In the 1960s, 65 percent of 503 American college men surveyed would not marry a woman whom they did not love—even if she had every trait they were looking for in a mate.[61] Women were more circumspect. Twenty-four percent of 576 college women said they would refuse to wed a man they did not love, even if he was an ideal partner; 72 percent were undecided.

Today these figures have changed. In a 1991 survey, 86 percent of men and 91 percent of women said they would unquestionably not wed someone they were not in love with.[62] More remarkable, today more than 50 percent of both sexes believe that if romantic passion fades, this is sufficient reason for divorce.[63]

Most Westerners see love as the very core of their emotional and social life. They feel deprived without it. To be sure, some still marry for status or financial gain. And many still cherish novels and

operas—where thwarted love predominates as it did among the troubadours. But when they climb into bed at night, they want to look
across the pillow at a sweetheart.

Their taste for romance is spreading around the world.

## "Free Love"

"Fall in love, fall into disgrace," a Chinese proverb says. The Chinese have long felt that matters of the heart were inconsequential
compared to an essential: the family. So across the centuries, countless millions of Chinese men and women married those whom their
parents chose. Honor, duty, and respect were paramount; one's ancestors and descendants were at stake.[64] As a Chinese slogan summed
it up, "You have only one family, but you can always get another
wife."[65]

Some lovers foiled their parents' plans by hurling themselves into
the family well or swallowing rat poison. Many went forth to their
arranged betrothals instead—often with a broken heart. The rich
chose concubines to love. And professional storytellers sang of this
passion in the markets and teahouses of imperial China.[66] But the
masses feared this profound and fickle passion.

"It is the heart always that sees, before the head can see," wrote
Thomas Carlyle. This idea began to emerge in China with the Opium
Wars of the nineteenth century. By the 1920s, some Chinese had
begun to pick partners for themselves—a tradition they called "free
love."

Times officially changed in 1952 with the Marriage Reform
Act. This law proclaimed, "Marriage shall be based upon the complete willingness of the two parties."[67] Chinese Communists regarded arranged marriages as barbaric: one should choose one's own
life mate.

Since 1976 more than five hundred new magazines have begun to
circulate in China—many devoted to courtship, romance, and wedding.[68] Currently, more than thirty-five television programs portray
love triangles and unrequited love. Today only 5.8 percent of young
men and women in Hong Kong say they would marry a person they
are not in love with—even if this person has all the other qualities
they desire in a partner.[69] Although Hong Kong is a cosmopolitan cen-

ter and does not reflect views in vast areas of China, these figures nonetheless mark a distinct change in attitude.

From hamlets in the Arctic to encampments in the Australian outback, men and women are choosing partners for themselves. In a study of thirty-seven societies, men and women ranked love or mutual attraction as the primary criterion for wedding.[70] Only in India and Pakistan, where the standard of living is low and the extended family is still exceedingly important to economic life, are some 50 percent of men and women willing to wed without this passion.[71]

Moreover, everywhere that marriages are still largely arranged, as in India, some Muslim countries, and sub-Saharan Africa, youths regularly meet their betrothed before their wedding day—to approve or reject the match.[72]

Arranged marriages, sometimes loveless, are on their way off this braid of human life.

## Polygyny Begone

So is polygyny—having more than one wife at a time.[73] Some 84 percent of societies still permit a man to take several wives; many even encourage it. But in most of these cultures, such as Muslim societies, only some 5 percent to 20 percent of men actually acquire enough wealth and status to create a harem.[74]

For these men, polygyny pays. Although they are undoubtedly unaware of the genetic benefits of harem building, polygynous husbands can impregnate several women within the same time period and spread their seed disproportionately.

Women in these societies traditionally joined a harem because they reasoned it was better to be the second or third wife of a rich man than the only wife of a poor one. Today, however, fewer and fewer women are willing to share a husband; they seek a romantic—and exclusive—partnership.

Many of these advocates of monogamy stood for hours in 1997 in Tehran to see the movie *Leila*, a story about a young Iranian woman who is deeply in love with her husband. The couple has what appears to be an enchanting marriage, until Leila discovers she is barren. Soon her mother-in-law begins to pressure Leila's husband to take a second wife, something he does not want to do. Finally he marries a second woman and fathers a child. Meanwhile Leila has fled to her parents' home. The new couple soon divorce, however, and the moviegoer is left wondering if Leila and her husband will reunite.

*Leila* caused an uproar in Tehran. Men and women waited hours outside movie houses to see the film. As eighteen-year-old Farima Sanati said to reporters about polygyny as she waited in a long line, "a woman cannot bear these things."[75]

## Pulp Love

Along with the opportunity to chose a partner for yourself come decisions. Not surprisingly, today both sexes are looking for guidance on how to court and choose a mate.

*The Bridges of Madison County,* a novel about a romance between a married woman and a traveling photographer, sold millions of copies in America during the early 1990s; its cinema version pulled in throngs of moviegoers, too. *The Rules,* a book that dictated explicit rules for courting, caught the American imagination like a forest fire. Television dramas and situation comedies about lovers or would-be lovers continue to proliferate as well.

TV talk shows, such as *Oprah,* have also skyrocketed in popularity. These fascinating forums offer the viewer a many-sided experience: psychologists who give advice, an audience that acts like a classical Greek chorus mouthing the mores of the culture, and a wrenching glimpse of the suffering that star-crossed lovers can experience.

The expanding worldwide imperative to be "in love" will undoubtedly create a thirst for more and more novels, self-help books, advice columns, movies, TV serials, and talk shows that script the glories and heartbreaks of the courting process. With their emotional sensitivity, their empathy, their curiosity about people, their linguistic skills, and their interest in relationships and romance, women will undoubtedly author or produce most of these treatises on romance.

Women will set the agenda for how many of us conduct our romantic lives.

## Picking Lovers

As women become more economically powerful, they may also make some changes in whom they choose to love.

Love is not random. "That first fine careless rapture," to borrow Robert Browning's phrase, is generally directed toward someone like oneself. Most women and men feel that magic for unfamiliar people of the same ethnic and social group, similar economic background, religion, and level of education, the same degree of physical attractiveness and level of intelligence.[76] They also tend to fall in love with individuals who have a similar sense of humor, the same political and social values, and similar beliefs and feelings about life in general.[77]

However, as the media broadcast more images of people from different backgrounds, and as more women have careers and money of their own, more may pick partners from different social or ethnic groups. In fact, in the United States interracial marriages increased some 800 percent between 1960 and 1990.[78]

Women may also become less interested in men's money—although the data on this issue are mixed. In a survey of 1,111 personal advertisements placed in American newspapers and magazines, women sought a partner with financial power some eleven times more frequently than men did.[79] Exceedingly rich women and high-achieving women often seek men with even more wealth and status.[80]

Nevertheless, some studies suggest that women's taste for men's resources is becoming tempered. In the 1980s, Japanese women—who generally had very little economic power of their own—valued a spouse's financial potential as roughly 150 percent more important than Japanese men did. But in Holland, where women were considerably more financially independent, women rated a mate's monetary status as only 36 percent more important than men did.[81]

### Virtual Love

In America today, 60 percent of men and women are introduced to their spouse through a friend.[82] But women are also pursuing love in a variety of other ways, including love on the Internet.

This is not as unusual as it might seem. People in India have a long tradition of advertising for spouses in the newspapers. Ever since European settlers began to trickle into North America, women from foreign lands have climbed aboard ships or airplanes to meet and marry men they have never seen before. But there is a difference between these arranged meetings and dating on the Internet. Even brides who wed through a modern agency have an intermediary who ostensibly has their best interests in mind. On the Internet, no one is facilitating the communication.

See no evil; hear no evil; touch no evil. When you date in cyberspace, all you have are words. What a haven for deceit.

Deception is part of courting, of course. The object is not honesty but illusion. One must impress. As Harry Truman once said, "If you can't convince 'em, confuse 'em." So males of many species strut, display their antlers, shimmer their feathers, shake their tails, charge their rivals, defend their surroundings, or just puff up to look important. Females display their buttocks, wag their heads, stretch their necks, or curl their bodies inward to signal approachability instead.

Humans are no exception. From fancy wristwatches to face-lifts, men and women deceive with hundreds of courting cues that camouflage or magnify who they really are.

But cyberspace is a veritable breeding ground for chicanery—as a woman in Virginia discovered.

In 1997 the Associated Press reported on a woman in Alexandria, Virginia, who fell in love with someone in a "chat room" on the Internet.[83] Soon daily e-mail messages became a barrage of telephone calls. She met her man in a romantic but chaste rendezvous in New Mexico. He proposed. She accepted. They made plans to wed. On their wedding day her spouse bound his chest with elastic bandages, claiming injuries suffered in a car accident. Soon after the wedding the skulduggery became evident: he wasn't Mr. Right; he wasn't even Mister. The new bride began proceedings to annul her marriage to a woman.

The Internet can be a useful tool for lovers, though. Many couples meet in person first, then begin romantic exchanges via e-mail. This new form of letter writing does allow people to express themselves in ways that they may be too shy to try in person. The Internet will certainly expand our opportunities to court a sweetheart and kindle the magic of romance.

### Homosexual Love

More women may also explore another path to romantic passion: homosexuality.

Although polls say that Americans are no more accepting of homo-sexuality today than they were in past decades, it seems quite obvious that same-sex love is becoming far less scorned in America and abroad. So as women gain economic independence, more of those who feel drawn to other women will feel free to express this taste.

Gay and lesbian romances differ in several ways. Gay men are far less likely to live with a partner. Fewer than half of gay men share a household with a mate.[84] And many of these men and their compan-ions have an implicit or explicit agreement that they will engage in oc-casional sex with others.[85] Lesbians more often seek permanent partnerships based on fidelity.[86] Some 75 percent of lesbians live in committed relationships, and lesbians express much more interest in affection and intimacy.[87] Like straight women, lesbians relish romance.

Lesbians are a tiny percentage of the population. As discussed in chapter 8, only 2.8 percent of American men and 1.4 percent of American women identify themselves as primarily homosexual.[88] But these men and women speak out. They march for their rights and broadcast their beliefs in a variety of other ways. Today many of our movies and books have gay themes.

These women and men are spreading what may well become a twenty-first-century ideal: the pursuit of happiness through romantic love.

## Senior Love: The Snowbirds

"But for real true love,—love at first sight, love to devotion, love that robs a man of his sleep . . . we believe the best age is from forty-five to seventy." So said Anthony Trollope in *Barchester Towers.*

Romance among the elderly is becoming commonplace.[89] Today more women and men live longer and remain healthier in their ad-vancing years. Many maintain their own homes rather than moving in with their children when they are widowed or divorced. They also mix at activities for senior citizens. They have the time, the energy, and the opportunity to find romance in their senior years.

Widower Harold Goodman and Marj Lintz met one evening as they were bowling. "She was it," he recalls. "I was overwhelmed by him," she remembers thinking. They have lived together for nine years. In

1998 he was aged ninety-two; she was eighty. As they say, "We are one."[90]

The most remarkable story I have heard about senior love, however, is of a man whose daughter insisted that he move into a home for the elderly; apparently she wanted his house for herself. He lived in the institution for several months. Then one morning he climbed on his bicycle and rode over a hundred miles to a trailer park in Texas he had heard about. Here senior citizens from all over the country rendezvous in their campers in the winter. "Snowbirds," these travelers call themselves. He met a woman and fell in love. They have been rolling across North America's byways in her camper ever since.

Romantic love is not, of course, only for the widowed. In one survey, men and women who had been married more than twenty years tested higher on romantic passion for each other than did those married only five years. In fact, their scores looked much like those of high school seniors.[91]

As women and men live longer, more and more may find a December love and say, "We are one."

## Polyamory: An Intimacy Network

A curious form of modern love is polyamory—having many loves or an "intimacy network."

Unlike swingers, who seek copulation with a variety of partners, those who engage in polyamory say they are interested in forming long-term loving relationships with more than one individual.[92] Most polyamorous people are deeply attached to a spouse. But as Brett Hill of Boulder, Colorado, an editor of *Loving More*, puts it, "one person is not going to meet all your needs."

So spouses agree to be honest with each other and handle these extracurricular relationships discreetly. Generally they establish rules. They may decide that each spouse must come home at night to sleep; no dates on Friday, family night; and no long phone conversations with a paramour until the children have gone to bed. Some groups of polyamorous individuals live in the same house and regard themselves as married to one another. In one "marital" celebration, six figures stood atop the wedding cake.

Polyamorous people say their lifestyle allows them to express different kinds of loving feelings: lusty sexuality, passionate infatuation, deep attachment. Avid participants have even formed a national association with an annual convention. And they endlessly discuss their complex love lives with other polyamorous individuals on the Internet.

Jealousy is a problem. In fact, at the San Francisco–based Sacred Space Institute, a center for polyamory, advocates of "responsible nonmonogamy" give workshops with exercises in which one practices feeling happy that a mate is in bed with someone else.

I am not surprised that jealousy plagues just about all polyamorous relationships. As you recall, a hallmark of romantic passion is a deep desire for sexual exclusivity.

### The Green Ey'd Monster

"Passion is a malady. It's possession, something dark. You are jealous of everything. There's no lightness, no harmony," wrote the French author Georges Simenon. Both sexes get jealous, in every society where scientists have studied love.[93] Shakespeare called it the "green ey'd monster." It is ubiquitous. And as romantic attraction becomes more and more acceptable, I think the world will see more and more jealous lovers.

Men and women become jealous over many of the same things. Hugging, flirting with, or dancing with another can rev up possessiveness in a mate or partner. Stumbling upon a partner in the act of coitus with a lover can drive both men and women berserk.[94] Moreover, men and women often handle their jealousy in the same ways. Both belittle their rival, attend to their mate's wants, guard their mate, and threaten their mate. Both also try to look richer, more important, sexier, or smarter than their rival.[95]

However, the sexes do show some differences in what triggers jealousy and how they manage a jealous heart. Women are more willing to overlook a one-night stand, even a brief affair, if they can convince themselves the dalliance was temporary and meaningless. If a beloved forms an emotional attachment to a rival, however, and begins to divert his resources to this contender, a woman can seethe with jealousy.[96]

As women tend to worry about the emotional connection between their mate and their rival, men are more likely to fume over real or imagined sexual indiscretions.[97] Men are much more likely to act overtly competitive toward their rival, with verbal or physical abuse. They also turn on their partner. In fact men's jealousy is the most common cause of wife battering and murder everywhere in the world.[98]

It is hard to love a jealous person. Havelock Ellis called jealousy "that dragon which slays love under the pretense of keeping it alive." Yet jealousy seems to have several reproductive payoffs. It can stimulate a partner to reassure his or her jealous mate with soothing words and comforting deeds—reassurances that contribute to the stability of the relationship.[99] Jealousy can also drive a couple apart, reducing the male's likelihood of being cuckolded and enabling the female to renew her search for a mate more to her satisfaction.

This unattractive emotion, jealousy, is probably spun tightly into the human brain, part of a constellation of feelings that men and women inherited to win the mating game.

Another seems to be the excruciating pain we feel when we are abandoned by a beloved.

### Lovesickness

"Of all the emotions, there is none more violent than love," wrote Cicero. Who hasn't been rejected? I have found only two people who told me they had never been "dumped" by a person whom they really loved. Both were men. Both were handsome, rich, successful, and quite shallow. Each had his problems. One was trapped in an ugly marriage to an alcoholic socialite. The other had been savagely maligned by business partners. But neither had been dropped by someone he adored.

I suspect these men are rare. When students at Case Western Reserve were asked about romantic rejection, 93 percent of both men and women reported that they had been discarded by someone with whom they had been deeply in love. Ninety-five percent of both men and women also said they had rejected someone who was wildly in love with them.[100] Few escape the feelings of emptiness, hopelessness, fear, and fury that abandonment can produce—anywhere in the world.

A rejected Chinese woman wrote of this, "I can't bear life. All my interests in life have disappeared."[101] A Polynesian woman moaned, "I was lonely and really sad and I cried. I stopped eating and didn't sleep well; I couldn't keep my mind on my work."[102] Poet Seamus Heaney described the feeling of rejection best, however: "In your presence time rode easy, anchored on a smile; but absence rocked love's balance, unmoored the days." He goes on to say, "You've gone, I am at sea. / Until you resume command, / Self is in mutiny."

Neither sex escapes this despair. Yet the sexes vary in how they deal with romantic rejection.

## Stalking

Men are more dependent on their romantic partners than women are,[103] probably because men have fewer ties to relatives and friends. Perhaps because of this, men are more likely to turn to drink, drugs, or reckless driving, and men are three to four times more likely to commit suicide after a love affair has ended.[104]

Men also stalk; they have a harder time letting go.[105] The U.S. Justice Department reports that more than a million women are stalked every year; the vast majority are between the ages of eighteen and thirty-nine—the height of their reproductive years. Fifty-nine percent are stalked by a husband, a former spouse, a live-in partner, or a boyfriend.[106] One out of twelve will be stalked by a man at some point in her life, usually by a former husband or lover.[107]

Some men besiege a coldhearted lover with letters, cards, flowers, faxes, e-mail messages, or presents. Some call incessantly in the middle of the night. Some wiretap the victim's telephone. Some follow in a car. Some leap from the bushes as a former sweetheart comes home from work, either to talk or to hurl insults. Some physically attack. Over 50 percent of stalkers threaten their victims; some 25 percent to 35 percent of them become violent; 2 percent actually end up killing their victims.[108] Most are men.

Women also have difficulty releasing a rejecting partner. The clingy type will not let go. She cries, feigns helplessness, sleeps on the man's doorstep, sends cards and letters, or telephones incessantly. "Let go or be dragged," an aphorism warns. These women choose to take the bumps. Some 370,000 men, most between the ages of eighteen and thirty-nine, were stalked in 1997.[109]

But rejected women do not display the physical aggressiveness of rejected men. They are more likely to fall into clinical depression. They also talk. Although women can get some relief from talking about their feelings, these endless conversations can backfire. As women dwell on the defunct relationship, they feed the ghost.

"Love is so short, forgetting is so long." Thus poet Pablo Neruda captured the suffering that people around the world feel when they have been rejected by a beloved.

### Controlling Love

The Tuareg Muslims of Nigeria call romantic passion *tamazai,* "an illness of the heart and soul." Many American psychologists go further, regarding romantic love as an addiction.[110] I agree. Moreover, I suspect that unrequited love drives up levels of dopamine and/or norepinephrine in the brain to a point where these natural stimulants actually produce the anxiety and despair that rejected lovers feel. Other brain chemicals probably kick in, adding depth, shading, and complexity to one's anguish.

Despite the chemical nature of this condition, I think you can control romantic passion, just as you can control fear or anger. But you must employ your intellectual faculties. Throw out your beloved's cards and letters. Don't call. Don't write. Flee if you see him or her in the office or on the street. Call friends. Get some exercise. Develop little sayings you can silently repeat to soothe or distract yourself. Do almost anything. But stay away from your drug of choice, your inattentive lover. Eventually the brain chemistry for this passion will wane.

But can you jump-start feelings of infatuation for someone with whom you would like to fall in love? Shakespeare played with this idea in *A Midsummer Night's Dream.* Puck is employed to sprinkle a magic potion on the dreaming eyelids of Titania, Queen of the Fairies—driving her to fall in love with the first creature she sees when she wakes up. Alas, she beholds Bottom, a man with the head of an ass.

We have all hoped, at one time or another, to own a magic charm that would help us or someone else to fall in love. Mandrake root, sea slugs, ginseng, anchovies, dried frog, mare's sweat, oysters, fleawort sap, goat's testicles: hundreds, probably thousands, of items and concoctions have been employed to catch or keep a lover.

None will ever work. Although the feeling of romantic attraction is a chemical experience, this passion flares only when the time is right and you find someone who fits within your love map. None of us falls in love randomly.

## Love in the Time of Woman

We will never know which sex loves more intensely, more enduringly, or more constantly. In a study of students at the University of Miami, 64 percent of women said they were in love, while only 46 percent of men reported being in love.[111] Among students surveyed in Russia and Japan, slightly more women than men reported that they were in love.[112] From these slim findings, women appear to be somewhat more inclined to indulge this passion.

Without question, however, women celebrate this emotion more regularly than do men. Discussions of love and dating dominate women's magazines. Romance novels are sold in fifty-two countries—almost exclusively to women. Women like their pornography laced with romantic plots. Some 85 percent of American valentine cards are bought by women.[113] And in their spare time, women tend to read or talk about love far more than men do.[114]

As arranged marriages become artifacts of history and romantic love sweeps into the marital expectations of young and old around the world, the twenty-first century will see more dating, more dating deception, and more avenues to meet potential partners, from ads in the personals to matchmakers of all kinds. Coming decades will also witness more songs, books, movies, TV serials, advice columns, and talk shows about love. Experimental kinds of love, such as polyamory and romance on the Internet, should proliferate. New holidays to celebrate love may emerge. More people will marry because they are passionately in love—and more will divorce when romance dies. More people will suffer from unrequited love; more will also be involved in crimes of passion. And more men and women will look for love again and again and again—in adolescence, midlife, and their senior years.

Hail the spread of romantic love, with all of its hopes and joys and sorrows. It has become unleashed in our modern world. With their natural talents, women will be our guides on this intoxicating voyage—even set the agenda for how, where, when, and with whom we express this ancient human passion.

# CHAPTER 10

# PEER MARRIAGE

## The Reformation of Matrimony

True love. Is it normal,
is it serious, is it practical?
What does the world get from two people
who exist in a world of their own?

WISLAWA SZYMBORSKA

Any marriage, happy or unhappy, is infinitely more interesting and significant than any romance, however passionate." I think W. H. Auden had it right. A long marriage is like an oriental rug, rich with intricate designs woven year after year as partners share their happiness and grief, their experiences and ideas. Beneath the kaleidoscopic pattern is the warp and weft, the sturdy grid of common goals and interests, shared memories and secrets. And threaded through this tapestry are humor, patience, compromise, and dogged determination.

Lust is a simple craving. Romantic love is a euphoric madness. Attachment is an ornate connection to another living soul.

Almost all adults know what attachment feels like: that sense of cosmic union as you hold hands along the beach, the calm satisfaction of talking at the dinner table, the sensation of security as you fold into one another's arms and kiss good night. As Antoine de Saint-Exupéry wrote, "Love does not consist in gazing at each other, but in looking together in the same direction."

This universal human emotion, attachment, is here to stay: it is embedded in the biology of the human brain. But marriage, that ancient human institution that celebrates attachment, is undergoing a historic reformation. The traditional male-headed patriarchal family—

the bastion of the agrarian lifeway for several thousand years—is metamorphosing into new family forms as women rise in economic power.

Signs of this change are everywhere. We are seeing more weddings between equals, what sociologists call "peer marriages." Intimacy is being redefined in feminine terms. Men and women are returning to ancient patterns of frequent divorce and remarriage—bringing more despair, as well as fresh opportunities for happiness. Female sexual expression, even adultery, is no longer being judged by harsher standards than male conduct. Whereas single women used to put their children in orphanages, they are now rearing them on their own until they wed. More households are temporarily headed by women. Women are keeping family networks intact and building "intentional" families of unrelated friends. There are even signs that a version of matriliny, the tracing of one's descent through the female line, may be emerging in the United States.

Underlying many of these important developments is a bedrock reality: women are becoming better educated, more independent, and more interesting than they have been at any time in human evolution. This will not undermine the profound human desire for attachment—or the institution of marriage. In fact, in this chapter I will conclude that men and women currently have the opportunity to make more emotionally and intellectually fulfilling marriages than at any time in history or prehistory.

## Marrying

Only 3 percent of all mammals pair up to rear their young. Humans are among them. Today some 90 percent of women marry by age fifty in all but a few countries.[1] Virtually all healthy men and women in traditional societies also wed.[2]

Americans are marrying somewhat later than they did a hundred years ago. In 1890, the median age at first marriage was 22.0 years for women and 26.1 for men.[3] In 1994, women in the United States married at a median age of 24.5, while men married at 26.7.[4] More men and women are living with a mate before they wed. And a remarkable number of women are having babies out of wedlock, then taking a husband several years later. Nevertheless, in 1994, 91 percent of all American women had married at least once by age forty-five.[5]

Even the irreverent American baby boomers wed. These men and women ushered in the sexual revolution in the 1960s. They marched for civil rights, grew beards, smoked pot, burned bras, ate tofu, blasted rock 'n' roll music across our airwaves, and thumbed their noses at big business, the establishment, and war. But 93 percent of them married. Many shunned traditional church weddings for be-trothals at backyard barbecues, on mountaintops, even while skydiv-ing. Some wed in bathing suits and hippie beads. But they tied the marriage knot.

"There is many a happy slave," Darwin mused.[6] As a young man he was circumspect about wedding. He meticulously listed all of the rea-sons why marriage did not suit him—including the financial strain, the loss of freedom, the constraints on time, and the inevitable anxi-ety and responsibilities of parenting. But eventually he settled down with Emma Wedgwood, his first cousin. Two things enticed him to the altar, he wrote, "a nice soft wife on a sofa" and his fear of being a "neuter bee."[7]

"Wedlock; padlock." So goes an old English aphorism. It was, and is, widely believed that women naturally want to be married while most men seek autonomy and adventure. I do not agree. I think the drive to form a strong attachment to a mate—a drive usually institu-tionalized as marriage—is a biological craving deeply embedded in the brains of both sexes.

### The Chemistry of Attachment

In the 1950s, British psychoanalyst John Bowlby proposed that hu-mans have evolved an innate attachment system consisting of specific behaviors and physiological responses.[8] Only recently, however, have neuroscientists begun to understand the chemistry of this remarkable emotion, attachment.

At least two closely related brain substances, vasopressin and oxy-tocin, seem to be involved. These are produced in the hypothalamus, a primitive region of the brain that governs what scientists call the "four Fs"—fighting, fleeing, feeding, and sexual intercourse. But to understand how these neurotransmitters produce feelings of attach-ment to a mate, you must meet some American midwesterners who live in lifelong unison with a single partner: prairie voles.

These furry, brown-gray, mouselike rodents live in a complex system of burrows on the grasslands of middle America. They are monogamous "by nature." They form pair-bonds to rear their young; some 90 percent mate for life.[9] The prairie vole's nuptial career begins soon after puberty as a male sets out to find a spouse. When he comes upon an appropriate female, he begins to court her. Sniffing, licking, darting, nuzzling, mounting: the couple copulate some fifty times in about two days.

Most curious, however, is what happens next. After their sexual spree wanes, the male begins to act like a young husband, building a nest for their forthcoming young, ferociously guarding his mate from rival males, and defending their precious real estate. When the newborns appear, he also huddles over them and retrieves them when they wander.

Sue Carter, behavioral endocrinologist at the University of Maryland, Tom Insel of the Yerkes Regional Primate Research Center in Atlanta, Georgia, and their colleagues have pinpointed the cause of these pair-bonding behaviors. As the male vole ejaculates, levels of vasopressin increase in his brain, triggering his spousal and parenting zeal.[10]

## The "Cuddle" Chemical: Oxytocin

Oxytocin, a closely related brain chemical, is equally important in creating attachment in mammals—particularly in females.[11]

Like vasopressin, oxytocin is made in the hypothalamus, as well as in the ovaries and testes. Unlike vasopressin, this chemical is released in women and other female mammals during the birthing process.[12] It initiates contractions of the uterus and stimulates the mammary glands to produce milk. Recently, however, scientists have come to think that oxytocin also stimulates the bonding process between a mother and her offspring—as well as between mating partners.[13] As Carter says about oxytocin and vasopressin in prairie voles, "They need those chemicals to form their pair bonds."[14]

Because humans share these basic bodily substances with all other mammals, it seems probable that vasopressin and oxytocin are also involved in the feelings of attachment in people.

You have probably experienced this yourself. Levels of vasopressin increase in men just after orgasm; levels of oxytocin rise in women at orgasm instead.[15] "Love is a quiet understanding and a fusion," wrote

Georges Simenon. That sense of fusion, intense closeness, and attachment you can feel just after making love is probably due to
heightened levels of these attachment drugs.

## Testosterone and Attachment

Testosterone seems to play a negative role in attachment.

Single men tend to have higher levels of testosterone than married
men.[16] Men with high baseline levels of testosterone also marry less
frequently, are more likely to be abusive during marriage, and divorce
more often.[17] If a man's marriage becomes unstable, his levels of
testosterone rise.[18] With divorce, a man's levels of testosterone rise
even more.

But as a man becomes more attached to family, his levels of testosterone can fall. When psychologist David Gubernick measured
the testosterone levels of nine expectant human fathers, for example,
their levels plunged after their child was born.[19]

The relationship between testosterone and attachment is particularly noticeable in birds. Male cardinals and blue jays flit from one female to the next; they never stick around to parent young. These
profligate fathers have high levels of testosterone. Males of species
that form pair-bonds with single females and help them rear their
young have much lower levels of this androgen. In fact, when scientists surgically pumped testosterone into male sparrows, these faithful fathers abandoned their nests, their young, and their spouses to
woo other females.[20]

Enduring attachment between human spouses would seem to be
associated with proportionately high levels of vasopressin and oxytocin and low levels of testosterone. This would explain why couples
often engage in less sex as they become more and more attached to
each other.

Wedding invitations, wedding rings, wedding dresses, wedding
dances, wedding songs, honeymoons: why do men and women go to
such extraordinary lengths to formally attach to one another? In my
last book, *Anatomy of Love,* I proposed that the human brain chemistry of attachment evolved millions of years ago. Because this theory
is pertinent here, I will review it briefly.

## The Evolution of Human Marital Attachment

The dead do speak. Beside the shallow lakes, on the grassy plains, in the gullies and the ravines of ancient East Africa, our ancestors left their bones and teeth. Today these fossils lie exposed in layers of dirt—as postcards from the past. From examining these fossils, anthropologists have established several essential things about our ancestry. Among them: By four million years ago our ancestors walked erect—on two feet instead of four.

Walking was humankind's most fundamental innovation. It enabled our forebears to start their march toward civilization. But it caused a crisis for females. With the evolution of the human stride, they were obliged to carry their infants in their arms instead of on their backs. How could a female carry the equivalent of a twenty-pound bowling ball with one arm, a protective stick or stone with the other arm, and still collect food? How could she defend herself from the snakes and cats that slumbered in the knee-high grass?

In the forest, their quadrupedal progenitors had carried their infants on their backs. Their hands were free to collect their daily fare, and they could easily escape into the foliage at the approach of predators. But as our forebears began to walk bipedally, carry tools and weapons, and collect their meals on the open plains, ancestral females began to need a mate to help them protect and feed their young.

As pair-bonding became critical to females, it became suitable to males. A male would have had considerable difficulty protecting and providing for a harem as he wandered the dangerous open plains. But he could defend and provide for a single female and her infant. With time, natural selection favored those with the tendency to form pair-bonds—and the human brain chemistry for attachment gradually evolved.

Much would stem from this remarkable adaptation. The husband, the wife, the father, the nuclear family, our myriad customs of courtship, our procedures for marriage and remarriage, our terms for kin, the plots in our operas, novels, plays, movies, and poems: hundreds of thousands of human traditions stem from the ancient human drive to pair and rear young children as a team. Attachment is the foundation stone of human social life.

But what we expect from our marital relationships changes with changing times. And as women gain economic power, the institution of marriage is undergoing a transformation.

## Peer Marriage: A Wedding of Like Minds

"All happy families resemble one another; every unhappy family is unhappy in its own fashion," Tolstoy wrote. I wonder whether the great Russian writer would say this today.

Unhappy marriages and dysfunctional families seem to have much in common: alcoholism, drug abuse, adultery, bickering about money, and arguing over how to rear children are all common themes. But most *good* marriages and happy families seem to be unique. I no longer know what to expect, for example, when I visit a happy couple for an evening in New York. Who has prepared dinner? Which spouse will be detained at the office? Who helped their daughter with her homework? Each marriage seems to be a novel mesh, an original collage pieced together by two busy, independent, yet deeply attached human beings.

Sociologist Pepper Schwartz of the University of Washington divides contemporary marriages into three varieties: "traditional" marriages, "near-peer" marriages, and "peer" marriages.[21] Traditional marriages, she says, are those in which the husband and wife play conventional roles. Generally the woman works full-time in the home and rears the young. The man is the sole breadwinner.

Near-peer marriages occur when both spouses have jobs, but the wife still does most of the household chores and tasks are allotted in more or less traditional ways. In many near-peer marriages, Schwartz reports, both partners are staunch supporters of equality between the sexes. But they don't seem to know quite how to achieve a true democracy in the home. The husband still makes the majority of the important financial decisions, for example. Most marriages today, she thinks, are of this variety.

Peer marriages are truly egalitarian matches. Each partner holds equal rank; each is equally responsible for the emotional and economic well-being of the household. The wife may have a more influential career and bigger salary than does her husband, or she may stay at home full-time. But both feel they have an equal say in making crucial financial decisions. Household chores are divided collaboratively and often unconventionally. And both partners feel they are in a fair, satisfying, durable, unique relationship. These partners, Schwartz notes, usually experience an intense sense of companionship.

The rise of peer marriages, a modern variant of what historian Lawrence Stone has called "companionate" marriages, can be traced back to the beginnings of the Western market economy and industrialization.[22] But social scientists believe these marriages, based on friendship, trust, similar values, common interests, and shared experiences, are sure to increase—because of women's increasing economic power and independence.[23]

The Bureau of Labor Statistics reports that by the year 2000, 51 percent of all American couples will be two-income families.[24] Women are pouring into the job market in almost every other society on record as well. In almost all cases, income providers gain status in the family. And social scientists say that where women are financially independent, men and women will form partnerships based only on social and emotional equality.[25] As sociologist Frank Furstenberg of the University of Pennsylvania puts it, the end of the twentieth century will be remembered as the time when "symmetrical marriages" proliferated.[26]

Attachment, attentiveness, companionship, equality, a bonding of like minds: hail the grit of peer marriages. Along with the rise of this marriage form has come a new interest in "intimacy."[27] But this intimacy is usually of the feminine variety.

## The Intimacy Gap

"You can be intimate only with your equal," it has been said. Agreed. But intimacy means different things to men and women.

Men are more likely to define emotional closeness as doing things side by side, while women often view intimacy as talking face-to-face.[28] Men like to go fishing, cheer at a ball game, or view a movie shoulder to shoulder.[29] You may have noticed how easily most men discuss difficult issues while driving in a car. Men become more talkative and relaxed when they cannot see their companion directly.[30] In videotapes of boys and men of all ages, they usually sit at angles and rarely look squarely into one another's eyes.[31]

Psychologists say that men form their sense of intimacy in childhood as they play sports side by side.[32] But I suspect that men's concept of intimacy has much deeper roots. After all, ancestral men faced their enemies; they worked and played side by side with friends.

Videotapes of girls and women of all ages show them sitting closer together, looking more directly into one another's eyes, expressing their emotions—and talking.[33] These emotional and verbal exchanges begin in childhood, when girls move face-to-face to share "small talk" and "deep talk."[34] But the intimacy women derive from talking face-to-face probably comes from deep history as well. Across the ages, ancestral women endlessly held infants in front of their faces, consoling, educating, and amusing their little ones with words.

Just as most women don't fully grasp why men get such pleasure from sitting side by side to watch football games on Sunday afternoons, most men don't understand why women spend hours with their girlfriends on the phone. But each taste probably comes across the ages from times long gone.

Each sex exploits the other's form of intimacy too. Men often court with intimate conversation. They write love letters, and they talk, talk, talk to their sweethearts—on the couch, at the bar, and on the pillow late into the night. Once the wedding knot has been tied, however, men tend to slip away from these penetrating, emotion-laden dialogues, back to their world of business, sports, and politics—intimacy with men.[35]

Women court men by going adventuring with them, doing things together. Hiking, swimming, sailing, skiing: some even sit side by side and cheer at TV sports with their chosen man. Yet after the wedding guests have all been thanked and a woman has spent a few months or years securing her marital relationship, she starts to skip sports events and outings to do woman things.

Women say that their marriages begin to sour when the talking stops.[36] But husbands must be disappointed when wives begin to decline their invitations to ball games and fishing trips.

Men also express closeness when they bring flowers, buy dinners, or give larger presents—helping by "doing." And men are four times more likely to relate coitus with intimacy.[37] As one man summed up this male view, "I feel we have really communicated after we have made love."[38] This seems preposterous to most women. But men's tendency to equate sexual intercourse with intimacy has a genetic logic. Sex is the single greatest gift a woman can give a man; coitus is his opportunity to spread his DNA into posterity. So when a man has received this precious present, he generally feels extremely close to the giver.

Women express intimacy and affection when they dress up to look attractive for a man. Women are more likely than men to regard sexual fidelity as a loving act.[39] And in the bedroom women derive more intimacy than men from talking to a partner—generally just before making love.[40]

If women deride men for associating the sex act itself with intimacy, men are astounded when women strike up a conversation just before making love. But this feminine penchant also has genetic logic. For millennia, women have needed emotional support from a beloved. This affirming precoital chat reassures them that their partner can listen, communicate, and demonstrate more than pure lust at important moments.

## The Feminization of Intimacy

The desire for intimacy has not always been regarded as central to marriage. Even what has been defined as intimacy has varied. In eighteenth-century America, for example, marital duty and mutual help were considered expressions of closeness.[41] Yet arranged marriages, segregated chores, rigid rules of social decorum, the subjugation of women, and many other factors have tended to undermine feelings of genuine togetherness between spouses throughout historic epochs in the West.[42]

Since men and women began to migrate into cities in the nineteenth century and near-peer and peer marriages started to emerge, however, intimacy has gradually become regarded as an important element of marital happiness, not only in the United States but in societies as diverse as Mexico, India, and China.[43]

The kind of intimacy currently in vogue, however, is the female version—involving intense emotionality and verbal disclosure. Male kinds of intimacy, including the sharing of physical and intellectual activities with a wife, helping out around the house, giving practical advice, making love, teasing, joking, and horsing around, are rarely regarded as genuine closeness today.[44]

The growing taste for feminine forms of intimacy may be tempered by a seemingly unrelated factor: the aging population.

In a study of 2,795 Swedish men and women aged fifteen to eighty, psychologist Lars Tornstam found that young women were more eager than young men to have deep, open, intimate conversations. However, middle-aged women were no more interested in these intense dialogues than men were.[45] Tornstam reasons that middle-aged women become more realistic in their marital expectations; they no longer feel the need for intense, emotional talk.

But hormonal changes may play a role in women's declining interest in intense, self-revealing, emotion-laden conversation. As discussed in chapter 7, middle-aged women become more assertive and independent—due, in part, to declining levels of estrogen and unmasked levels of the androgens. Perhaps this dampens their need to make deep, intense, verbal connections with others, too. Data on men corroborate this view. Middle-aged men begin to seek more tenderness and closeness with a wife.[46] Not coincidentally, I think, male levels of testosterone begin to decline in middle age, and men's levels of estrogen actually increase.[47]

"Grief can take care of itself, but to get the full value of a joy you must have someone to divide it with," Mark Twain wrote. Intimacy is sharing. As male and female baby boomers reach middle age in many societies, their definitions of intimacy may converge. This may serve to strengthen their near-peer and peer marriages.

## The Roving Eye

Alas, marriage has a darker side: adultery.

In a 1998 academic article I proposed that the brain circuitry for attachment is not closely linked to the brain circuitry for attraction, nor to the brain circuits associated with lust.[48] In short, we are capable of "loving" more than one person at a time. Humans are capable of feeling deep attachment to a long-term partner, *while* they feel attraction for someone in the office or their social set, *while* they feel lust when they see a stranger on the street.

Many do feel deep attachment for one individual and also have a roving eye. The most recent comprehensive poll of American sexuality, published by the National Opinion Research Center in 1994, reports that some 25 percent of men and 15 percent of women say they strayed at some point during marriage.[49] Other current studies report that from 30 percent to 50 percent of both married men and married women philander.[50]

Adultery is not an American specialty; it is noted in every society on record. In fact, I have come to believe that the American incidence of adultery is relatively low by world standards.[51] Typical of many are the Mehinaku of the Amazonian jungles, who call sex with extramarital partners *awirintya,* "delicious."[52]

Although different cultures define adultery differently, every society in the world has rules about what constitutes adultery, as well as means of punishing flagrant philanderers.[53] But despite the rules and penalties, men and women have slipped into bed with lovers for centuries—even when they believe that philandering is immoral, even when they stand to lose their family and friends, their job, their life savings, their stature in the community, their health, perhaps even their lives.

Why do men and women cheat? How will the rise of economically powerful women change this seemingly intractable human habit?

## Survival of the Faithless

A few natural rules govern living creatures—whether a beetle, an elephant, or a human being. One of them is "carpe diem," seize the day. Under favorable conditions, almost all living creatures seize mating opportunities.

Philandering is common among all kinds of "socially monogamous" creatures.[54] Songbirds are prime examples. Patricia Gowaty, a behavioral ecologist at the University of Georgia, reports that individuals in only 10 percent of some 180 species of socially monogamous songbirds are sexually faithful to a mating partner.[55]

The barn swallow, for example, pairs up in spring. Males arrive first and establish their homestead under the roofs and eaves of barns. Females appear later and choose among them. Together the mated pair copulate; daily she lays another egg. While she is fertile, her mate follows her constantly, a practice ornithologists call "mate guarding." Once she has begun to incubate their eggs, however, he turns his sights toward the neighbors—pursuing other females for a tryst.[56] Females of many species are often avid partners in these rendezvous. Female hooded warblers even have a special tune they use to attract a roving male.[57]

"A lot of birds are having a bit on the side," reports Jeffrey Black of the University of Cambridge in England.[58] Indeed, these "extra-pair copulations," known as EPCs or "sneakers," have genetic payoffs. Cheating females can acquire sperm from different males, as well as sperm from higher-ranking males, boosting their chances of bearing healthier or more varied young.[59] Males have an opportunity to spread their genes.

"No man knoweth who hath begotten him," says Telemachus, son of Odysseus, in Homer's *The Odyssey*. This is truer than many wish to think. Today scientists who screen people for genetic diseases typically find that about 10 percent of children tested are not the genetic offspring of their supposed fathers.[60]

In fact, adultery is so common around the world that a number of scientists have offered evolutionary explanations for this human proclivity.[61]

Like the males of many other species, ancestral men who secretly copulated with females from neighboring communities spread their seed. Hence those who philandered tended to father more young; these young survived, and through this process nature perpetuated those who cheated. Ancestral females who sneaked into the bushes with lovers tended to receive extra food and protection for their young. If they could entice better hunters or more charismatic leaders into assignations, they had the possibility of conceiving infants with better genes as well. At the very least, they acquired the seed of different men, creating genetic variety in their lineages. Those who philandered unconsciously reaped genetic payoffs—perpetuating a tendency toward adultery in women.

Women still pursue this tactic unconsciously. Adulterous women tend to have their rendezvous more frequently while they are ovulating—the time of peak fertility.[62]

"The chains of marriage are heavy. It takes two to carry them, sometimes three," said Oscar Wilde. Some say they cheat to supplement a good, but not perfect, marriage. Others who cheat are looking for an excuse to exit a bad marriage. Others want to get caught, hoping to revitalize a marriage. Some get bored when their spouse is out of town or lonely when they, themselves, are in a different city. Some want to solve a sex problem. Some want more sex. Some seek more attention or affection. Many want to feel more attractive, more masculine, or more feminine. Some want to be "understood." Some want to explore a different ethnic type, class, or age group. Some want excitement or variety. Some love a secret. Some enjoy a triangle and a tug-of-war. Some crave danger or independence. A few want revenge.[63]

Yet underlying all of these explanations for adultery may be a powerful inherited human desire, unconscious to be sure, to cheat in order to increase the survival of one's DNA.

"Darwin made me do it." So said an acquaintance to me as he explained his taste for adultery. I reminded him that during the course of evolution, humanity evolved sophisticated brain regions for making rational decisions. We are not puppets that do the bidding of our DNA. We can say no to adultery.

Nevertheless, it is remarkable how many people say yes.

## Gender Differences in Adultery

Men and women tend to seek somewhat different things from their clandestine affairs.

American men are more likely to engage in extramarital relations purely for sexual pleasure, while women are more inclined to seek emotional intimacy and commitment.[64] In one study of 205 adulterous married Americans, 72 percent of women as opposed to 51 percent of men said they sought a deep emotional connection—instead of just carnal satisfaction—in their extramarital affairs.[65] Women who have affairs are also more likely than men to believe their marriages are unhappy.[66]

Similar gender difference can be seen in other cultures. In countries as different as Zimbabwe, Australia, Finland, England, Japan, and the Netherlands, men are more likely to engage in short, loveless sexual encounters, while women tend to seek more emotional closeness with their lovers.[67]

This gender variation is relatively easy to explain.[68] Short, loveless sexual encounters can bring big rewards for men. The man who impregnates a woman during a one-night stand has expended little time, energy, or sperm. If his lover chooses to rear his child without him, he has won immortality. Every time a woman hops into bed with a secret lover, however, she risks the possibility of conceiving a child—and expending years of precious energy rearing this packet of DNA. If she can build an intimate connection with her lover, however, she may draw him into her web as potential father and provider.

## Male Mate Guarding

"Papa loved mama. / Mama loved men. / Mama's in the grave-
yard. / Papa's in the pen." Carl Sandburg's terse lines sum up another
gender difference in adultery: men go to greater lengths to guard the
vessel that will bear their seed.

Men tend to get more upset when a wife has engaged in a one-night
stand.[69] As mentioned in chapter 9, when they believe they have been
sexually betrayed, men are also much more likely than women to
become physically violent toward a spouse or rival. Worldwide, men
commit the vast majority of spousal homicides.[70] In dozens of societies, men are also more likely than women to divorce a spouse
for infidelity—undoubtedly because they risk having to rear another's
child when a wife philanders.[71]

Women become more deeply troubled if a husband has engaged in
a long, intimate affair.[72] Women are more likely to blame themselves.
They try to make themselves attractive to regain the love of their partner.[73] And they abandon the relationship less quickly than men do.
Before they depart, they attempt to discuss and understand the situation.[74] These feminine impulses to seduce back the philanderer and
to verbally explore the problems in the relationship may stem from
prehistory. Luring, talking, listening, and reconnecting are natural
ways that women get and keep a man.

Will patterns of adultery change as women's economic power rises?

## The Declining Double Standard for Adultery

I doubt that economically powerful women will engage in more one-
night stands or curb their desire for intimacy with extramarital lovers.
As discussed in chapter 8, women embed sex in a broader, more integrated social and emotional milieu than men do. Moreover, women
have a natural tendency to nurture and build relationships. So although many women are becoming financially capable of rearing infants by themselves, I think they will continue to seek intimacy and
commitment from their lovers.

One would expect that as women become more economically independent, they would seek more paramours. But the data on female
adultery are mixed.

Women are indeed starting their affairs earlier in marriage than they did in the past. In the 1950s, only 9 percent of wives under age twenty-five said they had philandered; in the 1980s, 25 percent of married persons of both sexes admitted to an extramarital affair by age twenty-five.[75] Still, the NORC study of American sexuality does not show an increase in the overall incidence of adultery for either sex since the 1950s.[76]

In fact, several social trends could actually be restraining the incidence of feminine adultery. Men and women are marrying later, divorcing more, and living longer. Hence they spend more time as single individuals. No marriage, no adultery. Moreover, today divorce is easy, contraception is widespread, paternity can be tested, and "illegitimacy" is more accepted. When divorce was difficult to obtain and paternity was impossible to prove, the cuckolded husband usually reared the child.[77] Now he can walk out. Today adultery has fewer perquisites than in the past.

Whether or not more powerful women will engage in more adultery remains to be seen. But one thing is clear: Society's views of female adultery are changing. Take the royals, Charles and Diana. Both had affairs. Yet Charles's devotion to Camilla Parker-Bowles has been widely regarded as unmanly, while Diana's affairs were often justified as acts of poetic despair brought on by a loveless marriage.[78] As author Katie Roiphe points out, today most adulterous men are regarded as sleazy villains, not the virile rogues of yesteryear. Philandering women, on the other hand, are often seen as striking a blow for feminine sexual freedom.

Across recorded history, especially in agrarian societies, women have received much heavier punishment for cheating.[79] Even in Christendom, where adultery by either sex was strictly prohibited, male philandering was often regarded as an understandable foible.[80] No more. The double standard for adultery is waning. In some circles, feminine adultery is even taking on a romantic, almost triumphant, air.

At the same time, economically powerful women are becoming less and less tolerant of adultery in their husbands.[81] I discovered this firsthand when I traveled to Aruba, in the Caribbean, to make a speech.

Until the mid-1980s, most Aruban women were housewives and

most Aruban men were employed by the Exxon Corporation, which had major operations in nearby Venezuela. Many an Aruban man also had a "byside," or paramour; often she bore him children, too. Wife and mistress lived in full knowledge of each other—unhappily. But in 1985 Exxon pulled up stakes, leaving a lot of Aruban men out of work. As a result, the island government launched a campaign to boost tourism. It proved successful.

Suddenly women began to find jobs in the rising hotels and entertainment centers. As Aruban wives gained economic independence, they became unwilling to overlook their husbands' affairs. The divorce rate soared.

I suspect that as women gain economic parity with men, as peer marriages increase, and as companionship, intimacy, and trust become more central to marital unions, women everywhere will become less and less likely to overlook their partners' dalliances. Instead, many more of those who feel betrayed will divorce.

## Divorcing

"The dark, uneasy world of family life—where the greatest can fail and the humblest succeed." Poet Randall Jarrell knew that lasting marriages take work. Nowhere in the world do men and women build enduring, mutually satisfactory marriages easily. In fact, almost all societies allow divorce under certain circumstances, and divorce rates are just as high in many traditional societies as they are in the United States.[82]

As might be expected, husbands and wives tend to end marriages for somewhat different reasons. In a study of 160 diverse societies by anthropologist Laura Betzig of the University of Michigan, the first reason that men gave for seeking divorce was blatant philandering by the wife; female barrenness was second.[83] Hence men, consciously or not, tend to marry to reproduce their genes—and divorce when this aim is thwarted.

This study and others have shown that women are more likely to seek divorce if a husband is sterile or cruel, if he fails to meet economic and domestic responsibilities, or if he is physically violent.[84] Women leave a marriage when a spouse threatens their ability to bear or rear their young.

Both sexes also give up on partners who are lazy, disrespectful, jeal-

ous, argumentative, nagging, sexually neglectful, boring, too talkative, or too busy watching television. Those who perceive that they are
giving more than they are getting, or feel they can get a better-quality
partner, tend to leave a marriage.[85] Those who made poor attachments to parents in childhood or grew up in stressful, unpredictable
households are more likely to make short-term attachments in adulthood.[86] In addition, as romantic love increasingly becomes the cen-
terpiece of modern marriage, more men and women have begun to
divorce when this passion wanes.[87]

There are dozens of reasons that men and women end a marriage.
But, as with adultery, I believe there are some underlying evolutionary forces associated with the human penchant to divorce. Although
I discussed these in detail in *Anatomy of Love*, I feel it is relevant to
summarize them here.

## The Evolution of Divorce

I arrived at my views on the evolution of divorce while studying the
demographic yearbooks of the United Nations.

Just about every ten years since 1947, the United Nations has published a yearbook devoted to numerical data on marriage and divorce
in some sixty countries. Hundreds of millions of people are involved.
I soon found several patterns in these data.

Men and women in cultures around the world have a remarkable
tendency to divorce during and around the fourth year of marriage,
while in their mid-twenties, and with no children or with one dependent child. As people age, as they bear more young, or as the marriage
endures past about three to seven years, they become more and more
likely to remain married for life.[88] Most divorced men and women
also remarry.

There were many exceptions to all these patterns. Nevertheless,
young people around the world tend to form a series of formalized attachments to different partners—serial monogamy.

A similar pattern is seen in other creatures. In the avian world, serial monogamy is common. Some 90 percent of birds pair up to rear
their young. But in more than 50 percent of those avian species, partners disband at the end of the mating season. Often they do not pair
with each other again the following year.[89]

The same pattern prevails among those few mammals that form

pair-bonds. Red foxes, for example, pair up in February and stay together until their young are out of infancy. But when the kits leave the
den for new worlds, the dog fox and the vixen go their separate ways.
Like many birds, red foxes pair only for the breeding season.

After considering these patterns, both in the wild and among
human beings, I came to believe that the human propensity to leave
a partner around the fourth year of marriage stems from our earliest
ancestry.

Soon after our forebears descended from the fast-disappearing
trees of Africa and began to walk bipedally, males and females started
to form attachments that lasted through the period of infancy and
lactation of a single child, about four years. Once a youngster had
been weaned and was able to join a play group with older children,
then juvenile siblings, aunts, grandmothers, and other members of
the band took up some of the burden of parenting. So if a couple
did not bear a second child, they were free to disband, find new
partners, and breed again—creating healthy genetic variety in their
lineages.

"And every bed has been condemned, not by morality or law, but by
time," wrote poet Anne Sexton. Century upon century, men and
women fell in love, paired, bore a child, reared it at least through infancy, then separated—selecting for the human propensity to have a
restless heart. Today's "four-year itch" is probably a remnant of an ancestral human breeding season.

## The Brain Physiology of Divorce

This restlessness in long relationships probably has a physiological
correlate in the brain. I suspect that either the receptor sites for attachment chemicals become overstimulated or the brain produces
less of these compounds—leaving one physiologically susceptible to
detachment.

Corroborating this view is evidence that divorce runs in families.[90]
Perhaps these kin inherit similar physiological processes for the production and absorpion of oxytocin, vasopressin, and/or testosterone,
and thereby are made more susceptible to restlessness and divorce.

## Social Forces That Contribute
## to Divorce: Money Walks

*How long* a couple have been wed, *how old* spouses are, and *how many children* they have produced all seem to be biological factors in divorce. We seem to have natural weak points in marriage, an inheritance from an ancient breeding strategy. But cultural forces and individual personality play enormous roles in influencing *how many* people leave a partner. Many, many social and psychological factors can speed or deter divorce.[91]

When individuals come from very different backgrounds, have different interests and goals, or are very young, they are more likely to divorce.[92] Spouses of markedly different ages and degrees of physical attractiveness tend to part.[93] Women with more education tend to walk out more frequently.[94] Couples who have a girl baby are more likely to break up than those who produce a boy. High alcohol consumption and low church attendance correlate with divorce. Moreover, the ways a woman and man negotiate, compromise, fight, show respect, and inject humor all play roles in marital separation.[95]

But of all of the social forces that contribute to marital instability, the most significant can be summed up in two words: working women.[96]

Where women own the rights to the local water holes in the Kalahari Desert of southern Africa, where they can harvest laden coconut palms in Polynesia, where they can make money on Wall Street, or where they own other valued goods or services, they depart unhappy unions. Why? Because they can. In the United States, the number of women in the workforce doubled between the early 1960s and late 1980s; the divorce rate more than doubled, too.[97]

Today almost 50 percent of American marriages are likely to end in divorce.[98] Working women themselves cannot be blamed entirely for the high divorce rate, however. Men are much more inclined to divorce wives who are economically solvent than ones who are dependent on them to survive.

This correlation between women's economic independence and divorce is seen in cultures around the world.[99] Between 1970 and 1990, women piled into the job market in many other industrial societies. Divorce rates in Canada, France, Greece, the Netherlands, England,

and Germany also doubled.[100] Today in Sweden some 48 percent of marriages are expected to end in divorce.[101] Some 40 percent to 60 percent of women in their forties in the Dominican Republic, Ghana, Indonesia, and Senegal divorce.[102] And in most other developing countries, at least one out of four marriages shatter.[103]

Where women are even somewhat economically independent, those caught in violent, alcoholic, abusive, sexually unfulfilling, or intolerably boring marriages generally vote with their feet. Money walks.

Such are the women of Barbados. In the hill villages of this Caribbean gem, many women are comparatively well-to-do. They leave their homes each morning to work in the resort hotels, the restaurants and markets that rim the emerald sea. They come home each evening with money. When anthropologist Connie Sutton of New York University asked a Barbadian man what he thought of women, the gentleman replied, "Oh, those women, they come to us; they make love to us; they have our children; and they leave us. No sense of commitment."

## The Emergence of Modern Divorce Patterns

Divorce rates were low in preindustrial America, Western Europe, and everywhere else where men and women worked the sod—except among the very poor and the very young who had no property or children.[104] But in farming cultures, husbands and wives were tied to the soil and to each other; no one could dig up half the farm and cart it off. Where can you go with a ton of wheat? A few bedeviled spouses walked out of bad marriages empty-handed. The rich paid to have distasteful weddings annulled. But to most farming men and women, "till death do us part" was an incontrovertible precept. They had no choice.

With the beginning of the Industrial Revolution, women gradually entered the paid labor force. What did they come home with? Money. Movable assets. Not coincidentally, divorce rates began their slow but steady climb.[105]

Divorce rates should continue to creep up. Women's participation in the paid workforce is increasing while men's is declining—almost everywhere in the world.[106] As a result, some demographers predict that in the near future some two thirds of all first marriages in the United States will end in divorce.[107] And what happens in the United States very often happens just about everywhere else.

How do the sexes handle divorcing?

## Breaking Up Is Hard to Do

Generally the wife is the first to realize that the relationship is in trouble.[108]

Women are more sensitive to the complex mosaic of interpersonal conflicts that contribute to divorce,[109] probably due to their capacity for web thinking. They usually can also give more intricate psychological explanations of why the partnership decayed—most likely because women tend to have keener insight into people and their motivations.

Men, on the other hand, are usually more confused about why the relationship has ended. And they offer more concrete external reasons for its demise, such as different daily schedules.[110]

The sexes also react differently when they divorce.

Women tend to cry and tell all their friends they are depressed. Not men. Men often deny that they feel vulnerable, empty, or sad.[111] They tend to run from loss, hoping to separate themselves from their despair. Divorcing men are more likely than women to turn to alcohol or drugs. They throw themselves into work, drive like maniacs, or endlessly replay maudlin nostalgic tunes.[112] Some take up crime; some obsess on sports; some womanize; some hole up and watch TV. A few kill their wives or themselves. But men don't talk about their sorrow. As one man summed up a common male response, "I can't put it into words."[113]

Several studies suggest that men are psychologically more dependent on a partner from an early age. Men and boys have fewer same-sex confidants.[114] So teenage boys are more emotionally dependent on girlfriends than vice versa.[115] Men are more emotionally dependent on sweethearts during a romance. And husbands become more emotionally dependent on their wives.[116] Being married adds more years to a man's life than to a woman's.[117] And men are at greater risk of dying after being widowed.[118]

Not surprisingly, men consistently say they are more satisfied with their marriages.[119] And men are roughly 25 percent more likely to abase themselves to keep a marriage going, giving way to a wife's requests and making elaborate promises to change.[120] Far fewer men than women initiate divorce.

## Remarrying

What I find most remarkable is the resiliency of the human animal.

After the last of the belongings have been parceled out and the memorabilia have been destroyed or tucked away, after the lawyers have been paid, and after the guilt, resentment, and longing have receded, both men and women renew the quest to attach to another. The vast majority remarry. In the United States some 75 percent of once-married women under the age of thirty wed again; 50 percent of those in their thirties remarry; and so do some 28 percent of those over age forty.[121] All ages considered, 72 percent of divorced women remarry and 80 percent of men tie the knot again—patterns that are similar to those in Japan.[122]

Few men or women leave a marriage without a great deal of thought. Yet some 54 percent of American women and 61 percent of American men who wed a second time eventually go through divorce again.[123] Indeed, in one out of every seven marriages in America, either the bride or the groom is marrying for the third time.[124] The number of those marrying for the third time has doubled in the past twenty-five years. Some 40 percent of third marriages also fail.[125]

"We outgrow love, like other things / And put it in the Drawer / Till it an Antique fashion shows— / Like Costumes Grandsires wore." Thus Emily Dickinson wistfully noted what so many have felt: attachment can wane—again and again.

As the constraints of farm living have lifted, the sexes are resuming an ancient human lifeway: serial monogamy, with all its pain and promise. Not everyone leaves a partner; some 50 percent of American marriages do not end in divorce. But today bad marriages *can* end. And deep in the human psyche is a restlessness, residing in the nerve endings that regulate the chemicals of attachment. More and more people are likely to have several partners in the course of their lives.

## Women-Centered Homes

"All things flow, nothing abides," said Heraclitus. It is true. Also on the rise is another ancient family form: the female-headed household.

For centuries, the male-headed patriarchal family reigned in all agrarian societies. But with women's growing presence in the workforce, the high divorce rate, and a host of other social forces, more and more female-centered households are emerging.[126]

In 1960, American women headed only 7 percent of all families with children. In 1992, 25 percent of all American families with children were headed by a woman.[127] This trend is common around the world. In Thailand and Brazil, for example, 20 percent of households are headed by women; in the Dominican Republic and Hong Kong, the figure is 26 percent; in Ghana it is 29 percent.[128]

Female-headed households are usually temporary. In the United States, children spend about five years, on average, in such a family; then the mother remarries.[129] Moreover, many women who are legally head of household have a live-in boyfriend, often the father of at least some of their children. In any case, the percentage of female-headed households is increasing worldwide. The traditional patriarchal family—headed by a man—is declining in America and around the world.[130]

## Women Producing Families by Themselves

The growing tendency of women to give birth out of wedlock is further weakening the father-centered home.

Between 1960 and 1993 the percentage of births to unmarried American women rose from 5 percent to an astonishing 31 percent. In 1994, nearly one third of American births were to unmarried women.[131] This is a worldwide trend. In 1995, some 50 percent of births in Sweden were to unmarried women. The figure was 46 percent in Denmark, 33 percent in France, 31 percent in Britain, and 23 percent in Canada.[132] Over 20 percent of women bear a child out of wedlock in Botswana, Kenya, and Tanzania as well.[133]

This is not new. But in past decades, the vast majority of unmarried, pregnant women in industrial societies had shotgun marriages. Or they put their babies into orphanages.[134] Today most single mothers choose to rear their infants by themselves. Some take up this lifestyle because the father of the child has abandoned the pair. Some prefer not to wed. But many have conceived a child with a man, usually quite young, who simply does not have the earning power to provide for a family.

In fact, many American women, particularly among the urban poor, are coming to believe that the best way to rear their young is to get some education, land a job, find decent day care, and live in a safe community. It's a struggle, but they reason that it is a safer solution than depending on a man.[135]

## The "Good Old Days"

After a trip to Germany, Mark Twain referred to Richard Wagner as "a musician who wrote music which is better than it sounds." In the same vein, the data cited above on divorce, female-headed households, and unwed mothers are not as dismal as they appear. In the "good old days," women's choices were often even worse.

In colonial America, obedience to a patriarchal, authoritative husband was expected—and widely considered to be ordained by God.[136] In England, until the nineteenth century, a woman, her property, her income, and her children were legally owned by her husband.[137] In past eras, few women had professional training or an education. Granted, some wives became influential in the home. But many had no choice but to do their chores and obey a man.

I hope you do not misunderstand me: I am not celebrating the rise of unwed mothers, female-centered households, or the incidence of divorce. Some of these cases are tragic; some are valiant endeavors to find happiness; many contribute to the feminization of poverty. But many Americans are caught up in what historian Stephanie Coontz of Evergreen State College in Washington calls the "nostalgia trap." Several social scientists who study trends in the family argue convincingly that, all things considered, more marriages are happy today than in the past.[138]

I would add that with the rise of peer marriages and the new emphasis on intimacy between partners, the world will see more happy unions. Each will be a unique tapestry of attachment woven by equals as a team.

## The Kin Keepers

T. S. Eliot once said that there was no vocabulary for the love between family members, calling this feeling "love that's lived in but not looked at."

In the 1980s, sociologists Alice and Peter Rossi set out to see how adult Americans actually relate to family members.[139] They collected data on over thirteen hundred randomly selected men and women aged eighteen or older in the United States. They confirmed what other sociologists had reported: Family members are dispersed—but they stay in touch.

In fact, some 60 percent of middle-aged married couples live within thirty-five miles of one or more of their elderly parents, and some 70 percent of their children live within thirty-five miles of them—less than a hour's drive.[140] Over 50 percent of middle-aged children see a parent at least once a week.[141] They also speak on the phone, send cards and letters, even e-mail one another. Grandparents are actually playing a greater familial role than they ever have—because more of them are living longer.

Women are at the center of these kinship webs. Fathers and middle-aged sons tend to give more advice and provide job leads and financial loans. But mothers and adult daughters give their kin more comfort, do more chores like watering plants and collecting mail, help more during illnesses, make and fix more household things, do more child care, give special gifts, and visit more frequently.[142]

Typically, an American wife also spends more time connecting her husband with her own parents, and connecting their children with maternal grandparents.[143] Women also build more relationships between their own nuclear family and stepchildren, nieces, aunts, cousins, and other relatives. "No man is an island, entire of it self," wrote John Donne. In the United States, mothers, daughters, sisters, and grandmothers build and maintain the social and emotional links among blood relatives.

But here's the key: These women favor maternal kin.[144] When a couple divorce, the woman generally builds even stronger ties to the maternal relatives while loosening ties to the father and his blood kin. And as women age, they intensify their focus on maternal relatives.

Rossi and Rossi argue that American women build strong ties to maternal kin because they depend on the child care, economic assistance, and emotional support that these blood relatives provide. Women usually suffer greater financial problems than men when they divorce.[145] Women live longer, too. So throughout their lives women are more likely to need the social and financial support of family members. As a result, even independent contemporary women nurse these maternal ties.

The feminine devotion to maternal kin is gradually making a remarkable change in American family life. As Rossi and Rossi sum it up, "The American kinship system has an asymmetrical tilt to the maternal side of the family."[146]

The tilt will be accentuated by working women interested in preserving their maiden name. Hillary Rodham Clinton is one of many who have done just that. In a 1997 survey conducted by *Bride's* magazine, some 22 percent of the women who responded said they planned to keep their birth name when they wed, as either a last name, a hyphenated last name, or a middle name.[147] These women are not retaining their maiden name purely to maintain strong kin ties, acquire security in old age, or even to make a statement about their independence. Many are career women who need to keep their professional identity.

As more women pursue careers, even more will preserve their birth names—and inadvertently strengthen their ties to their natal kin.

## Intentional Families

Women are also creating new kinds of families—what journalist Susan Ahern and psychologist Kent Bailey of Virginia Commonwealth University call "psychological kin" and "intentional families."[148] These are families by choice. Be they neighbors, colleagues, or friends, psychological kin invite you to celebrate holidays, bring food when you are sick, feed your cat while you are out of town, or pick up your child after school. They also join you regularly for meals and life events like birthdays and weddings.

"I have come to define family as the people who act like it," writes essayist Judith Viorst in *Necessary Losses*.[149] In one study of American family values, a whopping 74 percent of participants agreed, saying that a family is "a group of people who love and care for one another."[150] Today Americans have proportionately more of these psychological kin than in the past.[151] I am among them. My blood relatives are dispersed around the world. Yet I have a group of close friends who play the roles of local kin.

Given women's innate interest in people and their talent for building connections to others, I suspect women work harder at creating and maintaining these non-blood-kinship ties.

I am also convinced that this trend toward making intentional families is an exceedingly important innovation. A sense of community is essential to almost every human being on earth, especially to children. For eons, children grew up in local bands. They formed close bonds with some twenty-five individuals of all ages. If their parents divorced, youngsters remained in this stable social group. They had many adults to meet their needs.

Today children in industrial societies are often dependent on only two adults, the mother and father. This arrangement falls far short of human needs. And when parents divorce, children and parents are often left totally at sea. Growing up with only a single parent has serious disadvantages.[152] But life in the isolated nuclear family is not sufficient either. As the African proverb goes, "It takes a village to raise a child." This is correct. From the anthropological perspective, living in a familiar and supportive local community is an essential aspect of human life.

As women construct and maintain these intentional families, they are provided an essential social web in which their DNA can thrive. As Ahern and Bailey put it, these kin keepers are reinventing the hunting-and-gathering band.[153]

### The Rise of Matriliny?

The family is changing in many ways. Most noticeably, the male-centered patriarchal family unit is being supplemented by a variety of other family forms. In fact, we may be witnessing the beginning of a shift toward matriliny in the Western world.

Not to be confused with matriarchy, matriliny is the kinship system in which individuals trace their descent through the mother, through the female line. Today some 15 percent of cultures are matrilineal. In these societies, such as the Navajo of the American Southwest, women are often socially and economically powerful; they are generally the heads of households; and they maintain ties primarily with maternal kin.

Western societies have a long history of patriliny, the kinship system in which property and titles were largely passed through the father's line. This has changed. Today most families in industrial societies are bilateral: members acknowledge relatives and inherit property from both father and mother. But as more women become economically powerful, as more women become heads of households, and as more women build strong ties with maternal kin, many American families are taking on some of the lifeways associated with a matrilineal kinship system.

Predictably, a backlash has begun.

Southern Baptists, America's largest Protestant denomination, have added an amendment to their core statement of beliefs. It declares that all of its almost sixteen million church members should adhere to a literal interpretation of the scriptures requiring a wife to "submit herself graciously" to her husband's leadership; in exchange, a husband must "provide for, protect and lead his family."

As the Arabs say, "The dogs may bark but the caravan moves on." More attempts to curtail the power of women in the home will undoubtedly be made. But women will prevail. The Population Council lists six global trends for the twenty-first-century family: an increasing participation by women in the labor market, the decline of men's presence in the formal workforce, more women as heads of households, later marriage, later childbirth, smaller families, and more elderly dependents.[154]

All of these developments will bring women more power—and more responsibility—in the family and in society.

## Can the Family Survive?

Gloria Steinem reportedly once said, "A woman without a man is like a fish without a bicycle." Clever; but not accurate. To attach is human. The elegant human emotion of attachment evolved in the hominid brain millions of years ago; it is part of the bedrock of humanity. No social or political force will ever deter men and women from pairing with each other. If we survive as a species, marriage and the family will be with us a million years from now.

In fact, I have tremendous hope for the future of the family.

The traditional patriarchal family was not what nostalgic Americans like to think it was. First, it was never particularly stable or durable. Currently the median length of marriage is almost exactly the same as it was a hundred years ago.[155] Then, a partner died or deserted; today we divorce instead. Lawrence Stone regards the contemporary high divorce rate as the "functional substitute" for spousal death.[156] In fact, today American marriages are somewhat longer—because we are marrying later and living longer.[157]

Second, although the traditional patriarchal family had some merits, it was not an institution that was necessarily good for women. It denied many women the opportunity to express their natural talents and stifled their creativity. It left millions with little else but kitchen, church, and children. All too often it was also loveless.

Today the very essence of marriage is transforming. As women gain economic independence and power, they are making more egalitarian peer marriages based on genuine intimacy. Moreover, those caught in unhappy relationships can depart and try again. And both sexes are finally free to make intentional families or pursue other forms of unconventional family life. Human marriage may very well be in the process of a healthy and necessary reformation.

Most important, women are better educated than at any other time in human history. They also have more business opportunities, more personal and professional networks, fewer children, and more freedom to develop themselves socially and intellectually. Women are becoming capable, worldly, and interesting—as wives, as lovers, as friends, and as companions. If there ever was a time in human evolution when men and women have had the opportunity to make fulfilling marital attachments, that time is now.

# CHAPTER 11

# THE COLLABORATIVE SOCIETY
## Equality Regained

> The morning's the size of heaven.
> What will you do with it?
>
> MARK DOTY

There is a tide in the affairs of men, which, taken at the flood, leads on to fortune," Shakespeare wrote. We are entering a new world, a world in which the distinctive skills and aptitudes of women are becoming just as valuable in the marketplace and society as the abilities of men. As our forebears captured the power of fire, water, electricity, and atoms, today those who appreciate the natural talents of women—and make the most of this vital force—will catch the tide and profit.

Poet Ted Hughes once said of his relationship with poet Sylvia Plath, his wife, "We were like two feet, each one using everything the other did." Men and women were built to put their heads together, not only in their professional lives but in their personal relations. As the sexes come to understand their different strengths, each has the opportunity to gain priceless insight into the other's world; both have the opportunity to achieve new empathy and rapport.

It is time to honor our gender differences, enable women's natural talents to flourish in the workplace, build new understanding between men and women, and work together. Without this fundamental collaboration, both sexes are cheated. Society is cheated, too.

## The Gender War

Yet we live in what may be the only time in human evolution when a vast number of people, especially academics and intellectuals, have convinced themselves that the sexes are just about the same. They choose to ignore the growing body of scientific evidence about inherited gender differences, maintaining instead that men and women are born as blank sheets of paper on which childhood experiences inscribe male and female personalities.

As is often said of generals, these gender diehards are still fighting the last war. Many are troubled by the past. In former times, the sexes were almost universally viewed as different—and women were widely deemed inferior to men. So these doubters fear that if they concede that the sexes have inherently different traits and capabilities, they will just be offering male oppressors new weapons for keeping women in second place.

This kind of thinking is outdated and counterproductive. We live in an era when women's natural aptitudes are being documented. Moreover, today the marketplace needs the female mind. Women have become an enormous economic and social asset.

Society is in transition. The male-dominated patriarchal household is being replaced by a variety of new, egalitarian kinship forms. These new households need the determination and skills of both sexes as they remodel. Neighborhood connections have atrophied as people build personal networks through work, leisure activities, or the Internet. Communities need the energies of both sexes to redefine and strengthen local ties. Television is now the global campfire. As we sit around the TV trying to understand an array of complex issues, we benefit from hearing the views of women as well as those of men. Many companies, once structured as formal hierarchies, are now metamorphosing into hyborgs, or hybrid organizations; each is developing a unique composition. Most will need the abilities of both sexes to succeed.

Corporations, government offices, civil associations, the military, the law, medicine, police departments, classrooms: all of these and many other sectors of society are changing. Even our basic views of justice, health, charity, play, intimacy, sex, and romance are in transition. As we head into an epoch that will pose problems more complex and possibly more dangerous than any that humanity has yet experienced, we need the strengths of both sexes. Success will depend on the full participation of women as well as men. Success will depend on both sexes working as a team.

And women will be prominent team players. As I have emphasized throughout this book, many twentieth-century economic and social forces have conjoined to produce the remarkable rise of educated, economically powerful women. These forces will grow stronger as the next millennium proceeds, reinforced by two exceptional demographic realities that promise to increase the status—and participation—of women in society.

## The Only Child

In Canada, Western and Eastern Europe, Russia, Japan, Korea, Taiwan, China, Thailand, Cuba, and many other countries, fertility rates are currently at or below the population replacement level of 2.1. The United States has a slightly higher birthrate, due to massive immigration from Asia and Latin America.[1] Still, American birthrates are barely high enough to maintain the current population. Even in the developing world, fertility rates have declined from 6 to 3 infants per woman.[2] Demographers predict that the global fertility rate will drop to about 1.85 children per woman by the year 2050—well below the replacement level.[3]

This has broad implications for life on earth. Parents are going to be far less willing to send their only child into battle, for example. More important for women, parents will expend a great deal of time and energy rearing and educating their single child, be it a boy or a girl.

## Favoring the Girl Child

A second demographic factor has even wider consequences for the future participation of women in society. For the first time in human history, men's fertility rate is beginning to mirror that of women.[4] Both sexes are producing just about the same number of children. At first glance, this might seem to have little significance. But it is certain to enhance the status of women—for a curious biological reason.

In many cultures throughout recorded history, men, particularly upper-class men, often had several wives and clandestine lovers, as well as opportunities to copulate with servants, slaves, or concubines. Men could produce many young. Women, on the other hand, could bear only a limited number of babies.[5] For this fundamental biological reason, scientists propose, parents in agrarian societies tended to invest more time, money, and attention on sons. The boy child could potentially spread more of their DNA into the future.[6]

But in contemporary industrial societies, boys no longer grow up to produce more children than girls do. Daughters are becoming just as valuable as sons for spreading their parents' genes. "The incentive to favor sons over daughters is gone," says anthropologist Laura Betzig of the University of Michigan. "This Darwinian principle helps to explain why modern couples are eager to invest in girls."[7]

## The Capable Girl Child

Putting aside these unconscious biological motives, parents will also invest in daughters to achieve social and economic objectives.

In past centuries parents wanted to have sons for many practical reasons. Sons would come to own the resources needed to rear children and look after their parents in their dotage. Sons would acquire the education and experience that enabled them to run the family farm or business. Sons would have the personal networks required to protect family interests. And males would carry on the patriarchal family name. So our ancestors of the long agrarian era were elated when they heard the words "It's a boy!"

But today daughters not only bear just as many children as sons produce, they are also likely—due to their innate nurturing spirit—to expend more time and energy rearing children. Moreover, daughters may be more willing than sons to help parents in their old age. So more and more parents around the world will probably revel in the words "It's a girl!"

This thinking has even begun to spread in China, where male children were traditionally preferred. According to a *New York Times* report in 1998, some Chinese parents now think it is in their interest to have a daughter rather than a son. A girl, they reason, will be more compassionate to them in their advanced years.[8]

What is equally important, parents in many parts of the world will invest in girls because today women are becoming just as capable of financially supporting their families and aging parents as men are. A 1995 study of 130 societies by the United Nations Development Programme confirmed that women on every continent are moving toward economic parity with men. In industrial societies, a wave of educated, confident baby boomer women are also acquiring the "peaceful potency" of their postmenopausal years; many will have the time, energy, and money to assist their kin.

In their footsteps will be what could be an even more powerful generation of women. In the United States, men and women born between 1977 and 1994 are called the "echo boomers." Some seventy-two million Americans in all, they make up 28 percent of the population.[9] The women in this age group are expected to surpass their mothers in their pursuit of education and careers.[10] In other societies, millions more women of this age cohort are expected to break with the past, gain paid employment, and accumulate enough resources to support their children and their parents.

Women are on the march. They are shedding their status as the second sex, the role in which they were cast thousands of years ago as the agricultural era took hold. Their stature—and leadership—will increase. They are winning influential positions in business, education, the professions, government, and civil society. In some sectors of the economy they predominate; they are the first sex. They have also begun to express their sexuality and redefine romance and family life. Like a glacier, contemporary women are slowly carving a new economic and social landscape, building a new world.

This world, I believe, will go beyond the idea of the first sex or the second sex. We are inching toward a truly collaborative society, a global culture in which the merits of both sexes are understood, valued, and employed. The twenty-first century may be the first in the modern era to see the sexes work and live as equals—the way men and women were designed to live, the way men and women did live for so many millennia of our distinguished human past.

# NOTES

### Introduction. Deep History: An Immodest Proposal

1. A. Jost 1970; Nyborg 1994; Halpern 1992.
2. A. Jost 1970; Gorski 1980, pp. 215–22.
3. Gorski 1991, pp. 71–104; Nyborg 1994.
4. Nyborg 1994.
5. Nelson 1995.
6. Nyborg 1994.

### 1. Web Thinking: Women's Contextual View

1. McClelland 1975; Gilligan 1982; Tannen 1990.
2. Hall 1984; Silverman and Eals 1992, pp. 533–49.
3. Rosener 1995; Helgesen 1990; Duff 1993.
4. Ibid.
5. Helgesen 1990; Rosener 1995; Tannen 1990; Hampden-Turner 1994, p. 142; Duff 1993.
6. Eccles 1987; see Browne 1995, p. 1023.
7. Hampden-Turner 1994.
8. Seger 1996, p. 83.
9. Ibid., p. 137.
10. *Harper's* 1997, p. 53.
11. Masters and Carlotti 1993, p. 31.
12. National Foundation for Women Business Owners 1996, p. 4.
13. United Nations Development Programme 1995, p. 90.
14. Hall 1984.
15. Slatalla 1998.
16. Gilligan 1982.
17. Ibid., p. 35.
18. Ibid., p. 38.
19. Hampden-Turner 1994.
20. Tannen 1994.
21. Halpern 1992, p. 90.
22. Grafman, Holyoak, and Boller 1995, pp. 1–411.
23. Hendler 1995, pp. 265–76; Goldman-Rakic 1995, pp. 71–83.
24. Goldman-Rakic 1995; Holyoak and Kroger 1995, pp. 253–63.
25. Goldman-Rakic 1995; Damasio 1994; Hendler 1995.
26. Damasio 1994.
27. Della Salla et al. 1995, pp. 161–71; Guyton and Hall 1996.

28. Grafman 1989; Grafman and Hendler 1991, pp. 563–64; Holyoak and Kroger 1995, pp. 253–63; Grafman, Holyoak, and Boller 1995a, pp. 1–411.

29. Stuss et al. 1995, pp. 191–211; Posner 1994, pp. 7398–403; Posner and Dehaene 1994, pp. 75–79; Nichelli et al. 1995, pp. 161–71; Dehaene and Changeux 1995, pp. 305–19.

30. Skuse et al. 1997, pp. 705–8; Tucker, Luu, and Pribram 1995, pp. 191–211.

31. Pardo, Pardo, and Raichle 1993, pp. 713–19; Tucker, Luu, and Pribram 1995, pp. 191–211; George et al. 1996, pp. 859–71.

32. Schlaepfer et al. 1994, p. 170; George et al. 1996, pp. 859–71.

33. Goldman et al. 1974, pp. 540–42; Mitchell 1981.

34. Lacoste-Utamsing and Holloway 1982, pp. 1431–32; Witelson 1989, pp. 799–835; Allen et al. 1991, pp. 933–42; Holloway et al. 1993, pp. 481–98; Nyborg 1994.

35. Allen and Gorski 1991, pp. 97–104.

36. Gilinsky 1984; Barchas et al. 1984, pp. 131–50.

37. Hales 1998, pp. 49–51; Hales 1999.

38. Hales 1998, p. 51.

39. Lancaster 1994.

40. Hockhschild and Machung 1989.

41. Weiner and Brown 1997.

42. Rosener 1995; Helgesen 1990; Duff 1993; Seger 1996.

43. Helgesen 1990; Rosener 1995; Duff 1993.

44. Senge 1990; Byrne 1992, pp. 44–52.

45. Senge 1990, p. 68.

46. Hampden-Turner 1994; Senge 1990.

47. Worton 1996.

48. Kohlberg 1969; Piaget 1932; Lever 1976, pp. 478–87; Gilligan 1982.

49. Tannen 1990.

50. Kohlberg 1969; Lever 1976; Gilligan 1982; Piaget 1932.

51. Skuse et al. 1997, pp. 705–8.

52. Drucker 1992; Stewart 1997.

53. Damasio 1994; Fodor 1983; Gazzaniga 1988; LeDoux 1996.

54. Damasio 1994.

55. Bechara et al. 1997, pp. 1293–95.

56. Damasio 1994; Bechara et al. 1997, pp. 1293–95.

57. Simon 1987, pp. 57–63; Benderly 1989, pp. 35–40.

58. Simon 1974, pp. 482–88; see Klahr and Kotovsky 1989; Benderly 1989.

59. Gottman 1994, p. 12.

60. Rowan 1986, p. 3.

61. Agor 1986.

62. Simon 1987; Rosener 1995; Agor 1986; Rowan 1986.

63. Helgesen 1990; Hampden-Turner 1994.

64. Helgesen 1990, p. 25.

65. Simon 1998, p. A14.

66. Paine Webber 1997.

67. Simon 1998, p. A14.

68. Harris 1996, pp. 146ff.

69. Ibid., p. 153.

70. Paine Webber 1997.
71. Damasio 1994; Damasio 1995, pp. 241–51; Holyoak and Kroger 1995.
72. Senge 1990; Hampden-Turner 1994; Rosener 1995; McCorduck and Ramsey 1996; Drucker 1992; Stewart 1997; Helgesen 1990.
73. Boller et al. 1995, pp. 23–39.
74. Bergmann 1986; Coontz 1992.
75. McCorduck and Ramsey 1996; Coontz 1992.
76. Ibid.
77. *The Economist* 1996, pp. 23–26.
78. *The Economist* 1998, pp. 3–15.
79. Bergmann 1986.
80. Bruce et al. 1995; *The Economist* 1998, pp. 3–15.
81. Bergmann 1986; Posner 1992.
82. *The Economist* 1996; *The Economist* 1998.
83. Bergmann 1986; *The Economist* 1998.
84. Ibid.; Posner 1992.
85. Lewin 1995a; *The Economist* 1998a, pp. 3–15.
86. Russell 1995, p. 8.
87. Rosener 1995; Bergmann 1986; Harris 1996, pp. 146ff; *The Economist* 1998.
88. United Nations Development Programme 1995.
89. Ibid., p. 71.
90. Ibid.
91. Rosenthal 1998, p. A4.
92. Rosener 1995; United Nations Development Programme 1995.
93. United Nations Development Programme 1995.
94. Ibid.; Future Survey 1996, p. 11; Bruce et al. 1995; *The Economist* 1996.
95. Mydans 1997, p. A3.
96. United Nations Development Programme 1995, p. 78.
97. Karl 1995.
98. Seger 1996, p. 66.

## 2. The Organization Woman: Feminine Team Playing

1. See Hoyenga and Hoyenga 1979; Tannen 1990; Gilligan 1982; Rosener 1995; Helgesen 1990; Duff 1993; Chodorow 1974; Gilligan 1988; Seger 1996; Mitchell 1981; Tavris and Offrir 1977.
2. Darwin 1936, p. 873.
3. Rosener 1995; Helgesen 1990; Duff 1993.
4. See Pool 1994.
5. Chodorow 1974; Gilligan 1982.
6. Tannen 1990.
7. Lever 1976, pp. 478–87; 1978, pp. 471–83; Thorne 1993; Gilligan 1982.
8. Lever 1976; Tannen 1990, 1994.
9. Lever 1976, 1978; Thorne 1993; Tannen 1990.
10. Kohlberg 1981; Gilligan 1982.
11. Orenstein 1994.
12. Ibid., p. 13.

13. McCorduck and Ramsey 1996; Helgesen 1990; Rosener 1995; Hampden-Turner 1994; Duff 1993; Tannen 1994; Seger 1996.
14. Tannen 1990, 1994.
15. Auletta 1998, p. 75.
16. Duff 1993, p. 50.
17. Rosener 1995; Hampden-Turner 1994.
18. Tannen 1994.
19. Helgesen 1995, p. xxxiii.
20. Hampden-Turner 1994; Helgesen 1990; Rosener 1995.
21. Pool 1994; Kelly 1991, p. 100.
22. Helgesen 1990; Duff 1993; Daymont and Andrisani 1984, pp. 408–14; see Brown 1995, 973–1106.
23. Paine Webber 1997.
24. Piltch 1992a, pp. 6–7, 1992b.
25. Kohlberg 1981.
26. Tear 1995, p. A14.
27. See Hall 1984.
28. Ibid.
29. Tannen 1990.
30. Hall 1994.
31. Coates 1986; Tannen 1990, 1994.
32. Tannen 1994.
33. Ibid.
34. Monnet 1995, pp. 1–43.
35. Chodorow 1974; Gilligan 1982.
36. See Fedigan 1983, pp. 91–129; Silverberg and Gray 1992; Smuts 1986; Waal 1982.
37. Nishida and Hiraiwa-Hasegawa 1986.
38. Waal 1982.
39. Ibid.
40. Baker and Smuts 1994, pp. 227–42.
41. Smuts 1986, p. 402.
42. Waal 1982.
43. Ibid.
44. Symons 1979; Betzig 1988; Ellis 1992; Buss 1994.
45. Buss 1994.
46. Fedigan 1983, pp. 91–129; McMillan 1989, pp. 83–89.
47. Buss 1994; Betzig 1988.
48. Parish 1994, pp. 157–79; Smuts 1997.
49. Waal 1982.
50. Wrangham and Peterson 1996.
51. Parish 1994.
52. See Smuts 1986; Fedigan 1982; Low 1989, pp. 311–18.
53. Parish 1994.
54. Smuts 1997.
55. Pusey, Williams, and Goodall 1997, pp. 828–30.
56. Brown and Gilligan 1992; see Sommers 1994, p. 139.
57. Goldberg 1993.

58. Beach 1948.
59. Rose, Holaday, and Bernstein 1971, pp. 366–68; Rose et al. 1974; Sapolsky 1983, pp. 365–76; Velle 1982, pp. 295–315; Joslyn 1973; Cochran and Perachio 1977; Birch and Clark 1946.
60. Mazur and Lamb 1980, pp. 236–46; Mazur, Susmun, and Edelbrock 1997; Booth, Shelley, Mazur, Tharp, and Kottok 1989.
61. See Blum 1997, p. 176; Goleman 1990, pp. C1, 3.
62. Mazur, Susman, and Edelbrock 1997; Mazur, Booth, and Dabbs 1992, pp. 70–77; Booth et al. 1989, pp. 556–71.
63. Ibid.
64. Udry, Kovenock, and Morris 1992; See Edwards and Booth 1994.
65. Purifoy and Koopmans 1980, pp. 179–88; Bancroft et al. 1983, pp. 509–16.
66. Mazur, Susman, and Edelbrock 1997, pp. 317–26.
67. Dabbs 1992, pp. 813–24.
68. Udry, Talbert, and Morris 1986, pp. 217–27; Halpern 1992.
69. Several chemicals are associated with the fight for rank, including Vasopressin (DeVries et al. 1985, pp. 236–54), the precursors of the estrogens and androgens (Yalcinkaya et al. 1993, pp. 1929–31), and serotonin (McGuire, Raleigh, and Brammer 1982, pp. 643–61; Raleigh et al. 1991, pp. 181–90; Raleigh and Brammer 1993, p. 592; Frank 1985; Madsen 1994).
70. Kurtz and Zuckerman 1978, pp. 529–30; Ginsberg and Miller 1982, pp. 426–28.
71. Randall 1996; Paine Webber 1997, p. 12; Simon 1998, p. A14.
72. Zuckerman 1994.
73. Waal 1989a, pp. 3–39.
74. Duff 1993; Seger 1996; Worton 1996.
75. Seger 1996, p. 269.
76. Worton 1996.
77. Lagerspetz, Bjorkqvist, and Peltonen 1988, pp. 403–14.
78. Waal 1989.
79. Wilson 1993, pp. 3–26.
80. Duff 1993.
81. Bjorkvist, Lagerspetz, and Kaukiainen 1992, pp. 117–27.
82. Duff 1993.
83. Worton 1996, p. 22.
84. Bergmann 1986.
85. U.S. Department of Labor, Bureau of Labor Statistics 1996; Statistical Abstract of the United States 1996; *The Economist* 1996.
86. Ibid.
87. United Nations Development Programme 1995.
88. McCorduck and Ramsey 1996; Dobrzynski 1996a, p. D1f; Browne 1995, pp. 973–1106.
89. Wellington 1996.
90. Wellington 1997.
91. Ibid.
92. *Harper's* 1997, pp. 47–58.
93. Hayes 1997, p. A28.
94. Ibid.
95. Rosener 1995.

96. United Nations 1995c.

97. *Yearbook of Labor Statistics* 1994; Davidson and Cooper 1993; *The Economist* 1998a, pp. 3–15.

98. Browne 1995, p. 1079.

99. Townsend 1996, pp. 28–37; *Harper's* 1997, pp. 47–58.

100. Valian 1998, pp. 18–23.

101. Cowan 1989, p. A1f.

102. The New York Times 1997.

103. Helgesen 1995; Eccles 1987; Browne 1995; Townsend 1996, pp. 28–37.

104. Bergmann 1986; Helgesen 1995; Browne 1995.

105. Lawlor 1997, p. BU11.

106. United Nations Development Programme 1995.

107. *The Economist* 1998a, p. 12.

108. Helgesen 1990; Pasternack and Viscio 1998; Drucker 1992; Hey and Moore 1998.

109. Drucker 1988, pp. 45ff; Mills 1991; Katzenbach and Smith 1993; Naisbitt and Aburdene 1986; Pasternack and Viscio 1998; Fukuyama and Shulsky 1997; Weiner and Brown 1997; Stewart 1997; Hey and Moore 1998.

110. Pasternack and Viscio 1998.

111. Helgesen 1990.

112. Helgesen 1990; Stewart 1997; Drucker 1993, 1997.

113. Helgesen 1990; Fukuyama and Shulsky 1997.

114. Drucker 1992, p. 329.

115. Fukuyama and Shulsky 1997, p. x.

116. Weiner and Brown 1997, p. 93.

117. Helgesen 1990; Rosener 1995; Hey and Moore 1998.

118. Rosener 1995, p. 4.

119. Ibid.; Rosener 1990, pp. 119–25.

120. Townsend 1996, pp. 28–37.

121. Ibid.

122. Lawlor 1997, p. BU11.

123. Weiner and Brown 1997.

124. Ho 1997, p. B2; *The Economist* 1998a, pp. 3–15.

125. National Foundation for Women Business Owners 1996; Weiner and Brown 1997.

126. National Foundation for Women Business Owners 1996; Seger 1996.

127. Davidson and Cooper 1993.

128. Wilkinson 1996, p. 32.

129. United Nations 1995b.

130. Drucker 1997, pp. 20ff; Stewart 1997; Weiner and Brown 1997; Hampden-Turner 1994; McCorduck and Ramsey 1996; Pasternack and Viscio 1998; Hey and Moore 1998.

131. Rosener 1995, p. 20.

### 3. Women's Words: Educators in the Information Age

1. Hampson and Kimura 1993, pp. 357–400; Halpern 1992.
2. Horgan 1975; Shucard, Shucard, and Thomas 1987.
3. Ibid.; Halpern 1992; Hall 1984.
4. Maccoby and Jacklin 1974; McGuiness 1976b; McGuiness 1985; Martin and Hoover 1987, pp. 65–83.
5. Hampson and Kimura 1993; Halpern 1992.
6. Halpern 1992; Hedges and Nowell 1995, pp. 41–45.
7. Hampson and Kimura 1993.
8. Halpern 1992.
9. Hedges and Nowell 1995.
10. McGuiness, Olson, and Chapman 1990, pp. 263–85; Mann et al. 1990, pp. 1063–77.
11. McGuinness 1985, pp. 57–126; Mann et al. 1990.
12. Gallup Organization 1996.
13. Hall 1984; Tannen 1994.
14. Mitchell 1981.
15. Holden 1996, p. 1921; Witelson, Glezer, and Kigar 1995, pp. 3418–28.
16. McGuinness and Pribram 1979.
17. Shaywitz et al. pp. 607–9.
18. Lacoste-Utamsing and Holloway 1982, pp. 1431–32; Witelson 1989, pp. 799–835; Allen et al. 1991, pp. 933–42; Holloway et al. 1993, pp. 481–98.
19. Hines et al. 1992, pp. 3–14.
20. Kimura 1983, pp. 19–35, 1987, pp. 133–47.
21. Ibid.
22. LeDoux 1996.
23. Damasio 1994.
24. Ibid.; LeDoux 1996; Fodor 1983; Gazzaniga 1988.
25. Gould, Woolley, and McEwan 1991, pp. 67–84; Woolley et al. 1990, pp. 4035–39; Frankfurt 1994; Toran-Allerand 1986, pp. 175–211; See McEwens 1994, pp. 1–18; see Nyborg 1994.
26. Halpern 1992.
27. Hampson 1990b, pp. 26–43; 1990a, pp. 97–111; Kimura 1989, pp. 63–66.
28. Sherwin 1994, pp. 423–30; Sherwin and Phillips 1990, pp. 474–75; Phillips and Sherwin 1992, pp. 485–95; Barret-Connor and Kritz-Silverstein 1993, pp. 2637–41.
29. McCauley et al. 1987, pp. 464–73; Skuse et al. 1997, pp. 705–8.
30. Skuse et al. 1997, p. 707.
31. Hendricks 1998, pp. 12–19.
32. Fernald 1992.
33. Ibid.
34. Stern, Spieker, and MacKain 1983, pp. 727–35; Fernald and Simon 1984, pp. 104–13.
35. See Fernald 1992.
36. Ibid.
37. See Bruce et al. 1995, p. 51.
38. Hewlett 1992, pp. 153–76.

39. See Small 1998.
40. Hall 1984.
41. Mitchell 1981; McGuinness 1979.
42. Pinker and Bloom 1992, p. 484.
43. Deacon 1997, 1992; Falk 1992, pp.1–24.
44. Steenland 1987.
45. Robinson 1996, pp. 60–64.
46. Ibid., p. 63.
47. Moran 1998, pp. 38ff.
48. United Nations 1995.
49. Mifflin 1998, pp. D1ff.
50. Ibid.; United Nations 1995.
51. Seger 1996.
52. Steenland 1987.
53. Auletta 1998, pp. 72–78.
54. United Nations 1995.
55. Ibid.; Seger 1996.
56. United Nations 1995.
57. Ibid.
58. Steenland 1990, p. 237.
59. Statistical Abstract of the United States 1996.
60. United Nations 1995.
61. Carroll 1997, p. 7.
62. Ibid.
63. United Nations Development Programme 1995.
64. Seger 1996, p. xx.
65. United Nations 1995; Karl 1995.
66. Drucker 1992.
67. Seger 1996.
68. Passell 1995, p. A9.
69. Seger 1996.
70. Holmes 1996, p. A1f.
71. Seger 1996.
72. Ibid.
73. Karl 1995.
74. Seger 1996.
75. Bergmann 1986; Statistical Abstract of the United States 1996.
76. Ibid.
77. United Nations 1995.
78. United Nations Development Programme 1995.
79. Statistical Abstract of the United States 1996.
80. Ibid.
81. Heath 1997a, pp. 39–43.
82. *Futurific* 1995, p. 19.
83. Heath 1997b, p. 40.
84. Halpern 1992.
85. Heath 1997a.
86. United Nations 1995.

87. Western 1996; Tannen 1990; Tierney 1998, p. 14.
88. Campbell; Tierney 1998, p. 14.
89. Faison 1998, p. A4.
90. Fisher 1982, 1992.
91. Dunbar 1996.
92. Tierney 1998, p. 14.
93. Ibid.
94. O'Connor 1996, p. 12.
95. *New Scientist* 1997, p. 21.
96. Drucker 1992, p. 334.
97. Ibid.
98. Statistical Abstract of the United States 1997.
99. Ibid.
100. Greenwood 1996, p. 1987.
101. Browne 1995, pp. 973–1106.
102. *Futurific* 1996a, p. 4ff.
103. United Nations Development Programme 1995, p. 3.
104. Ibid.
105. Statistical Abstract of the United States 1996.
106. Rosener 1995.
107. Wessel 1996, p. A1ff.
108. Samuelson 1995, p. 61.
109. Russell 1996, p. 10ff.
110. Winerip 1998, p. 48.
111. Finn, Bierlein, and Mano 1996, p. 18ff; Orfield 1998, p. A17; Winerip 1998, p. 48.
112. Newman 1998, p. A21.
113. Applebome 1996, p. B7; Winerip 1998, p. 48.
114. Weiner and Brown 1997.
115. *The Economist* 1998b, p. 28ff.
116. Kantrowitz and Wingert 1998, pp. 64–70.
117. Applebome 1996, p. B7.
118. Lenzner and Johnson 1997, p. 127.
119. Bylinsky 1996, pp. 162Aff.
120. Byrne 1995, p. 64.
121. Weiner and Brown 1997.
122. Ibid.
123. Honan 1998, p. 4A:44.
124. Drucker 1992; Stewart 1997; Weiner and Brown 1997; Hey and Moore 1998.

#### 4. Mind Reading: People Skills at Your Service

1. Weinstein 1968; McGuiness 1976b; Galton 1894, pp. 40–42.
2. Heller 1997.
3. Gandelman 1983, pp. 1–17; Hall 1984.
4. Hall 1984.
5. See Hall 1984; Mitchell 1981.

6. Mitchell 1981.
7. Heller 1997.
8. Ibid., p. 38.
9. Small 1998.
10. Talbot 1998, p. 24ff; see Heller 1997.
11. Field et al. 1986, pp. 654–58; Schanberg and Field 1987, pp. 1431–47.
12. See Heller 1997.
13. Uvnas-Mogerg 1997, pp. 146–63.
14. Schanberg, Evoniuk, and Kuhn 1984, p. 135; Sapolsky 1997, pp. 1620–21; Liu et al. 1997, pp. 1659–62.
15. McGuinness 1972, pp. 465–73; Elliott 1971, pp. 375–80.
16. Gower 1998, p. 3.
17. Doty et al. 1984, pp. 1441–43; Doty et al. 1985 pp. 667–72; Doty 1986, pp. 377–413; Cain 1982, pp. 129–42.
18. Doty 1986, pp. 377–413.
19. Doty et al. 1984, pp. 1441–43; Doty et al. 1985, pp. 667–72.
20. Small 1998.
21. Goleman 1994, p. C1, 8.
22. Doty 1978, pp. 337–62.
23. Monneuse, Bellisle, and Louis-Sylvestre 1991, pp. 1111–17.
24. See Levenson 1995.
25. McGuinness 1976a, pp. 279–94.
26. McGuinness 1979.
27. McGuinness 1976c, 1985.
28. Brody 1997, p. F9.
29. Montagu 1953; Jacobs 1981; see Nathans, Thomas, and Hogness 1986, pp. 193–202.
30. Erwin, 1992, pp. 231–40.
31. Kolata 1995, p. C7.
32. Hall 1984; Brody and Hall 1993, pp. 447–60.
33. Babchuk, Hames, and Thompson 1983, pp. 89–102.
34. Hall 1984.
35. Ekman and Friesen 1971, pp. 124–29.
36. Hall 1984.
37. McCauley et al. 1987, pp. 464–73.
38. Goleman 1995a, pp. C1,9.
39. McGuinness and Pribram 1979.
40. Hall 1984; Goleman 1995a, pp. C1,9.
41. McGuinness and Pribram 1979; Hall 1984; Brody and Hall 1993, pp. 447–60.
42. Hrdy 1986, pp. 119–46.
43. McGuinness and Pribram 1979; Hall 1984.
44. Hales 1999.
45. Bever 1992; McGuinness and Sparks 1983, pp. 91–100; Miller and Santoni 1986, pp. 225–35; Gaulin and Fitzgerald 1989.
46. Silverman and Eals 1992, pp. 533–49.
47. Galea and Kimura 1993, pp. 53–65; Kimura 1987, pp. 133–47; Silverman and Eals 1992, pp. 533–49.

48. Silverman and Eals 1992, pp. 533–49.
49. Miller and Santoni 1986, pp. 225–35; Ward, Newcombe, and Overton 1986, pp. 192–213.
50. Williams and Meck 1991, pp. 155–76; Geary 1998.
51. Williams and Meck 1991, pp. 155–76.
52. Skuse et al. 1997, pp. 705–8; Tucker, Luu, and Pribram 1995, pp. 191–211; Damasio 1994; see Grafman, Holyoak, and Boller 1995.
53. Skuse et al. 1997, pp. 705–08.
54. Tucker, Luu, and Pribram 1995, pp. 191–211; Safer 1981, pp. 86–100.
55. Safer 1981, pp. 86–100.
56. Hittelman and Dickes 1979, pp. 171–84; Hall 1984.
57. McGuinness and Pribram 1979.
58. Ibid.
59. Mitchell 1981.
60. Hall 1984.
61. Rossi and Rossi 1990.
62. Hall 1984.
63. Ibid.
64. Maclay and Knipe 1972.
65. Hall 1984.
66. Ibid.
67. Weiner and Brown 1997; Pasternack and Viscio 1998; Rosener 1995.
68. Weiner and Brown 1997, p. 62.
69. Ibid.
70. Postrel 1997, pp. 4ff.
71. Saporito 1995, pp. 50ff.
72. Ibid.
73. Passell 1995, p. A9.
74. Ibid.; Weiner and Brown 1997.
75. Statistical Abstract of the United States 1996.
76. United Nations 1995c.
77. United Nations Development Programme 1995.
78. Kannapell 1995, p. C1.
79. Passell 1995, p. A9.
80. Statistical Abstract of the United States 1996; Harrington 1993.
81. Rosener 1995; Janofsky 1998, p. B14.
82. Rosener 1995, p. 132.
83. Rosener 1995; Janofsky 1998, p. B14.
84. Harrington 1993.
85. Rosener 1995.
86. Statistical Abstract of the United States 1996.
87. Rosener 1995, p. 22.
88. Bergmann 1986.
89. Statistical Abstract of the United States 1996.
90. Ibid.
91. United Nations 1995c.
92. *The Economist* 1997, p. 62.
93. Alexander 1995, pp. 42ff.

94. *Utne Reader* 1997, p. 71.
95. Ibid.; *The Economist* 1997; Pearce 1997.
96. Pearce 1997, p. 39.
97. Passell 1995, p. A9.
98. Crossette 1998b, p. WK5.
99. Weiner and Brown 1997.
100. Kishkovsky and Williamson 1997, p. A12.
101. McCorduck and Ramsey 1996; Statistical Abstract of the United States 1996.
102. Buchholz 1996.
103. Kay and Hagan 1998, pp. 728–43; Epstein 1981; Epstein et al. 1995, pp. 291–449.
104. Epstein 1981; Epstein et al. 1995.
105. Harrington 1993; Kay and Hagan 1998.
106. Ibid.
107. Harrington 1993.
108. Buchholz 1996.
109. Harrington 1993.
110. Ibid., p. 16.
111. Ibid.
112. Ibid.
113. Garry 1997, p. 10.
114. Dawley 1997, p. 66E16.
115. Garry 1997.
116. Dawley 1997.
117. Johnson 1995, p. B1.
118. Ibid.
119. Waal 1982.
120. Ibid.
121. Rosener 1995.
122. Ibid.
123. Jack and Jack 1989; Menkel-Meadow 1985, p. 39; Harrington 1993; West 1988, pp. 1ff; Rosener 1995.
124. Rosener 1995.
125. Harrington 1993.
126. Ibid.; Browne 1997, pp. 5–86.
127. Songer, Davis, and Haire 1994, pp. 425–39.

## 5. Heirs to Hippocrates: Women as Healers

1. Finerman 1995.
2. Kleinman 1980.
3. Finerman 1995.
4. Nordstrom 1995, p. 51.
5. Wedenoja 1995.
6. Strachey 1918, p 155.
7. Braus 1994, pp.40–47.
8. Rossiter 1995; Braus 1994.

9. Ibid.
10. *The Economist* 1996c, 23ff; Bergmann 1986; *The Economist* 1998a, pp. 3–15; U.S. Department of Labor, Bureau of Labor Statistics 1996; Braus 1994.
11. Ibid.
12. Ibid.
13. Ibid.
14. Ibid.
15. *The Economist* 1996; Braus 1986.
16. Gallup Organization 1996, p. 6.
17. Goleman 1995a.
18. Hall 1984; Gottman 1994.
19. Brody and Hall 1993, pp. 447–60.
20. Ibid.; Swain 1989; Tavris 1992, pp. 15–25; Stapley and Haviland 1989, pp. 295–308.
21. Swain 1989; Tavris 1992.
22. Brody and Hall 1993.
23. Gottman 1994.
24. Hatfield and Rapson 1996.
25. Gallup Organization 1996.
26. Gottman 1994.
27. Ibid.
28. Ibid.
29. LeDoux 1996.
30. Tucker, Luu, and Pribram 1995, pp. 191–211; LeDoux 1996.
31. Cummings 1995, pp. 1–13; Tucker, Luu, and Pribram 1995; Damasio, 1994.
32. Damasio 1995, pp. 241–51; LeDoux 1996.
33. Damasio 1995.
34. Damasio 1994.
35. Ibid.
36. Mlot 1998, pp. 1005–7; Tucker, Luu, and Pribram 1995; Damasio 1994.
37. Pardo, Pardo, and Raichle 1993, pp. 713–19; Tucker, Luu, and Pribram 1995; George et al. 1996, pp. 859–71.
38. Gottman 1994.
39. Gardner 1983.
40. Witkin 1995.
41. Maccoby and Jacklin 1974; Hoffman 1977, pp. 712–22; Brody and Hall 1993.
42. See Browne 1995, p. 1033.
43. Darwin 1936, p. 873.
44. George et al. 1996, pp. 859–71.
45. Goleman 1995a, p. C9.
46. Mlot 1998.
47. Ibid.
48. Brody and Hall 1993; Goleman 1995b.
49. Weissman and Olfson 1995, pp. 799–801; DSM III R 1994, pp. 317–91; Bower 1995b, p. 346.
50. Walsh 1987; Gove 1987; Johnson 1987.
51. Johnson 1987.

52. Bower 1995b; Gove 1987.
53. Brody and Hall 1993.
54. Brody and Hall 1993; Goleman 1995a; Gottman 1994.
55. Hoffman 1977; Hall 1984.
56. Hall 1984.
57. Ibid.
58. Stern 1987.
59. Mead and Newton 1967.
60. Rossi 1984, pp. 1–19; Katz and Konner 1981; Frayser 1985.
61. Rosenblatt 1995, pp. 3–25; Moltz et al. 1970.
62. Pedersen et al. 1992, pp. 1–492.
63. Brown et al. 1996, pp. 297–309; Cohen 1996.
64. Wade 1998, p. A17.
65. Darwin 1936, p. 873.
66. Drucker 1992; Stewart 1997.
67. Rossi 1984; Katz and Konner 1981; Frayser 1985.
68. McGuiness 1990, pp. 315–25.
69. Rosener 1995; Helgesen 1990; Duff 1993.
70. Paine Webber 1997.
71. Gallup Organization 1996.
72. McGrew 1981.
73. See Blum 1997.
74. Hampson and Kimura 1988, pp. 456–59; Kimura 1989, pp. 63–66.
75. Kimura 1989, pp. 63–66.
76. Kimura 1987, pp. 133–47.
77. McGrew 1981.
78. Nadler and Braggio 1974, pp. 541–50.
79. Mitchell 1981.
80. McGuinness and Pribram 1979; McGuinness 1985.
81. Ibid.; Kimura 1992, pp. 118–25.
82. Nyborg 1994; Geary 1998.
83. Burg 1966, pp. 460–66.
84. Maccoby and Jacklin 1974.
85. Hedges and Nowell 1995, pp. 41–45; Hyde, Fennema, and Lamon 1990, pp. 139–55; Halpern 1992.
86. See Benbow and Stanley 1983, pp. 1029–31; Mann et al. 1990, pp. 1063–77; Witkin and Berry 1975, pp. 4–87.
87. Nyborg 1994.
88. Janowsky, Oviatt, and Orwoll 1994, pp. 325–32.
89. Hampson and Kimura 1988; Hampson 1990b, pp. 26–43; Hampson 1990a, pp. 97–111.
90. See Nyborg 1994.
91. Ibid.
92. Nyborg 1994.
93. Udry, Talbert, and Morris 1986, pp. 217–27; Halpern 1992.
94. Braus 1994, pp. 40–47.
95. Braus 1994.
96. Ibid.

97. Zuger 1998b.
98. Ibid., p. WH20.
99. Braus 1994.
100. Zuger 1998b, p. WH20.
101. Braus 1994, p. 44.
102. Zuger 1998b, p. WH20.
103. Braus 1994; Redman et al. 1994, pp. 361, 368–69.
104. Braus 1994; Weisman et al. 1986, pp. 776–77.
105. Storch, personal communication.
106. Freudenheim 1997, pp. A1f.
107. Ibid.
108. Ibid.
109. Ibid.
110. Schenck-Yglesias 1995, pp. 18ff.
111. Weiner and Brown 1997.
112. House et al. 1988.
113. Ibid.
114. Goleman 1995a; Ornish 1998.
115. Ornish 1998.
116. Barton 1997, pp. 45ff.
117. Weiner and Brown 1997.
118. Barton 1997.
119. Stone 1997, p. 46.
120. Kolata 1996, pp. A1f; Duff 1997, pp. B1f.
121. Heath 1997, p. 27.
122. Ibid.
123. Dolan 1996, pp. 164ff; Smith 1997, pp. 169ff.
124. Reid 1995.
125. Ibid.; DeVries 1985.
126. Ibid.
127. See Trevathan 1987.
128. See Ibid.
129. Trevathan 1999.
130. Rooks 1997; Heller 1997.
131. Braus 1994, p 45.

#### 6. How Women Lead: Women in Civil Society and Government

1. Gallup Organization 1996.
2. McCorduck and Ramsey 1996; Huber 1996; Drobis 1997, pp. 281ff.
3. McCorduck and Ramsey 1996, p. 262.
4. Gellner 1994; Greene 1997, pp. 15–16.
5. Greene 1997, p. 15.
6. Coontz 1992; Fukayama 1995.
7. Tocqueville 1945, p. 225.
8. Karl 1995.
9. Ibid.
10. Ibid.

11. Fukuyama 1995.
12. Karl 1995, p. 19.
13. Belluck 1996, pp. 1f.
14. Weiner and Brown 1997.
15. *Wilson Quarterly* 1998, p. 126.
16. Weiner and Brown 1997.
17. Karl 1995.
18. Von Hoffman 1997, p. 14.
19. Weiner and Brown 1997.
20. Drucker 1992.
21. Drucker 1992, p. 227.
22. Ibid., p. 231.
23. Fukuyama 1995.
24. Browne 1995, pp. 973–1106; Rich 1998; Council on Foundations 1998, pp. 3–6; Bennett 1998, pp. 741–61.
25. Drucker 1992, p. 207.
26. Roger Pasquier, personal communication.
27. Browne 1995.
28. Rich 1998.
29. Ibid.
30. Council on Foundations 1998.
31. Lemann 1997, pp. 18ff; Fitzpatrick and Bruer 1997, p. 766.
32. Fitzpatrick and Bruer 1997.
33. Fukuyama 1995.
34. Samuels 1995, p. 28.
35. Jacoby 1997, pp. G1f.
36. Fitzpatrick and Bruer 1997.
37. Andina and Pillsbury 1997.
38. *The Economist* 1997a.
39. Kahn and Jordan 1995, p. A8.
40. Karl 1995.
41. Pearce 1994, p. 17.
42. Masini 1996, pp. 1ff.
43. Crossette 1998b, p. WK5.
44. Crossette 1998a, p. A17.
45. De Palma 1997, p. A1.
46. Chen 1996; McCorduck and Ramsey 1996.
47. Crossette 1998a, p. A6.
48. Ibid.
49. McCorduck and Ramsey 1996, p. 126.
50. Greene 1997, pp. 15–16.
51. Lewis 1998, p. B9.
52. Ibid.
53. Ibid.
54. Ibid.
55. McCorduck and Ramsey 1996, p. 15.
56. McCorduck and Ramsey 1996.
57. *The Economist* 1998, pp. 3–15; Doyle 1998; United Nations Development Programme 1995.

58. Bergmann 1986.
59. Doyle 1998; United Nations Development Programme 1995; *The Economist* 1998.
60. Ibid.
61. Ibid.
62. Crossette 1995a, p. A1.
63. Doyle 1998; McCorduck and Ramsey 1996; Bergmann 1986.
64. Karl 1995.
65. Doyle 1998; United Nations Development Programme 1995.
66. Crossette 1995b, p. A1; United Nations Development Programme 1995.
67. United Nations Development Programme 1995.
68. Ibid.
69. Ibid.
70. Ibid.
71. Seltzer, Newman, and Leighton 1997.
72. Lueptow, Garovich, and Lueptow 1995, pp. 509–30; Ayres 1997, pp. A1ff.
73. McCorduck and Ramsey 1996.
74. United Nations Development Programme 1995, p. 83.
75. Whyte 1978.
76. Fluehr-Lobban 1979, pp. 341–60; Gimbutas 1989.
77. Murdock 1949; Goldberg 1993; Whyte 1978.
78. Gallup Organization 1996.
79. Davis and Smith 1991.
80. Rosener 1995; Collins 1998, pp. 54–55.
81. Ayres 1997.
82. Karl 1995.
83. Lueptow, Garovich, and Lueptow 1995.
84. Ayres 1997.
85. Collins 1998.
86. Ibid., p. 56.
87. Gallup Organization 1996.
88. Whiting and Whiting 1975; McGuinness and Pribram 1979; Campbell 1993.
89. Wrangham and Peterson 1996.
90. Campbell 1993; *The Economist* 1996, pp. 23ff.
91. Wrangham and Peterson 1996.
92. Daly and Wilson 1988, p. 291.
93. Wrangham and Peterson 1996.
94. Campbell 1993; Zuger 1998a, pp. F1f.
95. Campbell 1993.
96. Simon and Landis 1991.
97. Campbell 1995, pp. 99–123.
98. Smuts 1986; Fedigan 1982.
99. Smuts 1986.
100. Mitchell 1981; see Smuts et al. 1986; Wrangham and Peterson 1996.
101. Chagnon 1988, pp. 985–92.
102. Gur et al. 1995, pp. 528–31.
103. Prentky 1985, pp. 7–55.
104. *The Economist* 1996; Archer 1991, pp. 1–28; Nyborg 1994.
105. Several other chemicals are associated with aggressiveness. Serotonin (see

Masters and McGuire 1994), monoamine oxidase (Cases,　et al. 1995, pp. 1763–99), vasopressin (DeVries et al. 1985, pp. 236–54; Koolhass et al. 1990, pp. 223–29), and the mix of androgens and estrogens (Simon and Masters 1988, pp. 291–95) have all been implicated.

106. See Karli 1991.
107. Udry, Talbert, and Morris 1986, pp. 217–27; see Halpern 1992.
108. Karl 1995.
109. See Wrangham and Peterson 1996.
110. *The Economist* 1997b, pp. 21ff.
111. Fukuyama and Shulsky 1997.
112. Ibid.
113. Whyte 1978; Murdock and Provost 1973, pp. 203–25.
114. Brown 1991.
115. Lueptow, Garovich, and Lueptow 1995, pp. 509–30.
116. Bergmann 1986; *The Economist* 1998a; United Nations 1995.
117. *The Economist* 1998; United Nations 1995; United Nations 1995a.
118. U.S. Department of Labor, Bureau of Labor Statistics 1996.
119. Statistical Abstract of the United States 1996.
120. *The Economist* 1998; United Nations 1995.
121. Halpern 1992.
122. Bergmann 1986.
123. Govier and Bobby 1994, pp. 179–86.
124. Ibid.; Govier and Boden 1997, pp. 27–32.
125. Ibid.
126. Dabbs 1992, pp. 813–24; Dabbs, de la Rue, and Williams 1990, pp. 1261–65; Nyborg 1994.
127. Udry, Kovenock, and Morris 1992; see Edwards and Booth 1994.
128. Hedges and Nowell 1995, pp. 41–45; Vogel 1996.
129. *The Economist* 1996; Statistical Abstract of the United States 1996; Rossiter 1995; United Nations 1995.
130. Braus 1994.
131. Bernstein 1996.
132. Harrington 1993.
133. See Nyborg 1994, p. 101.
134. Nyborg 1994.
135. United States Development Programme 1995; Bergmann 1986.
136. Farrell 1993.
137. Browne 1995, pp. 973–1106.
138. *The Economist* 1996; Statistical Abstract of the United States 1996; *The Economist* 1998.
139. *The Economist* 1996.
140. Greene 1997.

### 7. Tomorrow Belongs to Women:
### How Women Are Changing the Business World

1. *The Economist* 1996, pp. 23ff; United Nations 1995c.
2. Manuelito, personal communication.

3. Friedl 1975; Sacks 1979; Sanday 1973, pp. 1682–1700, 1981; Whyte 1978.
4. See Sanday 1981, p. 135.
5. Ibid.; Etienne and Leacock 1980; Dahlberg 1981; Reiter 1975; Sacks 1979; Weiner 1976; Klein and Ackerman 1995; Schlegel and Barry 1986, pp. 142–50; Whyte 1978; Leacock 1981; Boserup 1970; see Fisher 1992.
6. See Klein and Ackerman 1995, p. 32.
7. Shostak 1981; Howell 1979.
8. Slocum 1975; Sanday 1981; Whyte 1978; Leacock 1981; Fisher 1992; Lerner 1986; Maryanski and Turner 1992.
9. Diamond 1997, pp. 1243–44.
10. Jope 1956.
11. Ember 1983, pp. 285–304.
12. Hrdy 1986, pp. 119–46.
13. Ember 1983.
14. Ibid.
15. Whyte 1978.
16. Engels 1972; Leacock 1972; Sanday 1973; see Etienne and Leacock 1980; see Fisher 1992; Lerner 1986; Maryanski and Turner 1992; Burton and White 1984, pp. 568–82; Ember 1983; Boserup 1970.
17. Lerner 1986.
18. See Fisher 1992.
19. Darwin 1871, 1936, pp. 873–74.
20. Mosher 1997, p. A18.
21. McCorduck and Ramsey 1996.
22. Ibid.
23. Ibid.
24. Bergmann 1986; *Harper's* 1997, pp. 47–58; Lewin 1997, pp. A1f; *The Economist* 1998, pp. 3–15.
25. *The Economist* 1998.
26. Nash 1983; see Nash and Fernandez-Kelly 1983.
27. United Nations 1995a.
28. Drucker 1992; Stewart 1997.
29. Richburg 1997, pp. 6f.
30. United Nations 1995a.
31. Bergmann 1986, p. 39.
32. Coontz 1992.
33. Russell 1995a, p. 8; Mitchell 1995, pp. 22f.
34. Dychtwald and Flower 1989.
35. Benet 1974.
36. Ibid., p. 54.
37. Ibid.
38. Beidelman 1971, p. 61.
39. Hamilton 1970, pp. 17–20.
40. Jones and Jones 1976.
41. Lessa 1966.
42. Kehoe 1976, pp. 68–76.
43. Roy 1975.
44. Brown 1982, p. 23.

45. Ibid.; Amoss 1981, pp. 227–47; Levy 1967, pp. 231–38; Sinclair 1985, pp. 27–46; Quain 1948; Mead 1950; Herdt 1987; Murphy and Murphy 1974; Srinivas 1977, pp. 221–38; Wolf 1974, pp. 157–72; Mernisi 1975; see Kerns and Brown 1982.

46. Brown 1982.

47. Pavelka and Fedigan 1991, pp. 13–38.

48. Functioning ovaries produce from 5–25% of a woman's testosterone, as well as 45–60% of androstenedione and 20% of dehydroepiandrosterone (DHEA) (Longcope 1986, pp. 213–28; Van Goozen et al. 1997, pp. 359–82). During menopause, estrogen made in the ovaries drops twelvefold, while some of the ovarian androgens drop only a third to a half (Judd and Fournet 1994, pp. 285–98). The adrenal cortex also produces testosterone, androstenedione, and DHEA (Van Goozen et al. 1997). These androgens also decrease with menopause. But they do not drop as precipitiously as do the estrogens from the ovaries (Ganong 1993; Meldrum et al. 1981, pp. 624–28). Hence in women the ratio of androgens to estrogens increases with age (Judd and Fournet 1994).

49. Baucom, Besch, and Callahan 1985, pp. 1218–26.

50. Brody 1997, p. A25.

51. Williams 1957, pp. 32–39; Alexander 1974, pp. 325–83; Lancaster and King 1992; Pavelka and Fedigan 1991; Caro et al. 1995, pp. 205–20; Austad 1994, pp. 255–63; Hill and Hurtado 1991, pp. 313–50; Wood 1990, pp. 211–42.

52. Hill and Hurtado 1991.

53. Lancaster and King 1992; Walker 1995, pp. 59–71; Takahata, Koyama, and Suzuki 1995, pp. 169–80; Caro et al. 1995; Pavelka and Fedigan 1991.

54. Caro et al. 1995.

55. Lancaster and King 1992; Pavelka and Fedigan 1991.

56. Pavelka and Fedigan 1991.

57. Lancaster and King 1992; Pavelka and Fedigan 1991; Caro et al. 1995.

58. Lancaster and King 1992.

59. Pavelka and Fedigan 1991.

60. Lancaster and King 1992; Mayer 1982, pp. 477–94.

61. Russell 1995, p. 36.

62. Williams 1957; Alexander 1974; Gaulin 1980, pp. 227–32; Hamilton 1966, pp. 12–45; Mayer 1982; Lancaster and King 1992; Hawkes, O'Connell, and Blurton Jones 1989; Hawkes et al. 1998, pp. 1336–39.

63. Hawkes et al. 1998.

64. Hawkes, O'Connell, and Blurton Jones 1997, pp. 551–65.

65. Angier 1997, p. F1.

66. Menopause may have been a relatively easy process for ancestral females. Data from contemporary tribal cultures indicate that ancestral mothers bore their last infant around age 35 or 40, then they nursed this child for three to five years (Lancaster and King 1992). So prolactin and oxytocin, the hormones of nursing, may have masked the side effects of menopause. Females exercised regularly, another factor that may have reduced the side effects of menopause. They also spent about 15 of their reproductive years nursing, about four years in pregnancy, and only about four years at menstrual cycling. Women currently spend about 35 years in menstrual cycling; a condition associated with high

levels of estrogen (Short 1984; 1987). Contemporary hormonal profiles, as well as modern patterns of breast feeding, diet, and exercise may contribute to the side effects of menopause.

67. Rowe 1997, p. 367.
68. Kolata 1996, p. A1f; Rimer 1998, pp. A1f.
69. Rowe 1997.
70. Wattenberg 1997, pp. 60–62.
71. Ibid.
72. Pui-Wing 1998, p. B9C; *The Economist* 1995, pp. 52ff.
73. Ibid.
74. Navarro 1997, p. A16.
75. Rosenfeld 1992, pp. 46ff.
76. Russell 1996.
77. Ibid., p. 13.
78. Fukuyama 1998, p. 38.
79. Seltzer, Newman, and Leighton 1997; Russell 1996.
80. Seltzer, Newman, and Leighton 1997.
81. See ibid.
82. Manza and Brooks 1998, pp. 1235–66.
83. Seib 1995, pp. A1f.
84. Seltzer, Newman, and Leighton 1997.
85. Manza and Brooks 1998.
86. Seltzer, Newman, and Leighton 1997.
87. Ibid.
88. Manza and Brooks 1998; Seltzer, Newman, and Leighton 1997.
89. Seltzer, Newman, and Leighton 1997.
90. Manza and Brooks 1998; Seltzer, Newman, and Leighton 1997.
91. Seltzer, Newman, and Leighton 1997.
92. Russell 1996.
93. Russell 1996; Seltzer, Newman, and Leighton 1997.
94. Seltzer, Newman, and Leighton 1997.
95. Karl 1995.
96. Ibid.
97. Russell 1996.
98. Seltzer, Newman, and Leighton 1997.
99. Russell 1996.
100. Klein 1997.

## 8. Sexual Civility: The Feminization of Lust

1. Ganong 1993.
2. Judd and Yen 1973, pp. 475–81; Ganong 1993.
3. Nyborg 1994.
4. Sherwin and Gelfand 1987, p. 397.
5. Sherwin, Gelfand, and Brender 1985, pp. 339–51; Sherwin and Gelfand 1987.
6. Bancroft et al. 1980, pp. 327–40; Sherwin 1988, pp. 416–25, 1994, pp. 423–30; Persky et al. 1978, pp. 157–73.

7. Judd and Yen 1973; Van Goozen et al. 1997, pp. 359–82.
8. Sherwin 1988; Van Goozen, et al. 1997.
9. Edwards and Booth 1994; Mitchell 1981.
10. Kinsey et al. 1953; Ford and Beach 1951.
11. Money 1997.
12. Ellis and Symons 1990, pp. 527–55.
13. Ibid.
14. Laumann et al. 1994.
15. Ellis and Symons 1990.
16. See Blum 1997.
17. Geer and Manguno-Mire 1996, pp. 90–124.
18. Ellis and Symons 1990.
19. Geer and Manguno-Mire 1996; Ellis and Symons 1990.
20. Ellis and Symons 1990.
21. See ibid.
22. Reinisch and Beasley 1990.
23. Ibid.; Eibl-Eibesfeldt 1989; Laumann et al. 1994; Money and Ehrhardt 1972; Ellis and Symons 1990; Geer and Manguno-Mire 1996.
24. Gilfoyle, Wilson, and Brown 1992, pp. 209–30; Ellis and Symons 1990.
25. Ibid.
26. Barash and Lipton 1997; Wilson and Land 1981, pp. 343–46.
27. Laumann et al. 1994.
28. Eibl-Eibesfeldt 1989.
29. Ibid.
30. Darling, Davidson, and Cox 1991, pp. 3–21.
31. See Geer and Manguno-Mire 1996.
32. Witkin 1995.
33. Oliver and Hyde 1993, pp. 29–51; Laumann et al. 1994; Geer and Manguno-Mire 1996.
34. Kinsey, Pomeroy, and Martin 1948; Kinsey et al. 1953.
35. Reinisch and Beasley 1990.
36. Laumann et al. 1994.
37. See DeLamater 1995, pp. 501–3; Cherlin 1995, pp. 293–96; Presser 1995, pp. 296–98; Chancer 1995, pp. 298–302.
38. Laumann et al. 1994.
39. Ibid.
40. Oliver and Hyde 1993.
41. Laumann et al. 1994; Einon 1994, pp. 131–43.
42. Sherfey 1972.
43. Money 1997; Sherfey 1972.
44. Kinsey et al. 1953.
45. Witkin 1995.
46. Ellis and Symons 1990.
47. See Hatfield and Rapson 1996; Fowlkes 1994.
48. Metts and Cupach 1991, pp. 139–61; Laumann et al. 1994.
49. Witkin 1995, p. 46.
50. Edwards and Booth 1994; Kinsey et al. 1953.
51. Hällström and Samuelsson 1990, pp. 259–68.

52. Levy 1994; Hällström and Samuelsson 1990.
53. Hällström 1979, pp. 165–75; Channon and Ballinger 1986, pp. 173–80; Pfeiffer and Davis 1972, pp. 151–58; Pfeiffer, Verwoerdt, and Wang 1969, pp. 193–95.
54. Tavris and Sadd 1977.
55. Judd and Fournet 1994, pp. 285–98.
56. Masters and Johnson 1966; Edwards and Booth 1994.
57. Trivers 1972, pp. 136–79; Symons 1979; Buss 1994.
58. Bellis and Baker 1990, pp. 997–99.
59. Hrdy 1981; Smith 1984, pp. 601–59; Hill and Kaplan 1988, pp. 177–305; Fisher 1992; Smuts 1992, pp. 1–44; Parker 1970, pp. 525–67; Benshoof and Thornhill 1979, pp. 95–106.
60. Hrdy 1981; Smuts 1992; Wilson and Daly 1992.
61. Einon 1994, pp. 131–43.
62. Bullough and Bullough 1996, pp. 158–80.
63. Ibid.
64. Gilfoyle 1992.
65. Einon 1994.
66. Burley and Symanski 1981, pp. 239–74; Smith 1984, pp. 601–59; Symons 1979; Buss 1994.
67. Bullough and Bullough 1996, p. 171.
68. Laumann et al. 1994.
69. DeLamater 1995; Cherlin 1995, pp. 293–96; Laumann et al. 1994.
70. Hatfield and Rapson 1996.
71. Pattatucci and Hamer 1995, pp. 407–20.
72. Laumann et al. 1994; Coleman 1985, pp. 87–89; Fowlkes 1994, p. 168.
73. Bell and Weinberg 1978.
74. See Blum 1997, p. 139.
75. Danielsson 1956.
76. See Fisher 1992; Posner 1992.
77. See Stone 1977, 1990.
78. Tissot 1766/1985.
79. Posner 1992.
80. Laumann et al. 1994.
81. Darling, Davidson, and Cox 1991; Fisher 1980, pp. 27–35.
82. Blumstein and Schwarts 1983.
83. Edwards and Booth 1994.
84. Faison 1998a, p. A4.
85. Posner 1992.
86. Abelson 1995, p. 895.
87. Oliver and Hyde 1993, pp. 29–51; Kantner and Zelnik 1972, pp. 9–18; Udry, Baumann, and Morris 1975, pp. 783–87.
88. Davis and Smith 1991.
89. Buss 1989, pp. 1–49.
90. Liu, Ng, and Chou 1992.
91. Schlegel and Barry 1991.
92. See Ford and Beach 1951.
93. Money 1997.
94. Ibid.

95. Rossi 1994; Eveleth 1986.
96. Lancaster and King 1985; Short 1984, pp. 42–72, 1987, pp. 207–17.
97. Eveleth 1986.
98. Posner 1992; Laumann et al. 1994.
99. Smith 1994.
100. Posner 1992.
101. Smith 1994.
102. Posner 1992.
103. Ibid.
104. Francoeur 1996, p. 136.
105. Gabriel 1996, pp. C1f.
106. Harmon 1997.
107. Posner 1992.
108. McGinley, personal communication.
109. Davis and Smith 1987.
110. Posner 1992.
111. Smith 1994.
112. Paludi and Barickman 1991.
113. Ibid.
114. Ibid.; Web 1991.
115. McCorduck and Ramsey 1996.
116. Weiss 1998, pp. 43–47.
117. Web 1991.
118. Brown 1991.
119. See Fisher 1992.
120. Buss 1994, p. 145.
121. Buss 1994; Abbey 1982, pp. 830–38.
122. Geer and Bellard 1996, pp. 379–95.
123. Web 1991.
124. Browne 1997, pp. 5–86.
125. Weiss 1998, p. 47.
126. Weiss 1998.
127. Ibid.

## 9. Infatuation: Romantic Love in the Twenty-first Century

1. Tennov 1979.
2. Jankowiak 1995.
3. Wolkstein 1991.
4. Tennov 1979.
5. Harris 1995, p. 114.
6. Singer 1987.
7. Stendhal 1915.
8. Douglass and Atwell 1988.
9. Harris 1995, p. 113.
10. Plotnicov 1995; Hatfield, and Rapson 1996; Tennov 1979.
11. Davis and Davis 1995.
12. Tennov 1979; Hatfield and Rapson 1996.

13. Jankowiak 1995.

14. Bell 1995.

15. Liebowitz 1983; Fisher 1998, pp. 23–52.

16. Wise 1988; see Fisher 1998, pp. 23–52.

17. See Fisher 1998.

18. Ibid.

19. Ibid.

20. Ibid.

21. Ibid.

22. Ibid.

23. Darwin 1871/1936, p. 745.

24. Beach 1976, p. 24.

25. Hatfield and Rapson 1996; Tennov 1979.

26. Buss 1994.

27. Harrison and Saaed 1977, pp. 257–64.

28. Buss 1994; Symons 1979; Williams 1975.

29. Barber 1995.

30. Symons 1989, pp. 34–5.

31. See Barber 1995; Singh 1993, pp. 293–307.

32. Dion and Dion 1985; Peplau and Gordon 1985; Tennov 1979.

33. Buss 1994.

34. Sadalla, Kenrick, and Vershure 1987, pp. 730–38.

35. Kenrick et al. 1990, pp. 97–116.

36. Barber 1993.

37. Ibid.

38. Ellis 1992; Buss 1994.

39. Gregor 1985.

40. Buss 1994.

41. Tennov 1979.

42. Hopkins 1994, p. 20.

43. Harris 1995.

44. Dluzen et al. 1981.

45. Tennov 1979; Hatfield 1988.

46. Viederman 1988, pp. 1–14.

47. Shepher 1971, pp. 293–307; Spiro 1958; Fox 1980.

48. Wedekind et al. 1995, pp. 245–49.

49. Berreby 1998, p. F2.

50. Money 1997.

51. Frayser 1985; Friedl 1975.

52. Money 1997.

53. Ibid.

54. Hatfield and Rapson 1996.

55. See Money 1997, p. 144.

56. Stone 1988, pp. 15–26.

57. Hatfield and Rapson 1996.

58. Stone 1988.

59. Ibid.

60. Ibid.; Stone 1990; Goode 1982.

61. Kephart 1967, pp. 470–79.
62. Allgeier and Wiederman 1991, pp. 25–27.
63. Simpson, Campbell, and Bersheid 1986, pp. 363–72; Cancian 1987.
64. Mace and Mace 1980; Jankowiak 1995.
65. Collins and Gregor 1995.
66. Jankowiak 1995.
67. Yang 1959, p. 221.
68. Jankowiak 1995a.
69. Levine et al. 1994, p. 31.
70. Buss 1989, 1994.
71. Prakasa and Rao 1979, pp. 11–31.
72. Ibid.; Rosenblatt and Anderson 1981, pp. 215–50.
73. See Hatfield and Rapson 1996.
74. Lancaster and Kaplan 1994.
75. Jehl 1997, p. A4.
76. Murstein 1972, pp. 8–12; Buss 1985, pp. 47–51; Hatfield and Sprecher 1986; Rushton 1989, pp. 31–32.
77. Byrne, Clore, and Smeaton 1986, pp. 1167–70; Cappella and Palmer 1990, pp. 161–83; Lykken and Tellegen 1993, pp. 56–68.
78. Laumann et al. 1994; Lind 1998, pp. 38–39.
79. See Buss 1994; see Thiessen, Young, and Burroughs 1993, pp. 209–29.
80. Buss 1994; Wiederman and Allgeier 1992, pp. 115–24; Townsend 1989, pp. 241–53.
81. Buss 1994.
82. Laumann et al. 1994.
83. Associated Press 1997, p. A15.
84. Harry 1983, pp. 216–34.
85. Blumstein and Schwartz 1990, pp. 307–20.
86. Bell and Weinberg 1978; Fowlkes 1994.
87. Peplau and Cochran 1990; Fowlkes 1994.
88. Laumann et al. 1994.
89. Purdy 1995, p. A16.
90. Kankakee (Ill.) *Daily Journal* 1998, p. B7.
91. Knox 1970, pp. 151–57.
92. Hines 1998, pp. 24.
93. Buss 1994; White 1981, pp. 129–47; Buunk and Hupka 1987, pp. 12–22.
94. Buunk and Hupka 1987.
95. Buss 1994.
96. Ibid.
97. Ibid.; see Geary et al. 1995, pp. 355–83.
98. Buss 1994; Daly and Wilson 1988; United Nations Development Programme 1995c; Wilson and Daly 1992, pp. 289–326; Daly, Wilson, and Weghorst 1982, pp. 11–27.
99. Sheets, Fredendall, and Claypool 1997, pp. 387–402.
100. Baumeister, Wotman, and Stillwell 1993, pp. 377–91.
101. Jankowiak 1995a, p. 179.
102. Harris 1995, p. 113.
103. Baumeister, Wotman, and Stillwell 1993.

104. Walster and Walster 1978.
105. Hill, Rubin, and Peplau 1976, pp. 147–68.
106. Gugliotta 1997, p. 35; Meloy 1998.
107. Meloy 1998.
108. Ibid.; Walker and Meloy 1998, pp. 37–38.
109. Gugliotta 1997.
110. Peele and Brodsky 1975; Halpern 1982; Griffin-Shelley 1991.
111. Hendrick and Hendrick 1986, pp. 392–402.
112. Sprecher et al. 1994.
113. Tavris 1992.
114. Cancian 1987.

## 10. Peer Marriage: The Reformation of Matrimony

1. Bruce et al. 1995; Goode 1993.
2. Fisher 1989, pp. 331–54; see Fisher 1992.
3. Coontz 1992.
4. Furstenberg 1996, pp. 34ff.
5. Furstenberg 1996.
6. Lindholm 1995, p. 60.
7. See ibid.
8. Bowlby 1969, 1973, 1980.
9. Carter et al. 1997, pp. 260–72.
10. Winslow et al. 1993, pp. 545–48.
11. Pedersen et al. 1992, pp. 1–492.
12. Ibid.
13. Insel, Young, and Wang 1997, pp. 302–16.
14. Morell 1998, p. 1983.
15. Damasio 1994.
16. Booth and Dabbs 1993, pp. 463–77.
17. Ibid.
18. Ibid.
19. See Blum 1997.
20. Wingfield 1994, pp. 303–30.
21. Schwartz 1994.
22. Stone 1990; Cancian 1987.
23. Schwartz 1994; Stone 1990; Posner 1992.
24. Shellenbarger 1996, pp. B1f.
25. Posner 1992; Schwartz 1994; Stone 1977.
26. Furstenberg 1996.
27. Cancian 1987; Stone 1990.
28. Tavris 1992, pp. 15–25.
29. See Tavris 1992.
30. See Mitchell 1981.
31. Tannen 1990.
32. Tavris 1992.
33. Tannen 1994.
34. Tavris 1992.

35. Hatfield and Rapson 1996.
36. Tavris 1992; Riessman 1990; Gottman 1994.
37. Buss 1988.
38. Cancian 1987, p. 77.
39. Buss 1988.
40. Cancian 1987; Tavris 1992.
41. Cancian 1987.
42. Stone 1977, 1990; Posner 1992; Cancian 1987.
43. Cancian 1987; Hatfield and Rapson 1996.
44. Cancian 1986, pp. 692–709; Tavris 1992, 1997, p. A29; Swain 1989.
45. Tornstam 1992, pp. 197–217.
46. Cleveland 1981.
47. Nyborg 1994.
48. Fisher 1998, pp. 23–52.
49. Laumann et al. 1994.
50. Blumstein and Schwartz 1983; Thompson 1983, pp. 1–22; Gangestad and Thornhill 1997, pp. 69–88.
51. Fisher 1992.
52. Gregor 1985.
53. Frayser 1985; Daly, Wilson, and Weghorst 1982, pp. 11–27; Wilson and Daly 1992, pp. 289–326; see Fisher 1992.
54. Black 1996; Wittenberger and Tilson 1980; Mock and Fujioka 1990, pp. 39–43.
55. Morell 1998, pp. 1982–83.
56. Moller 1987, pp. 92–104.
57. Morell 1998.
58. Milius 1998, p. 153.
59. See Black 1996; Morell 1998.
60. Morell 1998.
61. Benshoof and Thornhill 1979, pp. 95–106; Symons 1979; Hrdy 1981, pp. 601–59; Smith 1984; Fisher 1992; see Wilson and Daly 1992.
62. Bellis and Baker 1990, pp. 997–99.
63. See Fisher 1992.
64. Glass and Wright 1992, pp. 361–87; Hatfield and Rapson 1996.
65. Spanier and Margolis 1993, pp. 23–48.
66. Glass and Wright 1985.
67. Lawson 1988; see Hatfield and Rapson 1996.
68. Buss 1994.
69. Ibid.
70. Daly and Wilson 1988; Wilson and Daly 1992; Daly, Wilson, and Weghorst 1982; United Nations Development Programme 1995.
71. Betzig 1989, pp. 654–76.
72. Buss 1994; see Geary et al. 1995, pp. 355–83.
73. Shettel-Neuber, Bryson, and Young 1978, pp. 612–15.
74. Nadler and Dotan 1992, pp. 293–310.
75. Blumstein and Schwartz 1983.
76. Laumann et al. 1994.
77. Posner 1992.
78. Roiphe 1997, pp. 54–55.

79. Daly, Wilson, and Weghorst 1982; Wilson and Daly 1992; Daly and Wilson 1988.
80. Stone 1990.
81. Hatfield and Rapson 1996.
82. Fisher 1992.
83. Betzig 1989.
84. Betzig 1989; Frayser 1985; Buckle, Gallup, and Rodd 1996, pp. 363–77.
85. Kerber 1994, pp. 283–97.
86. Belsky, Steinberg, and Draper 1991, pp. 647–70; Draper and Belsky 1990, pp. 141–62; Hill, Young, and Nord 1994, pp. 323–38.
87. Beach and Tesser 1988.
88. Fisher 1989, 1992, 1994, pp. 58–64.
89. Fisher 1992; Black 1996.
90. Pope and Mueller 1979; McGue and Lykken 1992, pp. 368–73.
91. See Fisher 1992; Gottman 1994; Goode 1993; Belsky, Steinberg, and Draper 1991, pp. 647–70; Stone 1990.
92. Fisher 1992; Gottman 1994.
93. Gottman 1994.
94. Goode 1993.
95. Gottman 1994.
96. Cherlin 1981; Levitan, Belous, and Gallo 1988; Glick 1975; Trent and South 1989, pp. 391–404; Furstenberg 1996; Espenshade 1985, pp. 193–245; Fisher 1992.
97. Furstenberg 1996.
98. Gottman 1994; Milbank 1996, pp. A1f.
99. Fisher 1992.
100. Judith Bruce et al. 1995.
101. *Futurific* 1994, pp. 23ff.
102. Bruce et al. 1995.
103. Lewin 1995; Bruce et al. 1995; Goode 1993.
104. Goode 1993; see Fisher 1992.
105. See Fisher 1992.
106. Wysocki 1996, pp. A1f; Bruce et al. 1995.
107. Martin and Bumpass 1989, pp. 37–51.
108. Hill, Rubin, and Peplau 1979, pp. 64–82.
109. Baxter 1984, pp. 29–48; Cupach and Metts 1986, pp. 311–34.
110. Hill, Rubin, and Peplau 1979.
111. Taffel 1990, pp. 49–53.
112. See Tavris 1992.
113. Ibid.
114. Barbee, Gulley, and Cunningham 1990, pp. 531–40; Duck 1991; Caldwell and Peplau 1982, pp. 721–32; Cancian 1987.
115. Ahern and Bailey 1996; Cancian 1987.
116. Hill, Rubin, and Peplau 1979; Stroebe and Stroebe 1987; Cancian 1987; Ahern and Bailey 1996.
117. Gottman 1994; Cancian 1987; Angier 1998, p. WH10.
118. Ibid.
119. Bernard 1972; Kelly 1982, pp. 304–37; Edwards and Booth 1994, p. 255.

120. Gottman 1994.
121. Goode 1993.
122. Gottman 1994; Tsubouchi 1984.
123. Glick 1984; Gottman 1994; Goode 1993.
124. Rosewicz 1996, pp. B1f.
125. Ibid.
126. Bruce et al. 1995; Cancian 1987.
127. Mitchell 1995, pp. 22f; Bruce et al. 1995.
128. Bruce et al. 1995.
129. Gottman 1994.
130. Bruce et al. 1995; Goode 1993; Furstenberg 1996; Popenoe, 1996.
131. *Wilson Quarterly* 1997; Russell 1995, p. 8.
132. Russell 1995a, pp. 22–41.
133. Bruce et al. 1995.
134. Coontz 1992.
135. Ibid.; Furstenberg 1996; Coontz and Franklin 1997, p. A23.
136. Coontz 1992; Stacey 1991.
137. Stone 1990.
138. Ibid.; Coontz 1992.
139. Rossi and Rossi 1990.
140. Ibid.
141. Ibid.; Coontz 1992.
142. Rossi and Rossi 1990; Salmon and Daly 1995, pp. 289–97; Schneider and Cottrell 1975; Cancian 1987.
143. Salmon and Daly 1996; Rossi and Rossi 1990.
144. Rossi and Rossi 1990.
145. Weitzman 1985.
146. Rossi and Rossi 1990, p. 207.
147. Pedersen-Pietersen 1997, p. F11.
148. Ahern and Bailey 1996.
149. Viorst 1986, p. 54.
150. See Coontz 1992, p. 21.
151. Ahern and Bailey 1996.
152. Popenoe 1996.
153. Ahern and Bailey 1996.
154. Bruce et al. 1995.
155. Stone 1988, p. 21, 1990; Goode 1993; Coontz 1994.
156. Stone 1990; Coontz 1992.
157. Ibid.

## 11: The Collaborative Society: Equality Regained

1. Drucker 1997, pp. 20ff.
2. Wattenberg 1997, pp. 60–62; Specter 1998, p. A1.
3. Wattenberg 1997, pp. 60–62.
4. Lancaster 1994; Lockard and Adams 1981, pp. 177–86.
5. Trivers and Willard 1973, pp. 249–53; see Hrdy 1987.

6. Dickemann 1979, 1992; Barash and Lipton 1997.
7. Lavia Betzig personal communication.
8. Eckholm 1998, pp. A1f.
9. Mitchell 1995, pp. 22ff.
10. Ibid.

# BIBLIOGRAPHY

Abbey, A. 1982. "Sex differences in attributions for friendly behavior: Do males mis-perceive females' friendliness?" *Journal of Personality and Social Psychology* 42:830–838.

Abelson, P. H. 1995. "Great Transitions." Editorial. *Science,* 10 November, 895.

Agor, W. H. 1986. *The logic of intuitive decision making: A research-based approach to top management.* Westport, Conn.: Quorum Books.

Ahern, S., and K. G. Bailey. 1996. *Family by choice: Creating family in a world of strangers.* Minneapolis: Fairview Press.

Alexander, M. 1995. "Vacation for the spirit." *Winning Strategies* (fall): 42ff.

Alexander, Richard D. 1974. "The evolution of social behavior." *Annual Review of Ecology and Systematics* 5:325–383.

Allen, Laura S., and Roger A. Gorski. 1991. "Sexual dimorphism of the anterior com-missure and the massa intermedia of the human brain." *Journal of Compara-tive Neurology* 312:97–104.

Allen, Laura S., Mark F. Richey, Yee M. Chai, and Roger A. Gorski. 1991. "Sex differences in the corpus callosum of the living human being." *The Journal of Neuroscience* 11(4):933–942.

Allgeier E. R., and M. W. Wiederman. 1991. "Love and mate selection in the 1990s." *Free Inquiry* 11:25–27.

Amoss, P. T. 1981. Coastal Salish elders. In *Other ways of growing old: Anthropologi-cal perspectives,* edited by P. T. Amoss and S. Harrell. Stanford, Calif.: Stan-ford University Press.

Andina, M., and B. Pillsbury. 1997. Trust: A new approach to women's empower-ment. Paper presented at the annual meeting of the Population Association of America, Washington D.C., 18 March.

Angier, Natalie. 1995. "Does testosterone equal aggression? Maybe not." *New York Times,* 20 June, C1, 3.

———. 1995a. "For baboons, rising to top has big cost in fertility." *New York Times,* 10 January, C1, 5.

———. 1995b. "Status isn't everything, at least for monkeys." *New York Times,* 18 April, C1, 6.

———. 1996. "Variant gene tied to a love of new thrills." *New York Times,* 2 January, A1f.

———. 1997. "Theorists see evolutionary advantages in menopause." *New York Times,* 16 September, F1.

———. 1998. "Men. Are women better off with them, or without them?" *New York Times,* 21 June, WH10.

Applebome, P. 1996. "New choices for parents are starting to change U.S. education landscape." *New York Times,* 4 September, B7.

Archer, John. 1991. "The influence of testosterone on human aggression." *British Journal of Psychology* 82:1–28.

Associated Press. 1997. "Bride finds her husband is a woman." *New York Times,* 13 January, A15.

Auletta, K. 1998. "In the company of women." *The New Yorker,* 20 April, 72–78.

Austad, Steven N. 1994. "Menopause: An evolutionary perspective." *Experimental Gerontology* 29(3/4):255–263.

Ayres, B. D. 1997. "Women in Washington statehouse lead U.S. tide." *New York Times,* 14 April, A1ff.

Babchuk, W. A., R. B. Hames, and R. A. Thompson. 1983. "Sex differences in the recognition of infant facial expressions of emotion: The primary caretaker hypothesis." *Ethology and Sociobiology* 6:89–102.

Baker, Kate C., and Barbara B. Smuts. 1994. "Social relations of female chimpanzees: Diversity between captive social groups." In *Chimpanzee cultures,* edited by R. Wrangham et al. Cambridge, Mass.: Harvard University Press.

Baker, R. R., and M. A. Bellis. 1995. *Human sperm competition: Copulation, masturbation and infidelity.* London: Chapman and Hall.

Bancroft, J., D. Sanders, D. Davidson, and P. Warner. 1983. "Mood, sexuality, hormones, and the menstrual cycle. III. Sexuality and the role of androgens." *Psychosomatic Medicine* 45:509–516.

Bancroft, J., D. W. Davidson, P. Warner, and G. Tyrer. 1980. "Androgens and sexual behavior in women using oral contraceptives." *Journal of Clinical Endocrinology* 12:327–340.

Barash, D. P., and J. E. Lipton. 1997. *Making sense of sex: How genes and gender influence our relationships.* Washington, D.C.: Island Press.

Barbee, A. P., M. R. Gulley, and M. R. Cunningham. 1990. "Support seeking in personal relationships." *Journal of Social and Personal Relationships* 7:531–540.

Barber, N. 1993. "The evolutionary psychology of physical attractiveness: Sexual selection and human morphology." *Ethology and Sociobiology* 16:395–424.

Barchas, P. R., W. A. Harris, W. S. Jose II, and E. A. Raso. 1984. "Social interaction and the brain's lateralization of hemispheric function." In *Social cohesion: Essays toward a sociophysiological perspective,* edited by P. R. Barchas and S. P. Mendoza. Westport, Conn.: Greenwood Press.

Barret-Connor, E., and D. Kritz-Silverstein. 1993. "Estrogen replacement therapy and cognitive function in older women." Journal of the American Medical Association 269:2637–2641.

Barton, L. 1997. "A shoulder to lean on: Assisted living in the U.S." *American Demographics* (July): 45ff.

Baucom, D., P. Besch, and S. Callahan. 1985. "Relation between testosterone concentration, sex role identity, and personality among females." *Journal of Personality and Social Psychology* 48:1218–1226.

Baumeister, R. F., S. R. Wotman, and A. M. Stillwell. 1993. "Unrequited love: On heartbreak, anger, guilt, scriptlessness, and humiliation." *Journal of Personality and Social Psychology* 64:377–394.

Baxter, L. A. 1984. "Trajectories of relationship disengagement." *Journal of Social and Personal Relationships* 1:29–48.

Beach, Frank A. 1948. *Hormones and behavior: A survey of interrelationships between endocrine secretions and patterns of overt response*. New York: Paul B. Hoeber, Inc.

———. 1976. "Sexual attractivity, proceptivity, and receptivity in female mammals." *Hormones and Behavior* 7:105–138.

Beach, S.R.H., and A. Tesser. 1988. "Love in marriage: A cognitive account." In *The psychology of love*, edited by R. J. Sternberg and M. L. Barnes. New Haven, Conn.: Yale University Press.

Bechara, A., H. Damasio, D. Tranel, and A. R. Damasio. 1997. "Deciding advantageously before knowing the advantageous strategy." *Science* 275:1293–1295.

Beidelman, T. O. 1971. *The Kaguru: A matrilineal people of East Africa*. New York: Holt, Rinehart and Winston.

Bell, A. P., and M. S. Weinberg. 1978. *Homosexualities: A study of diversity among men and women*. New York: Simon and Schuster.

Bell, J. 1995. Notions of love and romance among the Taita of Kenya. In *Romantic passion: A universal experience?*, edited by W. Jankowiak. New York: Columbia University Press.

Bellis, M. A., and R. R. Baker. 1990. "Do females promote sperm competition?: Data for humans." *Animal Behaviour* 40:997–999.

Belluck, Pam. 1996. "In an era of shrinking budgets, community groups blossom." *New York Times*, 25 February, 1f.

Belsky, J., L. Steinberg, and P. Draper. 1991. "Childhood experience, interpersonal development, and reproductive strategy: An evolutionary theory of socialization." *Child Development* 62:647–670.

Benbow, Camilla. 1988. "Sex differences in mathematical reasoning ability in intellectually talented preadolescents: Their nature, effects, and possible causes." *Behavioral and Brain Sciences* 11(2):169–183.

Benbow, C. P., and J. C. Stanley. 1983. "Sex difference in mathematical reasoning ability: More facts." *Science* 222:1029–1031.

Benderly, Beryl Lieff. 1989. "Intuition." *Psychology Today* (September):35–40.

Benet, Sula. 1974. *Abkhasians: The long-living people of the Caucasus*. New York: Holt, Rinehart and Winston.

Bennett, W. L. 1998. "The uncivic culture: Communication, identity, and the rise of lifestyle politics." *Political Science and Politics* 31 (4):741–761.

Benshoof, L., and R. Thornhill. 1979. "The evolution of monogamy and concealed ovulation in humans." *Journal of Social and Biological Structures* 2:95–106.

Berenbaum, Sheri A., and Melissa Hines. 1992. "Early androgens are related to childhood sex-typed toy preferences." *Psychological Science* 3 (3):202–206.

Bergmann, B. R. 1986. *The economic emergence of women*. New York: Basic Books.

Bernard, J. 1972. *The future of marriage*. New York: World.

Bernstein, N. 1996. "Study says equality eludes most women in law firms." *New York Times*, 8 January.

Berreby, D. 1998. "Studies explore love and the sweaty t-shirt." *New York Times*, 9 June, F2.

Betzig, L. 1988. *Despotism and differential reproduction: A Darwinian view of history*. Hawthorne, N.Y.: Aldine de Gruyter.

———. 1989. "Causes of conjugal dissolution: A cross cultural study." *Current Anthropology* 30:654–676.

Bever, Thomas. 1992. "The logical and extrinsic sources of modularity." In *Modu-*

*larity and constraints in language and cognition,* edited by M. Gunnar and M. Maratsos. Hillsdale, N.J.: Lawrence Erlbaum and Associates.

Birch, H., and G. Clark. 1946. "Hormonal modifications of social behavior. II. The effects of sex hormone administration on the social dominance status of the female castrate chimpanzee." *Psychosomatic Medicine* 8:320–331.

Bjorkvist, K., K. Lagerspetz, and A. Kaukiainen. 1992. "Do girls manipulate and boys fight? Developmental trends regarding direct and indirect aggression." *Aggressive Behavior* 18:117–127.

Black, J. M., ed. 1996. *Partnerships in birds: The study of monogamy.* New York: Oxford University Press.

Blakeslee, Sandra. 1992. "Why don't men ask directions? They don't feel lost." *New York Times,* 26 May, C1, 5.

Blum, D. 1997. *Sex on the brain: The biological differences between men and women.* New York: Viking.

Blumstein, P., and P. Schwartz. 1983. *American couples.* New York: William Morrow.

———. 1990. "Intimate relationships and the creation of sexuality." In *Homosexuality/heterosexuality: Concepts of sexual orientation,* edited by P. McWhirter, S. Sanders, and J. Reinisch. Vol. 2 of the Kinsey Institute Series. New York: Oxford University Press.

Boller, F., L. Traykov, M. H. Dao-Castellana, A. Fontaine-Dabernard, M. Zilbovicius, G. Rancurel, S. Pappata, and Y. Samson. 1995. "Cognitive functioning in 'diffuse' pathology: Role of prefrontal and limbic structures." In "Structure and functions of the human prefrontal cortex," edited by J. Grafman, K. J. Holyoak, and F. Boller. *Annals of the New York Academy of Sciences* 769:23–39.

Booth, A., and J. M. Dabbs. 1993. "Testosterone and men's marriages." *Social Forces* 72(2):463–477.

Booth, A., G. Shelley, A. Mazur, G. Tharp, and R. Kittok. 1989. "Testosterone, and winning and losing in human competition." *Hormones and Behavior* 23:556–571.

Boserup, E. 1970. *Women's role in economic development.* New York: St. Martin's Press.

Bower, Bruce. 1995. "Depression: Rates in women, men . . ." *Science News* 147:346.

Bowlby, J. 1969. *Attachment and loss: Attachment.* Vol. 1. New York: Basic Books.

———. 1973. *Attachment and loss: Separation.* Vol. 2. New York: Basic Books.

———. 1980. *Attachment and loss: Loss.* Vol. 3. New York: Basic Books.

Braus, P. 1994. "How women will change medicine." *American Demographics* (November): 40–47.

Brody, J. E. 1997. "Study says designed estrogen may be risk free." *New York Times,* 4 December, A25.

———. 1997. "When eyes betray color vision." *New York Times,* 21 October, F9.

Brody, Leslie R., and Judith A. Hall. 1993. "Gender and emotion." In *Handbook of emotions,* edited by Michael Lewis and Jeannette Haviland. New York: Guilford Press.

Broude, G. J., and S. J. Green. 1983. "Cross-cultural codes on husband-wife relationships." *Ethology* 22:273–274.

Brown, D. E. 1991. *Human universals.* Philadelphia: Philadelphia University Press.

Brown, Judith K. 1982. "Lives of middle-aged women." In *In her prime: New views of middle-aged women,* edited by Virginia Kerns and Judith K. Brown. Urbana: University of Illinois Press.

Brown, J. R., H. Ye, R. T. Bronson, P. Dikkes, and M. E. Greenberg. 1996. "A defect in nurturing in mice lacking the immediate early gene fosB." *Cell* 86:297–309.

Brown, Lyn Mikel, and Carol Gilligan. 1992. *Meeting at the crossroads: Women's psychology and girls' development.* Cambridge, Mass.: Harvard University Press.

Browne, Kingsley R. 1995. "Sex and temperament in modern society: A Darwinian view of the glass ceiling and the gender gap." *Arizona Law Review* 37 (4):973–1106.

———. 1997. "An evolutionary perspective on sexual harassment: Seeking roots in biology rather than ideology." *Journal of Contemporary Legal Issues* 8:5–86.

Brownmiller, S. 1975. *Against our will: Men, women and rape.* New York: Simon and Schuster.

Bruce, Judith, Cynthia B. Lloyd, and Ann Leonard, with Patrice L. Engle and Niev Duffy. 1995. *Families in focus: New perspectives on mothers, fathers, and children.* New York: The Population Council.

Buchholz, B. B. 1996. "Slow gains for women who would be partners." *New York Times,* 23 June.

Buckle, L., G. G. Gallup Jr., and Z. A. Rodd. 1996. "Marriage as a reproductive contract: Patterns of marriage, divorce, and remarriage." *Ethology and Sociobiology* 17:363–377.

Bullough, B., and V. L. Bullough. 1996. "Female prostitution: Current research and changing interpretations." *Annual Review of Sex Research* 7:158–180.

Burg, Albert. 1966. "Visual acuity as measured by dynamic and spatial tests: A comparative evaluation." *Journal of Applied Psychology* 50:460–466.

Burley, N., and R. Symanski. 1981. "Women without: An evolutionary and cross-cultural perspective on prostitution." In *The immoral landscape: Female prostitution in western societies,* edited by R. Symanski. Toronto: Butterworths.

Burton, M. L., and D. R. White. 1984. "Sexual division of labor in agriculture." *American Anthropologist* 86(3):568–583

Buss, D. M. 1988. "Love acts: The evolutionary biology of love." In *The psychology of love,* edited by R. J. Sternberg and M. L. Barnes. New Haven, Conn.: Yale University Press.

———. 1985. "Human mate selection." *American Scientist* 73(1):47–51.

———. 1989. "Sex differences in human mate preferences: Evolutionary hypotheses tested in 37 cultures." *Behavioral and Brain Sciences* 12:1–49.

———. 1994. *The evolution of desire: Strategies of human mating.* New York: Basic Books.

Buss, D. M. et al. 1990. "International preferences in selecting mates: A study of 37 cultures." *Journal of Cross-cultural Psychology* 21:5–47.

Buunk, B., and R. B. Hupka. 1987. "Cross-cultural differences in the elicitation of sexual jealousy." *Journal of Sex Research* 23:12–22.

Bylinsky, G. 1996. "Creating their own work forces." *Fortune,* 14 October, 162Aff.

Byrne, D., G. L. Clore, and G. Smeaton. 1986. "The attraction hypothesis: Do similar attitudes affect anything?" *Journal of Personality and Social Psychology* 51:1167–1170.

Byrne, J. A. 1992. "Management's new gurus." *Business Week,* 31 August, 44–52.

———. 1995. "Virtual b-schools." *Business Week,* 23 October, 64.

Cain, W. S. 1982. "Odor identification by males and females: Predictions vs. performances." *Chemical Senses* 7:129–142.

Caldwell, B. M., and R. I. Watson. 1952. "An evaluation of psychologic effects of sex hormone administration in aged women. Results of therapy after six months." *Journal of Gerontology* 7:228–244.

Caldwell, M. A., and L. A. Peplau. 1982. "Sex differences in same-sex friendship." *Sex Roles* 8:721–732.

Campbell, A. 1993. *Men, women and aggression.* New York: Basic Books.

———. 1995. "A few good men: Evolutionary psychology and female adolescent aggression." *Ethology and Sociobiology* 16:99–123.

Cancian, F. M. 1986. "The feminization of love." *Signs: Journal of Women in Culture and Society* 11(4):692–709.

———. 1987. *Love in America: Gender and self-development.* Cambridge, England: Cambridge University Press.

Cappella, J. N., and M. T. Palmer. 1990. "Attitude similarity, relational history, and attraction: The mediating effects of kinesic and vocal behaviors." *Communication Monographs* 57:161–183.

Caro, T. M, D. W. Sellen, A. Parish, R. Frank, D. M. Brown, E. Voland, and M. Borgerhoff Mulder. 1995. "Termination of reproduction in nonhuman and human female primates." *International Journal of Primatology,* 16 (2):205–220.

Carroll, R. 1997. "Today's media: What voice in foreign policy?" *Great Decisions.* New York: Foreign Policy Association.

Carter, C. S., C. DeVries, S. E. Taymans, R. L. Roberts, J. R. Williams, and L. L. Getz. 1997. "Peptides, steroids, and pair bonding." In "The integrative neurobiology of affiliation," edited by C. S. Carter, I. I. Lederhendler, and B. Kirkpatrick. *Annals of the New York Academy of Sciences* 807, 260–272.

Cases, O., I. Seif, J. Grimsby, P. Gaspar, K. Chen, S. Pournin, U. Muller, M. Aguet, C. Babinet, J. Chen Shih, and E. De Maeyer. 1995. "Aggressive behavior and altered amounts of brain serotonin and norepinephrine in mice lacking MAOA." *Science* 268:1763–1766.

Chagnon, Napoleon A. 1988. "Life histories, blood revenge and warfare in a tribal population." *Science* 239:985–992.

Chancer, L. 1995. "Unintended intimacies: Sex and sociology." *Contemporary Sociology* 24(4):298–302.

Channon, L. D., and S. D. Ballinger. 1986. "Some aspects of sexuality and vaginal symptoms during menopause and their relation to anxiety and depression." *British Journal of Medical Psychology* 59:173–180.

Chen, M. A. 1996. "Engendering world conferences: The international women's movement and the UN." In *NGO's, the UN, and global governance,* edited by T. G. Weiss and L. Gordenker. Boulder, Colo.: Lynne Rienner Publishers.

Cherlin, A. J. 1981. *Marriage, divorce, remarriage.* Cambridge, Mass.: Harvard University Press.

———. 1995. "Social organization and sexual choices." *Contemporary Sociology* 24 (4):293–296.

Chodorow, N. 1974. "Family structure and feminine personality." In *Woman, culture and society,* edited by M. Z. Rosaldo and L. Lamphere. Stanford, Calif.: Stanford University Press.

Cleveland, M. 1981. "Sexuality in the middle years." In *Single life: Unmarried adults in social context,* edited by P. Stein. New York: St. Martin's Press.

Coates, J. 1986. *Women, men and language: A sociolinguistic account of sex differences in language.* New York: Longman, Inc.

Cochran, C., and A. Perachio. 1977. "Dihydrotestosterone propionate effects on dominance and sexual behaviors in gonadectomized male and female rhesus monkeys." *Hormones and Behavior* 8:175–187.

Cohen, Jon. 1996. "Does nature drive nurture." *Science* 273:577–78.

Coleman, E. 1985. "Bisexual women in marriages." In *Bisexualities: Theory and research,* edited by F. Klein and T. Wolf. *Research on homosexuality,* vol. 11. New York: Haworth.

Collins, G. 1998. "Why the women are fading away." *New York Times Magazine,* 25 October, 54–55.

Collins, J., and T. Gregor. 1995. "Boundaries of Love." In *Romantic passion: A universal experience?* edited by W. Jankowiak. New York: Columbia University Press.

Coontz, S. 1992. *The way we never were: American families and the nostalgia trap.* New York: Basic Books.

———. 1997. "Divorcing reality." *The Nation,* 17 November, 21–24.

Coontz, S., and D. Franklin. 1997. "When the marriage penalty is marriage." *New York Times,* 28 October, A23.

Council on Foundations. 1998. "1998 grantmakers salary report: Executive summary." *Council on Foundations Newsletter* 17 (11):3–6.

Cowan, A. L. 1989. "Women's gains on the job: Not without a heavy toll." *New York Times,* 21 August, A1f.

Crenchaw, Theresa L. 1996. *The alchemy of love and lust.* New York: G. P. Putnam's Sons.

Crossette, B. 1995a. "Study finds worldwide decline in elections of women to office." *New York Times,* 27 August, A1.

———. 1995b. "U.N. documents inequities for women as world forum nears." *New York Times,* 18 August, A1.

———. 1997. "A manual on rights of women under Islam." *New York Times,* 29 December, A4.

———. 1998a. "Annan makes his bid to make his job count." *New York Times,* 8 March, A17.

———. 1998b. "Surprises in the global tourism boom." *New York Times,* 12 April, WK5.

———. 1998c. "Women see key gains since talks in Beijing." *New York Times,* 8 March, A6.

Cummings, J. L. 1995. "Anatomic and behavioral aspects of frontal-subcortical circuits." In "Structure and functions of the human prefrontal cortex," edited by J. Grafman, K. J. Holyoak, and F. Boller. *Annals of the New York Academy of Sciences* 769:1–13.

Cupach, W. R., and S. Metts. 1986. "Accounts of relational dissolution: A comparison of marital and non-marital relationships." *Communication Monographs* 53:311–334.

Dabbs, J. 1992. "Testosterone and occupational achievement." *Social Forces* 70:813–824.

Dabbs, J. M., Jr., D. de la Rue, and P. M. Williams. 1990. "Salivary testosterone and occupational choice: Actors, ministers and other men." *Journal of Personality and Social Psychology* 59(6):1261–1265.

Dahlberg, F., ed. 1981. *Woman the gatherer.* New Haven, Conn.: Yale University Press.

Daly, M., and M. Wilson. 1988. *Homicide.* Hawthorne, N.Y.: Aldine de Gruyter.

Daly, M., M. Wilson, and S. J. Weghorst. 1982. "Male sexual jealousy." *Ethology and Sociobiology* 3:11–27.

Damasio, A. R. 1994. *Descartes' error: Emotion, reason, and the human brain.* New York: G. P. Putnam's Sons.

————. 1995. "On some functions of the human prefrontal cortex." In "Structure and functions of the human prefrontal cortex," edited by J. Grafman, K. J. Holyoak, and F. Boller. *Annals of the New York Academy of Sciences.* 769:241–251.

Danielsson, B. 1956. *Love in the south seas.* Translated by R. H. Lyon. New York: Reynal and Company.

Darling, C. A., J. K. Davidson, and R. P. Cox. 1991. "Female sexual response and the timing of partner orgasm." *Journal of Sex and Marital Therapy* 17:3–21.

Darwin, Charles. 1936. *The origin of species and the descent of man.* Modern Library Edition. New York: Random House.

Davidson, M. J., and C. L. Cooper, eds. 1993. *European women in business and management.* London: Paul Chapman, Ltd.

Davis, D. A., and S. S. Davis. 1995. "Possessed by love: Gender and romance in Morocco." In *Romantic passion: A universal experience?* edited by W. Jankowiak. New York: Columbia University Press.

Davis, J. A., and T. Smith. 1987. *General social surveys. 1972–1987: Cumulative data.* Storrs: Roper Center for Public Research, University of Connecticut.

Davis, J. A., and T. W. Smith. 1991. *General social surveys, 1972–1991: Cumulative codebook.* Chicago: National Opinion Research Center.

Dawley, H. 1997. "And now, mad plaintiff disease." *Business Week.* 10 November, 66E16.

Daymont, T. N., and P. J. Andrisani. 1984. "Job preferences, college major and the gender gap in earnings." *Journal of Human Resources* 19:408–414.

Deacon, T. W. 1992. "The human brain." In *The Cambridge encyclopedia of human evolution,* edited by S. Jones, R. Martin, and D. Pillman. Cambridge: Cambridge University Press.

————. 1997. *The symbolic species.* New York: W. W. Norton.

Dehaene, S., and J. P. Changeux. 1995. "Neuronal models of prefrotal cortical functions." In "Structure and functions of the human prefrontal cortex," edited by J. Grafman, K. J. Holyoak, and F. Boller. *Annals of the New York Academy of Sciences* 769:305–319.

DeLamater, J. 1995. "The NORC sex survey." *Science* 270:501–503.

Della Sala, S., A. Baddeley, C. Papagno, and H. Spinnler. 1995. "Dual-task paradigm: A means to examine the central executive." In "Structure and functions of the human prefrontal cortex," edited by J. Grafman, K. J. Holyoak, and F. Boller. *Annals of the New York Academy of Sciences* 769:161–171.

De Palma, A. 1997. "As U.S. looks on, 120 nations sign treaty banning land mines." *New York Times,* 3 December, A1.

DeVries, G. J., R. M. Buijs, F. W. Van Leeuwen, A. R. Caffe, and D. F. Swaab. 1985. "The vasopressinergic innervation of the brain in normal and castrated rats." *The Journal of Comparative Neurology* 233:236–254.

DeVries, R. 1985. *Regulating birth: Midwifery, medicine and the law.* Philadelphia: Temple University Press.

Diamond, J. 1997. "Location, location, location: The first farmers." *Science* 278:1243–1244.

Dickemann, M. 1979. "Female infanticide, reproductive strategies, and social stratifications: A preliminary model." In *Evolutionary Biology and Human Social Behavior*, edited by N. Chagnon and W. Irons. North Scituate, R.I.: Duxbury Press.

———. 1992. "Phylogenetic fallacies and sexual oppression." *Human Nature* 3: 71–87.

Dion, K. K., and K. L. Dion. 1985. "Personality, gender and the phenomenology of romantic love." In *Review of personality and social psychology*, edited by P. Shaver. Vol. 6. Beverly Hills, Calif.: Sage Publications.

Dluzen, D. E., V. D. Ramirez, C. S. Carter, and L. L. Getz. 1981. "Male vole urine changes leutenizing hormone—releasing hormone and nerepinephrine in female olfactory bulb." *Science* 212:573–575.

Dobrzynski, J. H. 1996. "Somber news for women on corporate ladder." *New York Times*, 6 November, D1f.

———. 1996a. "Study finds few women in 5 highest company jobs." *New York Times*, 18 October.

Dolan, K. A. 1996. "When money isn't enough." *Forbes*, 18 November, 164ff.

Doty, Richard L. 1978. "Gender and reproductive state correlates of taste perception in humans." In *Sex and behavior: Status and prospectus*, edited by T. E. McGill, D. A. Dewsbury, and B. D. Sachs. New York: Plenum Press.

———. 1986. "Gender and endocrine-related influences on human olfactory perception." In *Clinical measurement of taste and smell*, edited by Herbert L. Meiselman and Richard S. Ravlin. New York: Macmillan.

Doty, Richard L., Paul Shaman, Steven L. Applebaum, Ronite Giberson, Lenore Siksorski, and Lysa Rosenberg. 1984. "Smell identification ability: Changes with age." *Science* 226:1441–1443.

Doty, Richard L., Steven L. Applebaum, Hiroyuki Zusho, and R. Gregg Settle. 1985. "Sex differences in odor identification ability: A cross-cultural analysis." *Neuropsychologia* 23(5):667–672.

Douglass, J. D., and F. C. Atwell. 1988. *Love, intimacy and sex*. New York: Sage Publications.

Doyle, R. 1998. "Women in politics throughout the world." *Scientific American*, January.

Draper, P., and J. Belsky. 1990. "Personality development in evolutionary perspective." *Journal of Personality* 58:141–162.

Drobis, D. R. 1997. "Borderless believability: Building trust around the globe." *Vital Speeches of the Day*, 15 February, 281ff.

Drucker, P. F. 1988. "The coming of the new organization." *Harvard Business Review* 66 (1):45ff.

———. 1992. *Managing for the future: The 1990s and beyond*. New York: Truman Talley Books/Plume.

———. 1997. "Looking ahead: Implications of the present: The future that has already happened." *Harvard Business Review*, September–October, 20ff.

DSM III R. 1994. *Diagnostic and statistical manual of mental disorders*. 4th ed. Washington, D.C.: American Psychiatric Association.

Duck, S. 1991. *Personal relationships and social support*. London: Sage Publications.

Duff, C. 1996. "Yuppies, independent widows boost single-dweller households in U.S." *The Wall Street Journal*, 10 December, A2.

———. 1997. "Indulging in inconspicuous consumption." *The Wall Street Journal*, 14 April, B1f.

———. 1998. "Census finds striking shift in families." *The Wall Street Journal,* 28 May, B1f.

Duff, C. S. 1993. *When women work together: Using our strengths to overcome our challenges.* Berkeley, Calif.: Conari Press.

Dunbar, R. 1996. *Grooming, gossip and the evolution of language.* Boston: Faber and Faber.

Dychtwald, K., and J. Flower. 1989. *Age wave: The challenges and opportunities of an aging America.* Los Angeles, Calif.: Jeremy P. Tarcher, Inc.

Eccles, J. S. 1987. "Gender roles and achievement patterns: An expectancy value perspective." In *Masculinity/femininity: Basic perspectives,* edited by S. Sanders, J. M. Reinisch, and L. A. Rosenblum. New York: Oxford University Press.

Eckholm, E. 1998. "Homes for elderly replacing family care as China grays." *New York Times,* 20 May, A1f.

*Economist, The.* 1995. "The economics of aging: The luxury of longer life," 27 January, 52ff.

*Economist, The.* 1996. "Tomorrow's second sex," 28 September, 23–26.

*Economist, The.* 1996a. "At your service," 14 December.

*Economist, The.* 1997. "Fun for the masses," 2 August, 62.

*Economist, The.* 1997a. "Microlending: From sandals to suits," 1 February, 75.

*Economist, The.* 1997b. "The future of warfare: Select enemy," 8 March, 21ff.

*Economist, The.* 1998. "For better for worse: A survey of women and work," 18 July, 3–15.

*Economist, The.* 1998a. "Philanthropy in America: The gospel of wealth," 30 May, 19ff.

*Economist, The.* 1998b. "Learning round the kitchen table," 6 June, 28ff.

Edwards, John N., and Alan Booth. 1994. "Sexuality, marriage, and well-being: The middle years." In *Sexuality across the life course,* edited by A. S. Rossi. Chicago: University of Chicago Press.

Eibl-Eibesfeldt, Irenaus. 1989. *Human ethology.* New York: Aldine de Gruyter.

Einon, D. 1994. "Are men more promiscuous than women?" *Ethology and Sociobiology* 15 (3):131–143.

Ekman, P., and W. V. Friesen. 1971. "Constants across cultures in the face and emotion." *Journal of Personality and Social Psychology* 17:124–29.

Elliott, Colin D. 1971. "Noise tolerance and extraversion in children." *British Journal of Psychology* 62:375–380.

Ellis, B. J. 1992. "The evolution of sexual attraction: Evaluative mechanisms in women." In *The adapted mind: Evolutionary psychology and the generation of culture,* edited by J. H. Barkow, L. Cosmides, and J. Tooby. New York: Oxford University Press.

Ellis, B. J., and D. Symons. 1990. "Sex differences in sexual fantasy: An evolutionary psychological approach." *The Journal of Sex Research* 27:527–555.

Ember, C. R. 1983. "The relative decline in women's contribution to agriculture with intensification." *American Anthropologist* 85:285–304.

Engell, J., and A. Dangerfield. 1998. "Humanities in the age of money." *Harvard Magazine,* May–June, 48–55.

Engels F. 1972. *The origin of the family, private property and the state.* New York: International Publishers.

Epstein, C. F. 1981. *Women in law.* 2d ed. Urbana: University of Illinois Press.

Epstein, C. F, R. Sauve, B. Oglensky, and M. Gever. 1995. "Glass ceilings and open doors: Women's advancement in the legal profession. A report to the committee on women in the profession, the Association of the Bar of the City of New York." *Fordham Law Review* 64:291–449.

Erwin, R. J., R. C. Gur, R. E. Gur, B. Skolnick, M. Mawhinney-Hee, and J. Smailis. 1992. "Facial emotion discrimination: I. Task construction and behavioral findings in normal subjects." *Psychiatry Research* 42:231–240.

Espenshade, T. J. 1984. "Investing in children: New estimates of parental expenditures." Washington, D.C.: Urban Institute Press.

———. 1985. "Marriage trends in America: Estimates, implications, and underlying causes." *Population and Development Review* 11 (2):193–245.

Etienne, M., and E. Leacock, eds. 1980. *Woman and colonization: Anthropological perspectives*. New York: Praeger.

Eveleth, P. B. 1986. "Timing of menarche: Secular trend and population differences." In *School-age pregnancy and parenthood: Biosocial dimensions*, edited by J. B. Lancaster and B. A. Hamburg. New York: Aldine de Gruyter.

Faison, S. 1997. "Door to tolerance opens partway as gay life is emerging in China." *New York Times*, 2 September, A1, 8.

———. 1998. "China lets 100 flowers bloom, in private life." *New York Times*, 22 June, A4.

———. 1998a. "Behind a great wall of reticence, some sex toys." *New York Times*, 5 March, A4.

Falk, D. 1992. *Evolution of the brain and cognition in hominids*. New York: American Museum of Natural History.

Farrell, W. 1993. *The myth of male power: Why men are the disposable sex*. New York: Simon and Schuster.

Fedigan, Linda Marie. 1982. *Primate paradigms: Sex roles and social bonds*. Montreal: Eden Press.

———. 1983. "Dominance and reproductive success in primates." *Yearbook of Physical Anthropology* 26:91–129.

Fernald, Anne. 1992. "Human maternal vocalizations to infants as biologically relevant signals: An evolutionary perspective." In *The adapted mind: Evolutionary psychology and the generation of culture*, edited by J. H. Barkow, L. Cosmides, and J. Tooby. New York: Oxford University Press.

Fernald, A., and T. Simon. 1984. "Expanded intonation contours in mothers' speech to newborns." *Developmental Psychology* 20:104–113.

Field, T. M., S. M. Schanberg, F. Scafidi, C. R. Bauer, N. Vega Lahr, R. Garcia, J. Nystrom, and C. M. Kuhn. 1986. "Effects of tactile/kinesthetic stimulation on preterm neonates." *Pediatrics* 77:654–658.

Finerman, R. 1995. "The forgotten healers: Women as family healers in an Andean Indian community." In *Women as healers: Cross-cultural perspectives*, edited by C. S. McClain. New Brunswick, N.J.: Rutgers University Press.

Finn, C., L. Bierlein, and B. Manno. 1996. "Finding the right fit." *The Brookings Review* (summer): 18ff.

Fisher, Helen. 1982. *The sex contract: The evolution of human behavior*. New York: William Morrow.

———. 1989. "Evolution of human serial pairbonding." *American Journal of Physical Anthropology* 78:331–354.

———. 1992. *Anatomy of love: The natural history of monogamy, adultery and divorce*. New York: W. W. Norton.

———. 1994. "The nature of romantic love." *The Journal of NIH Research* 6:58–64.

————. 1998. "Lust, attraction and attachment in mammalian reproduction." *Human Nature* 9 (1):23–52.

Fisher, S. 1980. "Personality correlates of sexual behavior in black women." *Archives of Sexual Behavior* 9:27–35.

Fitzpatrick, S. M., and J. T. Bruer. 1997. "Science funding and private philanthropy." Editorial. *Science,* 1 September.

Fluehr-Lobban, C. 1979. "A Marxist reappraisal of the matriarchate." *Current Anthropology* 20:341–360.

Foa, U. G., B. Anderson, J. Converse Jr., W. A. Urbansky, M. J. Cawley III, S. M. Muhlhausen, and K. Y. Tornblom. 1987. "Gender-related sexual attitudes: Some cross-cultural similarities and differences." *Sex Roles* 16:511–519.

Fodor, J. 1983. *The modularity of mind.* Cambridge, Mass.: MIT Press.

Ford, C. S., and F. A. Beach. 1951. *Patterns of sexual behavior.* New York: Harper and Row.

*Forecast.* 1998. "Not punching the clock," May, 3.

Fowlkes, M. R. 1994. "Single worlds and homosexual lifestyles: Patterns of sexuality and intimacy." In *Sexuality across the life course,* edited by A. S. Rossi. Chicago: University of Chicago Press.

Fox, R. 1980. *The red lamp of incest.* New York: E. P. Dutton.

Francoeur, R. 1996. "The guest room: Women are leading the next sexual revolution." *Forum,* February, 136ff.

Frank, R. M. 1985. *Choosing the right pond: Human behavior and the quest for status.* New York: Oxford University Press.

Frankfurt, M. 1994. "Gonadal steroids and neuronal plasticity: Studies in the adult rat hypothalamus." In "Hormonal restructuring of the adult brain: Basic and clinical perspectives," edited by V. N. Luine and C. F. Harding. *Annals of the New York Academy of Sciences* 743:45–60.

Frayser, S. 1985. *Varieties of sexual experience: An anthropological perspective on human sexuality.* New Haven, Conn.: HRAF Press.

Freudenheim, M. 1997. "As nurses take on primary care, physicians are sounding alarms." *New York Times,* 30 September, A1f.

Friedl, E. 1975. *Women and men: An anthropologist's view.* New York: Holt, Rinehart and Winston.

Fukuyama, F. 1995. *Trust: The social virtues and the creation of prosperity.* New York: The Free Press.

————. 1998. "Women and the evolution of world politics." *Foreign Affairs,* September–October, 24–40.

Fukuyama, F., and A. N. Shulsky. 1997. *The "virtual corporation" and army organization.* Santa Monica, Calif.: Rand.

Furstenberg, F. F. Jr. 1996. "The future of marriage." *American Demographics* (June): 34ff.

*Future Survey.* 1996. "The New Business Revolution," December, 11.

*Futurific.* 1994. "The family in transition," December, 23ff.

*Futurific.* 1995. "Knowledge unbound: Give credit where credit is due," March, 19.

*Futurific.* 1996. "Book bound: The world of 2044," June, 19ff.

*Futurific.* 1996a. "Toward global democracy: Europe," June, 4ff.

Gabriel, T. 1996. "New issue at work: On-line sex sites." *New York Times,* 27 June, C1f.

Galea, Lisa A. M., and Doreen Kimura. 1993. "Sex differences in rote learning." *Personality and Individual Differences* 14(1):53–65.

Gallup Organization. 1996. *Gender and society: Status and stereotypes: An international Gallup poll report*. Princeton, New Jersey.

Gandelman, R. 1983. "Gonadal hormones and sensory functioning." *Neuroscience and Biobehavioral Reviews* 7:1–17.

Gangestad, S. W., and R. Thornhill. 1997. "The evolutionary psychology of extrapair sex: The role of fluctuating asymmetry." *Evolution and Human Behavior* 18 (2):69–88.

Gangestad, S. W., R. Thornhill, and R. A. Yeo. 1994. "Facial attractiveness, developmental stability, and fluctuating asymmetry." *Ethology and Sociobiology* 15:73–85.

Ganong, W. F. 1993. *Review of Medical Physiology*. 16th ed. Norwalk, Conn.: Appleton and Lange.

Gardner, H. 1983. *Frames of mind*. New York: Basic Books.

Garry, P. 1997. "A nation of adversaries: How the litigation explosion is reshaping America." *Future Survey* (June): 10.

Gaulin, Stephen J. C. 1980. "Sexual dimorphism in the human post-reproductive life-span: Possible causes." *Journal of Human Evolution* 9:227–232.

Gaulin, Stephen J. C., and Randall W. Fitzgerald. 1989. "Sexual selection for spatial-learning ability." *Animal Behavior* 37:322–331.

Gazzaniga, M. S. 1988. "Brain modularity: Towards a philosophy of conscious experience." In *Consciousness in contemporary science*, edited by A. J. Marcel and E. Bisiack. Oxford: Clarendon Press.

———. 1995. "Gut thinking." *Natural History*, February, 68–71.

Geary, David C. 1998. *Male, female: The evolution of human sex differences*. Washington, D.C.: American Psychological Association.

Geary, David C., M. Rumsey, C. C. Bow-Thomas, and M. K. Hoard. 1995. "Sexual jealousy as a facultative trait: Evidence from the pattern of sex differences in adults from China and the United States." *Ethology and Sociobiology* 16:355–383.

Geer, J. H., and G. M. Manguno-Mire. 1996. "Gender differences in cognitive processes in sexuality." *Annual Review of Sex Research* 7:90–124.

Geer, J. H., and H. Bellard. 1996. "Sexual content induced delays in lexical decisions: Gender and context effects." *Archives of Sexual Behavior* 25:379–395.

Gellner, E. 1994. *Conditions of liberty: Civil society and its rivals*. New York: The Penguin Press.

George, M., T. A. Ketter, P. I. Parekh, P. Herscovitch, and R. M. Post. 1996. "Gender differences in regional cerebral blood flow during transient self-induced sadness or happiness." *Biological Psychiatry* 40(9):859–871.

Gilfoyle, J., J. Wilson, and S. Brown. 1992. "Sex, organs, and audiotape: A discourse analytic approach to talking about heterosexual sex and relationships." *Feminism and Psychology* 2:209–230.

Gilfoyle, T. 1992. *City of eros: New York City, prostitution and the commercialization of sex, 1870–1920*. New York: W. W. Norton.

Gilinsky, A. S. 1984. *Mind and brain*. New York: Praeger.

Gilligan, Carol. 1982. *In a different voice*. Cambridge, Mass.: Harvard University Press.

———. 1988. "Remapping development: Creating a new framework for psychological theory and research." In *Mapping the moral domain*, edited by C. Gilligan, J. V. Ward, and J. M. Taylor with B. Bardige. Cambridge, Mass.: Harvard University Press.

Gimbutas, M. A. 1989. *The language of the goddess*. San Francisco: Harper and Row.

Ginsburg, Harvey J., and Shirley M. Miller. 1982. "Sex differences in children's risk taking behavior." *Child Development* 53(2):426–428.

Glass, S. P., and T. L. Wright. 1985. "Sex differences in type of extramarital involvement and marital dissatisfaction." *Sex Roles* 12:1101–1120.

———. 1992. "Justifications for extramarital relationships: The association between attitudes, behaviors, and gender." *Journal of Sex Research* 29:361–387.

Glick, P. C. 1984. "Marriage, divorce, and living arrangements: Prospective changes." *Journal of Family Issues* 5:7–26.

———. 1975. "Some recent changes in American families." *Current Population Reports.* Social Studies Series P-23, no. 52. Washington, D.C.: U.S. Bureau of the Census.

Gllick, P., and S. Lin. 1986. "Recent changes in divorce and remarriage." *Journal of Marriage and the Family* 48:737–747.

Goldberg, Steven. 1993. *Why men rule: A theory of male dominance.* Chicago: Open Court.

Goldman, P. S., A. T. Crawford, L. P. Stokes, T. W. Galkin, and H. E. Rosvold. 1974. "Sex-dependent behavioral effects of cerebral cortical lesions in the developing rhesus monkey." *Science* 186:540–542.

Goldman-Rakic, P. S. 1995. "Architecture of the prefrontal cortex and the central executive." In "Structure and functions of the human prefrontal cortex," edited by J. Grafman, K. J. Holyoak, and F. Boller. *Annals of the New York Academy of Sciences* 769:71–83.

Goleman, Daniel. 1990. "Aggression in men: Hormone levels are a key." *New York Times,* 17 July, C1, 3.

———. 1994. "What men and women really want . . . to eat." *New York Times,* 2 March, C1, 8.

———. 1995a. "The brain manages happiness and sadness in different centers." *New York Times,* 28 March, C1, 9.

———. 1995b. *Emotional intelligence.* New York: Bantam Books.

Goode, W. 1993. *World changes in divorce patterns.* New Haven, Conn.: Yale University Press.

Goode, W. J. 1982. *The family.* Englewood Cliffs, N.J.: Prentice-Hall.

Gorski, Roger A. 1991. "Sexual differentiation of the endocrine brain and its control." In *Brain Endocrinology,* edited by Marcella Motta. 2d ed. New York: Raven Press.

———. 1980. "Sexual differentiation of the brain." In *Neuroendocrinology,* edited by D. T. Krieger and J. C. Hughes. Sunderland, Mass.: Sinauer Associates.

Gottman, John. 1994. *What predicts divorce: The relationship between marital processes and marital outcomes.* Hillsdale, N.J.: Lawrence Erlbaum and Associates.

Gould, Elizabeth, Catherine S. Woolley, and Bruce S. McEwen. 1991. "The hippocampal formation: Morphological changes induced by thyroid, gonadal and adrenal hormones." *Psychoneuroendocrinology* 16:67–84.

Gove, W. R. 1987. "Mental illness and psychiatric treatment among women." In *The psychology of women: Ongoing debates,* edited by M. R. Walsh. New Haven, Conn.: Yale University Press.

Govier, E., and M. Boden. 1997. "Occupation and dichotic listening performance." *Laterality* 2(1): 27–32.

Govier, E., and P. Bobby. 1994. Sex and occupation as markers for task performance in a dichotic measure of brain asymmetry." *International Journal of Psychophysiology* 18:179–186.

Gower, T. 1998. "Feel the burn, don't hear it." *New York Times,* Women's Health, 21 June, 3.

Grafman, J. 1989. "Plans, actions, and mental sets: Managerial knowledge units in the frontal lobe." In *Integrating theory and practice in clinical neuropsychology,* edited by E. Perecman. Hillsdale, N.J.: Lawrence Erlbaum and Associates.

Grafman, J., and J. Hendler. 1991. "Planning and the brain." *Behavioral and Brain Sciences* 14:563–564.

Grafman, J., K. J. Holyoak, and F. Boller, eds. 1995a. "Preface." In "Structure and functions of the human prefrontal cortex," edited by J. Grafman, K. J. Holyoak, and F. Boller. *Annals of the New York Academy of Sciences* 769:1–411.

———. 1995b. "Structure and functions of the human prefrontal cortex." *Annals of the New York Academy of Sciences* 769:1–411.

Greene, S. G. 1997. "Civic virtue vs. 'McWorld.' " *The Chronicle of Philanthropy,* 16 October, 15–16.

Greenwood, M.R.C. 1996. "Dancing with wolves." *Science* 271:1787.

Gregor, T. 1985. *Anxious pleasures: The sexual lives of an Amazonian people.* Chicago: University of Chicago Press.

Griffin-Shelley, Eric. 1991. *Sex and love: Addiction, treatment and recovery.* Westport, Conn: Praeger.

Gugliotta, G. 1997. "The stalkers are out there." *Washington Post Weekly Edition,* 8 December, 35.

Guyton, Arthur C. and John E. Hall. 1996. *Textbook of medical physiology.* 9th ed. Philadelphia: W. B. Saunders, Harcourt Brace Jovanovich.

Hales, Diane. 1998. "Lobe story: Why the female brain rules." New York *Daily News,* 9 July, 49–51.

———. 1999. *Just like a woman: How gender science is redefining what makes us female.* New York: Bantam Books.

Hall, Judith A. 1984. *Nonverbal sex differences: Communication accuracy and expressive style.* Baltimore: Johns Hopkins University Press.

Hällström, Tore. 1979. "Sexuality of women in middle age: The Göteborg study." *Journal of Biosocial Sciences, Supplement* 6:165–175.

Hällström, Tore, and Sverker Samuelsson. 1990. "Changes in women's sexual desire in middle life: The longitudinal study of women in Gothenburg." *Archives of Sexual Behavior* 19(3):259–268.

Halpern, Diane F. 1992. *Sex differences in cognitive abilities.* 2d ed. Hillsdale, N.J.: Lawrence Erlbaum and Associates.

Halpern, H. M. 1982. *How to break your addiction to a person.* New York: McGraw-Hill.

Hamilton, Annette. 1970. "The role of women in Aboriginal marriage arrangements." In *Woman's role in Aboriginal society,* edited by Fay Gale. Australian Institute of Aboriginal Studies, Australian Aboriginal Studies 36, Social Anthropology Series 6: 17–20.

Hamilton, W. D. 1966. "The moulding of senescence by natural selection." *Journal of Theoretical Biology* 12:12–45.

Hampden-Turner, C. 1994. "The structure of entrapment: Dilemmas standing in the way of women managers and strategies to resolve these." *The Deeper News* 5 (1):142. Emeryville, Calif.: Global Business Network.

Hampson, Elizabeth. 1990a. "Estrogen-related variations in human spatial and articulatory-motor skills." *Psychoneuroendocrinology* 15(2): 97–111.

———. 1990b. "Variations in sex-related cognitive abilities across the menstrual cycle." *Brain and Cognition* 14:26–43.

Hampson, Elizabeth, and Doreen Kimura. 1988. "Reciprocal effects of hormonal fluctuations on human motor and perceptual-spatial skills." *Behavioral Neuroscience* 102(3): 456–459.

———. 1993. "Sex differences and hormonal influences on cognitive function in humans." In *Behavioral endocrinology*, edited by J. B. Becker, S. M. Breedlove, and D. Crews. Cambridge, Mass.: The MIT Press.

Harmon, A. 1997. "For parents, a new and vexing burden." *New York Times*, 27 June.

*Harper's*. 1997. "Giving women the business: On winning, losing, and leaving the corporate game," December, 47–58.

Harrington, M. 1993. *Women lawyers: Rewriting the rules.* New York: Plume.

Harris, A. 1995. "Bully boy brokers." *Winning strategies* (April–June): 14ff.

Harris, D. 1996. "Why more women say . . . I don't need your money, honey." *Money* 25 (November): 146ff.

Harris, H. 1995. "Rethinking Polynesian heterosexual relationships: A case study of Mangaia, Cook Islands." In *Romantic passion: A universal experience?* edited by W. Jankowiak. New York: Columbia University Press.

Harrison, A. A., and L. Saaed. 1977. "Let's make a deal: An analysis of revelations and stipulations in lonely hearts advertisements." *Journal of Personality and Social Psychology* 35:257–264.

Harry, J. 1983. "Gay male and lesbian relationships." In *Contemporary families and alternative lifestyles: Handbook on research and theory*, edited by E. Macklin and R. Rubin. Beverly Hills, Calif.: Sage Publications.

Hatfield, E. 1988. "Passionate and companionate love." In *The psychology of love*, edited by R. J. Sternberg and M. L. Barnes. New Haven, Conn.: Yale University Press.

Hatfield, E., and R. L. Rapson. 1996. *Love and sex: Cross-cultural perspectives.* Needham Heights, Mass.: Allyn and Bacon.

Hatfield, E., and S. Sprecher. 1986. *Mirror, mirror: The importance of looks in everyday life.* Albany: State University of New York Press.

Hawkes, K., J. F. O'Connell, and N. G. Blurton Jones. 1989. "Hardworking Hadza grandmothers." In *Comparative socioecology: The behavioural ecology of humans and other mammals*, edited by V. Standen and R. A. Foley. Oxford: Blackwell Scientific Publications.

———. 1997. "Hadza women's time allocation, offspring provisioning, and the evolution of long postmenopausal life spans." *Current Anthropology* 38:551–565.

Hawkes, K., J. F. O'Connell, N. G. Blurton Jones, H. Alvarez, and E. L. Charnov. 1998. "Grandmothering, menopause, and the evolution of human life histories." *Proceedings of the National Academy of Science* 95 (3):1336–1339.

Hays, C. L. 1997. "Focus for M.B.A.s turns to women." *New York Times*, 14 November, A28.

Heath, R. P. 1997a. "Beyond the fringe in the 1990s." *American Demographics* (June): 27.

———. 1997b. "In so many words: How technology reshapes the reading habit." *American Demographics* (March): 39–43.

Hedges, Larry V., and Amy Nowell. 1995. "Sex differences in mental test scores, vari-ability, and numbers of high-scoring individuals." *Science* 269:41–45.

Helgesen, S. 1990. *The female advantage: Women's ways of leadership.* New York: Doubleday/Currency.

Heller, Sharon. 1997. *The vital touch: How intimate contact with your baby leads to happier, healthier development.* New York: Henry Holt and Company.

Hendler, J. A. 1995. "Types of planning: Can artificial intelligence yield insights into prefrontal function?" In "Structure and functions of the human prefrontal cortex," edited by J. Grafman, K. J. Holyoak, and F. Boller. *Annals of the New York Academy of Sciences* 769:265–276.

Hendrick C., and S. S. Hendrick. 1986. "A theory and method of love." *Journal of Personality and Social Psychology* 50:392–402.

Hendricks, M. 1998. "The origins of babble." *Johns Hopkins Magazine,* February, 12–19.

Herdt, Gilbert. 1987. *The Sambia: Ritual and gender in New Guinea.* New York: Holt, Rinehart and Winston.

Hewlett, B. S. 1992. "Husband-wife reciprocity and the father-infant relationships among Aka pygmies." In *Father-child relations: Cultural and biosocial contexts,* edited by B. S. Hewlett. Hawthorne, N. Y.: Aldine de Gruyter.

Hey, Kenneth R., and Peter D. Moore. 1998. *The caterpillar doesn't know: How personal change is creating organizational change.* New York: The Free Press.

Hill, C. T., Z. Rubin, and L. A. Peplau. 1976. "Breakups before marriage: The end of 103 affairs." *Journal of Social Issues* 32 (1):147–168.

Hill, E. M., J. P. Young, and J. L. Nord. 1994. "Childhood adversity, attachment security, and adult relationships: A preliminary study." *Ethology and Sociobiology* 15:323–338.

Hill, K., and A. M. Hurtado. 1991. "The evolution of premature reproductive senes-cence and menopause in human females: An evaluation of the 'grandmother hypothesis.' " *Human Nature* 2:313–350.

Hill, K., and H. Kaplan. 1988. "Trade-offs in male and female reproductive strategies among the Ache: Parts 1 and 2." In *Human reproductive behaviour: A Darwinian perspective,* edited by L. Betzig, P. Turke, and M. Borgerhoff Mulder. Cambridge, England: Cambridge University Press.

Hines, E. 1998. "Menage a . . . lot." *Jane,* August, 119–121.

Hines, M., L. Chiu, L. A. McAdams, P. M. Bentler, and J. Lipcamon. 1992. "Cogni-tion and the corpus callosum: Verbal fluency, visuospatial ability and language lateralization related to midsagittal surface areas of callosal subregions." *Behavioral Neuroscience,* 106 (1):3–14.

Hittelman, Joan. H., and Robert Dickes. 1979. "Sex differences in neonatal eye con-tact time." *Merrill-Palmer Quarterly* 25(3): 171–184.

Ho, R. 1997. "Gender gap narrows for credit-seekers, survey finds." *The Wall Street Journal,* 9 April, B2.

Hockschild, A. 1997. *The time bind: When work becomes home and home becomes work.* New York: Henry Holt and Co.

Hockschild, A., and A. Machung. 1989. *The second shift: Working women and the revolution at home.* New York: Viking.

Hoffman, Martin L. 1977. "Sex differences in empathy and related behaviors." *Psychological Bulletin* 84(4):712–722.

Holden, C. 1996. "Researchers find feminization a two-edged sword." *Science* 271:1919–1921.

Holloway, Ralph L., Paul J. Anderson, Richard Defendini, and Clive Harper. 1993. "Sexual dimorphism of the human corpus callosum from three independent samples: Relative size of the corpus callosum." *American Journal of Physical Anthropology* 92:481–498.

Holmes, S. A. 1996a. "Sitting pretty: Is this what women want?" *New York Times,* 15 December, 4, A1f.

———. 1996b. "Traditional family stabilized in the 1990s, study suggests." *New York Times,* 7 March, B12.

Holyoak K. J., and J. K. Kroger. 1995. "Forms of reasoning: Insight into prefrontal functions?" In "Structure and functions of the human prefrontal cortex," edited by J. Grafman, K. J. Holyoak, and F. Boller. *Annals of the New York Academy of Sciences* 769:253–263.

Honan, W. H. 1998. "The ivory tower under siege." *New York Times.* Education Supplement, 4 January, 4A.

Hopkins, Andrea. 1994. *The book of courtly love: The passionate code of the troubadours.* San Francisco: HarperSanFrancisco.

Horgan, D.M.D. 1975. Language development: A cross-methodological study. Ph.D. diss., University of Michigan, Ann Arbor.

House, J. S., K. R. Landis, and D. Umberson. 1988. "Social relationships and Health." *Science,* 241 (4865):540–545.

Howell, N. 1979. *Demography of the Dobe !Kung.* New York: Academic Press.

Hoyenga, K. B., and K. T. Hoyenga. 1979. *The question of sex differences.* Boston: Little, Brown and Company.

Huber, P. 1996. "Cyberpower." *Forbes,* 2 December.

Hunt, M. 1959. *The natural history of love.* New York: Grove Press.

Hrdy, Sarah Blaffer. 1979. "Infanticide among animals: A review, classification, and examination of the implications for the reproductive strategies of females." *Ethology and Sociobiology* 1:13–40.

———. 1981. *The woman that never evolved.* Cambridge, Mass.: Harvard University Press.

———. 1986. "Empathy, polyandry and the myth of the coy female." In *Feminist approaches to science,* edited by R. Bleier. New York: Pergamon Press.

———. 1987. "Sex-biased parental investment among primates and other mammals: A critical evaluation of the Trivers-Willard hypothesis." In *Child abuse and neglect: Biosocial dimensions,* edited by R. J. Gelles and J. B. Lancaster. Hawthorne, N.Y.: Aldine de Gruyter.

———. 1995. "Natural-born mothers." *Natural History,* December.

Hyde, Janet S., Elizabeth Fennema, and Susan J. Lamon. 1990. "Gender differences in mathematics performance: A meta-analysis." *Psychological Bulletin* 107:139–155.

Hyde, J. S., and E. R. Geiringer, and W. M. Yen. 1975. "On the empirical relation between spatial ability and sex differences in other aspects of cognitive performance." *Multivariate Behavioral Research* 10:289–309.

Insel, T. R., L. Young, and Z. Wang. 1997. "Molecular aspects of monogamy." In "The integrative neurobiology of affiliation," edited by C. S. Carter, I. I. Lederhendler, and B. Kirkpatrick. *Annals of the New York Academy of Sciences* 807:302–316.

Jack, R., and D. C. Jack. 1989. *Moral vision and professional decisions: The changing values of women and men lawyers.* New York: Cambridge University Press.

Jacobs, G. 1981. *Comparative color vision.* New York: Academic Press.

Jacoby, S. 1997. "Giving." *New York Times,* 9 December, G1f.

Jankowiak, W. 1995. "Introduction." In *Romantic passion: A universal experience?* edited by W. Jankowiak. New York: Columbia University Press.

———. 1995a. "Romantic passion in the people's republic of China." In *Romantic passion: A universal experience?* edited by W. Jankowiak. New York: Columbia University Press.

Janofsky, M. 1998. "Pittsburgh is showcase for women in policing." *New York Times,* 21 June, B14.

Janowsky, Jeri S., Shelia K. Oviatt, and Eric S. Orwoll. 1994. "Testosterone influences spatial cognition in older men." *Behavioral-Neuroscience* 108(2):325–332.

Jehl, D. 1997. "One wife is not enough? A film to provoke Iran." *New York Times,* 24 December, A4.

Johnson, K. 1995. "You're fired! See you out of court." *New York Times,* 29 March, B1ff.

Johnson, M. 1987. "Mental illness and psychiatric treatment among women: A response." In *The psychology of women: Ongoing debates,* edited by M. R. Walsh. New Haven, Conn.: Yale University Press.

Jones, Rex L., and Shirley Kurz Jones. 1976. *The Himalayan woman.* Palo Alto, Calif.: Mayfield Publishing Company.

Jope, E. M. 1956. "Agricultural implements." In *A history of technology,* edited by C. Singer, E. J. Holmyard, A. R. Hall, and T. I. Williams. Vol. 2. New York: Oxford University Press.

Joslyn, W. 1973. "Androgen induced social dominance in infant female rhesus monkeys." *Journal of Child Psychology and Psychiatry* 14:137–145.

Jost, A. 1970. "Hormonal factors in the sex differentiation of the mammalian foetus." *Philosophical Transactions of the Royal Society, London,* B. 119–130.

Judd, H. L., and S.S.C. Yen. 1973. "Serum androstenedione and testosterone levels during the menstrual cycle." *Journal of Clinical Endocrinology and Metabolism:* 36:475–481.

Judd, Howard L., and Nicole Fournet. 1994. "Changes of ovarian hormonal function with aging." *Experimental Gerontology* 29 (3/4):285–298.

Kahn, J., and M. Jordan. 1995. "Women's banks stage global expansion." *The Wall Street Journal,* 30 August, A8.

*Kankakee (Ill.) Daily Journal.* 1998. "Ageless love: Today's seniors say romance not just for young people," 15 June, B7.

Kannapell, A. 1995. "A snoop's story: The confessions of a private eye." *New York Times,* 27 August, section 13, PC1.

Kantner, J. F., and M. Zelnik. 1972. "Sexual experience of young unmarried women in the U.S." *Family Planning Perspectives* 4:9–18.

Kantrowitz, B., and P. Wingert. 1998. "Learning at home: Does it pass the test?" *Newsweek,* 5 October, 64–70.

Karl, M. 1995. *Women and empowerment: Participation and decision making.* New York: United Nations Non-Governmental Liaison Service.

Karli, Pierre. 1991. *Animal and human aggression.* New York: Oxford University Press.

Katz, M., and M. Konner. 1981. "The role of the father: An anthropological perspective." In *The role of the father in child development*, edited by M. Lamb. New York: John Wiley and Sons.

Katzenbach, J. R., and D. K. Smith. 1993. *The wisdom of teams: Creating the high-performance organization*. Boston: Harvard Business School Press.

Kay, F. M., and J. Hagan. 1998. "Raising the bar: The gender stratification of law-firm capital." *American Sociological Review* 63:728–743.

Kelly, J. B. 1982. "Divorce: The adult perspective." In *Families in transition*, edited by A. S. Skolnick and J. H. Skolnick. 5th ed. Boston: Little, Brown and Company.

Kelly, R. M. 1991. *The gendered economy*. Newbury Park, Calif.: Sage Publications.

Kenrick D. T., E. K. Sadalla, G. E. Groth, and M. R. Trost. 1990. "Evolution, traits and the states of human courtship: Qualifying the parental investment model." *Journal of Personality* 58(1):97–116.

Kephart, W. M. 1967. "Some correlates of romantic love." *Journal of Marriage and the Family* 29:470–479.

Kerber, K. B. 1994. "The marital balance of power and quid pro quo: An evolutionary perspective." *Ethology and Sociobiology* 15 (5/6):283–297.

Kerns, Virginia, and Judith K. Brown, eds. 1992. In her prime: *New views of middle-aged women*. Urbana: University of Illinois Press.

Kimura, Doreen. 1983. "Sex differences in cerebral organization for speech and praxic functions." *Canadian Journal of Psychology* 37 (1):19–35.

———. 1987. "Are men's and women's brains really different?" *Canadian Journal of Psychology* 28(2):133–147.

———. 1989. "How sex hormones boost or cut intellectual ability." *Psychology Today*, November, 63–66.

———. 1992. "Sex differences in the brain." *Scientific American* 267 (3):118–125.

Kinsey, A. C., W. B. Pomeroy, and C. E. Martin. 1948. *Sexual behavior in the human male*. Philadelphia: W. B. Saunders.

Kinsey, A. C., W. B. Pomeroy, C. E. Martin, and P. H. Gebhard. 1953. *Sexual Behavior in the human female*. Philadelphia, W. B. Saunders.

Kishkovsky, S., and E. Williamson. 1997. "Second-class comrades no more: Women stoke Russia's start-up boom." *The Wall Street Journal*, 30 January, A12.

Klahr, D., and K. Kotovsky, eds. 1989. *Complex information processing: The impact of Herbert A. Simon*. Hillsdale, N.J.: Lawrence Erlbaum and Associates.

Klein, J. 1997. "Tough mothering." *Mother Jones*, January–February.

Klein, Laura F., and Lillian A. Ackerman, eds. 1995. *Women and power in native North America*. Norman: University of Oklahoma Press.

Kleinman, A. 1980. *Patients and healers in the context of culture*. Berkeley: University of California Press.

Knox, D. H. 1970. "Conceptions of love at three developmental levels." *Family Coordinator* 19:151–157.

Kohlberg, L. 1969. "Stage and sequence: The cognitive-developmental approach to socialization." In *Handbook of socialization: Theory and research*, edited by D. A. Goslin. Chicago: Rand McNally.

———. 1981. *The psychology of moral development*. San Francisco: Harper and Row.

Kolata, Gina. 1995. "Man's world, woman's world? Brain studies point to differences." *New York Times*, 28 February, C7.

———. 1996. "New era of robust elderly belies the fears of scientists." *New York Times*, 27 February, A1f.

Koolhass, J. M., T.H.C. van den Brin, B. Roozendaal, and F. Boorsma. 1990. "Medial amygdala and aggressive behavior: Interaction between testosterone and vasopressin." *Aggressive Behavior* 16:223–229.

Kurtz, James P., and Marvin Zuckerman. 1978. "Race and sex differences on the sensation seeking scales." *Psychological Reports* 43(2):529–530.

Lacoste-Utamsing, C. de, and R. L. Holloway. 1982. "Sexual dimorphism in the human corpus callosum." *Science* 216:1431–1432.

Lagerspetz, K. M., K. Bjorkqvist, and T. Peltonen. 1988. "Is indirect aggression typical of females?" *Aggression and Behavior* 14:403–414.

Lancaster, J. B. 1994. "Human sexuality, life histories, and evolutionary ecology." In *Sexuality across the life course*, edited by A. S. Rossi. Chicago: University of Chicago Press.

Lancaster, Jane B., and Barbara J. King. 1992. "An evolutionary perspective on menopause." In *In her prime: New views of middle-aged women*, edited by Virginia Kerns and Judith K. Brown. Urbana: University of Illinois Press.

Lancaster, J. B., and H. Kaplan. 1994. "Human mating and family formation strategies: The effects of variability among males in quality and the allocation of mating effort and parental investment." In *Topics in Primatology*, Vol. 1: *Human Origins*. T. Nishida, W. C. McGrew, P. Marler, M. Pickford, and F. B. M. de Waal, eds. Tokyo: University of Tokyo Press.

Laumann, E. O., J. H. Gagnon, R. T. Michael, and S. Michaels. 1994. *The social organization of sexuality: Sexual practices in the United States*. Chicago: University of Chicago Press.

Lawlor, J. 1997. "Goodbye to the job. Hello to the shock." *New York Times*, 12 October, BU11.

Lawson, A. 1988. *Adultery: An analysis of love and betrayal*. New York: Basic Books.

Leacock, E. B. 1981. *Myths of male dominance*. New York: Monthly Review Press.

Leacock, E. B. ed. 1972. *The origins of the family, private property and the state, by Frederick Engels with an introduction by Eleanor Burke Leacock*. New York: International Publishers.

LeDoux, Joseph. 1996. *The emotional brain*. New York: Simon and Schuster.

Leigh, B. C. 1989. "Reasons for having and avoiding sex: Gender, sexual orientation, and relationship to sexual behavior." *Journal of Sex Research* 26:199–209.

Lemann, N. 1997. "Notes & Comment: Citizen 501(c) (3)." *The Atlantic Monthly*, February, 18ff.

Lenzner, R., and S. S. Johnson. 1997. "Seeing things as they really are." *Forbes*, 10 March, 122ff.

Lerner, G. 1986. *The creation of patriarchy*. New York: Oxford University Press.

Lessa, William A. 1966. *Ulithi: A Micronesian design for living*. New York: Holt, Rinehart and Winston.

LeVay, S. 1991. "A difference in hypothalamic structure between heterosexual and homosexual men." *Science* 253:1034–1037.

Levenson, Robert, et al. 1994. "The influence of age and gender on affect, physiology and their interrelations: A study of long-term marriages." *Journal of Personality and Social Psychology* 76.

Levenson, Thomas. 1995. "Accounting for taste." *The Sciences: Journal of the New York Academy of Sciences* (January–February).

Lever, Janet. 1976. "Sex differences in the games children play." *Social Problems* 23:478–487.

———. 1978. "Sex differences in the complexity of children's play and games." *American Sociological Review* 43:471–483.

Levine, R., S. Sato, T. Hashimoto, and J. Verman. 1994. "Love and marriage in eleven cultures." In *Love and sex: Cross-cultural perspectives*, edited by E. Hatfield and R. L. Rapson. Needham Heights, Mass.: Allyn and Bacon.

Levitan, S. A., R. S. Belous, and F. Gallo. 1988. *What's happening to the American family?* Baltimore: Johns Hopkins University Press.

Levy, J. 1967. "The older American Indian." In *The older rural Americans*, edited by E. Youmans. Lexington: University of Kentucky Press.

———. 1969. "Possible basis for the evolution of lateral specialization of the human brain." *Nature* 224:614–615.

Levy, J. A. 1994. "Sex and sexuality in later life stages." In *Sexuality across the life course*, edited by A. S. Rossi. Chicago: University of Chicago Press.

Lewin, T. 1995a. "Women are becoming equal providers." *New York Times*, 11 May.

———. 1995b. "Workers of both sexes make trade-offs for family, study shows." *New York Times*, 29 October.

———. 1997. "Women losing ground to men in widening income difference." *New York Times*, 15 September, A1f.

———. 1998. "Birth rates for teenage declines sharply in the 90s." *New York Times*, 1 May, A21.

Lewis, P. 1998. "Not just governments make war or peace." *New York Times*, 28 November, B9.

Liebowitz, Michael R. 1983. *The chemistry of love.* Boston: Little, Brown and Company.

Lind, M. 1998. "The beige and the black." *New York Times Magazine*, 16 August, 38–39.

Lindholm, C. 1995. "Love as an experience of transcendence." In *Romantic passion: A universal experience?* edited by W. Jankowiak. New York: Columbia University Press.

Liu, D., J. Diorio, B. Tannenbaum, C. Caldji, D. Francis, A. Freedman, S. Sharma, D. Pearson, P. M. Plotsky, and M. J. Meaney. 1997. "Maternal care, hippocampal glucocorticoid receptors, and hypothalamic-pituitary-adrenal responses to stress." *Science* 277:1659–1662.

Liu, D. L., M. L. Ng, and L. P. Chou. 1992. *Sexual behavior in modern China: A report of the nationwide "sex civilisation" survey on 20,000 subjects in China.* Shanghai: San Lian Bookstore Publishers.

Lockard, J., and D. Adams. 1981. "Human serial polygyny." *Ethology and Sociobiology* 2:177–186.

Longcope, C. 1986. "Adrenal and gonadal steroid secretion in normal females." *Journal of Clinical Endocrinology and Metabolism* 15:213–228.

Low, B. S. 1989. "Cross-cultural patterns in the training of children: An evolutionary perspective." *Journal of Comparative Psychology* 103:311–318.

Lueptow, L. B., L. Garovich, and M. B. Lueptow. 1995. "The persistence of gender stereotypes in the face of changing sex roles: Evidence contrary to the sociocultural model." *Ethology and Sociobiology* 16(6):509–530.

Lykken, D. T., and A. Tellegen. 1993. "Is human mating advantageous or the result of lawful choice? A twin study of mate selection." *Journal of Personality and Social Psychology* 65:56–68.

Maccoby, E., and C. Jacklin. 1974. *The psychology of sex differences.* Stanford, Calif.: Stanford University Press.

Mace, D., and V. Mace. 1980. *Marriage: East and west.* New York: Dolphin Books.

Maclay, G., and H. Knipe. 1972. *The dominant man.* New York: Delta.

Madsen, Douglas. 1994. "Serotonin and social rank among human males." In *The neurotransmitter revolution: Serotonin, social behavior and the law,* edited by R. D. Masters and M. T. McGuire. Carbondale: Southern Illinois University Press.

Mann, V. A., S. Sasanuma, N. Sakuma, and S. Masaki. 1990. "Sex differences in cognitive abilities; A cross-cultural perspective." *Neuropsychologia* 28(10): 1063–1077.

Manza, J., and C. Brooks. 1998. "The gender cap in U.S. presidential elections: When? why? implications?" *American Journal of Sociology* 103 (5):1235–1266.

Martin, David J., and H. D. Hoover. 1987. "Sex differences in educational achievement: A longitudinal study." *Journal of Early Adolescence* 7:65–83.

Martin, T. C., and L. L. Bumpass. 1989. "Recent trends in marital disruption." *Demography* 26:37–51.

Maryanski, A., and J. Turner. 1992. *The social cage: Human nature and the evolution of society.* Stanford, Calif.: Stanford University Press.

Masini, E. B. 1996. "Silently working for the future: Recognizing women as creators of social alternatives." *Futures Bulletin,* March 1ff.

Masters, R. D., and S. J. Carlotti Jr. 1993. "Gender differences in response to political leaders." In *Social stratification and socioeconomic inequality,* edited by L. Ellis. Vol. 2. Westport, Conn.: Praeger.

Masters, Roger D., and Michael T. McGuire, eds. 1994. *The neurotransmitter revolution: Serotonin, social behavior and the law.* Carbondale: Southern Illinois University Press.

Masters, W. H., and V. E. Johnson. 1966. *Human sexual response.* Boston: Little, Brown and Company.

Maybury-Lewis, D. 1992. *Millennium: Tribal wisdom and the modern world.* New York: Viking.

Mayer, Peter J. 1982. "Evolutionary advantage of the menopause." *Human Ecology* 10 (4):477–494.

Mazur, A., A. Booth, and J. M. Dabbs Jr. 1992. "Testosterone and chess competition." *Social Psychology Quarterly* 55 (1):70–77.

Mazur, A., E. J. Susman, and S. Edelbrock. 1997. "Sex differences in testosterone response to a video game contest." *Evolution and Human Behavior* 18 (5):317–326.

Mazur, A., and T. Lamb. 1980. "Testosterone, status, and mood in human mates." *Hormones and Behavior* 14:236–246.

McCauley, Elizabeth, Thomas Kay, Joanne Ito, and Robert Treder. 1987. "The turner syndrome: Cognitive deficits, affective discrimination and behavior problems." *Child Development* 58:464–473.

McClelland, D. C. 1975. *Power: The inner experience.* New York: Irvington.

McCorduck. P., and N. Ramsey. 1996. *The futures of women: Scenarios for the 21st century.* New York: Addison-Wesley.

McEwen, B. S. 1994. "How do sex and stress hormones affect nerve cells?" In "Hormonal restructuring of the adult brain: Basic and clinical perspectives," edited by V. N. Luine and C. F. Harding. *Annals of the New York Academy of Sciences* 743:1–18.

McGrew, W. C. 1981. "The female chimpanzee as a human evolutionary prototype."

In *Woman the gatherer*, edited by F. Dahlberg. New Haven, Conn.: Yale University Press.

McGue, M., and D. T. Lykken. 1992. "Genetic influence on risk of divorce." *Psychological Science* 3(6):368–373.

McGuinness, Diane. 1972. "Hearing: Individual differences in perceiving." *Perception* 1:465–473.

———. 1976. "Perceptual and cognitive differences between the sexes." In *Explorations in sex differences*, edited by B. Lloyd and J. Archer. New York: Academic Press.

———. 1985. "Sensorimotor biases in cognitive development." In *Male-Female differences: A bio-cultural perspective*, edited by R. L. Hall, P. Draper, M. E. Hamilton, D. McGinness, C. M. Otten, and E. A. Roth. New York: Praeger.

———. 1990. "Behavioral tempo in pre-school boys and girls." *Learning and Individual Differences* 2(3):315–325.

McGuinness, D., A. Olson, and J. Chapman. 1990. "Sex differences in incidental recall for words and pictures." *Learning and Individual Differences* 2(3):263–285.

McGuinness, D. and K. H. Pribram. 1979. "The origin of sensory bias in the development of gender differences in perception and cognition." In *Cognitive growth and development: Essays in memory of Herbert G. Birch*, edited by M. Bortner. New York: Brunner/Mazel.

McGuinness, Diane, and Janet Sparks. 1983. "Cognitive style and cognitive maps: Sex differences in representations of a familiar terrain." *Journal of Mental Imagery* 7:91–100.

McGuinness, K. 1990. "Women and the peace movement." In *The American woman 1990–1991: A status report*, edited by Sara E. Rix. New York: W. W. Norton.

McGuire, M., M. Raleigh, and G. Brammer. 1982. "Sociopharmacology." *Annual Review of Pharmacology and Toxicology*. 22:643–661.

McMillan, Carol A. 1989. "Male age, dominance, and mating success among rhesus macaques." *American Journal of Physical Anthropology* 80:83–89.

Mead, Margaret. 1949. *Male and female: A study of the sexes in a changing world*. New York: William Morrow.

Mead, M., and N. Newton. 1967. "Cultural patterning of perinatal behavior." In *Childbearing—Its social and psychological aspects*, edited by S. A. Richardson and A. F. Guttmacher. Baltimore: Williams and Wilkins.

Meldrum, D. R., B. J. Davidson, I. V. Tataryn, and H. L. Judd. 1981. "Changes in circulating steroids with aging in postmenopausal women." *Obstetrics and Gynecology* 57:624–628.

Meloy, J. R. 1998. "The psychology of stalking" In *The psychology of stalking: Clinical and forensic perspectives*, edited by J. R. Meloy. New York: Academic Press.

Menkel-Meadow, C. 1985. "Portia in a different voice: Speculations on a woman's lawyering process." *Berkeley Women's Law Journal* 1 (1):39 (fall).

Mernissi, Fatima. 1975. *Beyond the veil: Male-female dynamics in a modern Muslim society*. Cambridge, England: Schenkman.

Metts, S., and W. R. Cupach. 1991. "The role of communication in human sexuality." In *Human sexuality: The societal and interpersonal context*, edited by M. McKinney and S. Sprecher.

Mifflin, L. 1998. "After drought, networks put more women in top posts." *New York Times*, 24 August, D1f.

Milbank, D. 1996. "Blame game." *The Wall Steet Journal*, 5 January, A1ff.

Milius, S. 1998. "When birds divorce: Who splits, who benefits, and who gets the nest." *Science News* 153:153–155.

Miller, J. B. 1976. *Toward a new psychology of women.* Boston: Beacon Press.

Miller, Leon K., and Viana Santoni. 1986. "Sex differences in spatial abilities: Strategic and experiential correlates." *Acta Psychologia* 62:225–235.

Mills, D. Q. 1991. *Rebirth of the corporation.* New York: John Wiley and Sons.

Minot, Marilee. 1995. Implications of selected speech practices in the creation and/or perpetuation of gender identity in several cultures. Master's thesis, University of Cambridge.

Mitchell, C. 1981. *Human sex differences: A primatologist's perspective.* New York: Van Nostrand Reinhold.

Mitchell, S. 1995. "The next baby boom." *American Demographics* (October):22ff.

Mlot, C. 1998. "Probing the biology of emotion." *Science* 280:1005–1007.

Mock, D. W., and M. Fujioka. 1990. "Monogamy and long-term pair bonding in vertebrates." *Trends in Ecology and Evolution* 5 (2):39–43.

Móller, A. P. 1987. "Behavioral aspects of sperm competition in swallows (*Hirundo rustica*)." *Behaviour* 100:92–104.

Moltz, Howard, Michael Lubin, Michael Leon, and Michael Numan. 1970. "Hormonal induction of maternal behavior in the ovariectomized nulliparous rat." *Physiology and Behavior* 5:1373–1377.

Money, J. 1997. *Principles of developmental sexology.* New York: Continuum.

Money, J., and A. A. Ehrhardt. 1972. *Man and woman, boy and girl: The differentiation and dimorphism of gender identity from conception to maturity.* Baltimore: Johns Hopkins University Press.

Money, J., M. Schwartz, and V. G. Lewis. 1984. "Adult heterosexual status and fetal hormonal masculinization and demasculinization: 46,XX congenital virilizing adrenal hyperplasia and 46,XY androgen-insensitivity syndrome compared." *Psychoneuroendocrinology* 9:405–414

Monneuse, Marie-Odile, France Bellisle, and Jeanine Louis-Sylvestre. 1991. "Impact of sex and age on sensory evaluation of sugar and fat in dairy products." *Physiology and Behavior* 50:1111–1117.

Montagu, A. 1953. *The natural superiority of women.* New York: Collier Books.

Moran, S. 1998. ". . . But not at work." *American Demographics* (May):38ff.

Morell, V. 1998. "A new look at monogamy." *Science* 281:1982–1983.

Mosher, S. W. 1997. "Too many people? Not by a long shot." *New York Times,* 10 February, A18.

Murdock, George P. 1949. *Social structure.* New York: The Free Press.

Murdock, G. P., and C. Provost. 1973. "Factors in the division of labor by sex: A cross-cultural analysis." *Ethnology* 12:203–225.

Murphy, Yolanda, and Robert Murphy. 1974. *Women of the forest.* New York: Columbia University Press.

Murstein, B. I. 1972. "Physical attractiveness and marital choice." *Journal of Personality and Social Psychology* 22:8–12.

Mydans, S. 1997. "When the bartered bride opts out of the bargain." *New York Times,* 6 May, A3.

Nadler, A., and I. Dotan. 1992. "Commitment and rival attractiveness: Their effects on male and female reactions to jealousy arousing situations." *Sex Roles* 26:293–310.

Nadler, R. D., and J. T. Braggio. 1974. "Sex and species differences in captive-reared juvenile chimpanzees and orangutans." *Journal of Human Evolution* 3:541–550.

Naisbitt, J., and P. Aburdene. 1986. *Reinventing the corporation*. New York: Warner Books.

Nash, J. 1983. "Introduction." In *Women, men and the international division of labor*, edited by J. Nash and M. P. Fernandez-Kelly. Albany: State University of New York Press.

Nash, J., and M. P. Fernandez-Kelly, eds. 1983. *Women, men and the international division of labor*. Albany: State University of New York Press.

Nathans, J., D. Thomas, and D. S. Hogness. 1986. "Molecular genetics of human color vision: The genes encoding blue, green and red pigments." *Science* 232:193–202.

National Foundation for Women Business Owners. 1996. *Research Highlights*. Silver Spring, Md.: National Foundation for Women Business Owners.

Navcarro, M. 1997. "Elderly wield their might in Florida." *New York Times*, 19 October, A16.

Nelson, R. J. 1995. *An introduction to behavioral endocrinology*. Sunderland, Mass.: Sinauer Associates, Inc.

Newman, M. 1998. "In second year, charter schools continue to gain in New Jersey." *New York Times*, 12 September, A21.

*New Scientist* 1997. "Newswire: Surfer girls," 1 July, 21.

*New York Times* 1997. "Top female executive resigns." 28 September, A15.

Nichelli, P., K. Clark, C. Hollnagel, and J. Grafman. 1995. "Duration processing after frontal lobe lesions." In "Structure and functions of the human prefrontal cortex," edited by J. Grafman, K. J. Holyoak, and F. Boller. *Annals of the New York Academy of Sciences* 769:161–171.

Nishida, T., and M. Hiraiwa-Hasegawa. 1986. "Chimpanzees and bonobos: Cooperative relationships among males." In *Primate societies*, edited by B. B. Smuts, D. L. Cheney, R. M. Seyfarth, R. W. Wrangham, and T. T. Struhsaker. Chicago: University of Chicago Press.

Nordstrom, C. 1995. "It's all in a name: Local-level female healers in Sri Lanka." In *Women as healers: Cross-cultural perspectives*, edited by C. S. McClain. New Brunswick, N.J.: Rutgers University Press.

Nyborg, H. 1994. *Hormones, sex and society*. Westport, Conn.: Praeger.

O'Conner, P. T. 1996. "Like I said, don't worry." *Newsweek*, 9 December, 12.

Oliver, M. B., and J. S. Hyde. 1993. "Gender differences in sexuality: A meta-analysis." *Psychological Bulletin* 114:29–51.

Orenstein, Peggy, in association with the American Association of University Women. 1994. *Schoolgirls: Young women, self-esteem, and the confidence gap*. New York: Doubleday.

Orfield, G. 1998. "Charter schools won't save education." *New York Times*, 2 January, A17.

Ornish, D. 1998. *Love & survival: The scientific basis for the healing power of intimacy*. New York: HarperCollins.

Paine Webber. 1997. *Women and investing: An index of investor optimism special report*. New York: Paine Webber.

Palmaffy, T. 1998. "No excuses." *Policy Review*, January–February, 18ff.

Paludi, M. A., and R. B. Barickman. 1991. *Academic and workplace sexual harassment: A resource manual*. New York: State University of New York Press.

Pardo, J. V., P. J. Pardo, and M. E. Raichle. 1993. "Neural correlates of self-induced dysphoria." *American Journal of Psychiatry* 150:713–719.

Parish, A. R. 1994. "Sex and food control in the 'uncommon chimpanzee': How bonobo females overcome a phylogenetic legacy of male dominance." *Ethology and Sociobiology* 15 (3):157–179.

Parker, G. A. 1970. "Sperm competition and its evolutionary consequences in the insects." *Biological Review* 45:525–567.

Passell, P. 1995. "Job advice for 2005: Don't be a farmer, play one on TV." *New York Times*, 3 September, A9.

Pasternack, B. A., and A. J. Viscio. 1998. *The centerless corporation: A new model for transforming your organization for growth and prosperity.* New York: Simon and Schuster.

Pattatucci, A.M.L., and D. H. Hamer. 1995. "Development and familiality of sexual orientation in females." *Behavior Genetics* 25(5):407–420.

Pavelka, Mary S. M., and Linda Marie Fedigan. 1991. "Menopause: A comparative life history perspective." *Yearbook of Physical Anthropology* 34:13–38.

Pearce, F. 1994. "Trees are on the march?" *New Scientist*. 31 December, 17.

———. 1997. "Review: Life is a beach." *New Scientist* 4 January, 39.

Pedersen, C. A., J. D. Caldwell, G. F. Jirikowski, and T. R. Insel. 1992. "Oxytocin in maternal, sexual, and social behaviors." *Annals of the New York Academy of Sciences* 652:1–492.

Pedersen-Pietersen, L. 1997. "To have and to hyphenate: The marriage name game." *New York Times*, 16 March, F11.

Peele, S. 1988. "Fools for love: The romantic ideal, psychological theory, and addictive love." In *The psychology of love*, edited by R. J. Sternberg and M. L. Barnes. New Haven, Conn.: Yale University Press.

Peele, S., and A. Brodsky. 1975. *Love and addiction.* New York: Taplinger Publishing Company.

Peplau, L. A., and S. D. Cochran. 1990. "A relational perspective on homosexuality." In *Homosexuality/heterosexuality: Concepts of sexual orientation*, edited by P. McWhirter, S. Sanders, and J. Reinisch. Vol. 2 of the Kinsey Institute Series. New York: Oxford University Press.

Peplau, L., and S. Gordon. 1985. "Women and men in love: Gender differences in close heterosexual relationships." In *Women, gender and social psychology*, edited by V. O'Leary, R. Unger, and B. Wallston. Hillsdale, N.J.: Lawrence Erlbaum and Associates.

Persky H., H. Lief, D. Strauss, W. Miller, and C. O'Brien. 1978. "Plasma testosterone level and sexual behavior of couples." *Archives of Sexual Behavior* 7 (3):157–173.

Pfeiffer, E., A. Verwoerdt, and H. S. Wang. 1969. "The natural history of sexual behavior in biologically advantaged group of aged individuals." *Journal of Gerontology* 24:193–195.

Pfeiffer, E., and G. C. Davis. 1972. "Determinants of sexual behavior in middle and old age." *Journal of the American Geriatrics Society* 20:151–58.

Phillips, S., and B. B. Sherwin. 1992. "Effects of estrogen on memory function in surgically menopausal women." *Psychoneuroendocrinology* 17:485–495.

Piaget, J. 1932. *The moral judgment of the child.* New York: The Free Press. 1965.

Piltch. C. 1992a. Work and mental distress: A comparative analysis of the experience of women and men. Ph.D. diss., Boston University.

———. 1992b. "Work and stress." *The Radcliffe Quarterly* 78 (December): 6–7.

Pinker, S., and P. Bloom. 1992. "Natural language and natural selection." In *The adapted mind: Evolutionary psychology and the generation of culture,* edited by J. H. Barkow, L. Cosmides, and J. Tooby. New York: Oxford University Press.

Plotnicov, L. 1995. "Love, lust and found in Nigeria." In *Romantic passion: A universal experience?* edited by W. Jankowiak. New York: Columbia University Press.

Pool, Robert. 1994. *Eve's rib: Searching for the biological roots of sex differences.* New York: Crown.

Popcorn, F., and L. Marigold. 1996. *Clicking: 16 trends to future fit your life, your work and your business.* New York: HarperCollins.

Pope, H., and C. W. Mueller. 1979. "The intergenerational transmission of marital instability: Comparisons by race and sex." In *Divorce and separation: Context, causes, and consequences,* edited by G. Levinger and O. C. Moles. New York: Basic Books.

Popenoe, D. 1996. *Life without father.* New York: The Free Press.

Posner, M. 1994. "Attention: The mechanisms of consciousness." *Proceedings of the National Academy of Science* 91:7398–7403.

Posner M., and S. Dehaene. 1994. "Attentional networks." *Trends in Neuroscience* 17:75–79.

Posner, R. 1992. *Sex and reason.* Cambridge, Mass.: Harvard University Press.

Postrel, V. I. 1997. "The nail file." *Reason* (October):4ff.

Prakasa V. V., and V. N. Rao. 1979. "Arranged marriages: An assessment of the attitudes of the college students in India." In *Cross-cultural perspectives of mate-selection and marriage,* edited by G. Kurian. Westport, Conn.: Greenwood Press.

Prentky, R. 1985. "The neurochemistry and neuroendocrinology of sexual aggression." In *Aggression and Dangerousness,* edited by D. P. Farrington and J. Gunn. New York: John Wiley and Sons.

Presser, S. 1995. "Sex, samples and response errors." *Contemporary Sociology* 24 (4):296–298.

Pui-wing, Tam. 1998. "Graying of Asia in the next 30 years entices U. S. pension-fund providers." *The Wall Street Journal,* 16 March, B9.

Purdy, M. 1995. "A sexual revolution for the elderly." *New York Times,* 6 November, A16.

Purifoy, F., and L. Koopmans. 1980. "Androstenedione, testosterone and free-testosterone concentrations in women of various occupations." *Social Biology* 26:179–188.

Pusey, A., J. Williams, and J. Goodall. 1997. "The influence of dominance rank on the reproductive success of female chimpanzees." *Science* 277:828–830.

Quain, B. 1948. *Fijian village.* Chicago: University of Chicago Press.

Raleigh, M. J., and G. L. Brammer. 1993. "Individual differences in serotonin-2 receptors and social behavior in monkeys." *Society for Neuroscience Abstracts* 19:592.

Raleigh, Michael J., and Michael T. McGuire. 1994. "Serotonin, aggression and violence in vervet monkeys." In *The neurotransmitter revolution: Serotonin, social behavior and the law,* edited by R. D. Masters and M. T. McGuire. Carbondale: Southern Illinois University Press.

Raleigh, M., M. McGuire, G. Brammer, D. Pollack, and A. Yuwiler. 1991. "Serotonergic mechanisms promote dominance acquisition in adult male vervet monkeys." *Brain Research* 559:181–190.

Randall, Margaret. 1996. *The price you pay: The hidden cost of women's relationship to money.* New York: Routledge.

Rebhun, L. A. 1995. "Language of love in northeast Brazil." In *Romantic passion: A universal experience?* edited by W. Jankowiak. New York: Columbia University Press.

Redman, S. et al. 1994. "Determinants of career choices among women and men medical students and interns." *Medical Education* 28:361, 368–369.

Reid, M. 1995. "Sisterhood and professionalization: A case study of the American lay midwife." In *Women as healers: Cross-cultural perspectives,* edited by C. S. McClain. New Brunswick, N.J.: Rutgers University Press.

Reinisch, June M., and Ruth Beasley. 1990. *The Kinsey Institute new report on sex.* New York: St. Martin's Press.

Reiter, R. R., ed. 1975. *Toward an anthropology of women.* New York: Monthly Review Press.

Rich, E. H., ed. 1998. *The foundation directory 1998 edition.* 20th ed. New York: The Foundation Center.

Richburg, K. B. 1997. "Spreading the wealth." *Washington Post.* National Weekly Edition. 17 March, 6f.

Riessman, C. K. 1990. *Divorce talk: Women and men make sense of personal relationships.* New Brunswick, N.J.: Rutgers University Press.

Rimer, S. 1998. "As centenarians thrive, 'old' is redefined." *New York Times,* 22 June, A1f.

Robbins, C. C. 1998. "In southeast, doctor meets medicine man." *New York Times,* 15 September, H1.

Robinson, J. R. 1996. "Radio songs." *American Demographics* (September): 60–64.

Roiphe, K. 1997. "Adultery's double standard." *New York Times Magazine,* 12 October, 54–55.

Rooks, J. P. 1997. *Midwifery & childbirth in America.* Philadelphia: Temple University Press.

Rose, R. M., I. S. Bernstein, T. P. Gordon, S. F. Catlin. 1974. "Androgens and aggression: A review and recent findings in primates." In *Primate Aggression, Territoriality and Xenophobia,* edited by R. L. Holloway. New York: Academic Press.

Rose, R. M., J. W. Holaday, and I. S. Bernstein. 1971. "Plasma testosterone, dominance rank and aggressive behavior in male rhesus monkeys." *Nature* 231:366–368.

Rosenblatt, J. S. 1995. "Hormonal basis of parenting in mammals." In *Handbook of parenting. Vol. 2: Biology and ecology of parenting.* Hillsdale, N.J.: Lawrence Erlbaum and Associates.

Rosenblatt, P. C., and R. M. Anderson. 1981. "Human sexuality in cross-cultural perspective." In *The bases of human sexual attraction,* edited by M. Cook. New York: Academic Press.

Rosener, Judy B. 1990. "Ways women lead." *Harvard Business Review* (November–December): 119–125.

———. 1995. *America's competitive secret: Women managers.* New York: Oxford University Press.

Rosenfeld, J. P. 1992. "Old age, new heirs." *American Demographics* 14(5):46–49.

Rosenthal, E. 1998. "In China's countryside, it is time to grow rich." *New York Times,* 30 May, A4.

Rosewicz, B. 1996. "Here comes the bride . . . and for the umpteenth time." *The Wall Street Journal,* 10 September, B1f.

Rossi, A. 1984. "Gender and parenthood." *American Sociological Review* 49:1–19.

Rossi, A. S. 1994. "Eros and caritas: A biopsychosocial approach to human sexuality and reproduction." In *Sexuality across the life course,* edited by A. S. Rossi. Chicago: University of Chicago Press.

Rossi, Alice S., and Peter H. Rossi. 1990. *Of human bonding: Parent-child relations across the life course.* New York: Aldine de Gruyter.

Rossiter, Margaret W. 1995. *Women scientists in America: Before affirmative action 1940–1972.* Baltimore: Johns Hopkins University Press.

Rowan, R. 1986. *The intuitive manager.* New York: Berkley Books.

Rowe, J. W. 1997. "A new gerontology." Editorial. *Science,* 17 October, 367.

Roy, Manisha. 1975. *Bengali women.* Chicago: University of Chicago Press.

Rushton, J. P. 1989. "Epigenesis and social preference." *Behavioral and Brain Sciences* 12:31–32.

Russel, C. 1995a "The baby boom turns 50." *American Demographics* (December): 22–41.

———. 1995b. "Find the missing men." *American Demographics* (May):8.

———. 1995c. "Why teen births boom." *Future Survey,* 8 September.

———. 1996. "Going their separate ways." *American Demographics* (November): 10ff.

———. 1997a. "The Rorschack test." *American Demographics* (January):10–12.

———. 1997b. "The ungraying of America." *American Demographics* (July):12ff.

Sacks, K. 1979. *Sisters and wives: The past and future of sexual equality.* Urbana: University of Illinois Press.

Sadalla, E. K., D. T. Kenrick, and B. Vershure. 1987. "Dominance and heterosexual attraction." *Journal of Personality and Social Psychology* 52:730–738.

Safer, M. A. 1981. "Sex and hemisphere differences in access to codes for processing emotional expressions and faces." *Journal of Experimental Psychology: General* 110:86–100.

Salmon, C. A., and M. Daly. 1995. "On the importance of kin relations to Canadian women and men." *Ethology and Sociobiology* 17:289–297.

Samuels, D. 1995. "Philanthropical correctness." *The New Republic,* 25 September, 28.

Samuelson, R. J. 1995. "Judgment calls: Three cheers for schools?" *Newsweek,* 4 December, 61.

Sanday, P. R. 1973. "Toward a theory of the status of women." *American Anthropologist* 75:1682–1700.

———. 1981. *Female power and male dominance: On the origins of sexual inequality.* Cambridge, England: Cambridge University Press.

Sapolsky, R. M. 1983. "Endocrine aspects of social instability in the olive baboon." *American Journal of Primatology.* 5:365–376.

———. 1997. "The importance of a well-groomed child." *Science* 277:1620–1621.

Saporito, B. 1995. "What's for dinner?" *Fortune,* 15 May, 50ff.

Schanberg, S. M., and T. M. Field. 1987. "Sensory deprivation stress and supplemental stimulation in the rape pup and preterm human neonate." *Child Development* 58:1431–1447.

Schanberg, S. M., G. Evoniuk, and C. Kuhn. 1984. "Tactile and nutritional aspects of maternal care: Specific regulators of neuroendocrine function and cellular development." *Proceedings of the Society for Experimental Biology and Medicine* 175(2):135–146.

Schenck-Yglesias, C. G. 1995. "How many doctors does it take?" *American Demographics* (April): 18ff.

Schlaepfer, T. E., A. Y. Tien, P. E. Barta, G. J. Harris, and G. Pearlson. 1994. "Cortical gender dimorphism in healthy subjects." *APA New Research Abstracts* NR 435:170.

Schlegel, A., and H. Barry III. 1986. "The cultural consequences of female contribution to subsistence." *American Anthropologist* 88:142–150.

———. 1991. *Adolescence: An anthropological inquiry.* New York: The Free Press.

Schlesinger, J. M. 1997. "A slide in factory jobs: The pain of progress." *The Wall Street Journal,* 28 April, 1.

Schneider, M. D., and C. B. Cottrell. 1975. *The American kin universe: A genealogical study.* Chicago: University of Chicago Press.

Schwartz, Pepper. 1994. *Peer marriage: how love between equals really works.* New York: The Free Press.

Seger, L. 1996. *When women call the shots: The developing power and influence of women in television and film.* New York: Henry Holt and Company.

Seib, G. F. 1995. "Houses divided." *The Wall Street Journal,* 11 January, A1f.

Seltzer, R. A., J. Newman, and M. V. Leighton. 1997. *Sex as a political variable: Women as candidates and voters in U.S. elections.* Boulder, Colo.: Lynne Rienner Publishers.

Senge, P. 1990. *The fifth discipline.* New York: Doubleday.

Shaywitz, B. A., S. E. Shaywitz, K. R. Pugh, R. T. Constable, P. Skudlarski, R. K. Fulbright, R. A. Bronen, J. M. Fletcher, D. P. Shankweiler, L. Katz, and J. C. Core. 1995. "Sex differences in the functional organization of the brain for language." *Nature* 373:607–609.

Sheets, V. L., L. L. Fredendall, and H. M. Claypool. 1997. "Jealousy evocation, partner reassurance and relationship stability: An exploration of the potential benefits of jealousy." *Evolution and Human Behavior* 18:387–402.

Shellenbarger, S. 1996. "Work & family: Two income couples are making changes at work and at home." *The Wall Street Journal,* 14 February, B1f.

Shepher, J. 1971. "Mate selection among second-generation kibbutz adolescents and adults: Incest avoidance and negative imprinting." *Archives of Sexual Behavior.* 1:293–307.

Sherfey, M. J. 1972. *The nature and evolution of female sexuality.* New York: Random House.

Sherwin, B. B. 1988. "A comparative analysis of the role of androgen in human male and female sexual behavior: Behavioral specificity, critical thresholds, and sensitivity." *Psychobiology* 16:416–25.

———. 1994. "Sex hormones and psychological functioning in postmenopausal women." *Experimental Gerontology* 29(3/4):423–430.

Sherwin, B. B., and M. M. Gelfand. 1987. "The role of androgen in the maintenance of sexual functioning in oophorectomized women." *Psychosomatic Medicine* 49:397.

Sherwin, B. B., M. M. Gelfand, and W. Brender. 1985. "Androgen enhances sexual motivation in females: A prospective cross-over study of sex steroid administration in the surgical menopause." *Psychosomatic Medicine* 7:339–351.

Sherwin, B. B., and S. Phillips. 1990. "Estrogen and cognitive functioning in surgically menopausal women." *Annals of the New York Academy of Sciences* 592:474–475.

Shettel-Neuber, J., J. B. Bryson, and C. E. Young. 1978. "Physical attractiveness of the 'other person' and jealousy." *Personality and Social Psychology Bulletin* 4:612–615.

Short, R. V. 1976. "The evolution of human reproduction." *Proceedings, Royal Society* (London) Series B, 195:3–24.

———. 1984. "The role of hormones in sexual cycles." In *Hormones in reproduction*, edited by C. R. Austin and R. V. Short. Vol. 3. Cambridge, England: Cambridge University Press.

———. 1987. "The biological basis for the contraceptive effects of breast feeding." *International Journal of Gynaecology and Obstetrics Supplement* 25: 207–217.

Shostak, M. 1981. *Nisa: The life and words of a !Kung woman.* Cambridge, Mass.: Harvard University Press.

Shucard, D. W., J. L. Schucard, and D. G. Thomas. 1987. "Sex differences in electrophysiological activity in infancy: Possible implications for language development." In *Language, gender and sex in comparative perspective*, edited by S. U. Philips, S. Steele, and C. Tanz. Cambridge, England: Cambridge University Press.

Silverberg, James, and J. Patrick Gray. 1992. *Aggression and peacefulness in humans and other primates.* New York: Oxford University Press.

Silverman, Irwin, and Marion Eals. 1992. "Sex differences in spatial abilities: Evolutionary theory and data." In *The adapted mind: Evolutionary psychology and the generation of culture*, edited by Jerome Barkow, Leda Cosmides, and John Tooby. New York: Oxford University Press.

Simon, H. A. 1974. "How big is a chunk?" *Science* 183:482–488.

———. 1987. "Making management decisions: The role of intuition and emotion." *Academy of Management Executive* (February):57–63.

Simon, Neal G., and David B. Masters. 1988. "Activation of intermale aggression by combined estrogen-androgen treatment." *Aggressive Behavior* 14:291–295.

Simon, R. 1998. "Women outdo men in results in investing." *The Wall Street Journal*, 20 October, A14.

Simon, Rita J., and Jean Landis. 1991. *The crimes that women commit, the punishments they receive.* Lexington, Mass.: Lexington Books.

Simpson, J. A., B. Campbell, and E. Berscheid. 1986. "The association between romantic love and marriage: Kephart (1967) twice revisited." *Personality and Social Psychology Bulletin* 12:363–372.

Sinclair, K. P. 1985. "Koro and Kuia: Aging and gender among the Maori of New Zealand." In *Aging and its transformations: Moving toward death in Pacific societies*, edited by D. A. Counts and D. R. Counts. Lanham, Md.: University Press of America.

Singer, I. 1987. *The nature of love.* Vol 3: *The modern world.* Chicago: University of Chicago Press.

Singh, D. 1993. "Adaptive significance of female physical attractiveness: Role of waist-to-hip ratio." *Journal of Personality and Social Psychology* 65:293–307.

Skuse, D. H., R. S. James, D.V.M. Bishop, B. Coppin, P. Dalton, G. Aamodt-Leeper, M. Bacarese-Hamilton, C. Creswell, R. McGurk, and P. A. Jacobs. 1997. "Evidence from Turner's syndrome of an imprinted X-linked locus affecting cognitive function." *Nature* 387:705–708.

Slatalla, M. 1998. "In sex-role tangle, a woman's search." *New York Times*. Circuits, G11.

Slocum, S. 1975. "Woman the gatherer: Male bias in anthropology." In *Toward an anthropology of women*, edited by R. R. Reiter. New York: Monthly Review Press.

Small, M. F. 1998. *Our babies, ourselves: How biology and culture shape the way we parent*. New York: Anchor Books.

Smith, L. 1997. "Coming to a health plan near you: Yoga and belladonna." *Fortune*, 29 September, 169ff.

Smith, R. L. 1984. "Human sperm competition." In *Sperm competition and the evolution of mating systems*, edited by R. L. Smith. New York: Academic Press.

Smith, T. W. 1994. "Attitudes toward sexual permissiveness: Trends, correlates, and behavioral connections." In *Sexuality across the life course*, edited by A. S. Rossi. Chicago: University of Chicago Press.

Smuts, Barbara B. 1986. "Gender, aggression and influence." In *Primate societies*, edited by B. B. Smuts, D. L. Cheney, R. M. Seyfarth, R. W. Wrangham, and T. T. Struhsaker. Chicago: University of Chicago Press.

———. 1992. "Male aggression against women: An evolutionary perspective." *Human Nature* 3(1):1–44.

———. 1997. "Social relationships and life histories of primates." In *The evolving female: A life history perspective*, edited by M. E. Morebeck, A. Galloway, and A. Zihlman. Princeton, N. J.: Princeton University Press.

Smuts, B. B., D. L. Cheney, R. M. Seyfarth, R. W. Wrangham, T. T. Struhsaker, eds. 1987. *Primate societies*. Chicago: University of Chicago.

Sommers, Christina Hoff. 1994. *Who stole feminism? How women have betrayed women*. New York: Simon and Schuster.

Songer, D. R., S. Davis, and S. Haire. 1994. "A reappraisal of diversification in the federal courts: Gender effects in the courts of appeals." *The Journal of Politics* 56(2):425–439.

Spanier, G. B., and R. L. Margolis. 1983. "Marital separation and extramarital sexual behavior." *The Journal of Sex Research* 19:23–48.

Specter, M. 1998. "Population implosion worries a graying Europe." *New York Times*, 10 July, A1.

Spiro, M. E. 1958. *Children of the kibbutz*. Cambridge: Harvard Unversity Press.

Sprecher, S., A. Aron, E. Hatfield, A. Cortese, E. Potapove, and A. Levitskaya. 1994. "Love: American style, Russian style, and Japanese style." *Personal Relationships* 1:349–369.

Srinivas, M. N. 1977. "The changing position of Indian women." *Man* 12:221–238.

Stacey, J. 1991. *Brave new families: Stories of domestic upheaval in late twentieth century America*. New York: Basic Books.

Stapley, J. C., and J. M. Haviland. 1989. "Beyond depression: Gender differences in normal adolescents' emotional experiences." *Sex Roles* 20:295–308.

Statistical Abstract of the United States. 1996. *The American almanac 1996–1997*. Austin, Tex.: Hoover's, Inc.

Steenland, S. 1987. "Women in broadcasting." In *The American woman 1987–88: A report in depth*, edited by S. E. Rix. New York: W. W. Norton.

———. 1990. "Behind the scenes: Women in television." In *The American woman 1990–91: A status report*, edited by S. E. Rix. New York: W. W. Norton.

Stendhal, (Beyle, Henry). 1915. *On love*. Translated by Philip Sidney Woolf and Cecil N. Woolf. New York: Brentano's.

Stern, D. 1987. *The interpersonal world of the infant*. New York: Basic Books.

Stern, D. N., S. Spieker, and K. MacKain. 1983. "Intonation contours as signals in maternal speech to prelinguistic infants." *Developmental Psychology* 18:727–735.

Stewart, T. 1997. *Intellectual capital*. New York: Doubleday.

Stone, B. 1997. "Rx: Thirty minutes on the stairmaster twice weekly,." *New York Times*, 1 March, B4.

Stone, L. 1977. *The family, sex, and marriage: In England 1500–1800*. New York: Harper and Row.

———. 1988. "Passionate attachments in the west in historical perspective." In *Passionate attachments: Thinking about love*, edited by W. Gaylin and E. Person. New York: The Free Press.

———. 1990. *Road to divorce: England 1530–1987*. New York: Oxford University Press.

Strachey, Lytton. 1918. *Eminent Victorians*. Garden City, N.Y.: Garden City Publishers, Inc.

Stroebe, W., and M. S. Stroebe. 1987. *Bereavement and health: The psychological and physical consequences of partner loss*. New York: Cambridge University Press.

Stuss, D. T., T. Shallice, M. P. Alexander, and T. W. Picton. 1995. "A multidisciplinary approach to anterior attentional functions." In "Structure and functions of the human prefrontal cortex," edited by J. Grafman, K. J. Holyoak, and F. Boller. *Annals of the New York Academy of Sciences* 769:191–211.

Suggs, R. C. 1966. *Marquesan sexual behavior*. New York: Harcourt, Brace and World.

Swain, S. 1989. "Covert intimacy: Closeness in men's friendships." In *Gender in intimate relationships*, edited by B. J. Risman and P. Schwartz. Belmont, Calif.: Wadsworth.

Symons, D. 1979. *The evolution of human sexuality*. New York: Oxford University Press.

———. 1989. "The psychology of human mate preferences." *Behavioral and Brain Sciences* 12:34–35.

Taffel, R. 1990. "The politics of mood." *The Family Therapy Networker* (September–October): 49–53.

Takahata, Yukio, Naoki Koyama, and Shigeru Suzuki. 1995. "Do the old aged females experience a long post-reproductive life span?: The cases of Japanese macaques and chimpanzees." *Primates* 36 (2):169–180.

Talbot, M. 1998. "Attachment theory: The ultimate experiment." *New York Times Magazine*, 24 May, 24ff.

Tannen, D. 1990. *You just don't understand: Women and men in conversation*. New York: Ballantine Books.

Tavris, C. 1992. *The mismeasure of woman*. New York: Simon and Schuster.

———. 1994. *Talking from 9 to 5*. New York: William Morrow.

———. "The feminizing of love." In *Diverse voices of women*, edited by S. F., Ballentine and J. B. Inclan. Mountain View, Calif.: Mayfield Publishing Co.

———. 1997. "How friendship was 'feminized.'" *New York Times*, 28 May, A29.

Tavris, C., and C. Offir. 1977. *The longest war: Sex differences in perspective*. New York: Harcourt Brace Jovanovich.

Tavris C., and S. Sadd. 1977. *The Redbook report on female sexuality*. New York: Delacorte.

Tear, Jayne. 1995. "They just don't understand gender dynamics." *The Wall Street Journal*, 20 November, A14.

Tennov, D. 1979. *Love and limerence: The experience of being in love.* New York: Stein and Day.

Thiessen, D., R. K. Young, and R. Burroughs. 1993. "Lonely hearts advertisements reflect sexually dimorphic mating strategies." *Ethology and Sociobiology* 14:209–229.

Thompson, A. P. 1983. "Extramarital sex: A review of the research literature." *Journal of Sex Research* 19:1–22.

Thorne, B. 1993. *Gender play.* New Brunswick, N.J.: Rutgers University Press.

Tierney, J. 1998. "The upside of gossip." *New York Times Magazine,* 25 January, 14.

Tissot, S.A.D. 1766/1985. *Onanism.* New York: Garland Publishing.

Tocqueville, Alexis de. 1945. *Democracy in america.* New York: Alfred A. Knopf.

Toran-Allerand, C. D. 1986. "Sexual differentiation of the brain." In *Developmental neuropsychobiology,* edited by W. T. Greenough and J. M. Juraska. New York: Academic Press.

Tornstam, L. 1992. "Loneliness in marriage." *Journal of Social and Personal Relationships* 9:197–217.

Townsend, B. 1996. "Room at the top for women." *American Demographics* (July): 28–37.

Townsend, J. M. 1989. "Mate selection criteria: A pilot study." *Ethology and Sociobiology* 10:241–253.

Trent, K., and S. J. South. 1989. "Structural determinants of the divorce rate: A cross-sectional analysis." *Journal of Marriage and the Family* 51:391–404.

Trevathan, W. R. 1987. *Human birth: An evolutionary perspective.* New York: Aldine de Gruyter.

——. 1999. *Evolutionary obstetrics.* In *Evolutionary medicine,* edited by W. R. Trevathan, E. O. Smith, and J. J. McKenna. New York: Oxford University Press.

Trivers, R. L. 1972. "Parental investment and sexual selection." In *Sexual selection and the descent of man,* edited by B. Campbell.

Trivers, R. L., and D. E. Willard. 1973. "Natural selection of parental ability to vary the sex ratio of off-spring." *Science* 191:249–253.

Tsubouchi, Y. 1984. "Nuptiality." In *Population of Japan. Country monograph series no. 11 ST/ESCAP269.* United Nations Economic and Social Commission for Asia and the Pacific. New York: United Nations Publications.

Tucker, D. M., P. Luu, and K. H. Pribram. 1995. "Social and emotional self-regulation." In "Structure and functions of the human prefrontal cortex," edited by J. Grafman, K. J. Holyoak, and F. Boller. *Annals of the New York Academy of Sciences* 769:191–211.

Udry, J. R., K. E. Baumann, and N. M. Morris. 1975. "Changes in premarital coital experience of recent decade-of-birth cohorts of urban American women." *Journal of Marriage and the Family* 37:783–787.

Udry, J. R., J. Kovenock, and N. Morris. 1992. "A biosocial paradigm for women's gender roles." Paper presented at the Population Association of America Conference, Denver, Colorado.

Udry, J. R., L. Talbert, and N. Morris. 1986. "Biosocial foundations for adolescent female sexuality." *Demography* 23:217–227.

United Nations. 1995. *The world's women 1995: Trends and statistics.* New York: United Nations Publications.

——. 1995a. *Women in a changing global economy: 1994 world survey on the role of women in development.* New York: United Nations Publications.

———. 1995b. *Women: Looking beyond 2000*. New York: United Nations Publications.

United Nations Development Programme. 1995. *Human development report: 1995*. New York: Oxford University Press.

*Utne Reader*. 1997. "On the road again," July–August, 71.

Uvnas-Mogerg, K. 1997. "Physiological and endocrine effects of social contact." In "The integrative neurobiology of affiliation," edited by C. S. Carter, I. I. Lederhendler, and B. Kirkpatrick. *Annals of the New York Academy of Sciences* 807:146–163.

Valian, V. 1988. "Running in place." *The Sciences: Journal of the New York Academy of Sciences*. 38(1):18–23.

Van Goozen, S., V. M. Wiegant, E. Endert, F. A. Helmond, and N. E. Van de Poll. 1997. "Psychoendocrinological assessment of the menstrual cycle: The relationship between hormones, sexuality, and mood." *Archives of Sexual Behavior* 26(4):359–382.

Velle, W. 1982. "Sex, hormones and behavior in animals and man." *Perspectives in Biology and Medicine* 25:295–315.

Viederman, M. 1988. "The nature of passionate love." In *Passionate attachments: Thinking about love*, edited by W. Gaylin and E. Person. New York: The Free Press.

Viorst, J. 1986. *Necessary losses*. New York: Fawcett Gold Medal.

Vogel, G. 1996. "Asia and Europe top in world, but reasons are hard to find." *Science*, 22 November, 1296.

Von Hoffman, N. 1997. "The times are a-changing: We're starting to behave." *The New York Observer*, 7 August, 14.

Waal, F. de. 1982. *Chimpanzee politics*. New York: Harper and Row.

———. 1984. "Sex differences in the formation of coalitions among chimpanzees." *Ethology and Sociobiology* 5:239–255.

———. 1989. *Peacemaking among primates*. Cambridge, Mass.: Harvard University Press.

———. 1989a. "Commentary: Gender and political cognition: Integrating evolutionary biology and political science," by R. D. Masters. In *Politics and the Life Sciences* 8:3–39.

———. 1996. *Good natured: The origins of right and wrong in humans and other animals*. Cambridge, Mass.: Harvard University Press.

Wade, N. 1998. "Good maternal behavior is linked to the genes of a father." *New York Times*, 29 August, A17.

Walker, L. E., and J. R. Meloy. 1998. "Stalking and domestic violence." In *The psychology of stalking: Clinical and forensic perspectives*, edited by J. R. Meloy. New York: Academic Press.

Walker, Margaret L. 1995. "Menopause in female rhesus monkeys." *American Journal of Primatology* 35:59–71.

Walsh, M. R. 1987. "Are women more likely to be mentally ill?" In *The psychology of women: Ongoing debates*, edited by M. R. Walsh. New Haven, Conn.: Yale University Press.

Walster E., and G. W. Walster. 1978. *A new look at love*. Reading, Mass.: Addison-Wesley.

Ward, Shawn L., Nora Newcombe, and Willis F. Overton. 1986. "Turn left at the church or three miles north: A study of direction giving and sex differences." *Environment and Behavior* 18(2):192–213.

Wattenberg, B. J. 1977. "The population explosion is over." *New York Times Magazine*, 23 November, 60–62.

Web, S. 1991. *Step forward: Sexual harassment in the workplace.* New York: Mastermedia.

Wedekind, C., T. Seebeck, F. Bettens, and A. J. Paepke. 1995. "MHC-dependent mate preferences in humans." *Proceedings of the Royal Society of London* 260:245–249.

Wedenoja, W. 1995. "Mothering and the practice of 'balm' in Jamaica." In *Women as healers: Cross-cultural perspectives,* edited by C. S. McClain. New Brunswick, N.J.: Rutgers University Press.

Weiner, A. B. 1976. *Women of value, men of renown: New perspectives in Trobriand exchange.* Austin: University of Texas Press.

Weiner, E., and A. Brown. 1997. *Insider's guide to the future: The powerful forces shaping our future . . . and how to profit from them.* USA: Boardroom, Inc.

Weinstein, Sidney. 1968. "Intensive and extensive aspects of tactile sensitivity as a function of body part, sex and laterality." In *The skin senses,* edited by D. R. Kenshalo. Springfield, Ill.: Charles C. Thomas.

Weisman, C. S., M. A. Teitelbaum, C. A. Nathanson, G. A. Chase, T. M. King, and D. M. Levine. 1986. "Sex differences in the practice patterns of recently trained obstetrician-gynecologists." *Obstetrics and Gynecology* 67(6):776–777.

Weiss, P. 1998. "Don't even think about it. The cupid cops are watching." *New York Times Magazine,* 3 May, 43–47.

Weissman, M. A., and M. Olfson. 1995. "Depression in women: Implications for health care research." *Science* 269:799–801.

Weitzman, L. J. 1985. *The divorce revolution.* New York: The Free Press.

Wellington, S. 1996. *1996 census of women corporate officers and top earners.* New York: Catalyst, Inc.

———. 1997. *Women board directors of the Fortune 500: 1997 catalyst census.* New York: Catalyst, Inc.

Wessel, D. 1996. "Reaching back." *The Wall Street Journal,* 13 February, A1ff.

West, R. 1988. "Jurisprudence and gender." *University of Chicago Law Review* 55(1):1ff.

Westermark, E. 1922. *The history of human marriage.* Vols. 1–3. New York: Allerton Book Company.

Western, R. 1996. "Gossip is golden." *Psychology Today* 29 (July–August).

White, G. L. 1981. "Some correlates of romantic jealousy." *Journal of Personality* 49:129–147.

Whitehead, B. D. 1996. "Women and the future of fatherhood." *Wilson Quarterly* (spring): 31ff.

Whiting, B., and J. Whiting. 1975. *Children in six cultures: A psychocultural analysis.* Cambridge, Mass.: Harvard University Press.

Whyte, M. K. 1978. *The status of women in preindustrial societies.* Princeton N.J.: Princeton University Press.

Wiederman, M. W., and E. R. Allgeier. 1992. "Gender differences in mate selection criteria: Sociobiological or socioeconomic explanation?" *Ethology and Sociobiology* 13:115–124.

Wilkinson, H. 1996. "Cracks in the glass ceiling." *World Press Review,* September, 32.

Williams, Christina L., and Warren H. Meck. 1991. "The organizational effects of gonadel steroids on sexually dimorphic spatial ability." *Psychoneuroendocrinology* 16 (1–3): 155–176.

Williams, G. C. 1957. "Pleiotropy, natural selection, and the evolution of senescence." *Evolution* 11:32–39.

———. 1975. *Sex and evolution.* Princeton, N.J.: Princeton University Press.

Wilson, G. D., and R. J. Land. 1981. "Sex differences in sexual fantasy patterns." *Personality and Individual Differences* 2:343–346.

Wilson, James Q. 1993. "On gender." *The Public Interest* (summer): 3–26.

Wilson, M., and M. Daly. 1992. "The man who mistook his wife for a chattal." In *The adapted mind: Evolutionary psychology and the generation of culture,* edited by J. H. Barkow, L. Cosmides, and J. Tooby. New York: Oxford University Press.

*Wilson Quarterly.* 1997. "Shotgun solutions for the family crisis" (winter).

Winerip, M. 1998. "Schools for sale." *New York Times Magazine,* 14 June, 42–48.

Wingfield, J. C. 1994. "Hormone-behavior interactions and mating systems in male and female birds." In *The differences between the sexes,* edited by R. V. Short and E. Balaban. New York: Cambridge University Press.

Winslow, J. T., N. Hastings, C. S. Carter, C. R. Harbaugh, and T. R. Insel. 1993. "A role for central vasopressin in pair bonding in monogamous prairie voles." *Nature* 365:545–548.

Wise, R. A. 1988. "Psychomotor stimulant properties of addictive drugs." In *The mesocorticolimbic dopamine system,* P. W. Kalivas and C. B. Nemeroff, eds. *Annals of the New York Academy of Sciences,* 537:228–234.

Witelson, S. F. 1989. "Hand and sex differences in the isthmus and genu of the human corpus callosum: A postmortem morphological study." *Brain* 112:799–835.

Witelson, S. F., I. I. Glezer, and D. L. Kigar. 1995. "Women have greater density of neurons in posterior temporal cortex." *Journal of Neuroscience* 15 (5):3418–3428.

Witkin, Georgia. 1995. *The truth about women: Fighting the 14 devastating myths that hold women back.* New York: Viking.

Witkin, H. A., and J. W. Berry. 1975. "Psychological differentiation in cross-cultural perspective." *Journal of Cross Cultural Psychology* 6:4–87.

Wittenberger, J. F., and R. L. Tilson. 1980. "The evolution of monogamy: Hypotheses and evidence." *Annual Review of Ecology and Systematics* 11:197–232.

Wolf, Margery. 1974. "Chinese women: Old skills in a new context." In *Women, culture and society,* edited by M. Rosaldo and L. Lamphere. Stanford, Calif.: Stanford University Press.

Wolkstein, D. 1991. *The first love stories.* New York: HarperPerennial.

Wood, J. W. 1990. "Fertility in anthropological populations." *Annual Review of Anthropology* 19:211–42.

Woolley, Catherine S., Elizabeth Gould, Maya Frankfurt, and Bruce S. McEwen. 1990. "Naturally occurring fluctuation in dendritic spine density on adult hippocampal pyramidal neurons." *Journal of Neuroscience* 10:4035–4039.

Worton, B. 1996. *Women and work: Executive summary.* New York: Deloitte and Touche with the Fortune Marketing Research Group.

Wrangham, Richard, and Dale Peterson. 1996. *Demonic males: Apes and the origins of human violence.* New York: Houghton Mifflin.

Wysocki, B. Jr. 1996. "About a million men have left work force in the past year or so." *The Wall Street Journal,* 12 June, A1f.

Yalcinkaya, T., P. K. Siiteri, J-L. Vigne, P. Licht, S. Pavgi, L. G. Frank, and S. E. Glickman. 1993. "A mechanism for virilization of female spotted hyenas in utero." *Science* 260:1929–1931.

Yang, C. K. 1959. *The Chinese family in the communist revolution.* Cambridge, Mass.: MIT Press.

*Yearbook of Labour Statistics.* 1994. Vol. 53.

Zuckerman, M. 1994. *Behavioral expressions and biosocial bases of sensation seeking.* New York: Cambridge University Press.

Zuckerman, Sir S. 1932. *The social life of monkeys and apes.* London: Butler and Turner, Ltd.

Zuger, A. 1998a. "A fistful of hostility is found in women." *New York Times,* 28 July, F1f.

———. 1998b. "What doctors of both sexes think of patients of both sexes." *New York Times.* Women's Health, 21 June, 20.

# INDEX

## ABOUT THE AUTHOR

HELEN FISHER is an anthropologist at Rutgers University and the author of *The Sex Contract: The Evolution of Human Behavior* and *Anatomy of Love: The Natural History of Monogamy, Adultery, and Divorce.* For her books, articles, lectures, and television and radio appearances, Dr. Fisher received the American Anthropological Association's Distinguished Service Award in 1985.